New Media Poetics

LEONARDO

Roger F. Malina, series editor

New Media Poetics

Contexts, Technotexts, and Theories

Edited by
Adalaide Morris
and Thomas Swiss

THE MIT PRESS
CAMBRIDGE, MASSACHUSETTS
LONDON, ENGLAND

MIT Press books may be purchased at special quantity discounts for business or sales promotional use. For information, please email special_sales@mitpress.mit.edu or write to Special Sales Department, The MIT Press, 55 Hayward Street, Cambridge, MA 02142.

This book printed and bound in the United States of America.

Library of Congress Cataloging-in-Publication Data

New media poetics : contexts, technotexts, and theories / edited by Adalaide Morris and Thomas Swiss.
    p. cm.
  Includes bibliographical references and index.
  ISBN-13: 978-0-262-13463-7
  ISBN-10: 0-262-13463-2 (alk. paper)
  1. Computer poetry—History and criticism. I. Morris, Adalaide Kirby, 1942–
II. Swiss, Thomas, 1952–

PN1059.C6N49   2006
808.10285—dc22

                                                              2005057658

10 9 8 7 6 5 4 3 2 1

To treat [new media] as humble servants . . . of our established conventions would be as fatal as to use an X-ray unit as a space heater.

—MARSHALL McLUHAN, "ELECTRONIC REVOLUTION" (1959)

The physical universe is not all that decays. So do abstractions and categories. Human ideas, science, scholarship, and language are constantly collapsing and unfolding. Any field, and the corpus of all fields, is a bundle of relationships subject to all kinds of twists, inversions, involutions, and rearrangement.

—TED NELSON, "A FILE STRUCTURE FOR THE COMPLEX, THE CHANGING, AND THE INDETERMINATE" (1965)

The machine is not an *it* to be animated, worshipped, and dominated. The machine is us, our processes, an aspect of our embodiment.

—DONNA J. HARAWAY, "A CYBORG MANIFESTO" (1985)

Contents

Contents

viii

Series Foreword

The cultural convergence of art, science, and technology provides ample opportunity for artists to challenge the very notion of how art is produced and to call into question its subject matter and its function in society. The mission of the Leonardo book series, published by the MIT Press, is to publish texts by artists, scientists, researchers, and scholars that present innovative discourse on the convergence of art, science, and technology.

Envisioned as a catalyst for enterprise, research, and creative and scholarly experimentation, the book series enables diverse intellectual communities to explore common grounds of expertise. The Leonardo book series provides a context for the discussion of contemporary practice, ideas, and frameworks in this rapidly evolving arena where art and science connect.

To find more information about Leonardo/ISAST and to order our publications, go to Leonardo Online at <http://lbs.mit.edu> or send e-mail to <leonardobooks@mitpress.mit.edu>.

Joel Slayton
Chair, Leonardo Book Series

Book Series Advisory Committee: Annick Bureaud, Pamela Grant-Ryan, Michael Punt.

Leonardo/International Society for the Arts, Sciences, and Technology (ISAST)

Leonardo, the International Society for the Arts, Sciences, and Technology, and the affiliated French organization Association Leonardo have two very simple goals:

1. to document and make known the work of artists, researchers, and scholars interested in the ways that the contemporary arts interact with science and technology, and
2. to create a forum and meeting places where artists, scientists, and engineers can meet, exchange ideas, and, where appropriate, collaborate.

When the journal *Leonardo* was started some thirty-five years ago, these creative disciplines existed in segregated institutional and social networks, a situation dramatized at that time by the "Two Cultures" debates initiated by C. P. Snow. Today we live in a different time of cross-disciplinary ferment, collaboration, and intellectual confrontation enabled by new hybrid organizations, new funding sponsors, and the shared tools of computers and the Internet. Above all, new generations of artist-researchers and researcher-artists are now at work individually and in collaborative teams bridging the art, science, and technology disciplines. Perhaps in our lifetime we will see the emergence of "new Leonardos," creative individuals or teams who will not only develop a meaningful art for our times but also drive new agendas in science and stimulate technological innovation that addresses today's human needs.

For more information on the activities of the Leonardo organizations and networks, please visit our Web site at <http://www.leonardo.info>.

Roger F. Malina
Chair, Leonardo/ISAST

Acknowledgments

From its inception as an idea for a conference to its completion as a printed book, this project has benefited from the gift economy Mark Surman and Darren Wershler-Henry have called "commonspace." It emerged in a hum of exchange, collaboration, aggregation, argumentation, and play that happened over coffee, over email, and over time in both actual and virtual locations. We are deeply grateful to all the people who helped generate and sustain the collectivity that is now this book.

Support for the New Media Poetry Conference, held October 11–12, 2002, at the University of Iowa, came from a coalition of discipline-crossing ventures within the university. We owe special thanks to Christopher Merrill, director of the International Writing Program, Brooks Landon, then chair of the Department of English, Jay Semel, director of the Obermann Center for Advanced Studies, and Nataša Ďurovičová, editor of *91st Meridian*. The Office of the Provost at the University of Iowa, Iowa's Project on the Rhetoric of Inquiry, and Humanities Iowa also provided crucial financial assistance. Without their ideas, encouragement, and leap of faith, this collection of essays would not have materialized.

During the conference, we depended on the assistance of Sarah Townsend, Patrick Walter, and Joshua Weiss. Throughout the back-to-back twenty-four-hour days it takes to make a conference happen, they did everything from tech assistance to transport services. Thanks to Ingrid Ankerson, who helped with the conference poster and created splash pages for the New Media Cabaret, and to Merrie Snell of POROI and Gayle Sand of the

Department of English, who helped with the intricacies of closing the conference accounts.

During the editing phase of the book, appointments as Media Associates at the Obermann Center for Advanced Studies put us in the midst of the Center's lively intellectual environment, ample computing resources, and generous support services. We owe particular thanks to Karla Tonella, Obermann's academic technologies specialist, who kept our laptops functioning, wired and unwired them as necessary, created and managed the Web site used by the conference speakers, and answered every question we asked with wit and patience. We are grateful, last but not least, to Obermann's talented administrative assistants, Lorna Olson and Carolyn Frisbie, who helped with everything else.

For their astute bibliographical and editing assistance in the preparation of the manuscript, we are indebted to Sarah Townsend and Joshua Weiss, who helped with the initial editing, and to Jennifer Banash, Amit Baishya, Ben Basan, Gunnar Benediktsson, LeDon Sweeney, and Danielle Weiss, who helped format and prepare the final manuscript. For final preparation of the book's many images, we relied on Kelly McLaughlin's keen eye and technical expertise. Thom Swiss also wishes to thank Cynthia Lewis for her patience during this process.

Finally, as the manuscript became a book, we are grateful to our editors at MIT, Doug Sery and Kathleen A. Caruso, to the anonymous initial book proposal reviewers, and to MIT's excellent editorial staff.

Adalaide Morris
Thomas Swiss

New Media Poetics: As We May Think/How to Write

Adalaide Morris

There is singularly nothing that makes a difference a difference in beginning and in the middle and in ending except that each generation has something different at which they are all looking.
—GERTRUDE STEIN, "COMPOSITION AS EXPLANATION"

Gertrude Stein liked Fords and billboards, filmstrips, and the view from planes. The world perceptible at cruising speed, in the flicker of early cinema, or from a seat high over Midwestern wheat fields is "what is seen," Stein explains, and "what is seen depends upon how everybody is doing everything" (1998a, 520). Again and again in the most abstruse sections of her lectures on poetry and grammar, plays, portraits, and repetition, Stein reminds her audiences that they already know what she is saying. "But everybody knows that. Yes anybody knows that" (1998b, 292), she reiterates, "anybody can know that" (288).

The catch is the lag between two kinds of knowledge: what we know because it is what we see and do, and what we know because it is what we think. The first kind of knowledge is instinctive and unself-conscious, located in the body as it moves through the world; the second is categorical, located in the mind as it remembers and elaborates what it has been taught. For Stein, every generation composes and explains its life in terms developed by people who did not see what they now see or do what they now do. Stein's paradigm of this lag—and intimation of its consequences—is the battle plan conceived by World War I generals who imagined "a nineteenth-century war . . . to be fought with twentieth-century weapons" (1998a, 520). For Stein, we are, each and every one of us, nimble citizens of an always newly technologized, mediated world that hasn't yet entered, much less altered, our categories of thought. The trick, for Stein, is not to be *ahead* of one's time—"No one is ahead of his time," she says (521)—but *in* one's time.

Instead of the beginnings, middles, and ends that structured nineteenth-century linear narratives, Stein constructed for her writing a continuous present as additive as a drive in the country, as iterative as the frames in a filmstrip, as collaged as the view from a plane. Gathered under titles such as "Composition as Explanation," "Forensics," or *How to Write*, her self-reflexive essays present themselves as if they were a set of instructions or procedures— not necessarily concise, not necessarily clear—for carrying out a particular operation or using a particular piece of equipment. These writings are machines for cognition, "Thinkertoys"—to borrow Ted Nelson's term for his digital imaginings (1974, 330)—engineered to cognize the *now* she apprehended. "I was dead against her," Carl Van Vechten recalls a student saying when Stein's lecture tour hit Amherst College in 1934, "and I just went to see what she looked like and then she took the door of my mind right off its hinges and now it's wide open" (qtd. in Harrison 1974, 10).

What would the early twenty-first century look like if we did not conceptualize it in categories developed in the heyday of Fords, silent film, prop planes, and typewriters? What is it that we know but do not yet know we know? The most interesting thinkers about contemporary media are those who, like Stein, insist on a knowledge that exceeds current conceptual categories: the embodied knowledge, in our era, of a world in which children grow up playing with toys that have as much computing power as the giant IBM computers that sold for millions of dollars a generation ago.[1] What we see and do is conditioned by a technoenvironment of digital computers, cell phones, PDAs, video games, email, networked chatrooms, networked archives, and ubiquitous online banking and commerce; what we think is conditioned by concepts developed, for the most part, in a world of print.

Extending N. Katherine Hayles's important work on embodied knowledge in the "posthuman" world, Mark B. N. Hansen turns to cognitive psychology and phenomenology to examine the interplay between technology and the ways in which we grasp our world. Like Stein's, Hansen's focus is the gap between the concrete experiential effects of what we see and do, on the one hand, and the mental categories of what we know, on the other. Without any

self-conscious contribution from their users, without mediation by preexist-
ing cultural constructions, without any more sophisticated terminology than
hybrid phrases such as "horseless carriage" or "moving picture," the Fords and
films of Stein's world altered early twentieth-century sensory ratios as drasti-
cally as digital technologies are currently transforming the life-world of the
twenty-first century. Like Stein's World War I generals, however, we remain
"at least several generations behind [our]selves" (1998a, 521): what we do and
see does not match the inscriptional or representational conventions through
which we think.

To explain why new technologies are not readily assimilable in terms of
current cultural codes, both Hayles and Hansen draw on theories of neuro-
scientists and cognitive theorists who argue that we know what we see
and do through emotions, kinesthesia, proprioception, and other sensations
located in the lower brain, limbic system, and central nervous system, and we
know what we know at the level of the neocortex.[2] The first is the knowledge
that Stein says "everybody knows": it's in our fingertips and attention spans,
habits, suspicions, and predilections. The second is book knowledge, cultural
doxa, canonical convictions, and common sense. What Stein did to take the
door off the hinges of the Amherst student's mind was, for a moment, to
connect these two segments of his cognition. The fact that there is no auto-
matic link between seeing, doing, and knowing puts them into productive
negotiation with one another. For Stein—and also, as we will see, for many
new media artists and interpreters—aesthetic constructions are crucial ele-
ments in that negotiation.

There is, however, an aspect of contemporary cognition Stein could not have
articulated, one that is key to the new media poetics this book takes up. Where
in Stein's reckoning, cognition is distributed between different centers *within*
an individual, since the mid-1980s, notions of "distributed cognition" have
increasingly extended *beyond* the individual to focus on circuits or systems that
link human beings with each other, with their material artifacts and tools,
and, most important for our purposes, with their networked and program-
mable machines.

Stein's thinking, for all its hinge-busting force, remains within range of a
humanist paradigm that reserves room for concepts such as "masterpieces,"
"genius," and "English literature." Her insistence that what we see and do is
altered by the technologies with which we interact, however, anticipates the

thinking of two groups of post–World War II theorists whose ideas prepare the ground for a study of new media poetics. Responding to the omnipresence of electronic media in the 1960s, Walter J. Ong, Eric A. Havelock, Jack Goody, and Marshall McLuhan elaborated theories of orality, literacy, and secondary or electronic orality in order to describe how communication technologies not only extend human capacities but alter the ways in which we construct knowledge, construe our subjectivities, and interact with other human beings.[3]

Responding to U.S. techno-scientific culture during and immediately after World War II, in their turn, Claude Shannon, Norbert Wiener, John von Neumann, Donald MacKay, and the other participants in the postwar Macy Conferences on Cybernetics elaborated theories of the nature of information, information technologies, and the biological, social, linguistic, and cultural changes that initiate, accompany, and complicate the development of those technologies.[4] By 1985, when Donna Haraway published "A Manifesto for Cyborgs," it made both literal and metaphoric sense to think of the human subject in the emergent paradigm Hayles calls the "posthuman."

From a posthuman point of view, we are not the bounded, autonomous, coherent, and fully self-conscious beings imagined by Enlightenment thinkers but cybernetic organisms joined in continuous feedback loops with media and information technologies. If, in a literal sense, a good 10 percent of the current U.S. population is seamlessly articulated with machines—including, in Hayles's list, "people with electronic pacemakers, artificial joints, drug-implant systems, implanted corneal lenses, and artificial skin"—a much higher percentage of the population spends its day linked to machines in a metaphoric sense, among them, again in Hayles's list, "the computer keyboarder joined in a cybernetic circuit with the screen, the neurosurgeon guided by fiber-optic microscopy during an operation, and the adolescent game player in the local video-game arcade" (1999, 115). The term "cyborg" and, increasingly, the term "posthuman" pop up everywhere in contemporary journalism, popular fiction, cultural criticism, and academic discourse because they play for our era the role the phrases "horseless carriage" and "moving picture" played for Stein's: in their cobbled-together hybridity, these terms hold open a place for configurations for which we have as yet only a tentative vocabulary.

Although the term "posthuman" has been defined in various ways, the common element in its use is a synergy between human beings and intelligent machines.[5] As the chapters in this volume suggest, this synergy has profound implications for the category "literature" and its subset "poetry" as they enter into combination with networked and programmable machines to emerge in such amalgams as "electronic literature" or "e-poetries."[6] The reciprocal and complementary aims of this book are to extend the work of understanding the computer as an expressive medium by adding new media poetry to the study of hypertext narrative, interactive fiction, computer games, intermedia art, and other digital art forms, to showcase a series of visually arresting, aurally charged, and dynamic examples of this kind of writing, and to consider some of the ways in which these examples reconfigure the familiar field of poetry by bringing back into view vital but marginalized lineages of print and sound poetics, procedural writing, gestural abstraction and conceptual art, and activist and/or utopian communities formed by emergent poetics.

If, as the poet-critic Charles Bernstein suggests, "Poetics is the continuation of poetry by other means" (1992, 160), what is the continuation of poetry carried out in compositions variously known as "new media poetry," "e-poetry," "digital poetry," "computer-poems," "poemsthatgo," "net.art," "codework," or any of a half a dozen other strikes at this moving target? As is true at the opening of any conceptual terrain, debates over new media taxonomy are consequential and often vitriolic. Are the terms Aristotle developed to describe drama useful, as Brenda Laurel and others claim, in the study of human-computer activity? Is it productive, as Janet Murray and others hold, to subsume the study of computer games into the discipline of narratology?[7] Is the critical apparatus developed to discuss cinematic forms of observing the world, structuring time, narrating a story, and linking one experience to the next "the basic means," as Lev Manovich maintains, "by which computer users access and interact with all cultural data" (2001, xv)? Or, as Mark Hansen, Espen J. Aarseth, and other critics retort, are these and other importations of vocabulary from one field to another a surefire way to miss the newness of new media?[8]

The question Alan Filreis asks in chapter 6—does a course in new media poetry belong in the curriculum of a Department of English, a Communication Studies program, a School of Art and Art History, or a program in Intermedia Studies?—pushes the debate from theory to practices that bear on faculty hiring, equipment purchasing, allotment of server space, student head counts, and professional certification. As Filreis suggests, the debate over terms is acrid in part because what is at stake is not just discursive categorizations and their implications for interpretation and evaluation but the flow of resources within institutions and the reach and prestige of one's own discipline.[9]

The most generative approaches to discussions of the computer as an expressive engine tend to be those that work from bottom up rather than top down. Instead of mapping categories developed in literary or cinematic studies onto new media compositions, these approaches start with the characteristics of the machines digital composers use to generate textual experiences as physical artifacts. To give just three examples of such bottom-up methods, N. Katherine Hayles defines her "media-specific analysis" as "a kind of criticism that pays attention to the material apparatus producing the literary work as physical artifact" (2002, 29); Lev Manovich calls his method "digital materialism" because it "scrutinize[s] the principles of computer hardware and software and the operations involved in creating cultural objects on a computer to uncover a new cultural logic at work" (2001, 10); and, most playfully, in "Stops and Rebels," Brian Kim Stefans composes an algorithmically generated "computer-poem" that runs across the top of more than one hundred pages of footnotes dedicated to meditations on the nature of its own category.

The upshot of this bottom-up method is not "literacy," a knowledge we already "know," but a set of behaviors Gregory Ulmer calls "electracy," a knowledge citizens of networked cultures "see" and "do." Agile operators, willy-nilly, of computer keyboards, ATMs, cell phones, PDAs, Gameboys, iPods, and the other devices of our digital epoch, we are already, in an unreflective fashion and in various degrees, at ease with digitality.[10] "The nice thing about having such a term," Ulmer tells Talan Memmott,

is not only the efficiency, but the categorical effect it produces. For one thing, it helps us see the difference between ["electracy" and] "media literacy" ([a term] whose goal is to protect from or defend against electracy by means of forms and practices specific to the previous apparatus; the equivalent for an oral person calling literacy "alphabetic orality"). It also is generative in that, knowing by analogy with literacy that digital technological shift is just one part of an apparatus, we may notice that the other parts of the apparatus shift are also well under way. (Memmott 2000)

The choice of the term "new media poetics" as a title for this volume is meant to bring into view an ongoing, elastic, and capacious process rather than a taxonomically precise product: as befits the processual or process-driven nature of computers, the emphasis in the following chapters is on the act of making rather than the thing made, on forces rather than stable formations. At its broadest, new media poetics includes a wide variety of configurations of language, image, and sound produced, distributed, archived, accessed, and/or assimilated on computers. At its narrowest, it is such material positioned by its composers and/or its reader-users in a lineage of information-rich, dense, heightened discourse, often but not only, as *The New Princeton Handbook of Poetic Terms* puts it, "heightened forms of perception, experience, meaning, or consciousness in heightened lang[uage]" (Brogan 1994, 233). Unlike hypertext narrative, the digital poem does not normally depend on lexia or blocks of semi-autonomous text joined by hot links into variable user-driven configurations; unlike computer games, it does not usually depend on a combination of rules, a simulated game world, or traditions of game playing; unlike interactive fiction, it doesn't require a simulated world, or world model, and a built-in parser to accept and analyze natural language input from the interactor.[11] Unlike traditional print poetry, finally, new media poems are not often lineated[12] or rhymed, do not necessarily maintain stable or consistent configurations, and seem by nature to bend—if not break—the founding constraints of the lyric as violently as hypermedia, computer games, and interactive fiction bend or break the constraints of narrative.

Because what we are calling new media poems spend at least part of their life cycle in digitized form, they can assume a number of different configurations: at their simplest, these poems are electronic documents that can be traversed, navigated, and/or reconfigured by their "users," "operators," or "interactors," but they may include print materials newly accessible through digitized archives such as those at UbuWeb or the Institute for Advanced Technology in the Humanities (IATH); print and sound materials made newly visible, even pivotal, by their position in the lineages that have generated new media compositions, as, for example, the concrete poems of Haroldo and Augusto de Campos, the "potential literature" of OULIPO, or the constraint-driven compositions of John Cage and Jackson Mac Low; sound materials accessible in the archives of UbuWeb, the Electronic Poetry Center (EPC), and PENNsound, as well as programs such as Martin Spinelli's *Radio Radio*, examined in chapter 5 and linked into all three of these online archives; digital poems available through online journals such as Jennifer Ley's pioneering *Riding the Meridian*, discussed in chapter 4, Megan Sapnar and Ingrid

Ankerson's *poemsthatgo,* Thom Swiss's *The Iowa Review Web,* and Talan Memmott's *BeeHive;* and, finally, materials that exist simultaneously in differential forms on a page, in a museum installation, and/or in a webzine or online "subject village."[13] No longer, in the usual sense of the term *literature,* "printed matter of any kind," then, these writings are, in at least one of their instantiations, digitized for sight, sound, and/or movement by machines that use code, databases, and algorithms to mediate, permutate, and/or compute what a composer and a clicking, sampling, cutting-and-pasting, or morphing user cocreate. Our approach has been to open the hermeneutic circle with texts new media poets and critics of poetry include in the category of new media poetics in order to think about the contexts and theories within which these writings operate.

As Loss Pequeño Glazier emphasized in the first book-length study of this body of material, code is fundamental to the meaning-making structures of digital poetry. To use the media-specific terminology of digital poetics, all poems (oral, written, or electronic) combine the elements of information and presentation or data and display, draw on the databanks of a culture (its language, knowledge archives, symbol sets, and emotional networks), and take shape through a series of sometimes unacknowledged but nonetheless formulable procedures or algorithms.[14] What makes digital poetry different from poetry that takes place in the air or on the page is the coding used by the poet and/or her collaborator to prepare information for display on networked and programmable machines.

As the middle layer in a digital poem's three-part structure, code is located in a control file or set of control files that tells a machine how to display information. In Safari, Explorer, Netscape, Firefox, and other browsers, this layer can be seen by clicking on a menu item called "view source," "page source," or "reveal code." Written in any of several high-level languages that combine a vocabulary and set of grammatical rules, code enables programmers to write instructions that are more or less independent of any particular type of computer. Without operable code and the programs that compose it, a computer is useless.[15]

Because programming languages can be interpreted by both humans and computers, code is the link between wetware and hardware or human brains and intelligent machines. Accessed by a programmer, poet, or "interactor," a digital poem's source code can be parsed, tweaked, snatched, sampled, altered, and/or recycled into other poems and programs.[16] Accessed, in turn, by a compiler in the computer's hardware, it can be transformed into an intermediary called object code and then into a machine language that consists entirely of numbers and is therefore all but impossible for humans to interpret.[17]

Of the three inseparable components of a digital poem—data fields, code, and display—only the final element, the display, is immediately visible. For this reason, critics of print poetry often underestimate the otherness of new media writing, its resistance, excess, or supplementarity to print poetics, even to experimental poetics. As Talan Memmott and John Cayley emphasize in chapters 15 and 16 respectively, new media poetry is more than the simple migration of words from page to screen, ink to pixels, static to dynamic forms, more than a shift from black letters on white backgrounds to flickering patterns in millions of colors; it is, in important aspects, a different order of writing. Definitions of new media poetics that do not account for code miss the synergy crucial to its operations, its realm of discourse, and its self-reflexivity.

Prefatory to looking at the contexts, differential forms, and theories behind some of the compositions that fall into the category of new media poetics, it is important to linger for a moment on the human-machine interactions through which this work is composed, disseminated, archived, and/or assimilated. How do intelligent machines and human beings think together? What kind of logical operations do they most productively perform? Why is it important to learn to think with or through networked and programmable machines—to become conscious, that is, of how they may think? "How," in short—to apply Gertrude Stein's procedural question-statement to the twenty-first century's information-rich, algorithmically driven, multimedia discourse network—"to write" as we may think?

As Lev Manovich explains in *The Language of New Media*, his crucial study of digital programming, architecture, and procedures, "new media represents a convergence of two separate historical trajectories: computing and media technologies" (2001, 20).[18] Confirming this dual scientific and artistic lineage, Noah Wardrip-Fruin and Nick Monfort constructed their foundational *New Media Reader* (2003) as a mix of documents from both trajectories. Side by side with writings by Jorge Luis Borges, Italo Calvino, and William S. Burroughs, Nam June Paik and Bill Viola, Jean Baudrillard, Gilles Deleuze and Félix Guattari, Raymond Williams, Sherry Turkle, Donna Haraway, and other writers, artists, theorists, and cultural critics are a series of fresh and powerful documents by the visionary engineers Vannevar Bush, Alan Turing, J. C. R. Licklider, Douglas Engelbart, Ted Nelson, Tim Berners-Lee, and their colleagues, who began in the aftermath of World War II to think their way toward human-machine interactions, desktop and laptop computers, mice, windows, mixed text-graphic displays, hyperlinks, worldwide networks, voice interaction, wireless data connections, and portable information devices that structure what we see and do and inflect how we write and read in the day-to-day life of the early twenty-first century.[19]

Vannevar Bush's essay "As We May Think" appeared in 1945 in the *Atlantic Monthly*, the same magazine that had a decade earlier precipitated Stein's lecture tour by serializing her *Autobiography of Alice B. Toklas*. Like Stein's young man at Amherst, Bush's readers—among them, Doug Engelbart, who came across the essay in a Red Cross library for U.S. soldiers in the Philippines, and Ted Nelson, who could have heard his grandfather read it aloud at the dinner table[20]—felt the hinges give way. "The world has arrived at an age of cheap complex devices of great reliability," Bush writes, wrenching open a door for a generation of inventors, "and something is bound to come of it" ([1945] 2003, 38).

All four words in Bush's title do nontrivial work: *as* signals that the change in question has to do not just with process but also with the quality, degree, manner, and extent of thinking; *we* tells us this process is transpersonal, a force that links people with each other and with the intelligent machines they shape and are shaped by; *may* suggests Bush's hope that the physicists that engineered unprecedented destruction in World War II might now turn their energies toward generative directions; and, finally, in its strongest sense, *think* suggests that the mental activity in question does not reproduce a reality that would exist without it but rather itself intervenes in and creates the world around us.

With Stein's mix of common sense and vision, Bush looked at the linear, logical, stable categories into which we struggle to fit what we know we know and concluded "[t]he human mind does not work that way":

It operates by association. With one item in its grasp, it snaps instantly to the next that is suggested by the association of thoughts, in accordance with some intricate web of trails carried by the cells of the brain. . . . [T]he speed of action, the intricacy of trails, the detail of mental pictures, is awe-inspiring beyond all else in nature. ([1945] 2003, 44)

Bush called the device he imagined to supercede card catalogs, indexes, and other hierarchical sequencing and storing schema the "Memex." This Rube Goldberg contrivance was an "enlarged intimate supplement to . . . memory" in the form of a desk that instantly "brings files and material on any subject to the operator's fingertips," displays them on "slanting, translucent screens," records the researcher's longhand notes, sketches, and surmises and refiles them using "code numbers" that will facilitate speedy retrieval and recombination (45).

Bush's "associative indexing" ([1945] 2003, 45), of course, prefigures the operations of late twentieth-century desktop and laptop computers and their early twenty-first-century handheld and wearable equivalents. As Hayles emphasizes in titling her MIT Mediawork pamphlet *Writing Machines*, all writing involves inscription technologies that actively condition what we can see, do, and know, but there is an additional twist to her phrase. "'Writing machines,'" Hayles explains, invoking the phrase's noun-verb variant, "is . . . what technotexts do when they bring into view the machinery that gives their verbal constructions physical reality" (2002, 26). The difference between the pen, the printing press, and the computer, however, is the gist of Bush's vision: like the Memex, a computer is an intelligent machine, not just faster but more precise, more capacious, and more dynamic than a pen, typewriter, or print-ing press. In an important sense, it can be said to think with us—even in dystopic imaginings, for us or against us.

To explain this human-machine partnership, Hayles turns to the work of Edwin Hutchins, who generated the term "distributed cognition" during his research into the navigational systems of oceangoing ships. Like the antiair-craft gunners who were Norbert Wiener's early research subjects, navigators enter into an information circuit with their instruments. In Hayles's summary of Hutchins's point, "the cognitive system responsible for locating the ship in space and navigating it successfully resides not in humans alone but in the complex interactions within an environment that includes both human and nonhuman actors" (1999, 288). Hutchins, Hayles, and, following their lead, Hansen, then, press beyond Stein's model of cognition toward Bush's model: for them, the body is not just repositioned by new technologies but supple-mented, extended, and remade into a material-informational entity whose boundaries are continuously constructed and reconstructed in its interactions with instruments whose total cognitive capacity exceeds our individual knowledge.

In *Embodying* Technesis: *Technology Beyond Writing* (2000), his first book, Hansen's use of the term "technology" is general, pertaining as much to cars, airplanes, telegraphs, telephones, radios, and televisions as to computers, but in his second book, *New Philosophy for New Media* (2004), Hansen grounds his argument in the robust material and phenomenological mechanics of the twenty-first-century digital image. The objects of his analysis are installations and environments engineered by Bill Viola, Jeffrey Shaw, Robert Lazzarini, Kirsten Geisler, and other new media artists to do the same thing Stein set out to do with the torqued grammar of her sentences: to force the embodied viewer-participant to open the door between what he sees or hears or does and what he knows, to put his mind into a circuit with the technologized and mediated information he is always processing, to make him, in a sense, his own contemporary.

Hansen's historically situated and technologically specific account of the workings of the digitized image moves the discussion of the reception of new media beyond the literary categories George P. Landow and other early hypertext theorists utilized to construct the distinction between print and electronic literature. The objects of Landow's analysis were first-generation electronic texts such as Michael Joyce's *afternoon, a story* (1987), Stuart Moultrop's *Victory Garden* (1991), and Shelley Jackson's *Patchwork Girl* (1995), many of them published on disk and marketed in booklike folders by Eastgate Systems. Composed for the most part between 1985 and 1995 in programs such as Eastgate's Storyspace,[21] these narratives typically consisted of verbal text with little or no multimedia supplementation. The feature that exhilarated writers and readers alike was their built-in flexibility. Consisting of blocks of text joined in multiple paths at nodes a user clicks to switch between screens and navigate across fields, these hypertexts are "read"—even, in some sense, "written"—by interpreters threading their way through a textual maze.

To its advocates, hypertext appeared to materialize the still vibrant poststructuralist dream of processual, dynamic, multiple signifying structures activated by readers who were not consumers of fixed meanings but producers of their own compositions. "From the vantage point of the current changes in information technology," Landow asserts in his groundbreaking study *Hypertext: The Convergence of Contemporary Critical Theory and Technology,* "Barthes's distinction between readerly and writerly texts appears to be essentially a distinction between text based on print technology and electronic hypertext" (1992, 5). Although it provided a powerful launch for a newly technologized form of writing, however, Landow's mapping of the difference between print and digital media onto Barthes' division between code-driven classical realist narratives and innovative or experimental texts is a strategy that emerges, in Ulmer's terms, from literacy rather than electracy. Misleading in at least three consequential ways, this conflation overestimates the agency of the electronic reader, underestimates the complexity of print texts, and occludes the genuinely revolutionary behavior of the digitized image.

In their essays for this volume, Marjorie Perloff (chapter 7) and Brian Kim Stefans (chapter 3) put the case against first-generation claims for inter-activity in strong terms. Because clickable options are, by definition, prepro-grammed, the reader's claim to compositional agency is, in Perloff's judgment, a "sham." "Is such activity," she asks, "really any more 'interactive' than, say, *The Sims* games, which allow their players to 'decide' what sort of house the family will live in, what their furniture will look like, and what their 'per-sonalities' are?" In the closed system of "an overdetermined narrative—by its nature, linear and noninteractive—the choices," Stefans observes, "can have no more than trivial differences between them, and their results can be of no more than trivial importance." Although the term "interactivity," then, gave the new electronic literature a cachet associated with innovative texts and a magic associated with radically improved technology, it remained, Aarseth concludes, "a purely ideological term, projecting an unfocused fantasy rather than a concept of any analytical substance" (1997, 51).

If early hypertext theory overestimated the electronic reader's agency, it underplayed the complexity, energy, and undecidability of print and the fragility of the divide between Barthes' two categories. Not only were Barthes' exemplars of the writerly all, of course, challenging and self-reflexive print texts but many of them created, in their turn, new protocols for reading. Once their conventions had been recognized and classified, these texts became in their turn as "traversed, intersected, stopped, [and] plasticized by some sin-gular system" as any of Barthes' readerly texts (Barthes 1974, 5). As Stein herself observed, much to her amusement, many decades earlier, only a moment separates the outlaw from the classic.[22]

While critics of first-generation electronic literature drew much of their terminology from analyses of narrative classics, critics of second-generation electronic literature, when they draw on literary methodologies, tend to invoke strategies developed to read the texts of avant-garde or experimentalist poets.[23] This shift from narrative to poetic models makes sense, however, not in a literary context—a sudden preference, say, for the poem over the short story—but in a material one: in tandem with the growth of the Web, the rapid development of sophisticated programming software in the decade between 1985 and 1995 made it possible for writers to go beyond the plot-driven verbal lexia of Storyspace. Composed for the most part after 1995 in DHTML, JavaScript, Java, QuickTime, Macromedia Flash, Shockwave, and other programs that combine verbal elements with graphics, images, animation, sound, and other multimedia effects, second-generation electronic texts tend to be compressed, multilayered, and time-driven—closer to Mallarmé than to Balzac, more like Dickinson than Frost, riders in a posse that includes such enduring outlaws as Stein's *Tender Buttons,* Joyce's *Finnegans Wake,* the concrete and visual poetry of Augusto and Haroldo de Campos, Bob Brown's "Readies," John Cage's mesostics, and OULIPO's "potential literature."[24]

Although it is possible to find poems scattered through the lexia of first-generation electronic texts, little link-node poetry emerged between 1985 and 1995.[25] The associational leaps, paratactic construction, zigzag traverses, and connotative vectors hotlinks added to narrative in these years are alive in even the most traditional print poems. As high-energy linguistic constructs, poems in print generate multiple meanings through strategic use of line endings, crosscuts between syntactic and metrical units, densely aural patterning of rhyme, echoic allusions, and the variable visual patterning of page space. To a greater degree than most prose narratives, poems in print are always already hotlinked and jumpy.

The most robust and enduring connection between poetics and hypertext is not hypertext poetry but the documents made available through networked hypertext archives such as the Blake, Rosetti, Dickinson, and Whitman archives allied with the University of Virginia's IATH; the online journal and multimedia companion to Cary Nelson's *Oxford Anthology of Modern American Poetry* housed at the University of Illinois; the visual, aural, and textual resources in the EPC at SUNY Buffalo, the Digital Dada Library at the University of Iowa, and the PENNsound archive at the University of Pennsylvania; the Online Classroom of the Academy of American Poetry; and dozens of other excellent sites that have made hard-to-find poetic texts and manuscripts newly available, linked them to newspapers, photo archives, sound files, and other contemporary multimedia documents to make visible the historical contexts occluded by variorum print editions and, in many cases, opened ongoing productive dialogues such as those Alan Filreis describes (chapter 6) at Kelly Writers House and Kenneth Goldsmith (chapter 2) on UbuWeb. Nonetheless, however much hypertext archives such as these enrich and enliven the reading of poems, they are not and never claimed to be new media poems.

If critics and theorists of second-generation electronic texts are not focused on issues of interactivity, invested in the push-pull of writerly and readerly texts, or, as we will see in their emphasis on "differential poetics," prepared to herald—much less welcome—the end of books,[26] what then are their preoccupations? What can new media poetics tell us about thinking and writing in a world increasingly reliant on databases, algorithms, collaborative problem solving, instant retrieval and manipulation of information, the play of cutting, pasting, morphing, and sampling, and the ambient and nomadic aesthetics of a networked and programmable culture? How are these changes in the processes of thinking and knowing altering structures of subjectivity and patterns of emotion that were once the providence of the lyric poem?

One of the implications of the complex Mark Hansen (2004) calls "the digital image" is that the receiver of a new media poem cannot be, in any familiar sense, its "reader." If in print terminology to "read" means to decipher and interpret the letters and signs of a document, in computer terminology, it means to copy data from one storage medium or device to another. To keep data safe from corruption in such a transfer, it is customary to save it in a "read-only" format; to explore that data, on the other hand—to interpret it, interact with it, operate or use it—it's necessary to take a deep breath and change it. The essays in this volume suggest an array of terms for this act: to engage a digital text, one "samples" or "morphs" it (Goldsmith, chapter 2), "infects" or "inflects" it (Cayley, chapter 16), "aggregates" or "amplifies" it (Stefans, chapter 3), transforms it from "object to event" (Hayles, chapter 9), or performs its signs and sign regimes in a *mise en écran* as robust and transgressive as the *mise en scène* demanded by Antonin Artaud (Memmott, chapter 15).

Instead of looking at the digital image, assessing its match with memories of the represented world, gauging its accuracy, beauty, or truth, or otherwise fixing its meaning, users enter it by clicking, zooming, scanning, copying, cutting, pasting, sequencing, and/or framing it. As Manovich emphasizes in his discussion of the principles of new media, "All new media objects, whether created from scratch on computers or converted from analog media sources, are composed of digital code; they are numerical representations." For this reason, Manovich continues, all digital material can be described mathematically and subjected to algorithmic manipulation (2001, 27). The same set of data can appear visually, acoustically, or kinesthetically; it can be warped, streamed, or sampled, accelerated or slowed, supersaturated or attenuated. No longer conceived as a fixed viewpoint on "reality," the image in its digital form is defined by its almost complete flexibility and addressability and its constitutive virtuality. What distinguishes it is the way in which this manipulability turns a viewer into an active *user* or *operator*.

This may seem a back-door return to the ideal of interactivity in hypertext theory, but there is a crucial difference. In his 1997 book, *Cybertext: Perspectives on Ergodic Literature*, Aarseth replaces the term "hypertext," which he finds "as much an ideological category as a technological one" (79), with the term "cybertext," which gives him a fresh opportunity to draw the lineage of new media by invoking Norbert Wiener's book *Cybernetics; or, Control and Communication in the Animal and the Machine* (1948). Rather than emphasizing the supposed interpretive freedom and agency of the reader—for Aarseth, the hype in hypertext—the term "cybertext" foregrounds the organization of the text as a feedback loop. In a cybertext, users steer the text: they are, in this sense, closer to programmers, gamers, and performers than they are to print personae such as writers and readers.[27]

To engage a new media text is to activate, augment, or alter a sequence of signs, images, sounds, and movements. Taken metaphorically this might serve as a handy definition of the art of interpreting any semiotically charged text, but in the case of new media poetics it has literal as well as figurative import, for it signals, Aarseth emphasizes, "a work of physical construction that the various concepts of 'reading' do not account for" (1997, 1). The term Aarseth coins to mark the digital text—the adjective "ergodic"—is an amalgam of the Greek terms for "work" and "path": in nonergodic literature, Aarseth explains, "the effort to traverse the text is trivial, with no extranoematic responsibilities placed on the reader except (for example) eye movement and the periodic or arbitrary turning of pages," but ergodic literature requires "nontrivial effort . . . to allow the reader to traverse the text" (1–2).

In confirmation of Aarseth's intuition, the artist statements in this volume describe a series of contemporary new media poems—Loss Pequeño Glazier's

"Io Sono At Swoons" (chapter 10), Stephanie Strickland and Cynthia Lawson's "Vniverse" (chapter 8), William Poundstone's "3 Proposals for Bottle Imps" (chapter 12), and Giselle Beiguelman's *egoscópio* (chapter 14) and other compositions for billboards and handheld mobile devices—by providing accounts not of the poems' fixed form but of their performative operations, that is, the algorithmic calculations that comprised their writing, the clicking, mousing, dragging, dropping, and other manipulations that comprise their operation by a user.[28] Like the poems by Talan Memmott, John Cayley, Brian Kim Stefans, Caroline Bergvall, Jim Rosenberg, and others whose work animates this book, these cybertexts are carefully crafted poem-machines, innovative engines that reconfigure digital poetics as freshly as the print texts Steve McCaffery and bpNichol (1992) call "book-machines" reconfigure traditional print poetics.

The machinic, new media artists, philosophers, and cultural critics emphasize, is not to be confused with the robotic. In the process of turning an object into an event, a digital image is not just activated but also augmented, amplified, and filtered by the user's body. In chapter 11, Carrie Noland describes a variety of ways in which new media texts engage and extend the body's energies. For both Noland and Hansen, the most profound effect of digitization is this coordination between a user's living body and the digital text. Far from turning users into automatons, Hansen argues, digitized images enter into a circuit with them, making their bodies into laboratories or workspaces where digital information is converted into corporeally apprehensible images. In new media poems such as Memmott's *Lexia to Perplexia,* Cayley's *What We Will,* and Strickland and Lawson's Vniverse, the virtual space of the image is transformed from an impersonal cognitive schema—for example, a set of equations in Memmott's poem, a clock dial in Cayley's, a star map in Strickland and Lawson's—into an immediately graspable, profoundly personal experience, one played out through its interface with the proprioceptive and affective body of the user.

To make the transition from classical hypertext lexia to new media poetic perplexia is to move from navigating linked text blocks to participating in the activities of dynamic information structures. Talan Memmott's term for the components of second-generation electronic texts is exact: perplexia leave would-be users uncertain about their configurations, trouble would-be interpreters with doubt about their meanings, and distract, confuse, or puzzle those who venture past an initial click into sustained interaction. What forms of synergy between humans and intelligent machines do these poems invite? Why is it worthwhile to push beyond perplexity to play with or through these new media constructions?

The rapid evolution of software and hardware, the variety of uses they can be put to, and their roles in the constant flow of morphed and sampled data through global networks make it all but impossible to give the term "new media poem" a stable definition. In chapter 15, Memmott suggests that instead of a classificatory system, interpreters develop a flexible, mobile, and capacious applied poetics: not a taxonomy but, in his coinage, a *taxonomadism*. In that spirit, before concluding with a brief description of the three sections of essays that follow, it may be helpful to sketch a set of family resemblances between the networked and programmable constructions these chapters take up.

The term "family resemblance" comes, of course, from Wittgenstein, who rejected a search for fixed definitions in order to investigate how words function in everyday language. If we gather together five members of the same family, he argues, they will probably not share any one distinctive feature—two may have dark eyes, another two an aquiline nose, and three, one with dark eyes and two without, the same long torso—but we can, nonetheless, identify them as members of the same group.[29] If, by extension, there is no single defining characteristic of all exemplars of the category "new media poem," we can nevertheless recognize constructions that cluster under this rubric through a series of overlapping similarities and relationships.

As Hayles points out, Aarseth's typology of cybertexts invokes their similarities and relationships by itemizing variables such as links, perspective, access, determinability, transience, dynamics, and user function. "Combinations of these variables," she calculates, "yield 576 different variations, which can be plotted on a grid to locate a particular text's strategies within the cybertext domain" (Hayles 2002, 27–28). Instead of attempting to plot a grid for the subset of cybertextuality called new media poetry, I'd like to make two broad gestures toward a working definition—one negative, the other positive—that will, I hope, bring into view the dynamic new media compositions this volume takes up.

In this book, Brian Kim Stefans (chapter 3) and Barrett Watten (chapter 17) both evoke the conceptual artist Robert Smithson's "non-sites" in order to set up a definition of new media poetry as an active negation of and/or negotiation with prior representational practices. In these gallery installations, Smithson initiated a dialectical exchange between his constructions and the terrain they evoke. *Non-Site, Franklin, New Jersey*, for example, juxtaposes a segmented aerial map of a New Jersey township with five trapezoidal bins containing proportional amounts of ore from each of its parts: these bins are artifice and allusion, not the site but in their alterity from it a dialogue with the site. As Smithson explains to an interviewer, this simultaneous evocation of site and non-site expands the field of the art work in order to "de-mythify things" by "expos[ing] the fact that it is a system [and] therefore taking away the vaulted mystery that is supposed to reside in it" (1979, 159). In the interplay between site and non-site, negation undoes the aura that clings to "nature" and "art" alike. For Stefans, the poetics of his antiwar Web site, Circulars, lies in its dialectical exchange with contemporary notions of political community, technological journalism, and poetic rhetoric; for Watten, the poetics of radical groups such as the Language School and new media artists such as Talan Memmott lies in their negation of and negotiation with conventional forms of poetic language and structure.

Extending the arguments of Stefans and Watten, I want to position new media poems in an expanded field that is neither poetry nor not-poetry but an active exchange between two forms of discourse: the late romantic print lyric, on the one hand, and the networked and programmable poem, on the other. The lyric came into its present form at the same time as the nineteenth-century rise of the industrial economy; networked art developed during the late twentieth-century rise of a global informational economy.[30] Inhabiting the ground between these two forms, new media poets such as Memmott, Strickland, Cayley, Poundstone, Glazier, Bernstein, Beiguelman, and others "de-mythify" both the romantic Self and the global Internet, open poetry to its twenty-first-century contexts, and bend these contexts toward the making that is poetics.

The lyric has served for two centuries to articulate a private interior self. Taught in university writing programs, circulated in literary journals and magazines, performed on book tours financed by publishers, canonized in pedagogical anthologies, and idealized through myths surrounding real figures such as John Keats and imagined figures such as John Keating (the charismatic teacher in the movie *Dead Poets Society*), the lyric presents an array of characteristics that includes the ideology of a single author, a rhetoric of self-examination, self-justification, and self-restoration, an idealization of the mystery of one-of-a-kind art objects, and, not least, control of the distribution of artifacts through pedagogical customs, copyright protections, and expensive variorum print editions.[31]

As Loss Penqueño Glazier (2002a, 22) has suggested, there is something inherently inhospitable to the lyrical "I" in digital poetries. As presented in the chapters that follow, new media poems are often collaborations emerging from alliances between writers, artists, composers, and programmers; they replace romantic narcissism with the human-machine loops Memmott (2001) calls "narcisystems"; and, since the mid-1990s, they have circulated, for the most part, freely on the Internet. Like Ted Nelson's "Thinkertoys," these constructions might be best defined as "mental environments . . . [or] working places for structured activity" ([1974], 2003, 325): laboratories, in effect, in which the "I" of the lyric morphs into the polysemous, constantly changing, distributive "I" of the informational economy.

To turn from a negative to a positive definition opens questions about new media poetry's precursors, procedures, and interpretive contexts. What is the lineage of new media poetry? How do its constituents operate? What similarities animate and affiliate new media poems? What differences divide but do not divorce them? Of the three broad categories of new media poetry—hypertextual poems, poems composed for dynamic and kinetic manipulation and display, and programmable texts[32]—the essays in this volume focus primarily on the last two. To introduce the range and vitality of these nonlyric constructions, the following screenshots offer six snaps from a family album. As fixed black-and-white reductions of colorful kinetic materials, they are suggestive rather than exhaustive, descriptive rather than predictive. In their resemblances and differences, however, they convey some of the strangeness, variety, and excitement of new media poetics.

1. *Literal art:* One of the first things to note about new media poems is the frequency with which they feature not the stanza, the line, the phrase, or resonant word but tumbling, morphing, graphical, and semiotic letters. "Literal art" is John Cayley's term for this "alternative, radically formal tradition of letters projected from Mallarmé, through Dada into the currency of total syntax and post-Concrete visual poetry" (2004a). Composed in programs such as QuickTime, Flash, or Java, literal art can be as straightforward as an animated concrete poem or as complex as the most extravagant algorithmically generated Oulipian experiment. Examples include Ana Maria Uribe's

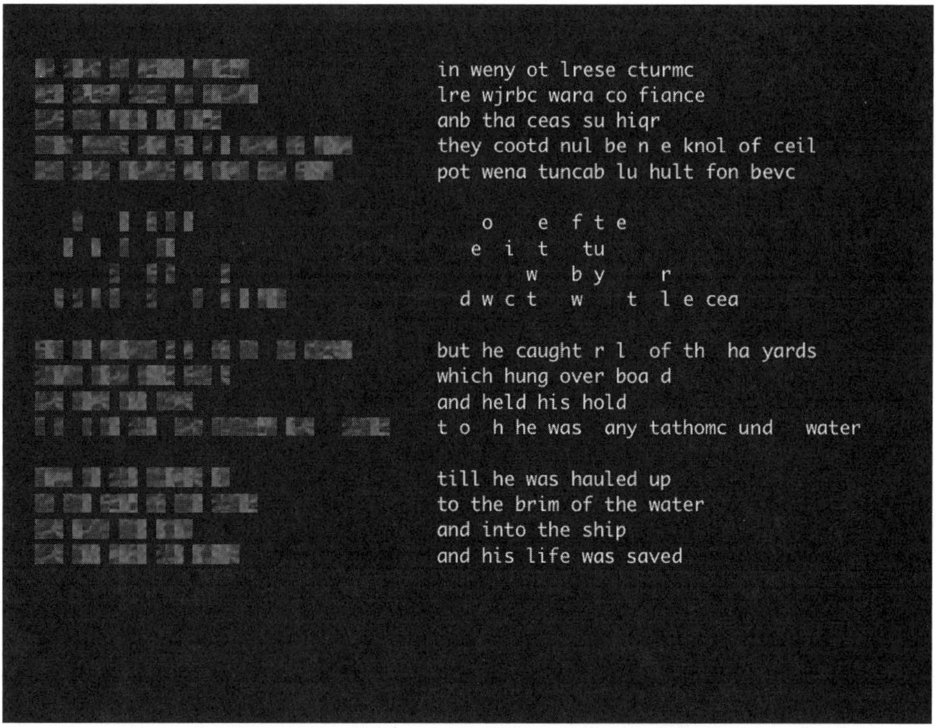

Figure 1.1 Screenshot from *overboard*. Courtesy of John Cayley.

alphabetic *Anipoems* (2003), Brian Kim Stefans's *the dreamlife of letters* (1999), and Jim Rosenberg's *Intergrams;* the screenshot above comes from a work-in-progress by John Cayley and Giles Perring entitled *overboard* (figure 1.1).

In one of its recent incarnations, *overboard* is a gallery installation Cayley describes as "a dynamic linguistic 'wall-hanging,' an ever-moving 'language painting'" (2004b). As time passes, the stable text underlying its changing display moves in and out of legibility, in Cayley's words "sinking, rising, and sometimes in part, 'going under' or drowning, then rising to the surface once again." Similar to Cayley's *riverIsland, overboard* depends on a series of "simple but carefully designed algorithms that allow letters to be replaced by other letters which are in some way similar to . . . those of the original text" (2004b). The music Giles Perring has composed for the piece follows similar generative procedures to provide an aural complement to the letter's visual morphing.[33]

As dynamic as *overboard*, the digital pieces Carrie Noland discusses in chapter 11 inflect the definition of literal art toward the kinetic energies of the body. In the pulsing, jumping, twisting, and rotating of animated letters, she argues, literal art is closely allied to dance and to the gestural abstraction of artists such as Cy Twombly and Robert Morris. By evoking the physical movements of a body engaged in the production of individual or connected letters, Noland argues, digital poetics reconnects the interactor with the embodied gestures of letter making and the status of writing as a performed activity.

2. *Poem-games:* While literal art can be a closed kinetic display, such as Uribe's *Anipoems* or Stefans's *the dreamlife of letters* (1999), or, similar to Rosenberg's *Intergrams* or Cayley's *riverIsland,* a text open to a user's mousing, clicking, dragging, and sequencing manipulations, poem-games are by definition interactive. Like the digital fictions Nick Montfort describes in his book *Twisty Little Passages* (2003b), poem-games are rule-driven ritual spaces dependent on an engaged player: briefer, faster, and less text-driven than interactive fictions, however, poem-games splice the appeal and conventions of computer and video games into the critical and creative traditions of poetry. The next screenshot comes from Jim Andrews's *Arteroids 2.5* (figure 1.2).

Introduced in the Literary Games issue of *poemsthatgo,* billed as "the battle of poetry against itself and the forces of dullness," *Arteroids* riffs off the classic arcade game *Asteroids* in which a lone fighter pilot shoots, rotates, thrusts, and pauses through deep space menaced at every turn by swarms of deadly asteroids. In Andrews's permutation, however, deep space is a poetic field, the projectiles are charged words or phrases, and the ship the player pilots is a term chosen from the arsenal of her creative or critical vocabulary. Struck by a poem-fragment, the player's term explodes into a piece of literal art, "a circular lettristic spray of letters"; shot by a player, the poem-fragment "vaporize[s] into ideas" (2002). The sound of language cracking open—the game's percussive phonotext—is Andrews's voice digitally altered to echo arcade bleeps, cartoon dialogue, sound poems, and radio art. As the player ascends through the game levels, the sounds accelerate in speed and pitch, and the projectile phrases—the poem's projective verses—increase in velocity and density.[34]

Similar to other creative software, *Arteroids* is continuously updated. Version 2.5 contains two "cantos" or divisions: a game mode with scores based on a mortal player's time and accuracy, and a play mode in which a player can choose to be mortal or deathless, compose her own poetic particles, adjust

Figure 1.2 Screenshot from *Arteroids 2.5*, showing the project in play mode, using language from Charles Olson's "Projective Verse." Courtesy of Jim Andrews.

their density, and throw them into warp speed or slow them into legibility. In play mode, Andrews explains, *Arteroids* turns into "a kind of visual/kinetic poetry display/composition device" (2003b). In showing his poem-game to audiences, Andrews positions it as an act that is at once creative and critical: "I try to drive it so that the sounds you get when you press the arrow keys are compositional of sound poetry," he explains to an interviewer, "then i run circles around the word 'poetry,' then i approach it and reverse, approach and reverse, then i blow it up from across the edge of the screen" (2004).[35]

3. *Programmable procedural computer-poems:* Unlike the poem-game, which enters new media poetics from the side of popular culture, the programmable procedural computer-poem (CP) emerges from avant-garde practices associated with groups such as Oulipo, Fluxus, and the Language poets, all thought to be hermetic or elitist in their nonlyric fervor. A procedural poem is a poem generated by the interplay between a body of information and a sequence of steps or, in new media terminology, a database and algorithm.[36] Long before computers, Raymond Queneau, François Le Lionnais, Georges Perec, Italo Calvino, Emmett Williams, John Cage, Jackson Mac Low, Ron Silliman, Lyn Hejinian, Bernadette Mayer, and many others devised ways to pursue the activity Kenneth Goldsmith calls "uncreative writing"[37]—that is, the composition of texts based on rules that force the writer to swerve from the authenticity of self-evaluation and/or self-justification, the mystery of beauty and truth, and the aura of creative genius and timeless masterpieces. The procedure, which can be as simple as eschewing the letter *e* (Perec) or as elaborate as tying the number of sentences in a textual unit to the progression of the Fibonacci sequence (Silliman), is a form of discipline that precedes and generates the body of the poem.[38] When the procedural poem meets the mechanisms of programming-as-writing, the outcome is a variant exemplified and theorized in Brian Kim Stefans's "Stops and Rebels or, The Battle of *Brunaburh*" (figure 1.3).

Printed in a thin strip across the top of a series of brilliantly self-reflexive footnote-essays, Stefans's CP is an image or final description of an algorithm's interaction with a database. The source files for "Stops and Rebels" are Alfred Lord Tennyson's translation of the Anglo-Saxon poem "The Battle of Brunaburh," Stefans's own phonetic rendition of the same poem, a paragraph from Leonard Schwartz's introduction to an anthology of contemporary poetry, a paragraph from Harold Bloom's *Anxiety of Influence,* and a paragraph from Roshi Philip Kapleau's *Three Pillars of Zen.*[39] The poem's workpath is the

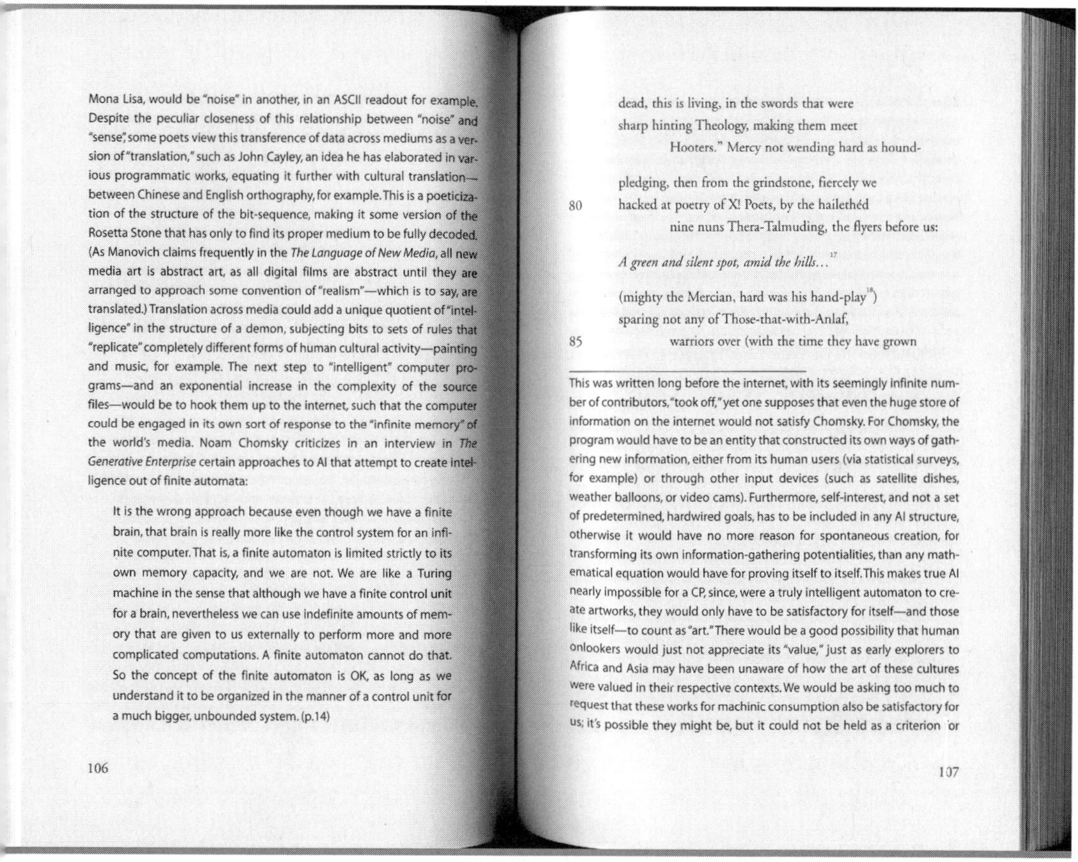

Mona Lisa, would be "noise" in another, in an ASCII readout for example. Despite the peculiar closeness of this relationship between "noise" and "sense," some poets view this transference of data across mediums as a version of "translation," such as John Cayley, an idea he has elaborated in various programmatic works, equating it further with cultural translation—between Chinese and English orthography, for example. This is a poeticization of the structure of the bit-sequence, making it some version of the Rosetta Stone that has only to find its proper medium to be fully decoded. (As Manovich claims frequently in the The Language of New Media, all new media art is abstract art, as all digital films are abstract until they are arranged to approach some convention of "realism"—which is to say, are translated.) Translation across media could add a unique quotient of "intelligence" in the structure of a demon, subjecting bits to sets of rules that "replicate" completely different forms of human cultural activity—painting and music, for example. The next step to "intelligent" computer programs—and an exponential increase in the complexity of the source files—would be to hook them up to the internet, such that the computer could be engaged in its own sort of response to the "infinite memory" of the world's media. Noam Chomsky criticizes in an interview in The Generative Enterprise certain approaches to AI that attempt to create intelligence out of finite automata:

> It is the wrong approach because even though we have a finite brain, that brain is really more like the control system for an infinite computer. That is, a finite automaton is limited strictly to its own memory capacity, and we are not. We are like a Turing machine in the sense that although we have a finite control unit for a brain, nevertheless we can use indefinite amounts of memory that are given to us externally to perform more and more complicated computations. A finite automaton cannot do that. So the concept of the finite automaton is OK, as long as we understand it to be organized in the manner of a control unit for a much bigger, unbounded system. (p.14)

106

dead, this is living, in the swords that were
sharp hinting Theology, making them meet
        Hooters." Mercy not wending hard as hound-

    pledging, then from the grindstone, fiercely we
80 hacked at poetry of X! Poets, by the hailethéd
        nine nuns Thera-Talmuding, the flyers before us:

A green and silent spot, amid the hills... [17]

    (mighty the Mercian, hard was his hand-play [18])
    sparing not any of Those-that-with-Anlaf,
85   warriors over (with the time they have grown

This was written long before the internet, with its seemingly infinite number of contributors, "took off," yet one supposes that even the huge store of information on the internet would not satisfy Chomsky. For Chomsky, the program would have to be an entity that constructed its own ways of gathering new information, either from its human users (via statistical surveys, for example) or through other input devices (such as satellite dishes, weather balloons, or video cams). Furthermore, self-interest, and not a set of predetermined, hardwired goals, has to be included in any AI structure, otherwise it would have no more reason for spontaneous creation, for transforming its own information-gathering potentialities, than any mathematical equation would have for proving itself to itself. This makes true AI nearly impossible for a CP, since, were a truly intelligent automaton to create artworks, they would only have to be satisfactory for itself—and those like itself—to count as "art." There would be a good possibility that human onlookers would just not appreciate its "value," just as early explorers to Africa and Asia may have been unaware of how the art of these cultures were valued in their respective contexts. We would be asking too much to request that these works for machinic consumption also be satisfactory for us; it's possible they might be, but it could not be held as a criterion or

107

Figure 1.3 Pageshot from "Stops and Rebels," in *Fashionable Noise: On Digital Poetics* (Berkeley, CA: Atelos Press, 2003), 106–107. Courtesy of Brian Kim Stefans.

sampling, mixing, and resequencing of these materials by an algorithm Stefans names the "demon." Having selected the materials and composed the algorithm, the poet's final task is to tweak the source texts, fine-tune the demon, and now and then jimmy the output to provide "the gaps in the flow—the black holes—through which the reader can enter the text and be 'activated' as interpreter" (97).[40]

"Stops and Rebels" lures the reader into its data field by accessing the energies of narrative and lyric poetry, but instead of offering an organic origin story or a teleological end point, it presents for inspection "an excavation of the sediment of language and a revelation of hitherto-unknown properties of the language" (64). Stefans's CP is a snapshot of the energies implied by Vannevar Bush's phrase "as we may think": a tantalizing, resistant, sometimes frightening, sometimes witty, always odd poetic interface between the contemporary mind, the workings of language, and cullings from the data bank of cultural poetics.

4. *Real-time reiterative programmable poems:* As the pageshot of "Stops and Rebels" suggests, the final stage of Stefans's CP is a trace or fossilization of a past activity. Because the demon performs its navigation prior to the reader's interaction with the text, its output looks more like a traditional literary work than a digital production. When the process plays out in the real-time flow of a computer screen, it is not visible on a print page and can therefore only be suggested by a screenshot from Loss Penqueño Glazier's "Io Sono At Swoons" (2002b) (figure 1.4).

In a real-time reiterative programmable poem such as "Io Sono," the demon coughs up for consideration endless algorithmic iterations of its source texts. Like "Stops and Rebels," the poem occurs at the crossroads of readability and resistance, but here the traffic is continuous: words and phrases move by like projectiles in *Arteroids,* dissolve in incoherence, or vaporize into ideas only to be pushed from the screen by more words and phrases. When Glazier performs this poem for new media audiences, he enacts the risk of the process by vocalizing the generated text as it materializes then disappears on the screen behind him.

Working in a lineage of innovative poetics that begins with Stein, Glazier is interested not in external thematic statements about an already-known world but in the ongoing, various, and vital iterations his poem-machine generates: "Io Sono" is, in this sense, not an outcome but a form of research into how we might think and write should we immerse ourselves in the contem-

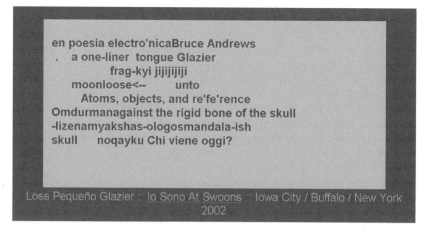

en poesia electro'nicaBruce Andrews
. a one-liner tongue Glazier
frag-kyi jijijijiji
moonloose<-- unto
Atoms, objects, and re'fe'rence
Omdurmanagainst the rigid bone of the skull
-lizenamyakshas-ologosmandala-ish
skull noqayku Chi viene oggi?

Loss Pequeño Glazier :: Io Sono At Swoons :: Iowa City / Buffalo / New York
2002

Figure 1.4   Screenshot of "en poesia electrónica" from "Io Sono At Swoons." Courtesy of
Loss Pequeño Glazier.

porary information flow. The poem's constitutive repetitions are not based on
rhetorical strategies, nor do they build toward coherence or closure: the poet,
the demon, and the source files perform the necessity of living with redun-
dancy, superfluity, and noise as well as meaningfulness and music, thus demon-
strating on the fly the art of survival by surfing and browsing rather than
perfecting and preserving.[41]

5. *Participatory networked and programmable poems:* By concocting the
demon and setting the source files for their poems, Stefans and Glazier produce
documents that move, like much other digitized information, from one source
to many recipients. Stefans's poem-on-the-page and Glazier's poem-on-the-
Web do not accept input from the user, who thus remains, for all his inter-
pretive zeal, the poem's end point rather than its partial generator. Computers,
however, have a potential for many-to-many interactions: they can build rela-
tionships, that is, in which they not only give but receive, store, and process
information. A participatory networked and programmable fiction such as *The
Impermanence Agent* by Noah Wardrip-Fruin, ac chapman, Brion Moss, and
Duane Whitehurst or a participatory networked and programmable poem-
structure such as *egoscópio* by Giselle Beiguelman invites interactors to con-
tribute to its source files, thereby ceding a measure of control in return for
gobbets of text the demon can devour. Beiguelman's instructions for *egoscópio*
suggest both the ethos and structure of this kind of project (figure 1.5).

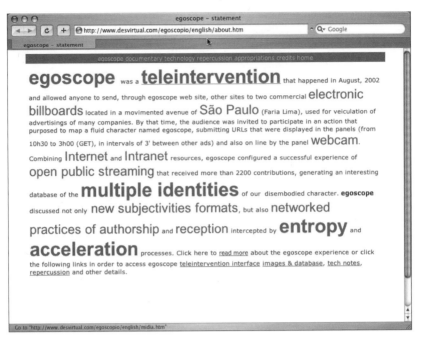

Figure 1.5 Screenshot from *egoscópio*.
http://www.desvirtual.com/egoscopio/english/about.htm.

In Beiguelman's teleintervention, which occurred between August 5 and August 20, 2002, members of the public submitted URLs to the egoscope website. These URLs were banked in a database hosted by a billboard company, converted to VGA format, saved as avi files for uploading, then streamed, in the sequence of their submission, to two billboard panels above a busy avenue in São Paulo. Dispersed among conventional advertisements, the poem's material was seen live by 120,000 passersby a day and made available through webcams to thousands more networked flâneurs. The "I" of *egoscópio*—"a fluid character named egoscope"—was a multiple, hybrid, fragmented, and public construction. Compounded of art, advertising, and information, it stands in for the open, processual "post-subject" of the informational age: not the ego analyzed by Sigmund Freud but the posthuman subject or narcisystem theorized by critics such as Marshall McLuhan, Manuel Castells, Donna Haraway, Judith Butler, N. Katherine Hayles, and Talan Memmott.

If the "ego" of *egoscópio* is communal and contingent, the "scope" is instrumental: Beiguelman's nonlyric is a device, like a telescope, helioscope, or radarscope, designed to bring into focus an emergent and chaotic phenomenon. Like other members of the new media family, the participatory networked and programmable poem is an inquiry into a global flow of trademarks, gadgets, and images that exists at the intersection of electronic commerce, networked personal computers, and ambient attention spans. The dispersed and morphing being named Egoscope has no gender, no age, and no nationality; it inhabits networked spaces and is available only to ambient or peripheral vision. As Beiguelman puts it, updating McLuhan, "The interface is the message" (2002a).

6. *Codework:* As programmatological writing, new media poems depend on a multilevel hierarchy of machine codes, compiler languages, and source codes: what we see on the screen is the result of cascading coordination between, in John Cayley's summary, "machine codes, tokenised codes, low-level languages, high-level languages, scripting languages, macro languages, markup language, Operating Systems and their scripting language, the Human Computer Interface, the procedural descriptions of software manuals, and a very large number of texts addressed to entirely human concerns" (2002a).[42] Except to those who click View Source on their browsers to display a screen's upper-level coding languages, the operations of code remain hidden. When code or code elements seep onto a screen to be read not by an intelligent machine but by a human audience, the result is a kind of digital composition Alan Sondheim calls "codework."[43] Excellent examples of this kind of new media writing include poems by Mez (Mary-Anne Breeze), John Cayley, Brian Lennon, Talan Memmott, Alan Sondheim, and Ted Warnell;[44] the final screenshot in this series comes from a Flash animation by Jessica Loseby entitled "code scares me" (figure 1.6).

For reasons Loseby's poem performs, code scares a lot of people. As a system of rules and regulations, it is frequently hidden and always instrumental: its purpose is to facilitate the execution of commands. Cybernetic code expresses information and gives instructions in a form usable by computers: in the proper context, a single keystroke is capable of altering the behavior of an entire system. By allowing machine-addressed code to sweep up and over language addressed to humans, Loseby destabilizes both levels. "If I could only get rid/of this darkness," the human-addressed text reads, "I could see you//and you could see/me." Although the underlying text, like most lyrics,

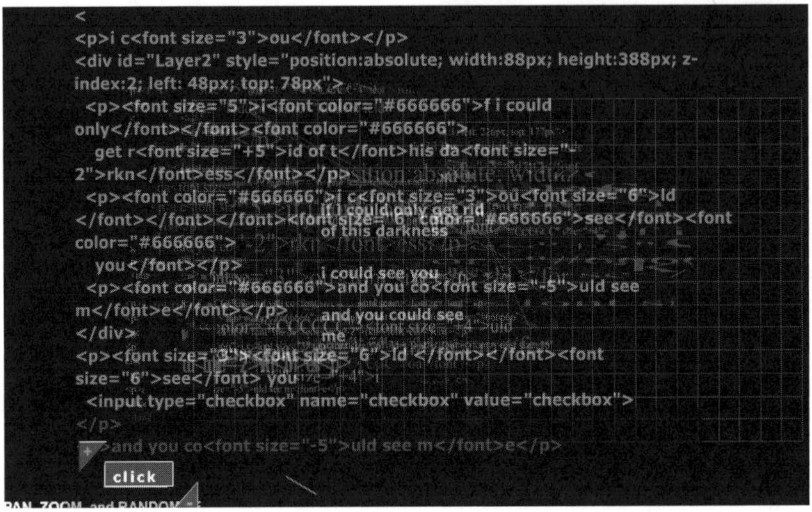

Figure 1.6 Screenshot from "code scares me." http://www.rssgallery.com/code.htm.

enacts a bond between "I" and "you," the code swarm negates the dream of transparency: the binary pair is cracked or hacked by the code of contemporary information culture. The questions this act generates are fundamental to new media poetics. Who is "I" and who are "you" in a cybernetic context? What is the feedback loop between humans and their machines? Which language is "natural," which "artificial"? Where does the darkness reside? What would it mean to "see"? In this juxtaposition of early twentieth-century free verse lyric language and twenty-first-century machine code, "what is seen," as Stein would say, "depends upon how everybody is doing everything" (1998a, 521). Code scares us at least in part because, as Stein suggests, it catches us in a cleft between what we "see" and what we "know."

The workpath in "code scares me" depends on a user or interactor who is neither robotic nor passive. Although the code in the interface text is not operative, Loseby (2001b) programmed the poem to give the interactor access to a code that changes its behavior: by using "the '+' and '−' buttons," she explains, "the wall of code can be increased or decreased until the text beneath can be seen, and read." In this interchange between human and machine, cognition is distributed and "the darkness," as the lyric puts it, "loses its potency." By granting the user access to the vocabulary of the machine, Loseby allows a trial of language. "code scares me" is an experiment in reconceptualizing the field of textuality as a porous, indeterminate, intertextual dialogue, simple in its structure but rich with implications for how we may think and write in the twenty-first century.

These six varieties of an emergent practice called new media poetics offer not a neat or exhaustive taxonomy but a restless taxonomadism. If these new media poems could be plotted on a grid, their characteristic links, perspective, access, determinability, transience, dynamics, user functions, and coding strategies would variously overlap and differ. What gives them their family resemblance is an imagination that mobilizes programming code as a poetic device. This is not the force traditionally figured as a muse or daemon: Stefans's demon looks nothing like Coleridge's nineteenth-century esemplastic imagination or Bloom's high modernist oedipal anxiety of influence. What drive these poems are the energy patterns of an age of information. For Johanna Drucker, it includes the "algorithmic imagination" (2002, 689), for Lev Manovich, the "database imagination" (2001, xxiv), but we might think of it more simply as the spirit of an informational age. Distinct from the encyclopedic imagination of the Enlightenment, it is the cyborganization that is now recalibrating how we write and how we think: "what is seen" when poets and critics catch up with "how everybody is doing everything" (Stein 1998a, 520).

However resistant they may seem to interpretation, the interfaces of new media poems are likely to be more familiar to contemporary game-playing, net-browsing undergraduates than the sonnets, sestinas, and villanelles that fill their poetry surveys. Like the innovative poets whose print work offers, in Alan Golding's words, "transitional materialities"—forms of visual text that test the limits of the page-based, word-centered poem—new media artists are, in Kenneth Goldsmith's phrase, a "bridge generation." As creators of marginal, elusive, and self-reflexive, ungainly texts, they belong to Stein's tradition of outlaws who prepare the way for a future that is already here.

Writing of the early twentieth-century transition marked by the emergent technologies of photography, cinema, and radio, Walter Benjamin refines this point: "One of the foremost tasks of art has always been the creation of a demand that could be fully satisfied only later. The history of every art form shows critical epochs in which a certain art form aspires to effects which could be fully obtained only with a changed technical standard, that is to say, in a new art form" (1969, 237).[45] The essays and artist statements in this collection participate in this ongoing transition. The materials in the three sections that follow look at the contexts of the production and dissemination of new media poems, the differential poetics of their presentation, and some of the theories that make it possible to grasp their potential.

The chapters in part I, "Contexts," look not at cyberculture—that is, the social phenomena associated with globalized networked communication—but at connected structures that produce, nourish, and circulate new media poetics. All five essays examine communities variously formed by electronic archives, digital Web sites, new media journals, sound-editing practices, and pedagogical innovations that shape and are shaped by information age technologies. Kenneth Goldsmith's UbuWeb, Brian Kim Stefans's Circulars, Jennifer Ley's *Riding the Meridian,* Martin Spinelli's *Radio Radio,* and Alan Filreis's Kelly Writers House are sites at which technological innovations shape and are shaped by cultural practices. The discourse they make possible is not just multimedia but multiauthored and multipurposed, open rather than owned, morphing rather than fixed.

The chapters in part II, "Technotexts," veer sharply from the apocalyptic celebrations of first-generation electronic literature: not only will digital writing not put an end to books, these essays suggest, it is not necessarily more subtle, more properly poststructural, more accomplished, more important, or even more interesting than print writing. Far from displacing print, in fact, new media texts frequently depend on a differential relationship with analogous or related print materials. "The most interesting exemplars of digital poetics to date," Marjorie Perloff writes in chapter 7, "have tended to be what I have called elsewhere *differential* texts—that is to say, texts that exist in different material forms, with no single version being the definitive one."[46] Just as the emphasis in part I is on communities rather than individual authors, the emphasis in part II is on a dynamic media ecology in which works exist in reciprocity rather than hierarchy, in collaboration rather than revolution or even evolution. As it moves between page and screen, screen and billboard, cell phone, or museum gallery, the flickering, doubling, and recombining energies of this work test how we write and suggest the many ways in which we may think.

The eight chapters in this section consider examples of print, digital, and/or installation art by composers such as Caroline Bergvall, Charles Bernstein, Philippe Castellin, Kenneth Goldsmith, Robert Grenier, Steve McCaffery, and Stephanie Strickland. For these makers of differential texts, each remaking is a rethinking. The reciprocal complications of the various iterations of these materials make them, in Hayles's term, "technotexts": texts that foreground and reflect on the inscription technologies used to produce them (2002, 25). As Alan Golding emphasizes in chapter 13, the "playful reciprocity" between print, digitized, and three-dimensional forms of the same material undoes the notion that one medium can supercede or even suppress another. Multiple instantiations of the same textual materials allow interpreters to consider what portion of meaning in print texts is challenged, intensified, or lost in digital environments, what memories of previous forms persist in their virtual transformations, and what new paradigms need to emerge in order to grasp what is in fact new in new media poetics.[47]

The chapters in part III, "Theories," all written by practicing poet-critics, develop a series of terms to address these and other nuanced and pressing questions concerning how to think about new media poetics. As he does in each piece he writes, Talan Memmott (chapter 15) generates multilayered terms to act as "liquid delimiters" for digital poetics, which he defines as "creative cultural practice through applied technology." Arguing that the ability to cause thinking is an essential part of digital poetics and rhetoric, he sees these poems as operational interfaces for systems of "signifying harmonics" or resonances between visual, auditory, lexical, computational, and performative signs and sign regimes. In the discipline of taxonomadism, as Memmott formulates it, categories remain open at their forward edge, at once altering and altered by the technologies that generate them.

"You will sense," John Cayley writes in chapter 16, "words shifting their meanings as I write/speak and you read/hear." Cayley's subject is the relationship between code and text in cultural objects that are classified as literary and composed from programmed signifiers. "The programmatological dimension of writing has always already been operative," Cayley writes, "and therefore the traditional temporally stunned conception of textuality has always already been inadequate to literary and especially to poetic practice. However, the coding applied to textuality *in new media* allows us to perceive, if not the coding itself, then the unambiguous effects and consequences of that coding." In his refinement of the thinking of Ted Nelson and his subtle analysis of the work of Jim Rosenberg, Cayley offers a phenomenology of reading that has important consequences both for print and for the now significant body of networked and programmable writing in which paraphrase, gloss, elaboration, annotation, and other acts of interpretation are coded into a time-based and successively revealed interface text.

In the final chapter of this collection, Barrett Watten challenges the habit of describing artistic practices in relation to fixed positions of form, genre, discipline, and cultural meaning and proposes instead a more inclusive and dynamic formulation of an expanded field of literary, visual, and digital practice. Beginning with the premise that the form of making is itself an intelligence, Watten lays out a structural logic common to radical poetics, conceptual art, and digital aesthetics. His lucid delineation of this logic emphasizes its double structuration in negative and positive practices: its dialectical and historical efforts to dismantle customary standards of judgment, on the one hand, and its generation of new cultural meanings and possibilities on the other. "The expanded field of poetics," Watten writes, "leads thereby to the making of art in new genres, as a self-reflexive moment within practice that creates grounds for new meaning." Watten's analysis returns us to a vision of new media poetics not as technologized bells and whistles but as a crucial form of thinking and writing in a cybernetic world.

The poets and critics in this volume share with thinkers such as Gertrude Stein, Walter Benjamin, Vannevar Bush, Ted Nelson, and Marshall McLuhan a keen sense of the consequences of the simple fact that, as Stein puts it, "each generation has something different at which they are all looking" (1998a, 520). The essays and artistic statements that follow register, each in its way, a seismic shake-up in the media that negotiate our experience. As familiar abstractions and categories collapse, the effects ripple across all forms of creative and critical practice. The difference, Stein would say, is "a difference in beginning and in the middle and in ending" (520). In this large, long-yielding context, how to write is to write as we may think. Our hope in this volume is to participate in the effort to provide models adequate to understanding this process.

Notes

1. In his book *Mindstorms: Children, Computers, and Powerful Ideas,* Seymour Papert predicted this would occur, as it did, "long before the end of the century" (1980, 416). In 2004, more money is spent on computer games than on cinema, networked intelligence is embedded in every kind of physical system, natural and artificial, everywhere, and wearable computers on retail shelves have the capacity to turn each of us into mobile subnetworks of larger networks. For a summary of these and other developments, see Mitchell 2003.

2. See, for example, Varela, Thompson, and Rosch 1991 and Damasio 1999.

3. For summaries of these theories, see Ong 1982, Havelock 1986, Goody 1987, and McLuhan 1962, 1964. Giving this thinking a contemporary turn, Friedrich A. Kittler formulates the notion of the *discourse network*, which he defines as "the network of technologies and institutions that allow a given culture to select, store, and produce relevant data" (1990, 369).

4. For a summary of this material, see "Contesting for the Body of Information," chapter 3 of Hayles 1999.

5. The term "intelligent machine" first gained currency in Alan Turing's landmark essay "Computing Machinery and Intelligence," published in the journal *Mind* in 1950, in which he proposed the imitation game as a test for machine intelligence. The definition of the term "intelligent machine" remains contested, but Hayles explains that she uses it in association with "the idea of machines performing tasks that require cognition, e.g., neural nets performing sophisticated decisions, expert systems making judgments, information-filtering ecologies selecting data, genetic programs designing electrical circuits, etc. I argue that any entity that can perform these tasks should prima facie be considered as thinking or intelligent" (email message to Adalaide Morris, October 5, 2004). I use the term here to mean any digital device capable of processing data and acting on the basis of that data.

6. The term "electronic literature" is most prominent in the name of the Electronic Literature Organization. The term "e-poetries" is central to Glazier 2002. The formulation "networked and programmable," which I use throughout this introduction, is John Cayley's long-standing designation for new media writing (see, e.g., Cayley 1998b).

7. For pertinent examples of these debates, see parts I and II of Wardrip-Fruin and Harrigan 2004.

8. For more on Manovich, see Hansen 2004, 32–46. For information on the relevance of narratology for game aesthetics, see Aarseth 2004.

9. Aarseth puts this imputation straightforwardly in "Genre Trouble": "Are games texts?" he asks. "The best reason I can think of why one would ask such a crude question is because one is a literary or semiotic theorist and wants to believe in the relevance of one's training" (2004, 47).

10. Although it is crucial to problematize the "we" in this sentence, computers are not a local but a global phenomenon, part of the architecture of a worldwide informational network. Networked and programmable machines are as essential to the activities of so-called terrorists as they are to stockbrokers, academics, military planners, and other agents in the cultures of contemporary capitalism.

11. I am drawing here on Nick Montfort's definition of interactive fiction in his book *Twisty Little Passages* (2003b).

12. Commenting on print media's new emphasis on visual rhetoric, J. David Bolter notes the influence of "the new visual rhetoric of electronic writing, in which words, images, and numbered elements easily occupy a single space. . . . Sedate rows of linear text are becoming the exception rather than the rule ([1991] 2003, 690).

13. "Subject village" is Loss Pequeño Glazier's useful term for "a site for the access, collection, and dissemination of poetry and related writing" on the Web (2002a, 3). In this function, subject villages such as UbuWeb, EPC, and PENNsound both overlap with and differ from the presses, books, magazines, and anthologies utilized to gather and disseminate print materials in the past.

14. For Manovich, databases and algorithms exist in a symbiotic relationship and form the two halves of the ontology of the world according to computers. For his discussion of "database logic," see Manovich 2001, 218–243.

15. For this reason, code often serves as a metonymy in essays on new media poetics for the otherness of digital poetry. For compelling examples of code that drives contemporary artwork, see the two installments of CODeDOC on Artport, the Whitney Museum Portal to Net Art, at http://www.whitney.org/artport/commissions/index.shtml.

16. For many of the artistic ramifications of this open-source possibility, see chapter 2. On the transformative potential of open-source programs for business, see Surman and Wershler-Henry 2001.

17. I return to the issue of code later in this chapter, but I want to emphasize here that, as John Cayley, N. Katherine Hayles, and Jerome McGann have all argued, print texts also contain markup code in the form of paragraph indentations, parentheses, and so forth. New media objects, however, are not only coded but their code is compiled and run by a machine prior to its engagement by a reader. For more on this topic, see McGann 2001, Cayley 2002, and Hayles 2005, chapters 2 and 4.

18. See his enumeration of the characteristics of new media in Manovich 2001 and Manovich 2003.

19. For a succinct survey of the profound shifts caused by these devices, see Mitchell 2003. For a wide sociological overview, see Castells 2000.

20. Montfort (2003, 35–36) makes these connections in his introduction to Bush's essay in *The New Media Reader*.

21. Now in Version 2, Storyspace is still billed as "the tool of choice for hypertext writers." (For a full description, see Eastgate's Web site at http://www.eastgate.com/ Storyspace2.html.)

22. "The creator of the new composition in the arts," Stein writes, "is an outlaw until he is a classic, there is hardly a moment in between and it is really too bad very much too bad naturally for the creator but also very much too bad for the enjoyer, they all really would enjoy the created so much better just after it has been made than when it is already a classic" (1998a 521).

23. For examples of this strategy, see especially Glazier 2002 and, in this volume, the essays by Alan Golding (chapter 13), Marjorie Perloff (chapter 7), and Barrett Watten (chapter 17).

24. In my definitions of first- and second-generation electronic texts, I am indebted to Hayles's *Writing Machines* (2002). For an excellent anthology of outlaw texts in poetics, see Rasula and McCaffery 1998. It is important to note, however, that a pivotal source of inspiration for second-generation electronic texts is not literature but the skill and swagger of advertisements, music videos, film credits, and other digital constructions in popular culture.

25. For an example of a hypertext poem composed in Storyspace, see Stephanie Strickland's *True North* (1998), and the discussion of this poem in her essay "Poetry in an Electronic Environment" (1997a). The poems in *True North* were also published in a print version (Strickland 1997b).

26. For this controversy on first-generation electronic texts, see especially Coover 1992 and Miller 1998.

27. Aarseth is clear about the implications of his terminology: "Especially," he writes, "I wish to challenge the recurrent practice of applying the theories of literary criticism to a new empirical field, seemingly without any reassessment of the terms and concepts involved. This lack of self-reflection places the research in direct danger of turning the vocabulary of literary theory into a set of unfocused metaphors, rendered useless by a translation that is not perceived as such by its very translators" (1997, 14).

28. In chapter 5, Martin Spinelli draws a parallel distinction between "listening carefully," characterized by the analog editor's desire to preserve sound through accurate reproduction, and "listening digitally," characterized by the digital editor's experimental recombinations of sound materials.

29. "If you look at [games]," Wittgenstein (1953) writes in a pertinent example, "you will not see something that is common to *all*, but similarities, relationships, and a

whole series of them at that. To repeat: don't think, but look! . . . And the result of this examination is: we see a complicated network of similarities overlapping and criss-crossing: sometimes overall similarities, sometimes similarities of detail" (31^e–32^e).

30. For a detailed elaboration of the descriptors *industrial* and *informational*, see Castells 2000. My point here is not that these formations are determinative but concomitant: the lyric did not create the bourgeois economy any more than new media networked writing created the informational economy, but both are intricately involved in the historical, cultural, and economic contexts in which they arose. "Our societies," Castells writes, "are increasingly structured around a bipolar opposition between the Net and the Self" (1:3). This opposition creates the expanded field of new media poetics.

31. It is easy to caricature this kind of poetry, which has been amply thrashed as bourgeois, suburban, conformist, and conservative but has nonetheless compelling and enduring effects. Although it is only the first of four zones the poet-critic Jed Rasula identifies in the contemporary American "poetry world"—respectively, Associated Writing Programs poetry, the New Formalism, Language poetry, and "various coalitions of interest-oriented or community-based poets" (1996, 440)—the mainstream lyric not only takes the lion's share of academic and popular prestige, resources, and publicity but has become, for the broad public, synonymous with poetry itself.

32. For more on this tripartite division, see Drucker 2002.

33. For a full description of this poem's algorithmic coding and rhetorical configuration, see Cayley 2004b. Examples of Uribe's work can be found at http://amuribe.tripod.com/. See also Megan Sapnar's interview with Uribe on *The Iowa Review Web*. For literal art in the form of an interactive multiuser computer poem, see "Just Letters" at http://web.okaygo.co.uk/apps/letters/flashcom/. See also Hennessey's (2004) "Jabber: The Jabberwoky Engine," a "dynamic nonsense word sound poem" that creates "a linguistic chemistry with letters as atoms and words as molecules." See also mIEKEL aND's haunting "seedsigns for philadelpho," an "intersign action" composed as an elegy to Philadelpho Menezes at http://cla.umn.edu/joglars/SEEDSIGN/.

34. In "Projective Verse," the manifesto that energized the New American Poetry of the 1960s, Charles Olson emphasizes the kinetics of field composition: "get on with it," he writes, "keep moving, keep in, speed, the nerves, their speed, the perceptions, theirs, the acts, the split second acts, the whole business, keep it moving as fast as you can, citizen. And if you also set up as a poet, USE USE USE the process at all points, in any given poem always, always one perception must must must MOVE, INSTANTER, ON ANOTHER!" (1966, 17).

35. For an example of a game in speculative computing designed to allow players to do the work of interpretation, see Drucker and McGann 2004.

36. For Manovich and other new media commentators, the term "programmable" means subject to algorithmic manipulation (see Manovich 2001, 27). As a number of commentators have pointed out, highly stylized forms such as sonnets, sestinas, and villanelles are generated by algorithms applied to an acceptable set of arguments—a database—about love, death, fame, and other standard subjects.

37. Goldsmith's course in "Uncreative Writing" was taught at the University of Pennsylvania in fall 2004. For his discussion of this term, see "Uncreativity as a Creative Practice" (2002–2003).

38. For astute analyses of procedural poetics, see Perloff 1991, chapter 5, and Conte 1991, part II.

39. To throw an additional twist into this mix, as Stefans points out, Tennyson's translation was plagiarized and remixed from his son's prose translation of the same Anglo-Saxon poem. "The creator of CPs," Stefans comments, "can spend as much, if not more, time working on the source files as he will on the poem itself, understanding them to have a symbiotic relationship to each other that corrupts normal cultural valuations of what 'code' is and what 'language' is" (2003, 64).

40. One of Stefans's interventions after the demon had run its course was to throw into the poem a few lines by Samuel Taylor Coleridge and William Carlos Williams, thereby flanking a Victorian poet with poet-theorists from the Romantic and Modernist innovative traditions. The inclusion of a paragraph from Kapleau's practical guide to Zen meditation ties Stefans's poem to a spiritual discipline of self-effacement important to Glazier, Stefans, and several other digital poets.

41. To borrow a term Stefans borrows from Tan Lin, "Io Sono" is an ambient poem: it generates information whether or not one attends to it, talks to a friend, washes the dishes, or sleeps. In this, it becomes, in Stefans's words, "a celebration of the activity of reading itself, as if the word were just a placeholder, a minor diversion in real-time, intended to let reading continue but not to the exclusion of other activities" (2003, 111).

42. Cayley uses the term "programmatology"—an extension of Derrida's "grammatology" and Gregory Ulmer's "applied grammatology"—to signify "the study and practice of writing . . . with an explicit awareness of its relation to 'programming' or prior writing in anticipation of performance (including the performance of reading)" (2002a, n. 1).

43. For important discussions of codework, see Raley 2002, Cayley 2002a, and Cramer 2001. In addition to functioning machine-addressed languages, code can include faked code or code elements that invade a screen to point to or stand in for the language-animating or language-generating programming in the layers below.

44. As Raley (2002) points out, digital composers give this practice a variety of names: "Mez composes in a neologistic 'net.wurked' language that she has termed m[ez]ang.elle; Memmott uses the term 'rich.lit'; Warnell names some of his JavaScript poems 'codepoetry'; Lennon refers to 'digital visual poetics.'"

45. For Manovich, the period Benjamin discusses—the period from 1915 to 1928—is more relevant to new media than any preceding period. "During these years," Manovich comments, "avant-garde artists and designers invented a whole new set of visual and spatial languages and communications techniques we still use today" (2003, 22).

46. For her elaboration of this term, see Perloff 2002.

47. On these topics, see especially Drucker 1998 and Manovich 2001.

Works Cited

Aarseth, Espen J. 1997. *Cybertext: Perspectives on Ergodic Literature.* Baltimore, MD: Johns Hopkins University Press.

Aarseth, Espen J. 2004. "Genre Trouble: Narrativism and the Art of Simulation." In *First Person: New Media as Story, Performance, and Game*, ed. N. Wardrip-Fruin and P. Harrigan, 45–55. Cambridge, MA: MIT Press.

aND, mIEKEL. 2000. "Seedsigns for Philadelpho." http://cla.umn.edu/joglars/ SEEDSIGN/ (accessed February 2, 2005).

Andrews, Jim. 2002. "Games, Po, Art, Play, and Arteroids 2.03." http://vispo.com/ arteroids/onarteroids.htm (accessed February 23, 2005).

Andrews, Jim. 2003a. "Arteroids 2.5." *poemsthatgo*, no. 14 (Fall). http://www. poemsthatgo.com/gallery/fall2003/arteroids/arteroids.htm (accessed October 24, 2004).

Andrews, Jim. 2003b. "Arteroids, Poetry, and the Flaw." *poemsthatgo*, no. 14 (Fall). http://www.poemsthatgo.com/gallery/fall2003/arteroids/article.htm.

Andrews, Jim. 2004. "Avant Auteur: An Interview with Jim Andrews." *Avant Gaming.* http://www.avantgaming.com/andrews.html (accessed February 4, 2005).

Barthes, Roland. 1974. *S/Z.* Trans. Richard Miller. New York: Hill and Wang.

Beiguelman, Giselle. 2002a. *egoscópio.* http://www.desvirtual.com/egoscopio/ (accessed February 11, 2005).

Beiguelman, Giselle. 2002b. *Egoscope.* http://www.desvirtual.com/egoscopio/english/ about_more.htm (accessed February 11, 2005).

Benjamin, Walter. 1969. "The Work of Art in the Age of Mechanical Reproduction." Trans. Harry Zohn. In *Illuminations*, ed. Hannah Arendt, 217–251. New York: Schocken.

Bernstein, Charles. 1992. *A Poetics.* Cambridge, MA: Harvard University Press.

Bolter, J. David. [1991] 2003. "Seeing and Writing." In *The New Media Reader*, ed. N. Wardrip-Fruin and N. Montfort, 680–690. Cambridge, MA: MIT Press.

Brogan, T. V. F., ed. 1994. *The New Princeton Handbook of Poetic Terms.* Princeton, NJ: Princeton University Press.

Bush, Vannevar. [1945] 2003. "As We May Think." In *The New Media Reader*, ed. N. Waldrip-Fruin and N. Montfort, 37–47. Cambridge, MA: MIT Press.

Castells, Manuel. 2000. *The Rise of the Network Society,* 3 vols. Oxford: Blackwell.

Cayley, John. 2002a. "The Code Is Not the Text (Unless It Is the Text)." *electronic book review.* http://www.electronicbookreview.com/v3/servlet/ (accessed February 17, 2005).

Cayley, John. 2002b. *What We Will.* http://www.z360.com/what/ (accessed February 23, 2005).

Cayley, John. 2004a. "Literal Art." *electronic book review.* http://www.electronicbook review.com/v3/servlet/ebr?command=view_essay&essay_id=cayley (accessed January 29, 2005).

Cayley, John. 2004b. "Overboard: An Example of Ambient Time-Based Poetics in Digital Art." http://www.dichtung-digital.org/2004/2-Cayley.htm (accessed February 9, 2005).

Conte, Joseph M. 1991. *Unending Design: The Forms of Postmodern Poetry.* Ithaca, NY: Cornell University Press.

Coover, Robert. 1992. "The End of Books." *New York Times Book Review,* June 21. http://www.tnellen.com/ted/endofbooks.html (accessed February 23, 2005).

Cramer, Florian. 2001. "Digital Code and Literary Text." *BeeHive Hypertext/ Hypermedia Literary Journal.* http://beehive.temporalimage.com/content_apps43/app_ d.html (accessed February 17, 2005).

Damasio, Antonio. 1999. *The Feeling of What Happens: Body and Emotion in the Making of Consciousness.* New York: Harcourt.

Drucker, Johanna. 1998. "Language as Information: Intimations of Immateriality." In *Figuring the Word: Essays on Books, Writing, and Visual Poetics*, 213–231. New York: Granary Books.

Drucker, Johanna. 2002. "Theory as Praxis: The Poetics of Electronic Textuality." Review of *Digital Poetics* by Loss Penqueño Glazier, *Electronic Texts in the Humanities* by Susan Hockey, and *Radiant Textuality* by Jerome McGann. *Modernism/Modernity* 9.4: 683–691.

Drucker, Johanna, and Jerome McGann. 2004. "IVANHOE: Design and Development." October. http://www.patacriticism.org/ivanhoe/credits.html (accessed February 23, 2005).

Glazier, Loss Pequeño. 2002a. *Digital Poetics: The Making of E-Poetries.* Tuscaloosa: University of Alabama Press.

Glazier, Loss Pequeño. 2002b. "Io Sono At Swoons." http://epc.buffalo.edu/authors/glazier/java/iowa/iosono.html (accessed February 12, 2005).

Goldsmith, Kenneth. 2002–2003. "Uncreativity as a Creative Practice." *Drunken Boat* no. 5 (Winter). http://drunkenboat.com/db5/goldsmith/uncreativity.html (accessed February 20, 2005).

Goody, Jack. 1987. *The Interface between the Written and the Oral.* New York: Cambridge University Press.

Hansen, Mark B. N. 2000. *Embodying Technesis: Technology Beyond Writing.* Ann Arbor: University of Michigan Press.

Hansen, Mark B. N. 2004. *New Philosophy for New Media.* Cambridge, MA: MIT Press.

Haraway, Donna. 1985. "A Manifesto for Cyborgs: Science, Technology, and Socialist Feminism in the 1980s." *Socialist Review* 80: 68–108.

Harrison, Gilbert A. 1974. "Introduction." In *Gertrude Stein's America*, ed. Gilbert A. Harrison, 9–17. New York: Liveright.

Havelock, Eric A. 1986. *The Muse Learns to Write: Reflections on Orality and Literacy from Antiquity to the Present.* New Haven, CT: Yale University Press.

Hayles, N. Katherine. 1999. *How We Became Posthuman: Virtual Bodies in Cybernetics, Literature, and Informatics.* Chicago: University of Chicago Press.

Hayles, N. Katherine. 2002. *Writing Machines.* Cambridge, MA: MIT Press.

Hayles, N. Katherine. 2005. *My Mother Was a Computer: Digital Subjects and Literary Texts.* Chicago: University of Chicago Press.

Hennessey, Neil. 2004. "Jabber: The Jabberwoky Engine." *poemsthatgo* 15 (Winter). http://www.poemsthatgo.com/gallery/winter2004/jabber/index.htm (accessed February 4, 2005).

"Just Letters." http://web.okaygo.co.uk/apps/letters/flashcom/ (accessed February 4, 2005).

Kittler, Friedrich A. 1990. *Discourse Networks 1800/1900.* Trans. Michael Metteer, with Chris Cullens. Stanford, CA: Stanford University Press.

Landow, George P. 1992. *Hypertext: The Convergence of Contemporary Critical Theory and Technology.* Baltimore, MD: Johns Hopkins University Press.

Loseby, Jessica. 2001a. "code scares me." http://www.rssgallery.com/code.htm (accessed February 17, 2005).

Loseby, Jessica. 2001b. "Commentary on 'code scares me.'" *New Media Line.* http://www.kanonmedia.com/news/nml/code.htm (accessed February 17, 2005).

Manovich, Lev. 2001. *The Language of New Media.* Cambridge, MA: MIT Press.

Manovich, Lev. 2003. "New Media from Borges to HTML." In *The New Media Reader,* ed. Noah Wardrip-Fruin and Nick Montfort, 13–25. Cambridge, MA: MIT Press.

McCaffery, Steve, and bpNichol. 1992. *Rational Geomancy: The Kids of the Book-Machine (The Collected Research Reports of the Toronto Research Group 1973–1982).* Vancouver: Talonbooks.

McGann, Jerome J. 2001. *Radiant Textuality: Literature after the World Wide Web.* New York: Palgrave.

McLuhan, Marshall. 1962. *The Gutenberg Galaxy: The Making of Typographical Man.* Toronto: University of Toronto Press.

McLuhan, Marshall. 1964. *Understanding Media: The Extensions of Man.* New York: McGraw-Hill.

Memmott, Talan. 2000. "Toward Electracy: A Conversation with Gregory Ulmer." *BeeHive* 3.4. http://beehive.temporalimage.com/archive/34arc.html (accessed October 7, 2004).

Memmott, Talan. 2001. "Narcisystems" (from "Delimited Meshings: A White Paper)" *Cauldron & Net* 3 (Spring). http://www.studiocleo.com/cauldron/volume3/

confluence/talan_memmott/delimited_meshings/meshings/narcisys.html   (accessed January 28, 2005).

Miller, Laura. 1998. "www.claptrap.com." *New York Times Book Review*, March 15, Bookends.

Mitchell, William J. 2003. *Me++: The Cyborg Self and the Networked City.* Cambridge, MA: MIT Press.

Montfort, Nick. 2003a. "[Introduction] As We May Think" by Vannevar Bush. In *The New Media Reader*, ed. N. Wardrip-Fruin and N. Montfort, 35–36. Cambridge, MA: MIT Press.

Montfort, Nick. 2003b. *Twisty Little Passages: An Approach to Interactive Fiction.* Cambridge, MA: MIT Press.

Nelson, Theodor H. [1974] 2003. "From Computer Lib/Dream Machines." In *The New Media Reader,* ed. Noah Wardrip-Fruin and Nick Montfort, 303–338. Cambridge, MA: MIT Press.

Olson, Charles. 1966. "Projective Verse." In *Selected Writings of Charles Olson,* ed. Robert Creeley, 15–26. New York: New Directions.

Ong, Walter J. 1982. *Orality and Literacy: The Technologizing of the Word.* New York: Methuen.

Papert, Seymour. [1980] 2003. "From *Mindstorms: Children, Computers, and Powerful Ideas*." In *The New Media Reader*, ed. N. Wardrip-Fruin and N. Montfort, 414–431. Cambridge, MA: MIT Press.

Perloff, Marjorie. 1991. *Radical Artifice: Writing Poetry in the Age of Media.* Chicago: University of Chicago Press.

Perloff, Marjorie. 2002. "'Vocable Scriptsigns': Differential Poetics in Kenneth Goldsmith's *Fidget* and John Kinsella's *Kangaroo Virus*." In *Poetry and Contemporary Culture: The Question of Value*, ed. Andrew Roberts and John Allison, 21–43. Edinburgh, Scotland: Edinburgh University Press.

Raley, Rita. 2002. "Interferences: [Net.Writing] and the Practice of Codework." *electronic book review.* http://www.electronicbookreview.com/v3/servlet/ebr?command=view_essay&essay_id=rayleyele (accessed February 4, 2005).

Rasula, Jed. 1996. *The American Poetry Wax Museum: Reality Effects, 1940–1990.* Urbana, IL: National Council of Teachers of English.

Rasula, Jed, and Steve McCaffery, eds. 1998. *Imagining Language: An Anthology.* Cambridge, MA: MIT Press.

Rosenberg, Jim. 1993. *Intergrams*. Watertown, MA: Eastgate Systems.

Sapnar, Megan. 2002. "'The Letters Themselves': An Interview with Ana Maria Uribe." *The Iowa Review Web*. http://www.uiowa.edu/~iareview/tirweb/feature/uribe/uribe.html (accessed February 4, 2005).

Smithson, Robert. 1979. "Smithson's Non-Site Sights: Interview with Anthony Robbin." In *The Writings of Robert Smithson*, ed. Nancy Holt, 157–159. New York: New York University Press.

Stefans, Brian Kim. 1999. *the dreamlife of letters*. http://www.ubu.com/contemp/stefans/dream/ (accessed February 23, 2005).

Stefans, Brian Kim. 2003. "Stops and Rebels or, The Battle of *Brunaburh*." In *Fashionable Noise: On Digital Poetics*, 63–169. Berkeley, CA: Atelos.

Stein, Gertrude. 1998a. "Composition as Explanation." In *Gertrude Stein: Writings 1903–1932*, ed. Catherine R. Stimpson and Harriet Chessman, 520–529. New York: Library of America.

Stein, Gertrude. 1998b. "Portraits and Repetition." In *Gertrude Stein: Writings 1932–1946*, ed. Catherine R. Stimpson and Harriet Chessman, 287–312. New York: Library of America.

Strickland, Stephanie. 1997a. "Poetry in the Electronic Environment." *electronic book review*. http://altx.com/ebr/ebr5/strick.htm (accessed February 1, 2005).

Strickland, Stephanie. 1997b. *True North*. Notre Dame, IN: University of Notre Dame Press.

Strickland, Stephanie. 1998. *True North* [hypertext version]. Watertown, MA: Eastgate Systems.

Surman, Mark, and Darren Wershler-Henry. 2001. *Commonspace: Beyond Virtual Community*. Toronto: FT Prentice-Hall.

Turing, Alan. 1950. "Computing Machinery and Intelligence." *Mind* 59 (October): 433–460.

Uribe, Ana Maria. 2003. *Anipoems*. http://amuribe.tripod.com/anipoems.html (accessed February 4, 2005).

Varela, Francisco J., Evan Thompson, and Eleanor Rosch. 1991. *The Embodied Mind: Cognitive Science and Human Experience*. Cambridge, MA: MIT Press.

Wardrip-Fruin, Noah, ac chapman, Brion Moss, and Duane Whitehurst. 1999. *The Impermanence Agent*. http://www.impermanenceagent.com/agent (accessed February 3, 2005).

Wardrip-Fruin, Noah, and Pat Harrigan, eds. 2004. *First Person: New Media as Story, Performance, and Game.* Cambridge, MA: MIT Press.

Wardrip-Fruin, Noah, and Nick Montfort, eds. 2003. *The New Media Reader.* Cambridge, MA: MIT Press.

Wiener, Norbert. 1948. *Cybernetics; or, Control and Communication in the Animal and the Machine.* New York: Technology Press.

Wittgenstein, Ludwig. 1953. *Philosophical Investigations.* Trans. G. E. M Anscombe and R. Rhees. Oxford: Blackwell Publishers.

Contexts

The Bride Stripped Bare: Nude Media and the Dematerialization of Tony Curtis

Kenneth Goldsmith

In May 2000, I received the following email at UbuWeb:

i really enjoyed your site. it made me think about different cultures other than the ones i experience daily living in a small texas town.—meredith

I can't imagine that many of UbuWeb's materials are available in Meredith's local library. Chances are that they don't have much, if any, sound poetry, and I'll bet that their concrete poetry section is lacking as well. Odds are that the local bookstore isn't chock-full of this stuff either. If Meredith were ambitious, she might try searching the Web and buying these items online. But then she'd have to fork out $125 to buy a used copy of Emmett Williams's (1967) *An Anthology of Concrete Poetry* or $90 to purchase the newly released *OU Revue* box set that compiles the entire run of the legendary French sound poetry magazine from the 1960s (Marghen 2002). Those two items comprise a miniscule amount of what's available to Meredith for free on UbuWeb, right in the comfort of her own living room.

Meredith's note succinctly summed up what I had wished to achieve with UbuWeb: the creation of a distribution center for out-of-print, hard-to-find, small-run, obscure materials, available at no cost and from any point on the globe. UbuWeb embraces the distributive possibilities inherent in the Web's original technologies: call it "radical forms of distribution."

When I began my engagement with this material in the late 1980s, there was not much of it to be found, even in New York City. Generally produced in small, poorly distributed editions during the 1960s and 1970s, sound and concrete poetry by the 1980s seemed to be a moribund genre. Over the next five years, though, I managed to track down a small but generative collection of books, journals, LPs, and tapes of concrete and sound poetry.

Over the next decade, through a confluence of interests (pop culture, nostalgia, the marketplace, and the Web), this situation would radically change. In January 1996, a friend showed me Netscape. The first image I saw appear on the screen was a slowly unfurling interlaced gif. And as the text and image filled in with alternating lines, it reminded me of sequential movement poems such as Jean François Bory's "The worldWord is . . . , " which, when printed across several pages, resembles a flipbook. Over the next few months, the proliferation of slick graphic images on the Web—most often used for advertising—also reminded me of concrete works such as bpNichol's "eyes" from the mid-1960s and Décio Pignatari's "beba coca cola" from the late 1950s.

History Completes Itself

UbuWeb was launched in November 1996. It felt right to move my collection to the Web: scanning the images and seeing them backlit by the computer screen made everything seem fresh, as did other recontextualizations of the work. Freed from the dusty bookstores and flea markets, sprung from their yellowing pages, these images were revitalized; concrete poetry was once again in dialogue with contemporary culture.

There was something formally astonishing about the way that the computer screen and concrete poetry seemed to work naturally together. It seemed a fulfillment of concrete poetry's original premise. In 1958, the Brazilian Noigandres Group defined concrete poetry as "[the] tension of thing-words in space-time" (de Campos, Pignatari, and de Campos 1958, 72). When we look at early concrete poetry manifestos, we can't help but recognize this Web environment. The physical attributes the Noigandres group found inspiring in various poetic precursors reappears in the space of the screen:

space ["blancs"] and typographical devices as substantive elements of composition. . . . ideogramic method . . . word-ideogram; organic interpenetration of time and space . . . atomization of words, physiognomical typography; . . . the vision, rather than the praxis . . . direct speech, economy and functional architecture (71).

As early as 1968, Mary Ellen Solt noted the relationship between commercial graphics and concrete poetry in the introduction to her book *Concrete Poetry: A World View*:

Uses of language in poetry of the traditional type are not keeping pace with live processes of language and rapid methods of communication at work in our contemporary world. Contemporary languages exhibit the following tendencies . . . : a move toward "formal simplification," abbreviated statement on all levels of communication from the headline, the advertising slogan, to the scientific formula—the quick, concentrated visual message. (1968, 10)

Early concrete poetry's hard-line allegiance to modernism adapts itself perfectly to the flat mediums of the interface and the screen. These poets adhered closely to Greenbergian modernist tenets concerning nonillusionistic space and full autonomy of the artwork. Looking through examples of early concrete works, in fact, none are illusionistic; instead, unadorned sans serif language inhabits the plane of the white page and, as Greenberg (1992) says, "[the] shapes flatten and spread in the dense, two-dimensional atmosphere" (558). In so doing, the emotional temperature is intentionally kept cool, perfectly adapting itself to the environment of the computer.

The interface design of UbuWeb is intentionally modeled to emphasize these same flat, cool, and minimal qualities. Illusionistic depth-of-space, three-dimensional modeling, and decoration of any sort is avoided. UbuWeb's form is meant to fit its function.

UbuWeb has moved a distance from its beginnings as a repository for visual, concrete, and sound poetry; we dropped the suffix "poetry" from our name. We're now simply UbuWeb. UbuWeb is becoming a clearinghouse for the avant-garde, something the Web sorely needs. By releasing ourselves from the obligation of just presenting one sort of poetry—or limiting ourselves to *only* poetry—we open ourselves up to worlds of related ideas, all of which are easily absorbed under UbuWeb's scalable umbrella.

The Bride Stripped Bare: Nude Media

Our sound section is the most popular section of UbuWeb, which is no surprise given the immense interest in MP3 file sharing over the past few years. What does surprise me, however, is that enormous numbers of people are actually interested in avant-garde sound works. But what I'm learning is that while many of these people are enjoying or studying these files as they are, many others are using them as source material for new compositions, remixes, or the process of stitching several tracks together that's come to be known as "bootlegging" or "smushing."

In thinking about the way that UbuWeb (and many other types of file-sharing systems) distribute their warez, I've come up with a term: "nude media." What I mean by this is that once, say, an MP3 file is downloaded from the context of a site such as UbuWeb, it's free or naked, stripped bare of the normative external signifiers that tend to give as much meaning to an artwork as the contents of the artwork itself. Unadorned with branding or scholarly liner notes, emanating from no authoritative source, these objects are nude, not clothed. Thrown into open peer-to-peer distribution systems, nude media files often lose even their historical significance and blur into free-floating sound works, traveling in circles that they would not normally reach if clad in their conventional clothing.

Tony Curtis Defrocked

All forms of traditional media that are morphed onto the Web are in some way defrocked. An article about Tony Curtis, for example, which appeared in the Sunday Arts & Leisure section of the *New York Times,* is fully clothed in the conventions of the *New York Times.* Everything from the typeface to the pull quote to the photo layout bespeaks the authority of the paper of record. There's something comforting about reading the Arts & Leisure section on Sunday that the visual presentation of the paper both produces and reinforces. The *New York Times* represents stability in every way (figure 2.1).

If we look at that same article on the *New York Times* Web site, however, we find that much of what gave the piece its rock steadiness in the traditional print version is gone. For starters, there's a big red sans serif "W" for Washington instead of the classic black serifed "T" for Tony. Thus, the message is that the place in which the interview happened has greater significance than the subject of the article. Other things have changed as well, most notably the size and character of the typeface. The default typeface on any browser is Times Roman, but if we look at the newspaper compared to the screen, we'll see that Times Roman is never New York Times Roman (figure 2.2).

At 77, Tony Curtis Still Likes It Hot

By MATTHEW GUREWITSCH

WASHINGTON

TONY CURTIS'S weight-control strategy, which seems to be working for him, is to avoid cooked foods as much as possible.

In late August, for several days running, he was following a regimen of oysters for breakfast, oysters for lunch, oysters for dinner. One Sunday at the venerable Old Ebbitt Grill, across 15th Street from the White House, he was tucking into the evening ration of a half-dozen bluepoints (accompanied by a wedge of iceberg drizzled with balsamic vinegar), when a waiter danced up from another station and introduced himself as Kevin.

"I've always admired your work, Mr. Curtis," Kevin said. "Are you in town for a show?"

"Yeah," Mr. Curtis said almost bashfully, in the Bronx accent immortalized by lines like "Yonder is the valley of the sun and my father's castle." (Contrary to various inconsistent authorities, Mr. Curtis attributes it to "The Prince Who Was a Thief," 1951.)

At 77, after more than 100 starring film roles and half a century before the cameras, Mr. Curtis seemed to be basking in the gleam of imaginary klieg lights. The glossy black hair has gray in it now, but thanks to what Mr. Curtis calls "an unexaggerated hair piece," it has turned white for the new show. The big ice-blue eyes can still stop traffic though. Across the table was the former Jill Ann VandenBerg, 32, the statuesque equestrian and American history buff

---

The sole surviving star of a Billy Wilder film classic takes the stage in its theatrical adaptation.

---

who is his fifth wife and with whom he lives in Las Vegas. For the first time, Mr. Curtis, who has painted all his life, even has an art studio.

"Starting Tuesday, we're doing this musical of 'Some Like It Hot' out at Wolf Trap," Mr. Curtis continued, his baritone a smoky mix of silk and husk.

The show is his first stab at singing and dancing since the film "So This Is Paris" (1954), which led Gene Kelly to advise him, "Keep fencing." (That was in Mr. Curtis's swashbuckling days.)

The lone surviving star of the original "Some Like It Hot," Billy Wilder's Hollywood comedy of 1959, Mr. Curtis now has the marquee to himself. He has given up the role of the saxophone player Joe, perhaps the most popular of his career, for that of the eccentric millionaire Osgood Fielding III.

Wilder's masterpiece has acquired something more than mere classic status since its release; in 2000, the American Film Institute ranked it the funniest American movie ever made. You'll remember the premise: having witnessed the St. Valentine's Day massacre in Prohibition Chicago, two down-on-their-luck musicians (Mr. Curtis and Jack Lemmon), fearing for their lives, dress up as women and run off to Palm Beach with an all-girl band in which Marilyn Monroe plays the ukulele.

The new version has a book credited to Peter Stone (leaning heavily on the original screenplay, by Wilder and I. A. L. Diamond) and songs mostly by Jule Styne and Bob Merrill, some recycled from the Broadway adaptation, "Sugar" (1972). The show, directed and choreographed by Dan Siretta, opened in June, as the inaugural attraction at the Hobby Center for the Performing Arts in

Scott Suchman

Houston, the new $100 million home of Theater Under the Stars. By August, it had made its leisurely way to the capital's Virginia suburbs and Wolf Trap.

On Tuesday, the real push begins: four weeks at the Golden Gate Theater in San Francisco, followed by dates in 21 other cities coast to coast. The New Jersey Performing Arts Center in Newark has the

Carol T. Powers for The New York Times

Tony Curtis sketches with pastels outside his McLean, Va., hotel in August before performing in "Some Like It Hot" at Wolf Trap in Vienna, Va., left. The show had played there as part of its national tour.

show from Feb. 4 through Feb. 9, and the Shubert Theater in New Haven from March 11 through March 16. (The tour schedule appears on the production's Web site, thehotmusical.info.)

Mr. Curtis's accumulated stage experience before the new "Some Like It Hot" adds up to less than

Continued on Page 22

Figure 2.1 Tony Curtis on paper. *New York Times,* print edition, Sunday, October 6, 2002.

The Bride Stripped Bare

Figure 2.2 Tony Curtis online. *New York Times,* online edition, Sunday, October 6, 2002.

The image of Mr. Curtis, too, is different. It's shoved over to the side and shrunken. The Starbucks ad, which appears nowhere in the print edition,[1] almost functions as a caption. I could go on, but I think the point is obvious. The Web version of the article might be termed scantily clad. While not entirely nude, the stability and authority of the *New York Times* brand is under siege.[2]

In the upper right-hand corner of the Web page is an option to email the article. When we do that, what arrives in our inbox is extremely stripped down compared to the Web page. It's just a text. The only indication that it comes from the *New York Times* is a line at the top that says "This article from NYTimes.com has been sent to you by. . . ." The Times font has vanished, to be replaced (at least in my inbox) by Microsoft's proprietary sans serif screen font Verdana. There are no images, no pull quotes, and no typographical treatments save the capitalization of the words "WASHINGTON" and "TONY CURTIS'S." How easy it would be to strip out the words "NYTimes.com." If

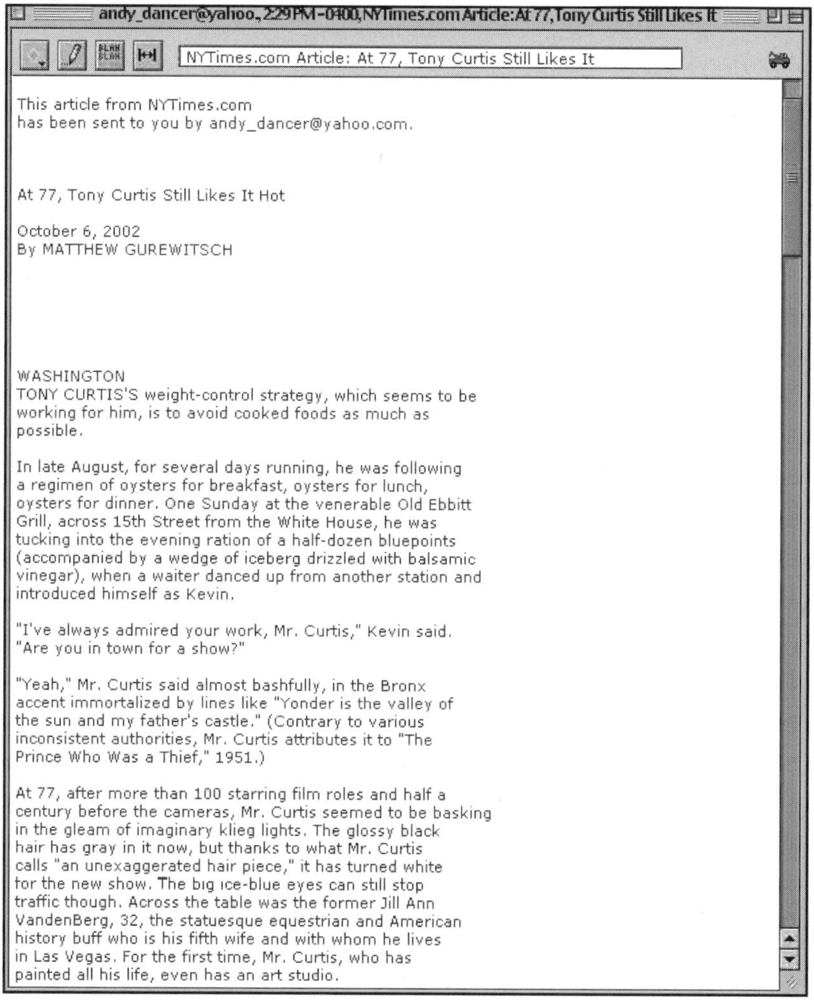

Figure 2.3 Tony Curtis as text. *New York Times,* text email.

we do that, this file becomes detached from any authority, completely naked. In fact, it is entirely indistinguishable from any number of text-based attachments that arrive in my inbox daily (figure 2.3).

To go one step further, if we cut and paste the *text* (and it is a text and no longer an "article") into Microsoft Word and run a primitive altering function on it (e.g., the auto summarize feature), we end up with something bearing minimal resemblance to the original article as printed in the paper or on the

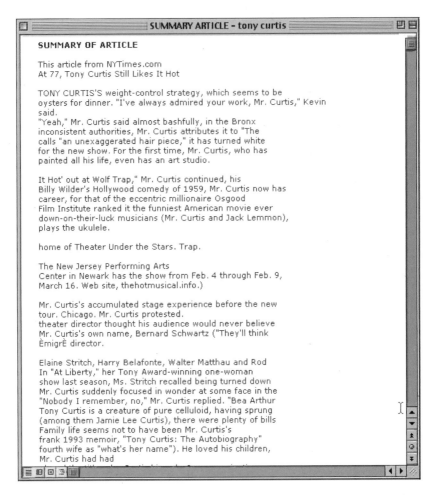

Figure 2.4 Tony Curtis summarized. Microsoft Word summary command.

Web. Now the lead line is "SUMMARY OF ARTICLE," followed by its provenance and then the headline. Curiously, the word "Washington," which figured so prominently in prior versions, is nowhere to be found. The body text, too, now becomes radically unhinged and stripped down (figure 2.4).

If I were to take this text and either email it to a number of people or enter it into an online text-mangling machine, the nude media game could continue ad infinitum. Think of it as an ever-evolving game of telephone. Free-floating media files around the net are subject to continuous morphing and manipulation as they become further removed from their sources.

Figure 2.5 Tony Curtis pornolized. http://www.pornolize.com.

When destabilized texts are recontextualized and reclothed back into "authoritative" structures, the results can be jarring. Examples of this include the Pornolizer machine, which turns all Web pages into smutty, pottymouthed documents while retaining their authoritative clothing (figure 2.5); or Brian Kim Stefans's (2002) recent series of détournements of *New York Times* articles, which intersperse leftist quotes with *Times* reportage, while still sporting the architecture of the *New York Times* site.

Disinformation Wants to Be Free

Believers in the inherent stability of media, regardless of its form, might argue that this phenomenon leads to little more than a tangle of disinformation. But recontextualization has been the basis for innumerable radical works of art. With the advent of file sharing, we've seen this approach explode.

On UbuWeb, although we encode our MP3s with the ID3 tags—which, on the MP3 player, identify the artist, the title of the cut, and so forth—we do not encode provenance information, such as "Courtesy of UbuWeb." When an MP3 leaves our site it is, in essence, returned to the common space of the Web: it leaves nude.

Flogging a Dead Poem

We can only guess what happens to our files after they leave our site, but I'd like briefly to consider the previous journey of an MP3 that can be found on UbuWeb. Over the course of the last half century, Henri Chopin's sound poem "Rouge" has been subjected to various mutations, both clothed and unclothed.

Chopin began his tape recorder experiments in the mid-1950s, and "Rouge," recorded in 1956, was one of his first pieces.[3] It's a literal sound painting, with the names of colors repeated with different emphasis, almost like varying brushstrokes. Manipulated audio techniques and track layering build up an increasingly dense surface. The piece reflects its time: think of it as an abstract expressionist canvas. It, too, is Greenbergian: its form is its content.

In its day, "Rouge" never made it to LP as an "official" release by a record label. It was born naked and remained that way—unreleased and without a publisher—until twenty-four years later, when it was put out by a German gallery.[4] Thanks to Chopin's highly visible work as a promoter and publisher of sound poetry, however, tapes of his work were making the rounds in advanced musical circles of the day.[5]

A decade after the recording of "Rouge," it curiously appears in the first "Region" of Karlheinz Stockhausen's 1966 composition *Hymnen*, an electronic and musique concrète mélange of national anthems. Although truncated, "Rouge" forms the basis for a short spoken-word section based around varieties of the color "red." Chopin's voice alternates with German-inflected voices reading a portion of a list of Windsor Newton paints. To listen to this excerpt alone and decontextualized, it sounds like an extension of Chopin's sound painting. But squeezed between magnetic tape deconstructions of "The Internationale" and "The Marseillaise," its meaning becomes very different. The nude poem is now clothed in the garments of leftist politics.

Twenty-three years later, in 1999, the sampling group called Stock, Hausen & Walkman (note the group's name) brought "Rouge" into an entirely different context: that of ironic pop in a cut called "Flogging" (flogging = flayed "rouge" skin). Amid the cheesy vocals, snappy drumbeats, and appropriated mathematical recitations from children's records, Chopin's piece is snatched away from Stockhausen's political agenda and returned closer to its formalist origins. But it's an emptying gesture: finally "Rouge" is just one sample of many, part of a noisy landscape in which sounds are easily obtained and just as easily manipulated. In such a landscape, no sound appears to have more meaning than any other.

Pop Goes the Avant-Garde

Stock, Hausen & Walkman is known for its graphical inventiveness. They understand how to create a package that visually approximates their musical practice. Packaging—or, in our terms, dressing—creates a context of value. Stock, Hausen & Walkman's redressing of "Rouge" places Chopin's poem back into circulation fully clothed.

In the clothed realm, popular culture's fetishizing of the historical avant-garde reached a plateau a few years ago when the rock band Sonic Youth released a CD called *Goodbye 20th Century* (1999). On it, the one-time rockers rattled their way through cover versions of some of the more difficult works by John Cage and George Maciunas, among others. Through a curious confluence of downtown sensibility and mass marketing, thousands of rock-loving, Lollapalooza-attending Sonic Youth fans bought the disc and were exposed to what until very recently has resided on the fringes of the historical avant-garde.

Through gestures such as these, the avant-garde becomes hip and well-marketed. Stroll through any good record store or museum gift shop, and you'll notice hundreds of artifacts of the historical avant-garde gorgeously repackaged to be snapped up by consumers.

As soon as these items are purchased, however, they can be recruited as nude media, via peer-to-peer file sharing. In the case of some of this material, what was originally created as an antiauthoritarian gesture has, thanks to the Internet, been restored to its original radical intentions. Due to the manipulative properties of digital media, such artworks are susceptible to remixing and mangling on a mass scale, hence never having *the* one authoritative version bestowed upon these objects in traditional media. They are ever-changing works-in-progress operating in the most widespread gift economy yet known.

Such circumstances raise many questions: How does having a variety of contexts influence the cultural reception of such objects? Who or what determines an avant-garde artifact's value, both commercially and intellectually? How does this in turn impact the artist's reputation, both commercially and intellectually? If artifacts are always in flux, when is an historical work determined to be "finished"?

It is a little too early to answer such questions. We are a bridge generation. Brought up on books and records—media in a clothed and stable form—it's hard for us to accept cultural artifacts in constant flux as "genuine." Once *Ulysses* arrived on our shelves, the only new versions of the book that came along were typesetters' corrections and annotated editions, which only reified our sense that Joyce was a singular genius. With the exception of Xeroxing and collaging, remixing texts on the scale of *Ulysses* was difficult.

While it's hard to predict how computer users who have come of age in this environment will assign values and form canons, it might be useful to look at how quickly bootleg remixes became legitimized. As a 2002 MTV article reports:

The art of bootleg remixes, mash-ups or sound clashes (take your pick) emerged as an Internet phenomenon two years ago but is now scratching its way into the commercial music market, especially overseas.

In Europe the pioneers of the movement, such as Kurtis Rush, Soulwax, Osymyso and Freelance Hellraiser, have become household names, headlining popular clubs and spinning their creations on radio shows. One mash-up artist, Richard X, even recently topped the UK singles chart with "Freak Like Me," which layers vocals from the Sugababes and Adina Howard over new-wave hero Gary Numan's "Are Friends Electric."

[. . .]

Electronic music luminary BT, who also produced 'NSYNC's "Pop," was so impressed with a mash-up of his "Mercury And Solace," he tracked down the remixer and released it.

"I love having people do unsolicited remixes of my stuff. In fact, I'm thinking about posting vocals of the whole next album on my Web site when it's done," BT said. "I believe that everyone uses sounds in a case-specific and different manner than other people who use the same sounds."

BT is especially fond of mash-ups that pair drastically different songs. "I'm an avid believer in crossing boundary lines and idiom subdivisions in the music-making process, and if we need to mix Willie Nelson with John Cage to push the envelope in the right direction, then bring it," he said. (MTV Asia News 2002)

When big business sniffs a trend—even one as formally "radical" as bootlegging—they invest in it, turning outlaws into stars overnight. It's not the first time this has happened with sampled material. Composer John Oswald's legendary 1989 CD *Plunderphonic* was destroyed after successful litigation from CBS Records and Michael Jackson for unauthorized use of images and samples. Soon afterward, however, Oswald received a call from the head of Elecktra Records, asking him to remix Elecktra's archive on the occasion of the company's fortieth anniversary. The subsequent release, *Rubáiyát*, was a fully legitimate, corporate-endorsed bootleg, which was just one of many records at the time comprised entirely of samples (big-selling hip-hop and Jamaican music had been employing the remix for several years).

When it comes to text, we haven't seen anything close to the bootlegging phenomenon. I'm hard pressed to come up with any peer-to-peer *text* sharing communities. But musical examples might hold clues as to how such systems might operate in the future. In this light, it's no surprise to see John Cage, an early advocate of intermedia and nude media, mentioned in the MTV context. As early as 1986, Cage predicted and embraced the idea of unstable electronic texts as potential source texts for remixing:

Technology essentially is a way of getting more done with less effort. And it's a good thing rather than a bad thing. . . . The publishers, my music publisher, my book publisher—they know that Xerox is a real threat to their continuing; however, they continue. What must be done eventually is the elimination not only of the publication but of the need for xeroxing, and to connect it with the telephone so that anyone can have anything he wishes at any time. And erase it—so that your copy of Homer, I mean, can become a copy of Shakespeare, mmm? By just quick erasure and quick printing, mmm? . . . Because that's the—electronic immediacy is what we're moving toward. (Bronzell and Suchomski 1986, 25)

While vast libraries containing intact texts are stored online, few offer textual remixes, even the sort that Cage alluded to twenty years ago. One encouraging example is the online webzine *xStream*. According to its mission statement, "Every issue consists of two parts: Regular issue, which is a selection of poetry submitted to *xStream*, and Autoissue, which is a computer-generated version of regular issue."

Although a step in the right direction, *xStream* doesn't go far enough. While the methodology regarding the computer-generated content is not made apparent, it appears that the manipulation was done by the editor of xStream and posted on the Web site. But unlike peer-to-peer systems, the text stops here. Certainly, one could cut and paste the text so as to continue the destabilization, but the site doesn't encourage it. Instead, even though the site's content is purposefully skewed, it remains on the site as securely as it was printed on the page. I could imagine another scenario: the computer-generated manipulations are available as text files to be downloaded. Then, in turn, they are remanipulated and re-uploaded for further processing by users.

. . . (And We've Got to Get Ourselves) Back to the Garden

How, then, do all these new conditions position a resource such as UbuWeb? Suddenly, our idea of "radical distribution" is changing again: UbuWeb is not *the* resource but instead just another *source*; our "radical distribution" might not be so radical after all. We've become subsumed in the mechanics of *redistribution*. It's apparent that our function has changed. Our authority has been undermined by our own process.

UbuWeb is now positioned on a two-way street. Imagine these altered files returning back to the source from which they came, clothed and housed momentarily before being sent back out into the world again. Like the files themselves, UbuWeb is becoming less stabilized in its identity as a center. Instead, we're just another brief stopover point on the road to instability and nudity.

Notes

1. The printed *New York Times* page is bereft of all ads.

2. Curiously, in a bid to regain control of these exact issues, the *New York Times* offers an option on its home page to "[s]ee it in the same format as the physical newspaper." What is offered is a clumsy proprietary reader, an enormous download, and no significant savings to readers of the newspaper.

3. "Rouge," a rather traditional sound poem, is quite unlike the type of electronic work based on bodily sounds that Chopin would be later be closely identified with.

4. Hundermark Gallery, Germany, 1981. "Rouge" has since been released many times on various compilations.

5. Chopin's energies as a publisher and enthusiast for electronic sound poetry were highly visible throughout the 1950s and 1960s, culminating in 1964 when his *Revue Ou* began publication and its work regularly aired on the BBC.

Works Cited

Bory, Jean François. 1968. "The worldWord is. . . ." In *Once Again*, ed. Jean François Bory, 86–95. New York: New Directions.

Bronzell, Sean, and Ann Suchomski. 1986. "Interview with John Cage." In *The Guests Go in to Supper*, ed. Melody Sumner, Kathleen Burch, and Michael Sumner, 20–27. Oakland: Burning Books.

Chopin, Henry. 1956. "Rouge." *UbuWeb Sound Poetry*. http://www.ubu.com/sound/chopin.html (accessed March 21, 2004).

de Campos, Augusto, Décio Pignatari, and Haroldo de Campos. 1968. "Pilot Plan for Concrete Poetry." In *Concrete Poetry: A World View*, ed. Mary Ellen Solt, 71–72. Bloomington: Indiana University Press.

Greenberg, Clement. [1940] 1992. "Towards a Newer Laocoon." In *Art in Theory, 1900–1990: An Anthology of Changing Ideas*, ed. Charles Harrison and Paul Wood, 558. Oxford: Blackwell Publishers.

Marghen, Alga. 2002. *Revue Ou: Sound Poetry, The Anthology*. 4 CD boxset. ALGA045.

MTV Asia News. 2002. "Bootleg Remixes: Music's Latest Craze." August 2. http://www.mtvasia.com/news/International/.

Nichol, bp. 1967. "eyes." In *An Anthology of Concrete Poetry*, ed. Emmett Williams, n.p. New York: Something Else Press.

Pignatari, Décio. 1968. "beba coca cola." In *Concrete Poetry: A World View*, ed. Mary Ellen Solt, 108. Bloomington: Indiana University Press.

Pornolizer. http://www.pornolize.com (accessed March 20, 2004).

Solt, Mary Ellen. 1968. "Introduction." In *Concrete Poetry: A World View*, ed. Mary Ellen Solt, 7–66. Bloomington: Indiana University Press.

Sonic Youth. 1999. *Goodbye 20th Century*. Sonic Youth Recordings. SYR 4.

Stefans, Brian Kim. 2002. [Index to *New York Times* Vaneigem détournements.] http://www.arras.net/vaniegem (accessed June 26, 2004).

Stock, Hausen & Walkman. 1999. "Flogging." *Ventilating Deer*. LP. Hot Air. QRMVDLPOO1.

UbuWeb. http://www.ubu.com/ (accessed March 20, 2004).

Williams, Emmett, ed. 1967. *An Anthology of Concrete Poetry*. New York: Something Else Press.

xStream. http://xstream.xpressed.org/ (accessed March 20, 2004).

Toward a Poetics for Circulars

Brian Kim Stefans

Introduction

The Web site Circulars was founded on January 30, 2003, to provide a focal point for poets' and artists' activities and reflections on the impending invasion of Iraq along with the politics of the media and civil liberties issues. Its format is a multiauthor weblog, or "blog."[1] The HTML design was based on a generic Movabletype template with customized coding added for the comments and archives sections. Original elements of the design included an unambitious header graphic and a Flash insignia—a vertical cylinder of rotating cogs that, when individually clicked, adopt different angles and sizes, courtesy of the freeware Flash site levitated.net—which I superimposed over Guy Debord's collage map of Parisian flows, "The Naked City," in reverse black and white (figure 3.1). Circulars was housed as a subsite of my Web site www.arras.net, devoted to new media poetry and poetics, though as a distinct entity. (Indeed, for the first several weeks, www.arras.net did not even contain a link to Circulars.)

For about four months, activity on the site was high, helped partly by stories about it in the *Village Voice* and *Publisher's Weekly*[2] and by email announcements to listservs and people in my address book. As many as twelve new stories were posted a day by several contributors around the world; the comments section was active, with several distinct threads running concurrently. Predictably, site activity—both posting and random traffic—dropped considerably after Bush announced the "end of hostilities" on May 1, as did

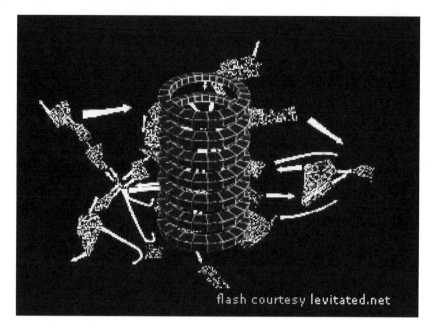

flash courtesy levitated.net

Figure 3.1 Circulars logo. http://www.arras.net/circulars/.

protest activity by poets and artists. Around May 15, I announced that the site would be put in "hibernation" mode at the end of the month—new stories would continue to appear, but the home page would consist of a text-only archive rather than the lively cacophony of material, much of it illustrated, that had been appearing during its peak.

The following paragraphs from the "mission statement" were written during a night of involuntary (i.e., insomniac) brainstorming and sent out to about twelve poets who I thought would be interested in being contributors:

CIRCULARS intends to critique and/or augment some conventional modes of express-ing political views that are either entirely analytical, ironic, or humanistic. These are all valuable approaches, of course, and not unwelcome on CIRCULARS, but our hope is to create a dynamic, persuasive idiom that can work in a public sphere, mingling elements of rhetoric and stylistics associated with the aforementioned modes—analytical, ironic, or humanistic.

CIRCULARS is, in this sense, a workshop—a place to explore strategies.

CIRCULARS was not created in the spirit of believing that all poets should be "political" or even "social" in nature. While such arguments are free to be made on the website and poems related to the themes of the site are (selectively) welcome, the focus is on articulating statements that are unique to the poetry community while not speaking for "poetry."

CIRCULARS holds no party line, nor is it particularly adherent to notions of the "avant-garde." All perspectives are welcome provided that they are articulated intelligently or (in some cases) amusingly and do not articulate perspectives or advocate actions that are, in the editors' judgment, of an entirely unethical nature.

CIRCULARS understands that, in the world of the internet, the link can be as powerful as word of mouth and is itself the prize of an effective rhetorical strategy. These are "Circulars" because they are circulated.

There's a lot to unpack in these concise, suggestive statements; I'll comment on some of these facets later. In general, I was interested in having the site be a place where poets could work out strategies of writing that were not necessarily "poems"—a category of writing that, in the minds of the public and even many poets, seems antithetical to "real world" issues, or at least impotent in the face of social conflict. I'd rather they relied on their skills as creative writers nurtured by a progressive, international artistic community that traditionally has affiliations with other disciplines, such as the social sciences, new media arts, and grassroots activism.

In this way, Circulars would stand in contrast to the Web site Poets Against the War (PAW), the organization started by Sam Hamill in the wake of the controversy over his being uninvited to a White House reading organized by Laura Bush after he had sent out an email request to other poets for antiwar poems he could read there. Whereas the PAW site focused on gathering and databasing thousands of poems opposing the war—which suggested to me that poems were being used as "votes" in an unofficial election or, at best, were general expressions of pacifist sentiment rather than fresh articulations of opposition—Circulars would highlight the poets' role as creative, even "revolutionary" (in a psychical sense) intellectuals, forcing the interaction of statements and activities by poets with interviews, opinion articles, open letters, and other writing mainly from left-leaning, independent media sites.

I contacted a small number of my friends, all of them poets, many from England and Canada, to become authors or *superusers*—that is, individuals with permission to add stories and make updates to the site—most of whom either had some experience in the creation of Web sites or had demonstrable interest in political activism and grassroots organization, "consciousness-raising," muckraking journalism, or simply writing about political issues in their poems and prose. Several poets responded immediately that they were interested in participating and offered valuable feedback on the initial proposal.

The number of authors on the blog reached about twenty, but only a handful became regular posters of stories, mostly those people who were already invested in Internet culture for work or other reasons. Darren Wershler-Henry transformed the site with his contributions; he is the author of several books on digital culture, including *Commonspace* (Surman and Wershler-Henry 2001) and *Free as in Speech and Beer* (2002), so this was right up his alley. David Perry, "Alfred Schein," Angela Rawlings, Jonathan Skinner, Patrick Durgin, and the Language poet and blogger Ron Silliman all made frequent contributions, mostly in the form of links but also in the postings of poems—Schein, for instance, appropriated a fiery piece by Antonin Artaud, "To Have Done with the Judgment of God." One poet, Carol Mirakove, made a very distinctive contribution to the site; three of her "Mirakove Relays"—highly researched, URL-laden, exposé-type emails with a matter-of-fact but persuasive tone on subjects such as the Guantanamo Bay detainees and the Patriot Act II—made their appearance.

A valuable contributor of links to the site was scholar Maria Damon, a tireless reader of alternative news sources. Thomas Mediodia, writer and student of Žižek, was a prolific depositor of redolent prose and poetry in the comments sections. Stephen Vincent, a California poet, made the most unanticipated contribution by sending me, sometimes two a day, his "Gothic News" items—satirical, hallucinogenic news accounts of potential occurrences that read like a cross between *The Onion* and the poetry of the Berkeley Renaissance. The poet Scott Pound sent in occasional journal entries from Turkey, where he was teaching. Essays and poems by Eliot Weinberger, Alan Gilbert, Kent Johnson, Carla Harryman, and Charles Bernstein also appeared. Barrett Watten's statement "War = Language" spurred one of the more energetic comments columns on the site, so active that some bloggers took to linking to this comments section rather than to the site itself.[3] The most active updates to the site were through the comments section itself, much of it contributed by casual passersby who had little interest in poetry per se.

Brian Kim Stefans

Besides the postings and writings of these authors, some artists and artist groups had a regular presence on the site, most importantly Paul Chan, originator of the Baghdad Snapshot Action that would tape or paste laser prints of digital photographs that Chan had taken in Iraq, where he had spent the January prior to the war as a member of Voices in the Wilderness.[4] Chan, also a Web programmer, distributed the photographs from his site (www .nationalphilistine.com); one artist couple, Lytle Shaw and Emilie Clark, were arrested while posting these photographs, news of which also appeared on Circulars.

As the "mission statement" suggests, my initial hope was to provide poets with a platform in which they could publish work relating to the war, as it seemed—with recent symposiums at places such as St. Mark's Poetry Project and the Bowery Poetry Club and the regular readings on the steps of the New York Public Library—that there would be a proliferation of writing and publishing activity by poets in the future months. There seemed to be a concern that poets were behind the times in not utilizing the Net for organizing or expressing their views (a reprimand usually made, ironically, by writers with little experience in Internet culture).

I hoped Circulars could answer this call and be a staging ground for these disparate activities, rubbing poetry and poets' statements up against news stories from both mainstream and alternative sources, digital art from other sites (often poster art and fake mirror sites such as whitehouse.org), opinion articles and interviews (by the likes of Noam Chomsky and Senator Robert Byrd), and so forth (figures 3.2 and 3.3). Poets are often criticized for speaking among themselves in languages that seem esoteric to the public; Circulars would be a place where the detailed critique specific to the poetry community could flourish while being channeled to, and challenged by, a nonpoetry readership.

Uncharacteristically, I promoted the investigation of "rhetoric" in poems that would be written in this time of war—not, of course, toward the goal of creating poems full of bluster and self-importance but to encourage poems that attempted to engage in tactics of persuasion, that had a rich variety of conceptual handles for even nonreaders of poetry to hook on to. I had no idea what these poems would look like (I was ready for anything), but I figured that, with Bush hiring an evangelical Christian to write his speeches, we had to counter that public rhetoric with something persuasive, charismatic, even manipulative, and not with merely fatalist, defeatist irony and plain old lefty

Figure 3.2   Ann Coulter Li'l Junior Miss Conservative Club.
http://whitehouse.org/initiatives/posters/ann_coulter_brownshirt.asp.

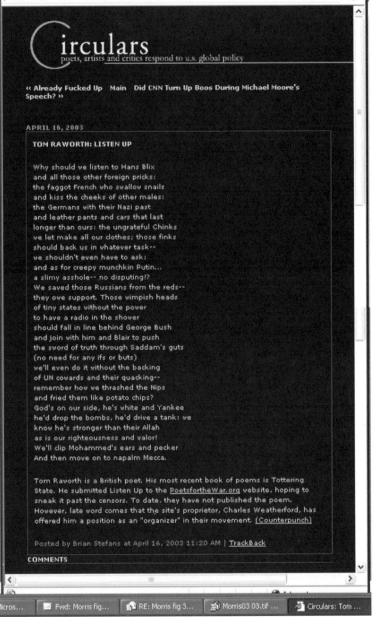

Figure 3.3 Screenshot of "Listen Up" by Tom Raworth.

http://www.arras.net/circulars/archives/000546.html.

rage. I wanted positive, detailed visions that could give confidence to those on the sidelines of the antiwar movement.

Email stories and jokes, not to mention political cartoons based on "remixes" of found material, were being zinged around daily on the Internet at that time. I thought: with the mere pressing of the "send" button to one's entire address book, one of these poems would be picked up by one of the many visitors to the site and turned into an anthem of dissent for millions— a lofty dream, of course, but nonetheless the guiding principle behind the name of the site.

None of the poems, so far as I know, became huge hits as "circulars"—certainly not as big as the ubiquitous hoax email petition whose first signatory was "Suzanne Dathe–Grenoble, France"[5]—though a few were picked up by newspapers. On that level, the site was a failure, but probably in the way that trying to light a match with a pair of reading glasses is a failure. I don't think the "war" (I'm not sure that it *was* one) lasted long enough for the involved writers to "develop new strategies," and with the exception of Vincent's "Gothic News" and Mirakove's "relays," most of the poetic writing that appeared on the site was not specifically geared toward the Internet.

What did happen with the site was unanticipated: it became an anthropological study of Internet protest culture, a consciously *unofficial* anthology of poetry from several generations of writers, a sort of warzone for the left and right (in the comments sections) fueled mostly by nonpoets, and, finally, a staging ground for ephemeral home pages that themselves had a certain poetic charge in the way the stories and images—many exclusive to the site, many merely links—associated with each other and *dissociated*[6] the reader from mainstream and government media, injecting at moments a spirit of laughter but also a sense of sublimity and possibility in the midst of some very bad news. The site obtained a "poetics": what I mean by this is the subject of the remainder of this chapter.

My fear is that this chapter will appear self-serving—I hope not. I see it as a way to record the moment, to theorize it a bit, and to think about what to do next. Because of Darren Wershler-Henry's important contribution during our brief run, I've asked him to help me write the second part of this chapter (which appears here as a confluent sidebar), with the hope of suggesting some of the dynamic of the "multiauthored" blog.

A Poetics for Circulars

What happens, then, in the situation of the decline of the Master, when the subject himself is constantly bombarded with the request to give a sign of what he wants? The exact opposite of what one would expect: it is when there is no one there to tell you what you really want, when all the burden of the choice is on you, that the big Other dominates you completely, and the choice effectively disappears—is replaced by its mere semblance. One is again tempted to paraphrase here Lacan's well-known reversal of Dostoevsky ("If there is no God, nothing at all is permitted"): if no forced choice confines the field of free choice, the very freedom of choice disappears (Žižek 1997, 153).

One of the facets of hypertext literature that is often celebrated by its proponents concerns the issue of *choice* and the malleability of a narrative based on a user's *interaction* with a text. The idea is that the reader, rather than being "passive," takes on a "writerly" position—an allusion to Roland Barthes usually appears here—by determining where the thread of the text (usually figured as a narrative) will go.

   It is arguable that a reader is truly given a choice in, say, a hypertext novel such as Michael Joyce's *afternoon* since "choices" have usually been preprogrammed by the writer. Outside of the parameters of an overdetermined narrative—by its nature, linear and noninteractive—the choices presented can have no more than trivial differences between them, and their results can be of no more

Exchange on Circulars (2003)

Brian Kim Stefans (BKS): I've come up with an awkward, unsettling title for this essay: "Circulars as Antipoem." I'm sure cries will be raised: So you are making a poem out of a war? The invasion was only interesting as content for an esoteric foray into some elitist, inaccessible cultural phenomenon called an "antipoem"? (There is, in fact, a lineage to the term "antipoem," but I don't think it's important for this essay.) This legitimate objection is to be expected, and I have no reply except the obvious: that a Web site is a cultural construct, shaped by its editors and contributors, and more specifically, Circulars had a "poetics" implicit in its multiauthoredness, its admixture of text and image, its being a product of a small branch of the international poetry community, and so forth. Of course, the title also suggests that this Web site has some relationship to a "poem," but perhaps as a non-site of poetry— as it is a non-site for war, even a non-site for activism itself, where real-world effects don't occur. But my point for now is that the fragmentary artifacts of a politicized investigation into culture—Gramsci's *Prison Notebooks* for example—has an implicit poetics to it, but standing opposite to what we normally call a "poem." This suggests roles that poets can play in the world quite divorced from merely writing poetry (or even prose, though it was the idea that poets could contribute prose to the antiwar cause—as speech writers or journalists, perhaps—that initially inspired the site.

Darren Wershler-Henry (DWH): Hey Brian: what are you using to count words? MS Word

than trivial importance. If there is only a shade of difference between the two options—the difference between clicking the word "Harry" or "Jane" or choosing the left door over the right—then one is not engaged in an issue of *choice* so much as partaking in *chance:* the chance that one link will lead to a more entertaining, substantial, or (in game worlds) utile or informative lexia than the other.

Ethical choices—such as "Would I have put an ice pick through that man's head were he to have killed my daughter?" or "Should I read this atheistic literature even though I am a practicing Catholic?"—are among the more compelling choices one might make in one's life and have been a staple of fiction, drama, and philosophy for centuries. Since most of us don't have to make choices about murder, or even about corrupting a purportedly pristine spiritual geography, there is an appeal to the vicarious experience of having to *decide*. Art can be compelling purely for this reason.

On the other hand, Internet activism, which on the face of it might seem to be all about such choices, could equally be deemed, from some perspectives, trivial. One of the criticisms of online activism—which can include "political" blogs and links sites, advocacy and organizational sites, independent media sites, and so on—is that the Internet has nearly nothing to do with "real world" traditional political activism. It doesn't involve going outside into the world and confronting physical events that can easily spiral into danger but remains stuck in

says the previous paragraph has 254 words; BBEdit says 259 (me, I'm sticking to BBEdit). Poets—particularly poets interested in working with computers—should be all about such subtleties. Not that we should champion a mechanically aided will to pinpoint precision (a military fiction whose epitome is the imagery from the cameras in the noses of U.S. cruise missiles dropped on Iraq during the first Gulf War), but rather, the opposite—that is, we should be able to locate the cracks and seams in the spectacle . . . the instances where the rhetoric of military precision breaks down. As such, here's a complication for you: why "anti-poem" instead of simply "poetics"? Charles Bernstein's cribbing ("Poetics is the continuation of poetry by other means") of von Clausewitz's aphorism ("War is the continuation of politics by other means") never seemed as appropriate to me as it did during the period when Circulars was most active. The invocation of Smithson's site/non-site dialectic is also apposite, but only in the most cynical sense. Is the U.S. bombing of Iraq and Afghanistan the equivalent of a country-wide exercise in land art? In any event, the relationship is no longer dialectical but dialogic; the proliferation of weblogs ("war blogs") during the Iraq War created something more arborescent—a structure with one end anchored in the world of atoms, linked to a network of digital non-sites.

BKS: I hesitate to tease out the "non-site" analogy—the *site* itself is too variable: for me, I was thinking of Circulars as being the non-site of activism, not just a corollary to the sweat and presence of people "on the streets" but a vision of a possible culture in which these activ-

the white box of the monitor, indissolubly "virtual." Internet activism is seen as absenting from the equation specificities encoded on the body—such as racial, gender, and class identity—that form the dynamite that explodes any sort of social cohesion and often aggravates social inequalities. The Internet is figured as a "gopherspace," and Internet activism is categorized as a form of living room radicalism, requiring little physical or mental effort—in other words, a voyeurism.[7]

My sense is that a site such as Circulars makes a step in creating an ethics of "choice" in hypertext literature but also that it makes a gesture toward creating a poetics of online activism, giving it a cultural tone beyond the merely critical or utilitarian. It never hoped to replace classic forms of social activism so much as to augment them and perhaps suggest new themes and angles. Circulars provides the interpretative bed in which events (protests, arrests, speeches) and personalities can be viewed outside of, even in conflict with, the interpretive strategies of the mainstream media, which are becoming increasingly consolidated under umbrella organizations with singular political viewpoints.

Thus, the site can be conceptualized as somewhere between a "poem" and a "community," as a place of shared laughter and contempt that infects and populates the private space with the concerns of the world. In this way, the site might be seen as motivated by a nostalgia for the oppositional "counterculture" of the sixties—not just its paraphernalia and pop songs—as it once

ities (otherwise abandoned to television) can exist, not to mention reflect and nourish culturally. That is, are our language and tropes going to change because of the upsurge in activity occurring around us—in the form of poster art, détourned "fake" sites, maverick blogging? I admit that some of what we've linked to is nothing more than glorified bathroom humor, but nonetheless if the context creates the content for this type of work as a form of dissent, I think that should be discussed, even celebrated. I haven't read too much about this yet. Thinking of Circulars as the "non-site" of the bombing itself is both depressing and provocative: it's no secret that one of the phenomena of this war was not the unexpected visibility of CNN but Salam Pax's Dear Raed blog, written by a gay man from the heart of Baghdad (even now he is remaining anonymous because of his sexuality). I could see Circulars as a "poetics," but I prefer to think of it as an action *with* a poetics, my own tendency being to think of poetry as the war side of the von Clausewitz equation, simply because poetics seems closer to diplomacy than a poem.

DWH: The variability and heterogeneity of the site was, I think, partly due to the infrastructural and technological decisions that you made when putting the site together, because those decisions mesh well with the notion of coalition politics. (I'm thinking of Donna Haraway's formulation here.) The presence of a number of posting contributors with varied interests, the ability of readers to post comments, the existence of an RSS feed that allowed anyone running a wide variety of Web software packages to syndicate the headlines, a

saturated everyday thinking with a need to imagine other forms of government, including self-government, one informed by an erotics as well as an egalitarian ethos.

What follows is a short list of descriptive categories that relates Circulars both to traditional activist/artistic practices (e.g., Brecht's "epic theater" and its genesis in the information-saturated theater of Erwin Piscator) and to issues of "electronic literature," work that relies for many of its effects upon its presentation through a digital medium. The list is meant to be suggestive rather than exhaustive. I don't necessarily hope to distinguish Circulars from other sites that might be informed by a "poetics" of political activism—several could be said to do that and a short essay such as this cannot double as a history. Though I believe all of the issues outlined below are embodied in the site, there will be no attempt, in this short space, to "prove" that Circulars does or did any of this—one can visit the site and find out.

Aggregation and Amplification

Regardless of one's opinion of the mainstream media, there can be no denying the trend of increased consolidation of major media organizations under umbrella groups such as the Turner Broadcasting System, Rupert Murdoch's empire, and, in radio, Clear Channel Communications. In the face of the semimonopolized state of the most successfully distributed forms of media in the United States and the proliferation of nefarious practices to gain marketable material

searchable archive, a regular email bulletin—these are crucial elements in any attempt to concentrate attention on the Web. Too seldom do writers—even those avowedly interested in collaboration and coalition politics—take the effect of the technologies that they're using into account, but they make an enormous difference to the final product. Compare Circulars to Ron Silliman's blog: on the one hand, you have a deliberately short-term project with an explicit focus that is built around a coalition of writers on a technological and political platform that assumes and enables dialogue and dissent from the outset; on the other hand, an obdurate monolith that presents no immediate and obvious means of response, organized around a proper name. Sure, the sites have different goals, but Silliman's site interests me because it seems to eschew all of the tools that would allow any writer to utilize the unique aspects of the Web as an environment for writing. And sadly, that's typical of many of the writers' blogs that exist.

BKS: I haven't been too bothered with those aspects of Silliman's blog for the mere fact that it would double his time having to respond to the comments, many of which could be vicious flames. I've deleted some of the comments on Circulars, in one case because the poster was making scandalous allegations (drugs, child molestation) about the head of an advertising agency, and another because the poster, in American fatwaesque fashion, deemed that I should have a rocket shoved up my ass. Of course, your point is well-taken—Silliman's blog could use some real-time play-by-play; I'm sure a diagnostic essay is forthcoming. I did set

(such as "embedded journalism" with its reality television overtones), there has been an increased reliance on, and desire for, alternative news sources, including overseas news services that are, in their native countries, relatively "mainstream."

But because, like homegrown butter, stories from fugitive or unknown presses don't have the stamp of officialdom, they only gain visibility and credibility by their reappearance on other Web sites that can contribute—via design, extensive readership, branding, and so forth—cultural capital. *Guardian UK* columnist Robert Fisk was probably one of the most read columnists by American antiwar advocates during the war, and yet, as far as I know, he has never had a regular column in an American publication. Reappearances on other sites, from ZNet to Common Dreams, gave him a visibility beyond that of other *Guardian* writers. A similar thing happened to the Dear Raed blogger, "Salam Pax," an Iraqi in Baghdad who was unofficial enough to have had his very existence questioned yet was read loyally by folks who discovered him through other Web sites (and who now writes a column for the *Guardian*).

The effect of a story reappearing across the Web in different contexts and thereby being *read* differently can be linked to the medieval rhetorical effect of "amplification,"[8] in which a basic descriptive trope—"he is the wisest king," for example—is revisited and teased out to give a grandiose air to the matter at hand. Though hardly in fashion today—the method is best lampooned in scenes of

Circulars up with the intention of there being subsets of discussion on the site, separate groups of people who would engage with each other over some time—"committees" of sorts, with their own story threads. This happened for a brief period: there was a lot of heat generated by one of Senator Byrd's speeches against the war, and there was a discussion about Barrett Watten's "War = Language." I was prepared to develop new sections of the site if anyone so requested, though I confess to being dictatorial about the initial setup, basically because I know more about the Web than most poets, and I hate bureaucracy. I was hoping that some of the more frequent poet bloggers who were writing political material would send their more considered material for posting to Circulars, but most simply posted to their own blogs without telling me.

DWH: I'm not suggesting that blogs and news forums should be about the abrogation of editorial control—far from it. It's always necessary to do a certain amount of moderation and housecleaning, which, as you well know, takes assloads of time. During its peak, I was spending at least two or three hours a day working on Circulars, and I'm sure you put in even more time than that, even with the help of the other industrious people who were writing for the site. Which takes me back to the value of the coalition model: a decent weblog *needs* multiple authors to work even in the short term. The classic example of a successful weblog is Boing Boing (www.boingboing.net), a geek news site that evolved from a magazine and accompanying forum on the WELL (www.well.com) in the late eighties/early nineties. Mark

sycophantic bombast by attendees of the court in Monty Python skits—it has been used effectively by such writers as Thomas Carlyle, who mated it with Protestant fury in such hypertroping essays as "Signs of the Times," and T. S. Eliot, who used it in his liturgical poems. It also reappears in hip-hop lyrics, often in a comic form of macho bragging in which recurring invention around a single lyrical trope gives proof of social power.

The argument that a rhetorical effect that reduplicates a turn of thinking is associated with the reappearance of a story on different Web sites depends on an understanding of Internet reading as an activity closer to "browsing"—in which the story might not be read until the third or fourth time it has been chanced upon—than it is to, say, reading a newspaper, which is discarded as soon as it is read. In this way, the more superficial aspects of a story (its headline, its byline, and so forth) become part of the poetics of a site such as Circulars, which featured the names of the last one hundred stories in a sidebar.[9]

Centrifugal and Centripetal Motions

Circulars had the benefit of being a simple site to understand—the navigation was easy, most of what you needed to see was right on the home page, and its perspective was clearly antiwar—yet it housed materials created by people in any number of fields taking any number of angles (satirical, poetic, pacifistic, Marxist, conservative, and

Frauenfelder, the original editor, has worked with many excellent people over the years, but the current group (including Canadian science fiction writer/Electronic Frontier Foundation activist Cory Doctorow, writer/video director David Pescovitz, and media writer/conference manager Xeni Jardin) presents a combination of individual talent and a shared vision. There's nothing *wrong* with personal weblogs, but, like reality television, they get awfully thin over time. Even when the current search technologies adapt to spider the extra text that blogging has created, the problem of anemic content isn't going to go away unless we start doing more collective writing online. The problem is partly a need for education; most writers are still in the process of learning how to use the Web to their best advantage.

BKS: I'm not sure that it's necessary for a blog to be multiauthored; what it really needs is a mandate, and it's possible that, were the mandate simply to produce rich, incantatory prose—imagine the Marcel Proust blog—a highly disciplined approach could work. Steve Perry's Bushwarsblog, for example, succeeds quite well on this level (not the Proustian but the muckraker), as does Tom Mantrullo's Swiftian Commonplaces. Both of them have "political" agendas, but they are also well-written and thoughtful for what are in effect news publications without an editor. It helps that these two are journalists and conceptualize their blogs as a distinct form of news writing alternative to the mainstream—the individual voice is sharpened by an informed sense of the social arena in which it will resonate (in which the message will ultimately become dulled). Just today, Tom posted

so forth) on the impending crisis. Some materials were outright offensive to some readers—the most notorious case being the poster art from the whitehouse.org Web site—while others might have appeared saccharine, obscure, reactionary, petulant, dismissive, even irrelevant.

My sense is that the very simple blog structure created a centripetal motion—that is, users were easily drawn deeper into its form to scroll downward to reach new stories, click comments links, avoid what they did not care to read, and so forth.[10] At the same time, in a centrifugal motion, the site constantly pointed outside toward other sites and toward the lack of centrality of the reader in the political event. (See the following "non-site" entry.)

Complexity and simplicity formed a dialectic, and the engagement between the two drew the reader into a questioning of motives. One can become part of a virtual community simply by showing up, but one only becomes implicated by moving in deeper and making choices about reading. There is clearly plenty of material to dissuade a reader from further engagement were this material figured as the dominating, monolithic content of the site, but because Circulars was unspecialized, the *culture* of the site was porous: readers who wanted to avoid poems could read, say, a speech by Senator Byrd or view a gritty satirical "remix," as each is contextualized as part of a single cultural mix.

a link to the [New York] *Times* story on corporate blogging—yecch!—and has coined this aphorism, a détournement from Foucault though sounding somewhat Captain Kirkish to me, to describe his project: "To blog is to undertake to blog something different from what one blogged before." A version of "make it new" but with the formal precedent being the blog itself—a vow not to let individual "multiauthoring" become equal to corporate monoglut. Perhaps the model blog is that which responds to the formal issues of other blogs as if they were social issues (i.e., beyond one's "community"), hence transforming the *techne* of the writer into a handling of hypertextual craft.

DWH: It's all too easy to imagine the Marcel Proust blog—Christ, what a nightmare (shades of Monty Python: "Proust in his first post wrote about, wrote about . . ."). Endless streams of novelistic prose, no matter how incantatory, are *not* what I want to read online. William Gibson, for one, thinks there's something inimical about blogging to the process of novel writing. I think that the paragraph-as-post is the optimal unit of online composition—and that an optimal online style would be some sort of hybrid of prose poetry and healthy geek cynicism (imagine a Slashdot [slashdot.org] full of Jeff Derksens). But I think I see your point, that it's possible for one writer to produce the kind of dialogic multiplicity that could sustain a blog. There is, however, a large difference between "possible" and "likely." In my opinion, as less stratospheric talents than the geniuses of high modernism, we stand a better chance of generating strong content collectively. Another model

Non-Site of Community

The artist Robert Smithson was best known for his large-scale earthworks such as the *Spiral Jetty* and the photos, films, and essays he used to document them. Equally celebrated, if not as freakishly grandiose, are his artworks consisting entirely of collected items which he calls "non-sites," such as the totemic *Non-Site, Pine Barrens, New Jersey* (1968), a hexagonal grouping of earth and industrial materials gathered at a disused airfield. He described his gallery-bound nonsites as

the absence of the site. It is a contraction rather than an expansion of scale. One is confronted with a very ponderous, weighty absence. . . .

The making of the piece really involves collecting. The container is the limit that exists within the room after I return from the outer fringe. There is this dialectic between inner and outer, closed and open, center and peripheral. It just goes on constantly permuting itself into this endless doubling, so that you have the nonsite functioning as a mirror and site functioning as a reflection. (Smithson 1996, 193)

This description addresses what might be called the active negation of Circulars, which is manifold:

• The site is the negation of community. For better or worse, the site replaced physical communion with virtual, while drawing attention to the absence of the reader

that I find promising is the Haddock Directory (www.haddock.org)—a site I've been reading daily for at least four years. Haddock has recently moved to a two-column format: standard blog description-plus-link on the left (maintained by the site's owner and editor-in-chief, if you will) and entries from the Haddock community blogs, identified by author, on the right. It's a very neat example of the effective aggregation of data within a particular interest group. And it seems to follow Stein's dicta: "I write for myself and for strangers."

BKS: I'm still curious about the line "generating strong content." What do you mean by "content"? My guess is not "writing" as we know it, but some admixture of links, intro paragraphs, pictures, and HTML formatting, that creates a dynamic, engaging, and timely space on the screen. "Content" moves from "writing" to the shape one creates by selectively linking to other sites serving, but also provoking, a "particular interest group." (I wrote earlier today in a dispute over blogs: "Circulars was a short-term effort [or as short term as the war] that was a response to what I sensed was or would be [or hoped to be] a moment of crisis in terms of American self-identification." Who would have thought, ten years ago, that a group of weblinks and writing could contribute to a crisis in national identity?) Most writers would probably feel demeaned to be referred to as "content managers," as if all writing were a versioning of some other writing (put it back in your pants, Harold), but, frankly, we're admitting for a whole lot of plagiarism in this concept of "content." I think the blog-ring model on haddock.org is strong,

from these time- and place-based forms of interaction, whether in protest activity or war itself.

- It is also the negation of technological power and the omniscience of "electric eyes": the site as a *willing myopia,* a metaphorical corrupting of the exactitude of satellite photography, and the guiding systems of smart bombs. Implicit in this is a critique of voyeuristically "engaging" in war via observing the embedded journalist on television, for example.

- It is also a negation of the poem. Despite a "poetics," there was no single rhetoric for the site, no way to recuperate it into an "author," no way to domesticate its contents into a confirmation of a bourgeois subjectivity. It targeted the very space of the "poem" in society. Further, it troubled language and narrativity, but in a way that did not require idiosyncratic reading strategies promoted by, among others, Language poets or the novelists of the Nouveau Roman.

Via these negations, reliant on a process of collecting—a "recovery from the outer fringes" that "brings one back to the central point"—Circulars had the effect of creating traffic between an inside and outside, fringe and centrality. That is, one was reminded of the monitor's limits as one is of the gallery's bounds in a non-site. The aura of the postmodern simulacra was actively dispelled via the extreme rhetoric of some of its contributors, overwhelming the irreality presented by the embedded journalists. The emphatic anger of many of the contributors, often

since it lets writers tend their gardens, deriving whatever classic satisfactions one gets from writing, and yet contribute unwittingly to a larger collective. I agree that some "types" of writing just *work* better online—claustrophobic syntax, also non sequiturs, drive readers back to hunt for hearty prose (though writers such as Hitchens seem to be as uncompromisingly belle-lettristic on-screen as on paper).

DWH: I like to think of myself as a malcontent provider. As someone who works regularly with found text, copping to the "plagiarism" that's at the heart of all "original" writing doesn't worry me at all; in fact, I'm beginning to think it's a necessary strategic position for artists at this particular moment in history. As thinkers such as Siva Vaidhyanathan and Lawrence Lessig have been arguing strenuously for the past few years, the concept of intellectual property is a relatively recent, regressive invention that has nothing to do with the reasons that copyright was established two hundred years ago and that it actually reverses copyright's original function—that is, to provide a short-term monopoly solely to drive innovative thought, not to create perpetual profit. Artists in many disciplines are increasingly moving toward creative processes based on appropriation, sampling, bricolage, citation, and hyperlinking, but the multinationals and the entertainment industries are driving legislation in the exact opposite direction by arguing that ideas can and should be owned. Artists and writers who have a large investment in their own "originality" do us all a serious disservice by refusing to recognize and protect the public

operating from the fringes of standard modes of expressivity—via avant-garde poetry, truly tasteless satire, and détournement—created the "reality" of the situation more adequately than the photoshopped images on the cover of the *Los Angeles Times*. One was not permitted to be a "political voyeur"—ironically, it was a non-site that taunted one into taking a position.

domain . . . the very thing that makes ongoing artistic activity possible. So by all means, yes, don't just "write" (a verb that in many cases bears the superciliousness of the romantic), build (mal)content. Bring on the hyperlinks, intro paragraphs, pictures, PHP scripts, and HTML formatting, especially if they help to demonstrate the mutual indebtedness that all creativity entails. Use Your Allusion.

Challenging Censorship and Making Dissent Palpable

In a climate of threatened civil liberties via the Patriot Act and the looming of its successor, the Patriot Act II, Circulars encouraged association with sites, individuals, and cultural traditions that engaged in nonacceptable, even antisocial, expressivity in a bid to contest the bounds of legal speech and encourage a discourse around what is permissible in U.S. publishing. The site intended to "sound out" what appeared to be, at times, an echo chamber of opinion and cultural evasions and to suggest that the practice of dissent for its own sake is worth refining.[11]

As Noam Chomsky and other critics from the left have argued, the conspiracy of silence and lack of risk taking in a prosperous democracy is voluntary, not forced. One legacy of Ralph Nader's experiment with American politics in the 2000 election was the discovery to many that, for the first time in recent history, a sort of "truth" could be expressed from behind a televised podium that was not compromised by million-dollar funding and that a language could be used in politics that was direct, detailed, and effective and appealed to an auditor's civic sense. Rhetoric was not being rendered anemic by the conflicting desires of special-interest lobbyists, nor was it being laced with subliminal religious assurances. That a reliably unanimated public speaker could draw such excited crowds was an event that couldn't be ignored.

Circulars encouraged an investigation of these fringe forms of expression and content not merely in an attempt to dissolve adherence to official perspectives and pry open the floodgates of political desire but, additionally, to create new semantic horizons beyond safe, well-worn, politically correct agendas. The zone between these two, in which pragmatic proposals and irrationality were in close consort, was where I expected the average reader of Circulars to flourish.

The Poem of Prose

Circulars offered a dynamic collage of visual and linguistic materials in a consistent but changeable structure. Even the most mundane inclusions, whether presented in excerpt form on the home page or as a full story once clicked through, contributed to this hypertext poem. In this egalitarian, psychically charged universe, the blandest Reuters update meshed with the most scurrilous opining in the comments section, their stylistics foregrounded as something crafted, purposeful, and aesthetically rich.

Several American poets since Walt Whitman and E. A. Robinson have experimented with using prose stylistics in poetry: Ezra Pound advocated turning to Gustave Flaubert and Ford Madox Ford to avoid "abstraction" and ambiguities inherited from the symbolist tradition, while John Ashbery and other New York School poets purposely flattened out the tone of their poems, moving even beyond the conversational to the bureaucratic to a degree that risked making the writer himself appear bored.

Such tactics might appear to be appealing to the avant-garde and no one else, but even the decidedly mundane prose stylist Chomsky observed that there is a transcendental beauty in the most pedestrian language. He expresses this through the following paraphrase of Schlegel's notion of the poetry intrinsic to everyday language:

Schlegel describes language as "the most marvelous creation of the poetic faculty of the human being." Language is "an ever-becoming, self transforming, unending poem of the entire human race." This poetic quality is characteristic of the ordinary use of language, which "can never be so completely depoeticized that it should find itself scattered into an abundance of poetical elements, even in the case of the most calculating and rational use of linguistic signs, all the more so in the case of everyday life—in impetuous, immediate, often passionate colloquial language. . . ."

The "poetical" language of ordinary language derives from *its independence of immediate stimulation* (of "the physically perceivable universe") and its freedom from practical ends. (Chomsky 2002, 61; my italics)

The growth of the Web site over several months correlates with this romantic notion of the growth of language through time, akin to Hegelian conceptions of history as an organic "becoming," similar to the growth of plants.[12]

More than a "poem containing history"—Pound's famous description of his *Cantos*—Circulars was able to permit sovereignty to its constituent elements while forcing them to exist together in a tight, even teleological, motion. But because it is the "non-site"—not the space of war or community itself but a pointing to it from within Plato's cave, hence "independent of immediate stimulation"—the site acquires poetical qualities that are akin to those of the lyric or elegy, remarking a material absence.

As a form safeguarding the right to trouble national self-identity "independent of immediate stimulation," Circulars can be seen not only as a "poem" but as a romantic and utopian one, even if its effects are nonlyrical and of an ambient nature.

Real-Time Détournement

"Détournement" is a word that appears frequently on the site, though in fact most of what is posted there is more properly "collage" or "political cartoons" or even "doodles."[13] The first writings on détournement by the Situationists noted that it must "go beyond any idea of scandal . . . drawing a moustache on the *Mona Lisa* is no more interesting than the original version of that painting" (Debord and Wolman [1956] 1981, 9). Further, "détourned elements, far from aiming at arousing indignation or laughter by alluding to some original work, will express our indifference toward a meaningless and forgotten original, and concern itself with rendering a certain sublimity" (9).

The products of the *Propaganda Remix Project* and www.whitehouse.org, while performing useful eviscerations of the underbelly of American classism and racism and the hypocrisy of a unified cultural front in prior war efforts, were not much concerned with effects of "sublimity." Most of these products were willing to be lowbrow, even exploitative, though there is, indeed, an implicit sublimity in the speed with which these "remixed" posters appeared on the scene. Many of the visual and textual remixes that appeared on Circulars were involved in a digital subterfuge in which imagery and textual elements were borrowed from "legitimate" Web sites (Tom Ridge's Homeland Security site was one immediate favorite) and reflowed into dystopic and dissociating mirrors.

However, the greater effect of détournement on Circulars happened on a less conscious level; items that had clear argumentative functions in isolation participated in a real-time documentary on the various home pages of the site.

As the Situationists wrote, "It is obviously in the realm of the cinema that détournement can attain its greatest efficacity, and undoubtedly, for those concerned with this aspect, its greatest beauty" (Debord and Wolman [1956] 1981, 12). They then move on to consider an "architectural" form of détournement: "Life can never be too disorienting: détournements on this level would really make it beautiful" (13).

Disorientation—both through time in its play-by-play commentary and through space in its architecture—might very well have been the modus operandi of Circulars, as its many authors contributed at ungoverned, merely opportune moments, thereby contributing in disparate concord to the ludic image of a collapsing social architecture.

Carnival

A Web site that collects such disparate materials by both marginal and central cultural figures can be seen as a stage on which to enact creative dissent. Via the mechanism of Web searches, links, and other forms of electronic word of mouth, the site begins to "contain multitudes" (to quote Whitman) and, in the process of simply acquiring more content, to become exponentially more visible to the various spiders and search engines that create Internet hierarchies of significance.

This snowballing effect, in which information and digitalized personalities (some of them salty) rub up against each other in dynamic fashion, is the effect of carnival. The term "carnival" is, of course, borrowed from Russian critic Mikhail Bakhtin's writing about the preservation of certain medieval social structures into the Renaissance and beyond. For Bakhtin:

The basis of laughter which gives form to carnival rituals frees them completely from all religious and ecclesiastic dogmatism, from all mysticism and piety. They are also completely deprived of the character of magic and prayer; they do not command nor do they ask for anything. Even more, certain carnival forms parody the Church's cult. All these forms are systematically placed outside the Church and religiosity. They belong to an entirely different sphere. (1984, 7)

While I'm not proposing that Circulars displaced community into cyberspace, the site did present an "anything goes" atmosphere, complete with video games, bawdy songs, dissident literature, and commentary by any number of geographically unlocatable (often pseudonymous) *citoyen* congregated there for no other reason than a particular focus on the war. On such a stage, via the violent yoking together of spontaneous acts of creation, is enacted the singular affect of a virtual community's political desire—a real-time, polyvalent performance of dissent that has, as its goal, the puncturing of what seemed like a monolithic expression of international prowar policy motivated by a bullying U.S. government.

While the future of the Internet is uncertain, this activity can be said to have been subsidized by this very "monoculture," which relies on the free trade of information to keep business culture fluid.[14] Circulars allowed the expression of political affections outside of the confines of understood party affiliations, even outside of standards of aesthetics and taste, in a cacophony that, upon inspection, reflected remarkably coherent wishes and needs. It focused a current of passions and gave an operatic scale to what might otherwise have been a series of "drive-by" expressions of political will.

Conclusion

In many ways, Circulars wasn't original or very effective, and it remained, for the most part, read and contributed to by a clique of people related to the poetry community, though a few right-wingers did attempt to use the site as a stage for their own agendas.[15] But perhaps this sketch of the site can inspire future efforts and even provoke that leap from screen to street that seems to lurk as some promise behind all Internet cultural activity, helping to catalyze, as I note in my dialogue with Wershler-Henry, that "crisis in national self-identity" that I think is important at this time when our notions of democracy are being subsumed under purely economic, often transnational, interests.

On the Web, "writing" is often a matter of creating links, inserting images, parody (both through writing and graphic design), and the creation of several flavors of détournement. As Wershler-Henry emphasizes in our dialogue, a liberated public domain is necessary to maintain the type of free-wheeling, free-*borrowing* Internet discourse necessary in a heteroglot "democracy." Though the point of the site was to articulate ideas regarding war and government, it also made a political point by the mere exploitation of digital—and by extension social—means, contributing to the sort of fervor one might associate with a "revolutionary" (I prefer the term "renaissance," as in "reborn") culture.

Appropriation, with its hint of criminality, was one surprisingly popular means, and I think the torrent of remixes and détournements leading up to the war put center stage a seething but as yet underground counterculture, an entire population of unrepresented people, that shares new views on intellectual property (one of which is that few of us outside of the corporations *have* it). This angle on property and how it can be recombined into new cultural products could be a key aspect of a new shared sensibility, one that, indeed, might frown upon classically romantic notions of creativity (the "transparent soul," for instance) but could unearth others that will take their place.

But "original" poems survive, even thrive, in this mix also: Tom Raworth's poem "Listen Up," written in the voice of a bigoted warmonger in tight couplets and submitted as a joke to the Web site Poets For the War was perhaps stronger for being sui generis as a tactic—a poem used as an ethical Trojan Horse, a virus of words (figure 3.3). The power of writing, rather than being overwhelmed by the very celerity with which text is produced and zinged around the Internet, was often buttressed in its classic qualities by the inherent properties of its formal, however (relatively) antiquated, construction (provided it was done well). Writing, and not Macromedia Flash, was the darkling plain upon which the invisible armies of civic night waged their heated but melancholic debates.

Circulars is perhaps best understood as an exploration in genre—where a Web site could figure in relation to pop songs, movies, television, and the novel and poem, but also where it figures in the social realm of opinion and in the dissemination of knowledge. What the site *was* and how that could be exploited for the future is the big question for me now. It illustrated, I hope, the potential power of community-created sites in times of crisis to be provocative, popular cultural tools and to put our heritage in avant-garde poetics to the service of a specific cultural effort. But, of course, motives are neither here nor there.

Notes

1. Readers interested in more technical aspects of blogs can refer to www.blogger.com. The URL for Circulars is http://www.arras.net/circulars.

2. See Clover 2003 and Sharf 2003.

3. This comments section periodically digressed into the internecine debates about literary politics that have stifled any sort of productive activity about poetry on the

Internet. Hence, I didn't necessarily applaud the severing, through direct linking, of this post from the site as a whole. But at its best, this comments section, with active participation from Watten, was one of the few instances of the spin-off subsites that I anticipated becoming part of Circulars culture in its inception. The page can be found at http://www.arras.net/circulars/archives/000417.html.

4. For a description of Voices in the Wilderness, see http://vitw.org/.

5. This email petition can still be found on several blogs and Web sites or via a search for "Suzanne Dathe Grenoble France."

6. "Dissociation" is a concept Ezra Pound (1996, 11–29) adopted from the French poet and critic Remy de Gourmont. It is, in their view, the act of divorcing readers from their outworn or unexamined ideas and unrealistic associations—such as the confusion of "education" with "intelligence"—that is a necessary prelude to cultural epiphany. It is a predecessor of Brecht's "V-effekt" among other versions of modernism's fascination with making reality "strange" in order to bring about new perceptions.

7. An example of such a critic is John Lockard. In his essay "Progressive Politics, Electronic Individualism and the Myth of Virtual Community," he writes,

> In the skeptical view, global cyberspace lends itself to an elite political voyeurism more readily than to effective activism. Distant lives translate into a gopherspace file organized into a collectivity of deprived subjects and absent even the materiality of yesterday's newspaper. (Lockard 1997, 229)

> Now as then, emergent cyberspace ideologies commonly promote credence in machine-mediated social relations and their benefits, together with mystifications of individual, community, and global relations. Progressive politics should seek to analyze, clarify, and demystify these relations. (Lockard 1997, 230)

8. This term can be found in Geoffrey de Vinsauf's "New Poetics" of 1210, a treatise on style that was influential on writers for centuries: "If you choose an amplified form," de Vinsauf writes,

> proceed first of all by [repetition]: although the meaning is one, let [it] not come content with one set of apparel. Let it vary its robes and assume different raiment. Let it take up again in other words what has already been said; let it reiterate, in a number of causes, a single thought. Let one and the same thing be concealed under multiple forms—be varied and yet the same. ([1210] 1974, 391)

9. RSS (Rich Site Summary) feeds, a method for syndicating news and the content of news-like sites, automatically put these headlines on other sites as well.

10. Indeed, part of the appeal of blogs is the *conventionality* of the navigation and the information-laden home pages, which is why they are so popular for public diaries: the screen becomes a window upon the soul, begging to be deeply examined by the viewer purely for the vanity of upping the hits count. Circulars co-opted this "open soul" aspect to become a window onto an undercurrent of American political life.

11. This is a point of political philosophy involving dialectics and identity that I can only touch on here but which is important and also runs against common sense. "The educator must be educated," writes Christopher Hitchens in *Letters to a Young Contrarian,* and follows with this anecdote:

> I have a dear friend in Jerusalem. . . . Nothing in his life, as a Jewish youth in pre-1940 Poland and subsequent survivor of indescribable privations and losses, might be expected to have conditioned him to welcome the disruptive. Yet on some occasions when I have asked him for his impression of events, he has calmly and deliberately replied: "There are some encouraging signs of polarisation." Nothing flippant inheres in this remark; a long and risky life has persuaded him that only an open conflict of ideas and principles can produce any clarity. (2001, 30–31)

12. Indeed, multiauthor blogs offer a vision of anarchist syndicalism in action, though I hesitate to make the transference of informational architectures to visions of societal organization (as others did during the time of the dot-com bubble). At the core of Chomsky's anarchistic politics are his beliefs that what is common to all humans is a striving for self-realization and that government oppression of linguistic self-realization is nefarious. Paraphrasing German linguist Wilhelm von Humboldt, Chomsky writes:

> The urge for self-realization is man's basic human need (as distinct from his merely animal needs). One who fails to recognize this "ought justly to be suspected of failing to recognize human nature for what it is and wishing to turn men into machines." But state control is incompatible with human need. It is fundamentally coercive, and therefore "it produces monotony and uniformity, and alienates people's actions from their own character." (2002, 67)

This paragraph suggests why Chomsky, who distrusts an analysis of "motives" to interpret world events and who is often criticized for emphasizing the negative in lieu of an argument for "what we should do," nonetheless exercises his faculty as a discerning and articulate political thinker above and beyond what might be considered standard cultural bounds—indeed, taking these bounds as his target. The act of utilizing language ethically is synonymous with being *human.*

13. Tom Raworth coined this term for the political cartoons and other societal lampoons that appear on his Web site at http://tomraworth.com/doodles.html. A more

popular coinage for these sorts of artifacts, when done entirely digitally—in Adobe Photoshop rather than with scissors and glue and thus devoid of the rough borders of collage—is "remix." As for détournement, the Situationist International (SI) was quite specific about what could not qualify:

> *Détournement is less effective the more it approaches a rational reply.* . . . The more the rational character of the reply is apparent, the more indistinguishable it becomes from the ordinary spirit of repartee, which similarly uses the opponent's words against him. . . . It was in this connection that we objected to the project of some of our comrades who proposed to détourne an anti-Soviet poster of the fascist organization "Peace and Liberty"—which proclaimed, amid images of overlapping flags of the Western powers, "Union makes strength"—by adding onto it a smaller sheet with the phrase "and coalitions make war." (Debord and Wolman [1956] 1981, 10–11; italics in original)

14. The passage that inspired this observation is Simon Schama's portrait of the ways in which aspects of carnival managed to survive well past the Enlightenment into the embryonic "information age." Schama notes that in the censorship-free zones of the Palais-Royal—"the most spectacular habitat for politics and pleasure in Europe" (1989, 136)—information and theater, role playing and revolution had a potentially volatile marriage:

> One could visit wig makers and lace makers; sip lemonade from the stalls; play chess or checkers at the Café Chartres (now the Grand Vegour); listen to a strolling guitar-playing Abbe (presumably defrocked) who specialized in bawdy songs; peruse the political satires (often vicious) written and distributed by a team of hacks working for the Duc; ogle the magic-lantern or shadow-light shows; play billiards or gather around the miniature cannon that went off precisely at noon when struck by the rays of the sun. . . .
>
> Louis Sebastien Mercier, who had railed against the boulevards for encouraging feeble-minded dissipation among "honest citizens," adored the Palais-Royal, where he witnessed "the confusion of estates, the mixture, the throng." (136)

15. A short treatise could be written about the politics of banning or deleting comments from a blog. In general, if I felt the comment was both indulgent and violent, a version of "hate speech"—this happened with some frequency—I deleted it. If the commenter continued to post to the blog and did not respond to my email petitions to tone it down (or to post less frequently, as certain commenters felt obliged to respond to each story going up), I blocked the IP from using the blog, which I don't view as a public service but a Web site project that I am paying for and invest time in maintaining. Even were it a public service, like a park, I would challenge anyone to argue that violent or pornographic graffiti is a version of "free speech" and thus should be welcome there.

Works Cited

Bakhtin, Mikhail. 1984. *Rabelais and His World.* Bloomington: Indiana University Press.

Chomsky, Noam. 2002. *Cartesian Linguistics: A Chapter in the History of Rationalist Thought.* Christchurch: Cybereditions.

Clover, Joshua. 2003. "American Ink." *Village Voice,* February 19–25. http://www.villagevoice.com/issues/0308/clover.php (accessed June 30, 2004).

Debord, Guy, and Gil J. Wolman. [1956] 1981. "Methods of Détournement." In *Situationist International Anthology,* ed. Ken Knabb, 8–14. Berkeley, CA: Bureau of Public Secrets.

de Vinsauf, Geoffrey. [1210] 1974. "Poetria Nova." Trans. Margaret F. Nims. In *Classical and Medieval Literary Criticism: Translations and Interpretations,* ed. Alex Preminger, O. B. Hardison, Jr., and Kevin Kerrane, 226–239. New York: Frederick Ungar.

Gourmont, Remy de. 1966. "The Dissociation of Ideas." In *Selected Writings,* 11–29. Ann Arbor: University of Michigan Press.

Hitchens, Christopher. 2001. *Letters to a Young Contrarian.* New York: Basic Books.

Joyce, Michael. 1990. *afternoon* [electronic resource]. Watertown, MA: Eastgate Systems.

Knabb, Ken, ed. 1981. *Situationist International Anthology.* Trans. Ken Knabb. Berkeley, CA: Bureau of Public Secrets.

Lockard, John. 1997. "Progressive Politics, Electronic Individualism and the Myth of Virtual Community." In *Internet Culture,* ed. David Porter, 219–232. New York: Routledge.

Poets Against the War. http://www.poetsagainstthewar.com. Redirected to Living Poets Society webpage (accessed June 28, 2004).

Schama, Simon. 1989. *Citizens: A Chronicle of the French Revolution.* New York: Knopf.

Scharf, Michael. 2003. "Nations of the Mind: Poetry, Publishing and Public Debate." *Publisher's Weekly,* March 31, 29–32.

Smithson, Robert. 1996. *The Collected Writings.* Berkeley: University of California Press.

Stefans, Brian Kim. 2003. Circulars. http://www.arras.net/circulars (accessed June 29, 2004).

Surman, Mark, and Darren Wershler-Henry. 2001. *Commonspace: Beyond Virtual Community*. Toronto: FT Prentice-Hall.

Voices in the Wilderness. http://vitw.org/ (accessed June 21, 2004).

Wershler-Henry, Darren. 2002. *Free as in Speech and Beer: Open Source, Peer-to-Peer, and the Economics of the Online Revolution*. Toronto: FT Prentice-Hall.

Žižek, Slavoj. 1997. "Cyberspace, or, The Unbearable Closure of Being." In *The Plague of Fantasies*, 127–167. New York: Verso.

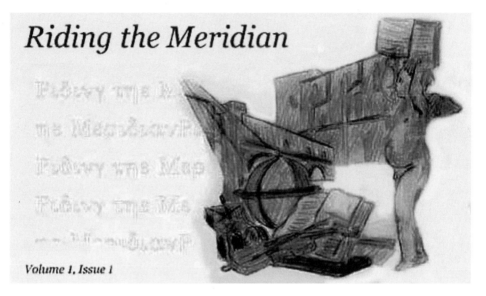

Riding the Meridian. Courtesy of Jennifer Ley.

Riding the Meridian

Jennifer Ley

Riding the Meridian, the online journal I created and edited, debuted in the late 1990s at a time when baud speeds were increasing to 56k (prebroadband) and programming tools such as Javascript and DHTML were just becoming popular. Importantly, *Meridian* was not intended to be simply a distribution portal for new media literature nor a site offering literary works that could just as easily be distributed on paper as on the Web. Its aim was to explore the myriad ways the mechanics of the Web could be used to create new forms of literary expression. This goal gave the editorial staff a mandate to seek out and promote the work of writers who were choosing to use the Web as an integral part of their creative process.

In order to bring electronic literature into dialogue with criticism, each issue featured a roundtable discussion as well as interviews and articles specific to the issue's "theme." Early Net access—email communication, MOOs, and online chat—allowed writers and theorists real-time access to each other's thoughts, facilitating a baud flow of collaborative, creative, and critical dialogue about how best to harness the new medium's creative opportunities. Early HTML language was relatively easy to learn, freeing writers from the need to invest in costly software programs before they could begin to experiment with reconstructing the literary process using hyperlinks, Javascript effects, and other elements of Web programming. When *Meridian* was founded, few online publishing opportunities existed for writers who had chosen to create what Christy Sheffield Sanford, in a 1999 trAce online workshop, dubbed "Web-specific literature." Creating a site in which work by these authors could be seen side-by-side with analytical articles helped stir up creative inquiry. Early Web magazine sites such as *Meridian* were the virtual equivalent of a Left Bank Parisian café or New York's Algonquin Round Table.

The first issue, guest edited by Peter Howard and available in spring 1999 (see chapter frontispiece on p. 94), focused on the global reach of the Internet and was subtitled "Nationality or Not." The late Alaric Sumner contributed a rich Sound/Text section to the next issue of *Meridian*, which appeared in fall 1999. The second issue also included John Cayley's first Web-specific work, as well as work from an international group of Web innovators—including Germany's Reiner Strasser, France's Annie Abrahams, and Australia's Diane Caney and geniwate.

In spring 2000, *Riding the Meridian* turned its focus to Women and Technology, an issue I'm especially proud of having compiled with the help of Margie Luesebrink and Carolyn Guertin. Designed to show that the Web of the new millennium was not just a boy's toy, the issue featured creative work by Shelley Jackson, Deena Larsen, Tina La Porta, mez, and Sue Thomas, among others. The roundtable discussion gave theorists, writers, and editors Katherine Hayles, Marjorie Perloff, Diane Greco, Linda Carroli, and Shelley Jackson an opportunity to debate gender and technology issues. Titled *The Progressive Dinner Party*, this survey of Web-specific writing by women was patterned on Judy Chicago's late-1970s sculptural *Dinner Party* and still serves as a testament to the depth and breadth of talent women bring to the new media writing table.

Two technological issues—Web browser language and the hyperlink—had a strong impact on the development of the online literary community and its publications. *Meridian* debuted at a moment when many writers from the hypertext community who had previously created stand-alone CD-ROM publications were moving to codework that used Web browser language instead of platform-specific coding software such as StorySpace.

The hyperlink, essential to nearly every decision readers make on the Web, was crucial to the construction of the labyrinth of interconnected literary Web sites that exists online today. By making it common practice to publish links to other online magazines, by coding live hyperlinks into authors' bios, by a willingness to risk site "stickiness" through offering one-click access to another author's work or publisher's Web site, online publishers helped build an audience for a diverse range of digital literature. When Google, the search engine of choice for a new generation of Web readers, chose to make links in and out of Web sites the barometer for page ranking, this choice served the online writing community exceedingly well.

While editors of some long-established print magazines continue to debate whether readers want to read online (audience statistics make clear that they do, especially when the digital writing engages them interactively), Web publishers are more interested in such issues as how we'll cope with the accelerated software obsolescence curve, and, importantly, how we will continue to fund online publications.

Because most literary Web sites do not charge a subscription fee to readers, the economics of Web publishing is complicated. It seems unlikely that the sizable audience for new media work that now exists could have been built if Web sites charged readers for access. However, as any online literary writer, editor, or publisher can tell you, a certain amount of capital is required to keep online publishing sites running. Not least among these is the capital of time.

One of the things online publishers most prized about the early Web was its position outside the world of traditional publishing, but now, ten years and counting into this brave new world, outsider status has taken a certain toll. Carpal tunnel syndrome and repetitive stress injuries affect more early practitioners than many people realize. The "log on anytime" freedom Web access originally gave writers and publishers has been supplemented by many conferences and events at which an increasing number of aesthetic, technical, and creative questions about the field are discussed, but these conferences require an editor to have time and funding to travel. Early Web writers needed nothing more than a computer, a text editor, an online connection, a free copy of Netscape, and a willingness to learn how to code for the Web. Today, a new generation of Web-content creation software can set a writer back over two thousand dollars, while the housekeeping inherent in keeping thousands of HTML files and their embedded links current has humbled even the most fastidious site editors.

Riding the Meridian is now on hiatus from publishing new work, but I remain committed to maintaining access to the works we have published. I will always be tremendously proud of the creativity so many writers, theorists, and editors committed to a project that, though it may have been mine to conceive, was ours to shape, promote, and enjoy. That so many of these people are still part of the new media discussions readers will find in the pages of this book is a great source of satisfaction to me.

Riding the Meridian

5

Electric Line: The Poetics of Digital Audio Editing

Martin Spinelli

While an aesthetic of "linearity" is now largely anachronistic in contemporary literature and criticism, there is one small corner of the American literary scene where it remains more than a wispy phantasm. The presentation of poetry in radio programs and now in webcasts is dogged by the watchwords "flow," "continuity," "narrative," and "linear," a situation rooted in the link between established radio semantics and traditional radio editing technology.[1] A particularly linear semantics evolved out of the analog production technology that dominated radio from the late 1940s through the mid-1990s: quarter-inch electromagnetic tape editing. Because this semantics became essential to and essentialized in conceptual models for radio and because professional and critical radio discourse never addressed technology's role in its evolution, it has been transposed without reflection into contemporary speech radio in general and literary/poetry presentation in particular.

Any project intent on demonstrating how an analog poetics born out of a relationship to a given production technology continues to affect literary presentation after a move away from that technology and inviting an exploration of current digital production technology with a view to describing a new digital poetics leaves itself open to the charge of technodeterminism. But an analysis of several key historical moments in the theorization and practice of sounded literature reveals that an analog semantics/poetics was in no way a foregone conclusion.

Modernist experiments in audio poetry that involved recording and editing technology constitute a critical mass onto which it is possible to graft a new digital poetics. It is, however, feasible to argue that writers such as William S. Burroughs, who experimented with analog sound technology throughout the mid-twentieth century, hit a kind of technological glass ceiling when their *digital* imagination of poetry and criticism dramatically outpaced the possibilities offered by reel-to-reel tape. Drawing from these earlier projects, the work of contemporary practitioners, and my own literary broadcasting work, I propose a vocabulary and open-ended taxonomy to help develop and evaluate a poetics of digital audio editing.

Today it is hardly radical to observe that poetry *is*—or at least is inseparable from—the means by which it is produced and distributed or transmitted. Recent scholarship charts this connection, and much of it speaks directly to sounded poetry's relationship to its technology. In her introduction to *Sound States: Innovative Poetics and Acoustical Technologies* (1997), Adalaide Morris characterizes much of sounded poetry's earlier critical tradition as constipated on the printed page: her goal is to "unstop" literature, to sound it by giving it voice and plumbing its depths. Borrowing the term "phonotext" from Garrett Stewart, Morris describes an "underestimated dimension of textuality" found in the aural, a dimension of slippage and polyvalence beyond the reach of a traditional critical vocabulary (1–2).

What Morris begins to suggest here is the complex array of social relationships that follow from poetry's relationship to technology: the relationships between interviewer, interviewee, and eavesdropper and between poem and listener through which meaning is generated.[2] This approach requires us to refocus our critical attention to the space between an audio text and a response to it. More than a Saussurian study of the unstable or arbitrary nature of the sign, it involves positioning instability not as a moment of anxiety but as a moment of poetic (and, in some cases, utopian) opportunity. For the most part, this opportunity has not been taken up by the producers of literary audiocasts.

My contention, then, is simple: given that the reception of sounded poetry has been considerably unstopped in recent years, our production and presentation of sounded poetry, especially in the digital environment of the Web, should not continue to reproduce the stopped-up presentational modes familiar to a radio tradition and the semantics of a disused technology.[3] A sea change has occurred in radio production during the past fifteen years—almost everything that was once produced on quarter-inch reel-to-reel tape today is produced using a computer-based digital audio editor—but our criticism of literary radio, our systems of radio semantics, and the form and shape of radio language have failed to keep pace. The technological shifts that have brought enormous production changes have yet to generate the conceptual changes that have attended other digital literatures and poetics.

If our new conceptual model for digital poetics must avoid technodeterminism, a poetic practice enhanced, encouraged, and even enabled by technological advances must avoid technofetishism. The problem in Gregory Whitehead's words is "to not be thought by the technology" (2003). Jacques Attali sounds an even more cautionary note about the excesses of computer music and, we may easily extrapolate, the digital audio editing of speech in a poetic context:

An acoustician, a cybernetician, he [the contemporary composer] is transcended by his own tools. This constitutes a radical inversion of the innovator and the machine: instruments no longer serve to produce the desired sound forms, conceived in thought before written down, but to monitor unexpected forms. . . . The modern composer . . . is now rarely anything more than a spectator of the music created by his computer. He is subjected to its failings, the supervisor of an uncontrolled development.[4] (1985, 115)

Attali's elaboration of technofetishism in music contains within it an implicit critique of the lackluster character of so much digital art across genres. In an arena where anything seems technologically possible, very little engages. When interest in how digital technology can process speech or music or image completely eclipses the cognitive or semantic work that might be activated through that speech or music or image, we are not likely to get beyond marveling at what computers can do. The safeguard for a poetics of digital audio editing is to focus on the relationships that accrue around meaning rather than on gee-whiz pyrotechnics. The trick is not only to recognize that the technological transposition of language always opens new possibilities for exchange but also to develop, expand, and articulate the parameters of that exchange.

In his 1936 essay "The Work of Art in the Age of Mechanical Reproduction," Walter Benjamin observed that audio had a unique place among the arts in that it allowed "the original to meet the beholder halfway" (220), requiring participation from an audience for its completion. Three years earlier, F. T. Marinetti and Pino Masnata proclaimed in their manifesto, "La Radia" ([1933]

1992), that radio was to be built on the ashes of narrative. Despite this critical lineage and these radio dreams, however, contemporary radio production theory—the theory taught in courses on radio production, for example—is much more narrowly defined.

Based on texts that have calcified around established radio forms and neglected the field's intellectual and creative history, contemporary production theory is marked by an anachronistic linearity. Perhaps the most widely read text in this context, Andrew Crisell's *Understanding Radio* establishes a taxonomy of radio signs that is incapable of dealing with the possibilities proposed by Benjamin, Marinetti, and Masnata. Interestingly, Crisell borrows a semiological system that predates broadcasting itself. Following turn-of-the-century pragmatist C. S. Peirce, Crisell places all radio emanations under three rubrics: the iconic, that which resembles the object it represents; the indexical, that which provides some direct link to its object; and the symbolic, that which has no obvious connection to its object. This plain vanilla, late nineteenth-century semiology poses real problems both for experimental presentation of poetry on radio and for its attendant critical discourse.

Crisell argues that because all radio signs are auditory, "they consist simply of noises and silences, and therefore use *time*, not space as their major structuring agent" (2000, 210). This temporal emphasis means Crisell interprets radio in terms of continuity and flow, a strategy predisposed to privilege discursivity and narrative. In his micrological analysis of radio language, Crisell argues that words have a dual semiological status: they are symbols of the things they represent but also indices of the person speaking, which means they provide direct access to the object that produces the sound.

At this point, it is possible to make an intervention into Crisell's schema that provides a first step in elaborating a radio poetics more receptive to extranarrative qualities, modernist radio history, and the digital sensibility. Words on radio—indeed, all sounds on radio—are not indices of some original voice or authentic sound producer but indices of radio technology. In other words, what is directly available through radio is a series of receiving, transmitting, editing, and recording devices. Not only are voices and words always created through technological mediation, but plenty of radio is possible through technology that does not depend on a person or musical instrument.[5]

Crisell, however, would resist this emendation. For him, sound is almost always referenced to narrative, never to the production of narrative and certainly never to the production of radio. He is uncomfortable, for example, discussing an old radio trick that threatens to expose its connection to the actual material of radio production: the technique of rustling a ball of crinkled reel-to-reel tape to provide the sound effect for a person walking through dry grass comes too close to indexing the technology of radio production, which must remain inaudible in the service of the continuous delivery of narrative. Crisell's blind spot is caused by an attachment to the "real" that he inherits from Peirce: using coconut shells to create the sound of a horse galloping cannot be indexical because there is no real horse involved. But neither a recording nor even a live broadcast of an actual horse would be as indexical as Crisell imagines because he is unable to recognize the mediating apparatus.

A production theory couched in such a tradition is not capable of dealing with a vast array of radio broadcasts, literary and otherwise, on their own most basic terms. It can no more readily address the complex semantic potential introduced by the digital than it can account for the most famous broadcast in the history of American radio, the 1938 production of *War of the Worlds*, whose art resided in semantic play that unsettled its audience's expectations of radio communication and its relationship to radio as a cultural institution. For Crisell, however, activating relationships of interpretation is less important than relating information or telling a story in a manner that does not complicate or problematize the medium. This is not to say that such an activation would be anathema to him, only that his analog sensibility, a sensibility thoroughly organized around time, has not positioned him to explicate or develop it.[6]

How did we arrive at a situation in which new digital tools are used not to experiment but to replicate old forms, thereby lodging professional radio discourse in an analog time warp? The answer lies, at least in part, in the fact that digital audio technology itself was designed to address the analog concern of maximum fidelity to an "original" and thereby to make the technology itself inaudible: in radio parlance, the aim of this technology is to maximize the "signal-to-noise ratio." In fact, the twenty-year history of digital audio has been almost exclusively about silencing technology in order to achieve a better delivery of something else: more direct access to the human voice, less noise, less distortion, less evidence of process. Today digital audio recording and editing software is sold as the apex of fidelity, not only better than Memorex but better than the live event because of its ability to remove all extraneous Cagean sounds and allow direct access to the pure voice.

To describe the digital as the capstone of analog's quest for fidelity traps the notion of fidelity in an analog consciousness. In this consciousness, access to unmediated sound or speech is prized largely because of its persistent and audible impossibility. An understanding of this history is necessary for us to appreciate what is at stake in the transposition of an analog into a digital aesthetics: if our aim is to recover a lost original or repair ontological shortcomings deemed essential to recorded speech, there will be little incentive to invite technology to do anything other than fetishize the "real."

Under such a regime, it is unacceptable to interfere with the project of providing access to "the voice," "the conversation," or "the poem" and blasphemous to foreground audio technology in an effort to complicate communication. In Jonathan Sterne's words, "Attending to differences between 'sources' and 'copies' diverts our attention from processes to products; technology vanishes, leaving as its by-product a source and a sound that is separate from it" (2003, 3). The concept of fidelity is "necessary for the medium to function as a vanishing mediator and thereby construct a relation of social correspondence among the sounds emanating from musicians' instruments and the sounds emanating from radios" (282). As such, the "best" medium is the one that is "least there." Functionally and ironically, however, the less we hear the medium, the more work it is doing to erase itself and, therefore, the more present it is.[7]

At this point, it may be useful to describe the differences between analog tape editing and digital audio editing. When producing a program using tape, in most cases, we record audio onto tape through a tape machine then edit this single linear continuum of sound by using a razor blade to cut out any undesired sound. This process creates a seamless, inaudible edit that carves direct speech out of a jumble of David Antin–like talk. If such a technique does not have what one might call built-in linearity, it nonetheless demonstrates a tendency toward linearization.

In digital audio editing, by contrast, there is no single line of sound from which offending elements are removed. Digital editing is a technique of addition rather than subtraction. Because numerous audio tracks are available on the same screen, it is as easy to add sound to multiple tracks as it is to add sound to one track; individual pieces of sound can be cut and layered in overlapping positions, and visual representations of waveforms that zoom in to a ten-thousandth of a second make enormously complex mixing jobs simple.

In much the same manner that the first moveable typefaces mimicked the monks' handwriting, our approach to audio editing transposes an aesthetics and semantics developed for one production technology onto a newer and different technology. The use of digital technology to realize an analog aesthetic extends beyond aspirations for linearity and fidelity. The perception that digital technology has largely accomplished unmediated delivery of the voice means the voice itself now becomes the next obstacle to clear communication. The human residue of the voice—Barthes' "grain of the voice"—is today heard as an impediment to the meaning that the language riding on it denotes. In an effort to force the voice to articulate meaning without the slippage of the phonotext, an impressive array of digital filters, de-essers, compressors, equalizers, and other processors—all with analog antecedents—have been developed to cleanse it.

Poetry played a crucial role in the development of analog semantics. From the very first experiments in recording and telephony, poetic cadences, forms, and familiarity helped language cross extremely high-resistance technologies by cuing listeners in on what to expect. It was not a coincidence that Edison's first recording onto a wax cylinder was a poem, and not just any poem but one learned by most English speakers as they learned to speak: "Mary Had a Little Lamb." Had Edison tried to record a grocery list or even a newspaper story, what would have passed as our first "recording" might have been significantly delayed. The only text capable of penetrating the static and noise of the first primitive recorders was something ingrained. Poetry's use at speech recording's birth both provides insight into the development of analog semantics and suggests a future sphere of engagement for digital poetics.

Analog semantics presupposes familiarity as a condition of communication. Even today, it is rightly assumed that one must be familiar with the form of a radio interview program to make sense of it. Our evolving digital audio poetics renegotiates rather than rejects this condition. Indeed, familiarity with language forms is necessary for a digital poetics to succeed. As I will discuss shortly, a poetics of digital audio editing works best when expectations for a language form are extremely strong or even naturalized to the point of being unacknowledged. Only in such circumstances will disruption or denial of expectation be effective. We might say, then, that a digital audio poetics is a parasite attached to established semantics: it is something that processes a system of meaning rather than just the sound of recorded speech.

What I have been describing as an "analog" aesthetic is not necessarily a function of analog technology. Modernist efforts to foreground the production and transmission technology of an art event in the event itself offer numerous useful analog examples. The technologization of spoken poetry that Steve McCaffery describes as the third phase of Western sound poetry (1997, 149) marked a move from expressivist voice experiments such as Antonin Artaud's screams or François Dufrêne's "cri-rhythmes" to a more specialized use of a then relatively new recording technology. Tape allowed sound poetry to surpass the limits of human expression in much the same way that the digital allows a presentation of poetry to exceed the limits of linearity and discursivity, but only when it is conceived outside analog notions of semantics and recording.

In the 1957 "Pêche de Nuit," his first technologically mediated "audio poem," Henri Chopin processed a core text of fish names audibly by putting the tape through a number of speed changes and intentionally overmodulating the recording. The voice was microphoned so close and hot as to be virtually unrecognizable, and the speed changes overwhelmed and degenerated normal speech cadences: the words were lost for the sound.[8] In "Pêche de Nuit," language's materialization back into sound makes it impossible to tell where voice ends and technology begins. A listener is denied sensible language but can still hear an unmistakably human voice in very small mouth sounds. In distinction, then, to the analog aesthetic, Chopin's microphonemes suggest a different (digital) register in which technology is grafted onto and accentuates the body rather stripping the voice from a body to erase its "grain" and transmit meaning more clearly.

Created over the next thirty years, Chopin's later audio poems move from manipulations of the voice through recording technology into a poetics of audio editing that completely removes speech from a linear framework. In his *Le Corpsbis* collection (1983), mouth sounds in speech have been spliced so small as to be arrangeable into natural sounds (such as dripping water) that become the sole elements in the creation of artificial soundscapes (as, e.g., a damp cavern). If this technique were reduced in intensity but enlarged in scale, it might be described as a predecessor of recent experiments in digital audio poetry in which extracted speech fragments are used to create dense, spatial listening experiences. But rather than using phoneme, word, or phrase fragments to punctuate faux soundscapes, contemporary poetic practices often interject them on top of or in the gaps of otherwise normally presented sound bites in order to accentuate or complicate a prevailing idea. At the moment when "cutting" comes to be heard as a compositional practice divorced from linearity, it is possible to begin describing a digital poetics.

Like Chopin, William Burroughs was a precursor in the poetics of digital audio editing. Expanding the practical possibilities of inventive tape editing and making an earnest attempt to describe its effects in print, Burroughs' most ambitious engagement with the potential for a new semantics emerging from tape technology is his novel/prose poem *The Ticket That Exploded* (1987). In fact, *Ticket* contains descriptions and sketches for language-tape possibilities that far exceed his own tape art experiments.[9]

While Burroughs experimented with the cut-up, fold-in method of composition in *Naked Lunch* and *Soft Machine*, *Ticket* contains his most intense use of accidental juxtaposition, fragmentation, and random sequencing as compositional practices. *Ticket*'s opening scene is a straightforward allegory of the critical and social power of such aleatory gestures. The narrator captures his opponent's queen early in a chess game by making a series of random moves. Despite going on to lose the game because of his lack of interest, the narrator (and Burroughs) makes a crucial point: even though a narrative or game might conclude as expected, disruption of its teleology—by haphazardly capturing a queen, for example, or puncturing a story's flow with incongruous language—carries an unsettling power. In this disruption, Burroughs provides a prototype for our practice and semantics of editing. It is the rupturing of recognizable form that most draws our attention and invites modes of reading not prima facie part of a familiar meaning system: in Barthes' terms, these techniques make for more "writerly" texts.

The aleatory effects enabled by technological mediations of the spoken word activate the kind of engagement previously described as essential to a poetics that aspires to leave the analog behind. One of Burroughs's favorite technological chance operations was moving tape erratically over the playback head, a technique he used to provide "liberation from old associational locks" (qtd. in Hayles 1997, 90). In the following passage from *Ticket*, Burroughs both describes this mediation of language and attempts to render its effects on the printed page:

"Now listen to this." The words were smudged together. They snarled and whined and barked. It was as if the words themselves were called into question and forced to give up their hidden meanings. "Inched tape . . the same recording you just heard pulled back and forth across the head . . You can get the same effect by switching a recording on and off at very short intervals. Listen carefully and you will hear words that were not in the original text: "do it—do it—do it . . yes I will will will do it do it do it . . really really really do it do it do it . . neck neck neck . . oh yes oh yes oh yes . ." (1987, 21)

The significance of this whining and barking can only be fully appreciated in context; we are enjoined to "listen to this" before the "hidden meanings" of this method can jerk forward into the world. This is not just an injunction to listen carefully: it is also an injunction to listen digitally, to be prepared to do more than the typical share of semantic work. *Ticket*, then, is not just a discussion and/or presentation of a production technique but a primer for a new mode of listening. A digital semantics is (like any semantics) necessarily bifurcated: here it is a set of techniques for rendering audio speech *in conjunction with* a mode of listening tuned in to those techniques. This is hardly an unreasonable or dramatic demand: it amounts to asking that the mind's years of training in the textural complexities of pop music, commercials, television, and film—the persistent and polyvalent inputs of postindustrial life—be used to engage with recorded and radio speech.

While resonances of Burroughs's own audio art experiments are evident here, *Ticket* contains two larger movements that suggest a digital poetics Burroughs did not develop on tape. One is a technique that resembles a musical fugue. After a page-and-a-half of dense, overlapping, interwoven, oblique references to previously unfamiliar themes, orders, and instructions, the prose slows down. When the narrative flow resumes, the lines that appeared as nonsensical fragments in the fugue begin to appear in situ. As we recognize them now, however, they are not just components of the narrative but also echoes of the confusion we experienced in the density of the earlier cut-up collage. Repeated in the more discursive passages, these phrases—"a male with female laughter," "St Louis Encephalitis," "muttering like burlap," "sperm tanks drained," and so forth—carry with them an unsettling familiarity that interferes with our absorption into the more formally traditional parts of the story.

Repetitions such as these point to a second feature in *Ticket* that might be adopted in a poetics of digital audio editing: the looping of large sections of narrative with slight alterations. For example, the sentence "the man caught his ejaculation in a jar" degenerates into "the man caught his spurts like a pack of cards," mutating in repetition from direct speech into analogy. In much the same way that repeated copying of a sound recording on tape moves away from an "original," a degree of fidelity has been lost. Clear information is replaced with an emptiness that the analogy invites us to fill through our own creative engagement.[10] These gentle, almost absent-minded repetitions occur not in close proximity to earlier iterations but pages later as questionable echoes. Contemporary poetic digital editing uses this technique of altered looping to elicit a slight sense of familiarity with spoken passages while prompting uncertainty about how they should be familiar and what the tiny changes might signify.

While analog tape editing typically draws language into its temporal flow, digital audio editing—labeled "nonlinear" in its marketing material—diffuses language and invites a more spatial interpretation and appreciation. Although webcast poetry programming might seem ideal for the elaboration of a digital aesthetic, however, it has generally adopted the presentational framework of its radio predecessors.[11] Webcasts feature a wide range of poetic types and genres: religious poetry, love poetry, local, slam, or ethnic poetry, as well as poetry more resistant to categorization. While it is not my intention to critique the poetry, I am concerned to describe the troubling, anachronistic way in which it is handled. In these programs' unacknowledged adoption of an analog semantics, the phonotext is not released or sounded but transcribed and stabilized by a technology that turns it into a kind of hissing graphotext.

Rather than developing a digital aesthetic, these programs typically use digital technology in an analog fashion. This is evident in all the most popular poetry webcasts listed through major Internet search engines. *The Spoken World Show* on Anthology Internet radio is an hour-long weekly program that airs CDs and tapes of recorded poetry readings as well as live readings from poets in the local Phoenix area. Although this program is occasionally quite interesting in its efforts to describe local poetry in terms of international and historical trends, similar to the programs I discuss later, it functions mainly as an eclectic spoken word jukebox. A commercial corollary, *Book Crazy Radio* is a 24–7 literary Internet station with poetry slots largely devoted to selling "how to" books about publishing. In its themed shows about "dream poetry," "your psychic IQ," and other new age topics, poetry is a decoration for a middle-class lifestyle—one stated aspiration is to have your own verse finely-bound and available on your shelf—and little attention is paid to the details of the programming, which consists most often of tentatively introduced poetry recordings. A third webcast, *Vocalized Ink,* is driven by pop-up ads that often interfere with the audio player. It airs mostly CDs of urban slam poetry performances and occasionally produced readings with break-beat music under them. Beyond setting spoken-word performances to music, little is done in terms of production. Another program, *October Gallery*, has a more diverse schedule with a fine arts focus, but technical and/or capacity problems with its server mean that the webstream often degrades into something that sounds like a loop of a Burroughs cut-up.[12]

Perhaps the most interesting webcast poetry station is *WSLM Slam Radio*.[13] Run without live content via a computer database, *WSLM* features poetry recordings, music, dramatic vignettes, monologues, and (often out-of-date) promotional announcements for poetry festivals. The promos constitute the most ambitious elements of its programming in their attempt to engage with the production technology and emulate techniques common to radio commercials. *WSLM* is the descendant of a now defunct webcast program called *Go Poetry!* organized by the poet Bob Holman and largely a vehicle for the slam poetry he has been involved with for many years.

Some of the more absorbing slam pieces aired on these webcasts come from Bob Holman and Paul Skiff's CD *Nuyorican Poets Symphony* (2000). While a number of performances in this collection are undeniably energetic, however, the technology is for the most part blank and quiet. In fact, in one instance, a performer seems readier to cultivate a digital semantics than Holman, Skiff, and their production engineers. At one point on the "Loisaida" track (Christian Haye, Jose Figueroa, Dael Orlandersmith, and Ed Morales), two speaking breaths come self-consciously one after the other in a live-to-tape technique that mimics an effect often created with a digital audio editor—or even with tape used in an unanalog way—to accentuate a processing. Here, the performer interpolates digital production values in a way that the CD producers have not yet managed.[14]

On other tracks such as "Sex" (Kimiko Hahn, Thaddeus Rutkowski, Eliza Galaher, Diane Spodarek, Kathe Burkhart, and Evert Eden) and "Rant" (Carl Watson, J. D. Rage, David Huberman, Jill Rappaport, and Barbara Henning) two recordings are overlapped, but little thought seems to have been given to how these simultaneous readings might be sculpted in order to interact with or comment on each other, let alone invite a different, digital mode of listening. Both lines of speech contain their original cadences, and, in the end, it's unclear why such an overlapping was used. Given slam poetry's investment in the expression through "voice" of individual artistic egos, it is not surprising that digital technology has not been used to shift it out of an analog semantics: complicating or questioning the voice through technological play, inviting its disintegration en route to a more relational engagement, runs counter to slam ideology.[15]

Contemporary efforts to develop a digital semantics for the spoken word began, famously, with John Oswald. Nearly thirty years ago, Oswald started using early sampler technology to create "plunderphonics," a genre of music without an analog pedigree. One early piece done in the 1970s is a resampling of William Burroughs's speech entitled "I Got." Following Burroughs's own tape cut-up method and editing techniques suggested in his writings, Oswald loops Burroughs saying the phrase "I got" (a phrase that is an acoustic palindrome when Burroughs speaks it) forward and backward a number of times. "I got" is repeated on its own and in a number of larger phrases until it is impossible to ascertain whether it is being played normally or in reverse.

The complications of voice and listening Oswald instantiates here proliferate in the better-known plunderphonic musical works in which he takes a familiar song, splices it into microsonic pieces, then rearranges the pieces to create a new song. What is most interesting about these pieces is not the technological resampling so much as the sampling and morphing of the cultural context of his sources. His interpretations of these pop songs always conflate, confuse, or tease sentiments the originals intended to invoke. In keeping with a digital semantics, they are plays on expectation.

The work of Scanner and DJ Spooky (individually and in collaboration) moves beyond the keyboard sampler and single pop song, yielding a wider range of cultural resonances and a greater complexity in their pieces. In their "mixes" of genres and styles, Scanner and DJ Spooky are less interested in reactivating sentiments that have accrued around famous pop cultural moments and more focused on the broad potential of *combination*. "Edison" and "Uncanny," two consecutive tracks on their collaboration *The Quick and the Dead* (1999), narrativize one hundred years of recording and broadcasting technology, tease out a Brechtian-utopian hope for that technology, and simultaneously remind us of the potential bankruptcy of such a hope.

In these tracks, Edison's recording of "Mary Had a Little Lamb" bleeds into a speech about the emancipation of the "machine age," a recording from a space flight, a 1970s-era black radio DJ, and old-school hip-hop. This two-minute morphing is flagged along by warbling sine waves, feedback, distortion, and early synthesizer noise, giving the whole a kitschy, sci-fi quality punctuated by outbursts that pass so quickly as to be indecipherable. DJ

Spooky's solo mixes in particular are often mediated speech "conversations" about a media-driven world between Marshall McLuhan and blaxploitation film soundtracks, television cartoon character voices and Alfred Hitchcock, even police sirens and the birds that mimic them. These curious and interrupted pairings force us to struggle to remember what we were just listening to. The computer's storage capacity and ease of access allow Spooky to create mixes in which the intensity and variety of juxtaposition exceed traditional interpretive strategies for both music and the spoken word.

Taking up and modifying many of these principles for the spoken word, the performer and composer Erik Belgum has developed a genre of speech recording and broadcast he calls "ambient" writing. His narratives, monologues, and dialogues, often composed with Burroughs-esque cut-up techniques, are designed to fade into the background while subtly changing the environment in which they are played. Belgum's works are not typically subjected to extensive technological processing; in fact, the relative plainness of the production style serves to hide more established forms of literary play such as cut-up or character shifts. His ambient piece *Blodder* provides a good example of this austerity.[16] The lack of technological razzle-dazzle and the consistent—almost monotone—quality of the speech mean the listener is not readily absorbed in these pieces.

In some of Belgum's ambient pieces, and more regularly in his audio interpretations of the works of other writers, this disaffecting veneer is punctured in a way that helps expand our evolving conception of a digital poetics. The flow of the monologue is often extremely simple and the voicings neutral or nonexpressive; the pieces sound like overly familiar stories (even if a forced close listening reveals formal experimentation). As soon as this state of vacant attention—hearing but not listening—is established, it is jostled by a wildly disjointed insertion or overlay. In Belgum's interpretation (1998) of Ray Federman's *Take It or Leave It*, for example, an antianalog or digital edit is used not to pop a listener out of a frame of absorption but to draw the listener *into* something previously distant. In this antislam model, the cultivated expectation of boredom and alienation is disrupted by an editing practice that exalts in its role as technological mediator of the voice.

As the "First Pretext" of *Take It* begins, the narrative is interrupted by tiny processed glitches recognizable as finer and more digitally distorted Chopin-like speech sounds. The tiny fragments that pepper the story are small enough to make listeners wonder whether the narrative was interrupted or the glitch was a problem in their playback system, something heard from some Cagean other place, even something added by their brains. This process exposes and inverts traditional analog semantics. Once a transparent high-fidelity communication circuit is established, an analog listener's role within it is naturalized and ultimately taken for granted; Belgum's digital interruptions, by contrast, remind listeners of their perpetual semantic work at the same time as they confuse the semantic process and complicate its completion.

Throughout Belgum's version of *Take It*, there is also an amusing narrative and technological self-reflexivity. At the "Second Pretext," parts of the story split between the stereo channels and are confusingly and intensely feathered together until "one more word and it's too much, everything is lost"; at which point, the split stereo field is once again centered. Left and right channel overlap significantly, each carrying a phrase of the story, but the effect is one of near incomprehensibility, of pure wordplay. Ironically, however, when the story becomes understandable again, "everything is lost." The clear narration of the story comments on the technological play: while the editing has gotten us lost, the attempt to return to the narrative only reiterates our condition as lost listeners. Alternatively, the phrase "one more word and it's too much" might signal that Belgum knows he is pushing the limits of listening and that he will calm things down before dissociation sets in. Following this reading, "everything is lost" might resonate with his sadness at having to abandon his playfully electrified project for the sake of our listening, for our desire for discursivity. Ultimately, then, his work might be seen to comment on our need to have expectations met.

Christof Migone is the contemporary artist who has done the most to synthesize and extend the digital practices and aesthetics developed by his contemporaries and their modernist predecessors. Migone's digital translations—or "machinations"—of the writing of the mentally ill in his radio/audio/CD project (1996) *Hole in the Head* share an attention to the microsonic level of the word-sound or prephoneme with Chopin and Chopin's predecessor, Dufrêne.[17] Migone, however, works with a broader range: in his vacillation between whole words—indeed whole and semicontextualized conversations—and prephonetic fragments, we hear in vivid detail a movement from meaning to sound. This electrocution of spoken language is perceptible only in relation to the normative conversation that surrounds it. By vacillating between recognizable narrative or discursive speech and speech fragments, Migone develops a digital poetics for radio language: presenting the same words and word particles as constituents of traditional meaning-making structures *and* as something outside of those structures, he produces transitions between analog and digital semantics that allow us to hear the shifts in the engagement we are asked to make throughout the piece.

In *Hole in the Head*'s companion essay, "Head Hole: Malfunctions and Dysfunctions of an FM Exciter," Migone explains his technological efforts to amplify "the noise of the brain" and demonstrate the aesthetics of a gradually increasing demand for interpretation through different modes of listening (2001, 42–52).[18] After a phonetic translation of some of Artaud's French glossolalia, which exposes an acculturated mind's disposition to slip back into analog semantics, he provides a summation that can stand as a definition for a wide range of digital poetic tactics: "They do not pretend to find universal meaning in a hermetic language but rather intrude, corrupt, and disarticulate the original. There is a certain paradoxical faithfulness in this approach, for it does not strive for accuracy, nor does it fabricate a neutral voice toward *literaturization* of the embodied text" (48). It is not a text or an interpretation or even a shift in modes of listening but a tendency toward meaning that constitutes the material of Migone's poetry.

What is required at this stage in the unfolding of a digital audio poetics is a taxonomy for radio speech editing that recognizes the characteristics of digital technology, respects a listener's ability to approach material with variegated interpretive strategies, and expands literary programming's engagement with the relationship at the core of radio.

Against the seamlessness sought in the razor-blade edit, we might posit the following techniques: the *breathless edit*, which splices two parts of speech unnaturally close to each other in violation of proper spoken rhythm to heighten the speed of a single line of speech; the *weave edit*, in which two or more separate lines of thought are cut into pieces and rearranged in an interlocking manner to create an artificial dialogue or parallel absorptions into parallel discursive flows followed by a disruption of that absorption; the *very slow fade to silence*, which gradually concentrates listening; the *cross-fade*, in which two or more separate lines of thought overlap and interfere with each other until one becomes the other; the *repeat cut*, in which two or more versions of the same speech echo each other or follow one after another; the *acoustic match*, in which one piece of speech or sound is transformed into another sound of similar pitch and rhythm to invite a meditation on the technologization of voice or some other idea of combination; the *stuttered edit*, in which a line of speech is broken by sporadic and uneven returns to earlier points in that line; the *interjection*, in which a small fragment of related or unrelated speech interrupts a longer line of thought; the *layered elaboration* or *exaggeration*, in which processing or added speech elements enhance or comment on semantic work being done by the language or the voice;[19] the *dense fugue*, in which the same line of speech or versions or alterations of it are layered in increasing density to the point where spoken language is nearly returned to sound or approaches music; and the *distant echo*, in which parts of speech offered first out of context reappear in the discursive flow from which they have been extracted to prime the cognitive pump for a complex idea.

Numerous additional edits might be gleaned from studying contemporary television, early film, and other media that have made a broad range of editing strategies part of their semantics. This nod to film and television, however, also reminds us that the aesthetic and critical potential of the digital edit is necessarily short-lived. In Attali's terms, "a noise [in this case our proposed digital edit] that is *external* to the existing code can also cause its mutation" (1985, 35). As "the network modifies the code within which messages are expressed" (35), the hope that the digital edit can mutate the existing format into something more engaging risks its own success. If it succeeds in modifying the code, it loses its status as noise.

Hence the techniques we develop must be deployed sparingly to be effective: not a ringing in the ears that quickly fades into the background but a practice that entices then dislodges absorption, something—similar to Belgum's first tiny fragments—that happens so quickly we wonder if what we heard was a mistake or even if it happened at all. In contrast then to the seamless analog edit, we might describe the digital edit as *spangled*. The spangled edit undoes the temporal nature of radio assumed by Crisell and invites a spatial or sculptural appreciation. In such an edit, elements of voice are removed from their linear flow and built into highly considered patterns that invite new modes of listening.

Debates about innovative arts often describe the attempt to insert a sign of the apparatus of communication into the message it carries in political terms. In foregrounding physical materiality through self-consciously audible processing, we draw attention to the social materiality supported, enabled, and typically obscured by the technology, including the relationships of host-guest, announcer-listener, and program producer-audience; issues of access; the potential for social influence; and the setting of terms for public discourse. In a broadcasting day that strategically mystifies social materiality, our proposed digital audio poetics is a tactical/technical glitch that forces unwanted questions.

Although this formulation captures the ideology of digital audio poetics, however, it presents two problems: first, the difficulty of making physical materiality invoke social materiality—not an automatic function by any stretch of the imagination[20]—and second, the implication or hope that observations promoted through these techniques will lead to a change in social relations. Systems of incorporation seem to appropriate an aesthetics only after purging it of its unsettling politics.

After nearly one hundred years in the wallpaper business, radio has developed many delightful patterns for flattening out both the information it conveys and its own material presence.[21] Yet there are counterexamples that are more often than not surprisingly low-tech. When William Gillespie debuted the series *Radio Radio* in the United States on WEFT in Illinois, his presentational manner was more critically charged than anything in the series itself. Before airing the first program, he told the story of how he met me at the conference that gave rise to this book; he recounted how he told me about his radio show, and I told him about *Radio Radio*; he brought the box that I had sent him containing the programs on CD out in front of his microphone, opened it with a pen knife (describing all his actions as he did so), read over the air the note I included in the box, dropped in a CD, and pressed "play." In Borgesian fashion, Gillespie thus described and enacted the final and most important (and most mysterious) facet in literary radio's social network: getting a program on the air.

Notes

1. This essay addresses itself primarily to radio programs and regularly scheduled webcast audio programs that present and/or discuss poetry. (On subsequent pages, these Internet and radio programs are collectively referred to as "audiocasts.") Despite the specificity of focus, this essay may offer useful conclusions and vocabulary for other studies of new media poetries as well as for broadcast criticism in general.

2. This issue has been usefully addressed by other critics with slightly different emphases. What Morris calls the phonotext, Charles Bernstein in his study of poetry readings describes as the "audiotext"—the point of departure from an aural poem into

a social exchange (1998, 12). Similarly in *The Audible Past,* his social history of recording technology, Jonathan Sterne argues that any "medium" is necessarily a set of relationships: a communication technology appreciated in the social context of its invention and use (2003, 182). But most important to my interests has been Gregory Whitehead's emphasis on the "network of radio" in which he asserts that the actual materiality of radio is not sound but the series of relationships it enables between producers, listeners, and gatekeepers ("Program 1").

3. For useful recent contributions to the study of sounded literature, see (in addition to *Sound States* and *Close Listening*) Douglas Kahn 1999 and Allen Weiss 1995, 2002.

4. Morton Feldman articulates the problem with characteristic clarity in a discussion about electronic music with John Cage: "Unfortunately," Feldman notes, "with permissiveness usually comes a very quick type of boredom" (1995, 260).

5. An excellent example of this is provided by David Tudor's resonating circuits.

6. Jonathan Sterne notes that while temporal descriptions of the sense of hearing have been naturalized through what he calls the visual/audio "litany" that echoes throughout the past century of media studies, "spatial" appraisals of hearing are just as valid. Invoking just this possibility, DJ Spooky (2003) refers to his radio/audio collages as "audio sculptures." Even with a cheap mono-speaker transistor radio, the layering and texturing of sound through editing can invoke, metaphorically and actually, sound shapes rather than a temporal or musical line. Although time is still an organizing principle in Glenn Gould's 1967 language-based radio piece *The Idea of North,* for example, Gould's composition reduces speech to delinearized words and phrases that occasionally build into a density of overlap, interference, and repetition that can only adequately be described in dimensional rather than temporal terms.

7. Some historians and theoreticians seek to undermine the digital's claim to fidelity by arguing that analog reproduction is more faithful to an "original." Unlike digital, they maintain, analog technology contains traces of the music itself. Vinyl, in particular, etches in its grooves the vibrations of the original sound. Electronic recording and reproduction (tape and radio) add a stage of mediation by transforming these vibrations into electricity, while the digital (DAT, hard drive, CD, etc.) involves a third-order mediation by transforming those electrical impulses into ones and zeros. While this line of argument complicates claims for digital fidelity, it is not directly useful in efforts to elaborate a digital poetics because of its participation in the fetishization of the real. Rendered in literary vernacular, *analog* is to *digital* as *analogy* is to *metaphor:* an analog recording aspires to be *like* the voice/source (vibrations exist in both), while a digital recording translates that voice/source into something else entirely (ones and zeros). The digital's self-conscious act of translation exists

in stark opposition to the transparency proposed by the analog. Recognizing that semantic change is inherent to translation allows the further step of experimenting with those changes to activate the play of relationships central to an evolving digital poetics.

8. For a detailed description of "Pêche de Nuit" within the history of sound poetry, see McCaffery 1997, 158.

9. For examples, see Burroughs's portrayal of two voices being spliced together twenty-four times per second (1987, 22) and the echoing of slightly altered versions of the same subliminal language throughout the text. These effects would have been extremely difficult to realize in the analog technology of his day.

10. Gregory Whitehead's "Degenerates in Dreamland," commissioned for New American Radio in 1991, is an extended radio study of the potential of this kind of tape degeneration.

11. To further elaborate on the differences between a poetics influenced by the analog and one influenced by the digital, it is useful to note the units of measure each technology uses: in analog work, the primary measurement is speed (inches per second of tape traveling across a playback head); in digital work, the primary measurement is information density or "bit-depth." While not determining interpretive strategies appropriate to each editing technology, these units suggest different production possibilities and semantic emphases.

12. cris cheek (1999) has produced an interesting piece that plays on the phenomenon of faulty Internet streaming. In "how can this hum be human," produced for the online magazine *Riding the Meridian,* instead of a conventional online poetry reading we hear something distorted, glitchy, and stuttering. cheek's discussion and presentation of this piece can be heard through the *Radio Radio* archive on UbuWeb.

13. The following webcasts were audited the first two weeks of May 2003: *The Spoken World Show* (http://www.anthology.org), *Book Crazy Radio* (http://www.bookcrazy.net), *Vocalized Ink* (http://www.vocalizedink.org), *October Gallery* (http://www.octobergallery.com/pages/octoberlive.html), and *WSLM Slam Radio* (http://www.gotpoetry.com/wslm).

14. McCaffery (1997) notes that Bob Cobbing used early tape recorders in a similar manner to expand his vocal repertoire for performance. Cobbing would speed up, slow down, and amplify recordings of his performances in order to discover new soundings to use in subsequent performances. "Where the tape-recorder leads," Cobbing said, "the human voice can follow" (qtd. in McCaffery 1997, 157–158).

15. In Whitehead's aesthetic and ideological critique of this kind of expressionist mode on radio,

> the voice becomes an onanistic fetish-object with which to explore the subjectivity of the one who speaks. To my ears, work in this tradition typically flattens out everything that is distinctive in an individual voice. . . . The fact is, we cannot find our voice just by using it: we must be willing to cut it out of our throats, put it on the autopsy table, isolate and savor the various quirks and pathologies, then stitch it back together and see what happens. The voice, then, not as something which is found, but as something which is written. (2001, 92)

16. See Belgum 1999.

17. McCaffery describes sound poetry's transition from Dufrêne to Chopin in terms of a willingness to embrace technology as a compositional tool for poetry rather than as primarily a recording tool (1997, 154–161).

18. What Migone calls the "post-digital" is an acceptance of the creative potential of the *digital aesthetic*: technology not engaged in its own disappearing act, nonantiseptic in its relation to the voice, and concerned with developing rather than correcting potential semantic errors.

19. An example of the technique of layered elaboration can be found in Belgum's seizing the O's in Federman's "bravo" as an opportunity for ecstatic multilayered soundplay.

20. A successful example of this connection is Michael Basinski's (2003) *Radio Radio* program in which he uses editing to engender a quickening of listening while the material being edited is an argument about how one of his poems should be announced.

21. The notion of radio wallpaper is borrowed from David Moss, who is quoted in Migone 2001, 42.

Works Cited

Attali, Jacques. 1985. *Noise: The Political Economy of Music*. Trans. Brian Massumi. Minneapolis: University of Minnesota Press.

Basinski, Michael. 2003. "Program 9." *Radio Radio*. http://www.ubu.com/sound/radio_radio/index.html (accessed September 22, 2005).

Belgum, Erik. 1998. *Raymond Federman's Take It or Leave It*. Smart Noise CO173.

Belgum, Erik. 1999a. *Blodder*. Innova Recordings CD 26708 65272.

Belgum, Erik. 1999b. "Erik Belgum. Interview by Dan Warburton. September 1999." *Paris Transatlantic Magazine*. http://www.paristransatlantic.com/magazine/interviews/belgum.html (accessed June 6, 2003).

Benjamin, Walter. 1969. "The Work of Art in the Age of Mechanical Reproduction." In *Illuminations*, trans. Harry Zohn, 217–251. New York: Schocken Books.

Bernstein, Charles. 1998. "Introduction." In *Close Listening: Poetry and the Performed Word,* ed. Charles Bernstein, 3–26. New York: Oxford University Press.

Burroughs, William S. 1987. *The Ticket That Exploded*. London: Paladin Books.

cheek, cris. 1999. "how can this hum be human." *Riding the Meridian*. http://www.heelstone.com/meridian/cheek.html (accessed June 29, 2004).

cheek, cris. 2003. "Program 4." *Radio Radio*. http://www.ubu.com/sound/radio_radio/cheek.html (accessed June 29, 2004).

Chopin, Henri. 1983. *Le Corpsbis*. Audio recording. http://www.ubu.com/sound/chopin.html (accessed June 29, 2004).

Crisell, Andrew. 1994. *Understanding Radio*. London: Methuen.

Crisell, Andrew. 2000. "Radio Signs." In *Media Studies: A Reader*, ed. Paul Marris and Sue Thornham, 210–219. New York: New York University Press.

DJ Spooky [Paul Miller]. 2003. "Program 12." *Radio Radio*. http://www.ubu.com/sound/radio_radio/miller.html (accessed June 29, 2004).

DJ Spooky, and Scanner. 2000. *The Quick and the Dead*. Sulfur Records. CD BBSUL 004.

Feldman, Morton. 1995. "Radio Happenings." In *Exact Change Yearbook*, ed. Peter Gizzi, 254–261. Boston: Exact Change.

Gould, Glenn. 1967. *The Idea of North*. Audio recording. http://www.gould.nlc-bnc.ca/ineye/eeye2.htm (accessed May 27, 2002).

Hayles, N. Katherine. 1997. "Voices Out of Bodies, Bodies Out of Voices: Audiotape and the Production of Subjectivity." In *Sound States: Innovative Poetics and Acoustical Technology*, ed. Adalaide Morris, 74–96. Chapel Hill: North Carolina University Press.

Holman, Bob, and Paul Skiff. 2000. *Nuyorican Poets Symphony*. Knitting Factory. Audio CD 138.

Kahn, Douglas. 1999. *Noise, Water, Meat: A History of Sound in the Arts*. Cambridge, MA: MIT Press.

Marinetti, F. T., and Pino Masnata. [1933] 1992. "La Radia." Trans. Stephen Sartarelli. In *Wireless Imagination: Sound, Radio, and the Avant-Garde*, ed. Douglas Kahn and Gregory Whitehead, 265–268. Cambridge, MA: MIT Press.

McCaffery, Steve. 1997. "From Phonic to Sonic: The Emergence of the Audio Poem." In *Sound States: Innovative Poetics and Acoustic Technologies*, ed. Adalaide Morris, 149–168. Chapel Hill: University of North Carolina Press.

Migone, Christof. 2001. "Head Hole: Malfunctions and Dysfunctions of an FM Exciter." In *Experimental Sound and Radio*, ed. Allen S. Weiss, 42–52. Cambridge, MA: MIT Press.

Migone, Christof. 1996. *Hole in the Head*. OHM/AVATAR AB-AVTR005-CD.

Morris, Adalaide. 1997. "Introduction." In *Sound States: Innovative Poetics and Acoustical Technologies*, ed. Adalaide Morris, 1–14. Chapel Hill: University of North Carolina Press.

Spinelli, Martin, prod. 2003. *Radio Radio*. Radio series. http://www.ubu.com/sound/radio_radio (accessed June 29, 2004).

Sterne, Jonathan. 2003. *The Audible Past*. Durham, NC: Duke University Press.

Weiss, Allen S. 1995. *Phantasmic Radio*. Durham, NC: Duke University Press.

Weiss, Allen S. 2002. *Breathless: Sound Recording, Disembodiment, and the Transformation of Lyrical Nostalgia*. Middletown, CT: Wesleyan University Press.

Whitehead, Gregory. 1991. "Degenerates in Dreamland." Radio program commissioned for New American Radio. http://www.somewhere.org/NAR/work_excerpts/whitehead/main.htm (accessed June 28, 2004).

Whitehead, Gregory. 2001. "Radio Play Is No Place." In *Experimental Sound and Radio*, ed. Allen S. Weiss, 89–94. Cambridge, MA: MIT Press.

Whitehead, Gregory. 2003. "Program 1." *Radio Radio*. http://www.ubu.com/radio/whitehead.html (accessed June 30, 2004).

6

Kinetic Is as Kinetic Does: On the Institutionalization of Digital Poetry

Alan Filreis

Anyhow I know where you can get a lot of words for potentially nothing, though you'll have to figure a way to get them home.
—ROBERT CREELEY, DAY BOOK OF A VIRTUAL POET, REFERRING TO THE WEB

Print is similar to the lecture.
—DIANA LAURILLARD, RETHINKING UNIVERSITY TEACHING

"The Truth About Us"

"How ever do you teach 'The pure products of America/go crazy'?" asked one of the conference participants of the vexed poem, also called "To Elsie," which William Carlos Williams published in *Spring and All* (1923), "especially the passage in which the poem makes a seemingly rushed rhetorical turn, using the conditional phrase 'as if' to veer off in a new direction?" The passage in the poem to which the questioner referred is this:

some Elsie—
voluptuous water
expressing with broken

brain the truth about us—
her great
ungainly hips and flopping breasts

addressed to cheap
jewelry
and rich young men with fine eyes

as if the earth under our feet
were
an excrement of some sky (Williams 1986, 218)

I listened hard for answers, partly because I had been giving a lecture about the poem, more or less unsuccessfully, for fifteen years. "You can't teach that poem by lecturing," one conference participant offered. "The digression at 'as if' is very hard to understand," another observed, "and still harder to teach. The best answer may be: you need more time than you have to teach it. Start with that assumption."

"First our students have to understand the 'as if' of digression generally," I found myself adding.

Poetry that goes where it needs to go, rather than where we—in a fifty-minute or hour-and-twenty-minute session—need it to go, toward some fixed state, arrived-at destination. Somewhere here is what the poem is saying about modern culture. Its kineticism, its interactivity. You want to say to your students: think about it, and come back again next year when culture has again changed. You want them to understand the digressive act of language, over time and across real space, and you cannot easily convey that in a room in a semester, given the task of teaching and learning the poem right there and then.

The conference, hosted by the poet Joan Retallack and others at Bard College, was called "Poetry & Pedagogy: The Challenge of the Contemporary," sponsored by the Institute for Writing & Thinking in June 1999. Its purpose was to bring together university scholars, experimentalist poets, and teachers of poetry from secondary schools to grapple with possible new relations between innovative poetry and teaching.

At only two moments during the four-day conference did any speaker or participant mention digital media as relevant to the issue of new poetry's connection to new modes of teaching. One was my own talk, in which I described a series of overlapping poetry-and-pedagogy projects—face-to-face for-credit courses; free noncredit workshops and poetry readings open to anyone; a salon or loft-space-like learning community open seven days and six nights per week; online for-credit courses; and a series of live interactive webcasts in which the for-credit students, the workshop participants, volunteer teachers, the hangers-on at the salon, and people worldwide tuning in via webcast all participate more or less together—at the Kelly Writers House (http://www.writing.upenn.edu/wh), a superwired 1851 Tudor-style cottage on the campus of the University of Pennsylvania.

The other moment when digital media were mentioned at the Bard conference was during a plenary session on poetry and cold-war politics, at a point when the group got itself stuck, collectively feeling nostalgic for dissident literary groupings such as those that some participants had convened in the Bay Area, yet unable to say specifically how these communities could be formed anew, given aesthetic and geographical displacements—other than, as someone improvisationally suggested, "perhaps on the Web."

I left the conference pondering the notion that "To Elsie" could be taught if we had more time (and I'll add space) in which to teach it. I decided to explore a lectureless poetics—poetics at the end of the lecture—and thus to discern the extent to which Diana Laurillard was right when she suggested what for me was an implicit analogue to digital writing: print is similar to the lecture.

Such conditions—more time and space—do exist. I observe that when I am working in them I am much more successful teaching the big problem posed by Williams's "To Elsie" than when I am a teacher in one place at one time. The reason is fundamental: I try not to "teach" the poem in any conventional sense of the term. I invite others to teach it for me and join them here and there as they do so. The problem of a digressive or disjunctive writing is not well learned at any given moment: my students and other learners (and practitioners) who join us have to learn it synchronously and asynchronously at once, in time and over time.

The Teacher as an Audience

The development of an iterative technology-infused practice I want to describe has coincided with the emergence of a partly virtual/partly local community of teachers, poets, and scholars who by behaving the way they do with poetry invite students to join them in the emerging community as they discuss experimental writing in a way that strikes the students as being the rhetoric of learners. Synchronously and asynchronously, over a distance and in person, students and unofficially affiliated community members have been involved in discussions about this poetry with a heterodox mix of poets and teachers, near and very far, academic and nonacademic—among them Edwin Torres, Cid Corman (in Japan), Carl Rakosi (in San Francisco), Temple University's Jena Osman, Robert Creeley, Alan Golding, June Jordan, Patrick Durgin (*Pundits Scribes Pupils*), Louis Cabri (curator of PhillyTalks, which itself developed into a live webcast series), Tony Green (a poet participating from New Zealand), Robert Martin (a businessman living in China), Marjorie Perloff, Ron Silliman, the students of Jonathan Monroe and Joel Kurzai at Cornell, Jodi Wilgoren of the *New York Times*, Andrew Levy, Joan Retallack, legal scholar David Skeel, the Providence-based editor of *Combo* Mike Magee, Jim Andrews (creator of vispo.com), Linh Dinh (the Vietnamese American poet then residing in Vietnam), Joe Farrell (a specialist in Latin writing), scholar-critic Jessica Burstein (in Seattle), Aaron Levy (founder of Slought Networks), and about four hundred others.

Let me continue with "To Elsie." Two weeks after returning from the Bard conference, I convened a small group to lead a several-hour discussion of the poem. I had the naïve notion that we would say everything one could say about the poem and be done with it. The session would be webcast live from the Writers House. The local discussants were poets Bob Perelman, Kristen Gallagher, and Shawn Walker. I invited anyone, anywhere to join us at the appointed time. I also invited people who were in Philadelphia or could easily travel to the Kelly Writers House to join us in that space, a synchronous, in-person audience. The four of us were each other's first audience (we had not at all planned what we were going to say); those who came to the Kelly Writers House were also of course an audience in the most conventional sense; then there were those who viewed and heard the webcast. There were also those who viewed the recording of the webcast at any later moment, an actually quite vast asynchronous audience that continues to grow to this day.

The recording of the webcast (http://www.writing.upenn.edu/~afilreis/88/ webcast-elsie.html), linked to the Writers House site immediately after the session ended, was in turn linked to the text of the poem; we widely announced the convergence. A fifth audience would be the students formally enrolled in my course, working through the difficult digressiveness of "To Elsie" in a class. These five audiences continue to interact; my email inbox alone testifies to this daily. I have long forgotten which of these people were once classified as students.

The first time I taught "To Elsie" in a face-to-face synchronous class after that, I asked the students to view the webcast recording of our discussion. When we in turn discussed the poem, I invited several of the poets and teachers who had participated in the webcast to join us virtually and in the room. What the new discussion added to the earlier discussion I posted to the course Web page so that students taking the course in subsequent semesters could benefit from that too, as well as anyone else who came across that material. It is widely linked.

The next time I read "To Elsie" with students, my course was being taught all online. Forty-nine participants were situated everywhere. They ranged from a high school junior in Texas to a sixty-two-year-old psycholinguistic therapist in Michigan and a businessman traveling in Asia, and included several young poets and two experienced teachers of poetry. Class sessions were held asynchronously (discussions by way of listservs) but also, about once per week, by way of a live webcast, with far-flung learners participating via telephone, chat room, and email. When we turned to "To Elsie," I had the students view the recording of the first discussion, read the results of the second group's discussion of the first, and then I invited teachers, scholars, and poets to join us during the new webcast. These people in effect helped me teach the poem, but so, in specific ways, did others who had participated before. I was delighted by the way in which the new students' questions about the poetry began roughly where the earlier discussions had left off. Consider the point in purely pedagogical terms: to accomplish this in the conventional university setting, one would have to describe what previous learners had learned— not typically an auspicious way of enticing new students into a discussion. Among the new group of nonstudent participants were a few people who had originally participated, among them the poet Shawn Walker, who had helped lead the first discussion, and also some of those who had viewed the webcast recording and had been discussing the poem with me by email in the previous weeks and months. The new live webcast was also recorded and became available as an additional resource.

Without any such specific goal in mind and using a university's resources for at least partially traditional purposes, I had helped create a "subject village" rather precisely on the analog of what Loss Pequeño Glazier (2002) argues is "central to the success" of digital poetry itself—a subject village that provides "a gathering ground" of poeisis, "a site for the access, collection, and dissemination of poetry" that bears out possibilities implicit in innovative poetry for many years before the digital age, namely, as Glazier puts it, "poetry's engagement with making, its mode of production, but also its means of dissemination" (2–3).

Problems of Conversion

Associated with digital poetics at the university is an incidental categorical problem that can soon become a prohibitive institutional problem. It is hard to tell the two problems apart, yet I contend it is helpful to do so, especially in the context of great expectations raised by claims for the interactive newness of electronic poetry, such as those of Glazier (2002), who begins *Digital Poetics* with the hyperauspicious rhetoric of manifesto: "[T]he making of poetry has established itself on a matrix of new shores." He writes, "[T]here is a tangible feel of arrival in the spelled air" (1).

No necessarily positive connection inheres between digital poets and the academy; many—if not, arguably, most—important contributors to the digital poetry scene are productively unaffiliated with the academy. But universities' strong network and huge server resources are alluring for artists who otherwise must pay for—or beg or "borrow"—server space from intentionally or unintentionally generous ISPs. Digital poets who find themselves in the academy tend to collaborate interestingly with colleagues in universities' information technology (IT) departments, creating relationships of a sort unusual for other poets. This extradisciplinary social fact in itself affords us a chance to press for changes in the way we read, interpret, teach, and write poetry. Yet for many reasons, such change has not come. One is disciplinary fit. Where within the curriculum does digital poetry belong? Is it a "fine art"? Is it, as many imply through curricula, a component of the study of literature (to be listed in the English department, along with the rest of poetry)? Is it "creative writing," inside or outside English? Is it "communications"? Is it "theory"? The most compelling of these seemingly superficial categorical questions is this: Is digital poetry part of the newly developing (and relatively well-funded) IT curriculum? Is it subject, in short, to the territorialization of knowledge required (for literal certification) of all "new subjects"? One way around these questions is to assert the claim that digital poetics is a new medium within an old subject matter—but that, as it turns out, marks it out as a territory nonetheless (within English or literature).

The moment a set of taxonomic decisions is made (arbitrary but necessary according to the way universities as institutions are budgeted), another opportunity for innovation is easily lost. Funds flow most freely through connections to traditional curricular structures, such as the for-credit course. Those who want, with university dollars, to make, disseminate, and encourage discussion of digital poems seek and get grants through the development of new courses or the digitalization of old ones, into which the digital poetries they make and those by others they admire can be inserted—similar to any block of what is called academic "content" fitted into curricular holes or slots. These ought to be new kinds of courses, but, alas, typically, they are not. Funds for "Web development" go to what IT administrators and a few newfangled academic deans call "content innovation." Where such funds are really needed is in truly different modes of reading, teaching, learning, responding, and discussion, and a consciously altered sense of who the learners are—that is, modes that break the rules of time and space that have long governed the medieval-agrarian "semester" durational legacies of the I know/you don't, I have/you want, I give/you receive, I write/you read structural technologies characteristic of the era of the book, print being similar to the lecture.

Courses in digital poetics have taken insufficient advantage of the revolutions in reading and learning and community-building practices that are in fact the radical basis of this aesthetic medium. Again, a college or university course that includes digital poetry is not by any means the necessary condition for the server space, Web design, keyboarding assistance, and network speed that digital poets need and crave, but the tie is advantageously real and can be reckoned creatively. This reckoning has not been as formally inventive as the digital poetry produced from the relationship. The irony unintentionally suggests to digital poetry's many doubters that such a poetics is the aesthetic and political equivalent of all other poetries, only presented via displayed packets of ones and zeroes (and thus needlessly more expensive and organizationally threatening).

At the Kelly Writers House, which I and others founded in 1995 as a stand-alone literary learning community situated *within* a university but in most ways independent of the curriculum and of curriculum-dependent dollars, I initiated the series of live interactive webcasts featuring discussions between and among contemporary poets, students, readers, critics, and teachers. I undertook this project with the modest—if not also conservative—notion that what we produced, after the live or synchronous interactive session was finished and uploaded into a world-viewable recording, would become, like most of the literary writing on the Web, a fixed record, just there, interesting, locatable, and possibly useful—certainly more widely available than poetry and discussions of experimental writing have been, but sufficient, done, permanent, and rather unkinetic. My assumption was founded on the institutional reality I have begun to describe. I managed the costs of my first interactive webcasts (and created the Web materials, bought the equipment needed to produce live video and audio streaming outward from the Writers House, installed a phone line to take calls from participants, learned to "patch" the incoming calls out to the digital stream as well as into the room full of onsite participants, etc.) from "course development" funds provided to me to (quoting the terms of the grant) "put up on the Web" my already established course on modernist and contemporary American poetry (which in its nondigital mode already included a section on digital writing). The "conversion" (another term of the grant) to the status of an "online course" of a course that already in part featured materials originally written online was supposed to be a matter of moving "old" content to "new" media; it was assumed by my funders that the *kind* of course I was teaching and most aspects of the pedagogy were going to be unchanged. Indeed, if I did alter the kind of course I was teaching, I risked formal decertification by a committee of colleagues that oversees all curricular expansion. If the online course were not demonstrably "like" the earlier version of the course, it might have to be categorized as a "new course," and, I was warned, a "new course" might not be approved since it would raise a question that the committee might answer in the negative—namely, Did students' "contact time" with me as their singly identifiable teacher pass the minimum quantitative standard? (That standard presumed I would meet with all the readers of the poetry in person, in the same physical space. Challenging the definition would require an entirely new set of procedures and a discrete political strategy.) So for public consumption, the medium would change but not much else. This we might call the "media conversion fallacy," and I will return to it. Generally, I had to face a series of limitations put up by rules that were essentially irrelevant to the quality of my enterprise—the very sort of limitations from which Kenneth Goldsmith (2000) proclaims he is free whenever he as a critic writes about, or "to," UbuWeb as a noninstitution.

Yet, as I have already described, something remarkable happened once I took these webcast sessions on contemporary poetics out of the curriculum and opened them up to participants anywhere, to members of the vastly extended Writers House community, mostly writers and readers unaffiliated with the "course" as such. I found that I had partially liberated the reading and discussion of the poetry from categorical constraints. (Although if I had to get further funding, I would have to gesture back toward the curriculum and do the dance of being inside and outside a constituted writing community at once.)

My modest experience with all this has taught me to want something from digital poetics that might help realize its implicit promise to resituate poetry within an institution where all pedagogical structures and most research structures have derived from centuries of naturalization of the technology of the book. I want "poetry on the Web," for instance, to disclose and contribute to the dynamism—both collaborative and agonistic—that is characteristic of the community of readers, poets, editors, interpreters, programmers, and teachers (many of them institutional players) who produce and support digital poetry.

Obviously there are models other than the synchronous-asynchronous, present-distant webcast interanimations hosted by the Writers House. One is what Katherine Parrish (2002) has achieved through "Teaching in the Splice" and through the collaborative virtual learning environment she built under the auspices of the University of Toronto. Janet Murray taught a course at MIT on the interpretation of nonlinear and interactive narrative starting in 1992, an experience that surprises the participants by, halfway through, turning from a reading into a writing course; these formative experiences now extend to the graduate program in information design she runs at Georgia Tech for the "arts- and humanities-based" creation of digital artifacts (see http://www.lcc.gatech.edu/idt/index.html). In the complex relationship between Glazier's course on the "Poetics of Programmable Language" at SUNY Buffalo and the Electronic Poetry Center, there is a fourth instance (see http://epc.buffalo.edu/authors/glazier/syllabi/2003s/606.html; http://wings.buffalo

.edu/epc/). Cybergraphia, a relatively new project at Bard College founded as a follow-up to the conference-retreat hosted by Joan Retallack on relation-ships between alternative poetry and alternative pedagogy, might soon prove to be another model (see http://cg.bard.edu/). Cybergraphia was created in order to bear out the main assumption of the present essay—the "conviction that as education is the place where we confront and instruct how to negoti-ate today's world, contemporary writing has much to contribute to this dis-cussion" (Bard College 2000).

All of these are, aesthetically and pedagogically, gift and giving spaces. They challenge the I give/you receive, I write/you read formulations that helped secure the fortress of Creative Writing in the postwar American uni-versity. They are never going to be as utopian as Goldsmith's almost utterly independent UbuWeb. The site Goldsmith (2000) calls, with apt pride, "essentially a gift economy" is indeed "the perfect space," as he puts it, "to practice utopian politics." Yet the spaces I've mentioned above, although less utopian by feel and located far from the freest districts, can be within as well as without the institutions traditionally set up for teaching only insiders (tuition payers). Writers within universities have all along written mostly for readers who are outside the space created for the isolated community of non-readers or neophyte readers who are tuition payers. Yet teachers of the same work, including those very writers acting in their roles as teachers in the for-credit curriculum, have taught this work restrictively. The animated redefin-ition of readerships augured by digital poetry has not extended to the pedagogical relationships that many contend the new modes of writing make possible. The interaction that I used to call teaching can extend outward in much the same way as the writing. Kinetic is as kinetic does.

To get to that animated outward extension we must subject ourselves to higher standards—or at least better definitions—of what constitutes this interactivity in or through the writing. (What this means in terms of writing programming code and literal networking others are in a better position to say than I, but I would insist that there is indeed an aspect of this problem being adequately addressed through innovative programs and wider net-works.[1]) Here, I can return to what I called the "media conversion fallacy"; earlier, I described the insufficiency of the model, a course with its assigned books, handouts, and lectures is "put online." Can we really say it is thus "online"? The lecture, for one, exists as ever—a block of knowing, uninterac-tive—perhaps a sound file available on the Web any time day or night but one that partakes (as sound) of none of the specific "aural opulence," for instance, that Adalaide Morris (1997) has identified in the modernist era of wireless acoustics or that Martin Spinelli evinces in *Radio Radio* (2003). I want to draw an analogy between what Marjorie Perloff has said on this topic and this particular but common fallacy that, among doubters on the faculty, has become associated with the presumed failure of the "Internet revolution" in the area of teaching and learning. "Does the medium disappear in this art?" Perloff (2002) asked in a recent conference presentation. "Yes and no. Language is generated off the page but by the time we see it, it may be back on it, the point being that, to be effective, digital poetics must be much more than transcribing an already written poem from one medium to another." Even if and when such writing does get beyond its tendency to "be back on" the page, there is an analogous conservatism in the way it has come to be understood at the university, in what often passes for—and is funded as—the "digitalization of the course."

Closing the Door to Protect the Professor

The development of digital poetics might help to alter structures that have tended to entrap the socioaesthetics of "To Elsie" in the university classroom. Much will depend on how and why the digitizing gets done. We must first get past the hype. We must bohemianize the electronic classroom to the extent possible. We must concede that the university might never be a haven for this work. And, finally, we must understand that the problems are as old—and at the same time precisely as "new"—as modernism. Let me take these requirements in turn.

First, the hype. Painting the alluring picture of an HTML-writing poet with two windows open, one Unix and the other Netscape, in which what one writes in the first becomes world-readable in the second, Glazier likens the experience of sudden total exposure, of the ultimate instant free press such as Ben Franklin never experienced, to Golden Age visual simulcasting: "The process has all the risks of live television" (2002, 5). This passing analogy should interest us because it implies a comparison of daring newnesses. Is the digital poet the twenty-first-century equivalent of Sid Caesar, inventing instantaneously and with brilliant avant-garde immediacy, exposing compositional practices as (hilariously) part of the product, but giving way, in a few short years, to canned schlock, commercialism and—most powerfully—genre consolidation? Claims for television's newness were oversold by a generation of mostly well-meaning people. The risks of synchronous exposure were real, but they gave way, in the same medium, to unself-consciousness and pure product.

I am pleased to say that Glazier's book participates in the hype only in its opening pages; he then gets down to the specific work of description and analysis of a new practice. Yet Johanna Drucker, who at least when she assembled the essays in *Figuring the Word* (1998) was not sanguine about a future of immaterial writing, surely was not wrong to suspect all the hyperbole, describing our "moment of electronic hyper-hype, in the throes of a pre-millennial techno-fascination, on the verge of making virtual everything we never needed in the real" (222). The end—or at least the lessening of—the hype about the electronic word roughly coincides with the most excessive of the rhetorical utopianism purveyed by university "reformists." Almost every grand online education scheme of the mid- to late 1990s—most of them were just that, schemes, a few of them true scams—has come crashing down. What is left is hard, actual work, use of the means at hand (programming, which is to say writing, dissemination, organizing, publishing in the new media, faster but just as complex as ever). Reform is no easier than it ever was.

Bohemianize the Classroom

For some, the productive new institutional space seems to be the "electronic classroom." I doubt that myself, and freely advise academic deans not to fund them until the utopianism gets fleshed out a little. Instead, I would say to such decanal presences: fund the renovation of a cottage, wire it through fat twenty-first-century conduits but then hide the wiring; administratively situate the space outside the academic departments; install comfy couches and a coffee pot; give it over to the digerati—in short, establish a technologized physical space that is nonetheless as much unlike an electronic classroom as possible.

Proponents of the electronic classroom are not wrong to argue that the old teaching methodology (in which the knowledgeable one tells the not-yet-knowledgeable one how and what to know) can be replaced. But by what, actually? Even a theorist of "hypertext writing communities" as keen as Michael Joyce, in an otherwise perspicacious study that puts a "hypertext poetics" near its center, never quite makes it clear what remains when, with "the convergence of electronic classrooms and writing environments," we are ridded of "expert-novice distinctions between groups of writer-learners (including the expert-novice distinction of teacher-learner)" (1995, 67).

As William Doll (1993) notes, we must acknowledge first that there will be "Curriculum Carryovers" (45). To the problem of the classroom, we can apply Jethro Lieberman's radical insight that by "putting the experts in charge" we forego changes urging from "a multitude of sources" in favor of the maintenance of a profession, "its image, health, membership, reputation" (1970, 5). But without a plan that concedes some form of authority (not pedagogical but institutional), the tyranny easily reasserts itself. I take it that this scenario is what makes skeptics so nervous.

Critics of the whole electronic text enterprise, such as Barry Sanders, would have it that the hundreds of screens full of lively, persuasive, responsive prose and verse that my students have posted electronically to their fellow students, to a worldwide network of poets and lay readers, and to me in the course of studying contemporary poetics are really authored by the Silicon Valley folks who wrote the software for the email text editor we use. *They* control the real (which is to say, operational) language, Sanders fears. Such a view seriously underestimates the reader's potential as a writer and his or her level of engagement and diverts attention from our responsibility as teachers (though not as tyrants), which, as I see it, is to find or create a means by which students can experience and learn from aesthetic authority by assiduously responding to it. Authors and teachers have as a new tool a kind of text that can "meander" (for Sanders, a hateful readerly quality) by virtue of its form as well as its content, inviting the reader to make choices at every turn. To the extent that we can resist the easy characterization of this mode of reading and learning as inhuman and "dictatorial"—with its anxious view of cultural authority as residing not in the individual creator of text but in the creator of the system syntax, and, as Glazier shows, even to employ that syntax—then, I think, we will be better able to face a few of our problems as teachers of reading. And, as the hypermedia writer M. D. Coverley puts it, "[n]ew 'writing possibilities' cannot really manifest themselves without new reading strategies" (Coverley, qtd. in Swiss 2002, 99).

The real electronic classrooms—for the purposes of the production of digital poetry, anyway—are located eight or ten blocks from campus, in hyper-wired, or wireless-networked, student-rental garrets that otherwise resemble the counterinstitutional digs that have in many eras produced emergent writing. And the new poetry is sent in electronically from there—a *copy* is sent, I should say—to the teacher, on its way well beyond the university toward some independent editor or creative e-forum such as UbuWeb. "We receive a submission Monday morning," Goldsmith recently boasted in the journal *NC1*, "and it's published Monday afternoon." Goldsmith contends that "an historical literary movement has, after a half century, found its ideal medium" (Goldsmith, qtd. in Swiss 2002, 108). He freely sets up an institution, or a noninstitution, that healthily accommodates that convergence. The university can also accommodate it, but only as it begins to focus energy as much on what might be called the software of responsiveness as on the new hardware it keeps accumulating.

Is the University a Haven?

If the university is to be a site relevant to the aesthetic problems posed by the special disjunctiveness of "To Elsie"—which is to say, of modern American culture as it is lived—we must concede that it might never sufficiently adapt to modes of interactivity needed for digital poetries to flourish there or that incentives (promotion, tenure, and other rewards; the restructuring of "teaching load") will never be great enough to create the speed (and enthusiasm) of responsiveness daily evinced by Goldsmith. For every one Writers House there are ten classes such as the graduate-level cybertext course that Katherine Parrish took; "we closed the door when class was in session," Parrish recalls, "to protect our professor from the teasing of his passing colleagues." I am speaking here about the university as a big undeniable fact—and as an institution I deem worthy of the changes that would suit social ideas about writing, reading, and learning implicit in digital poetics—but I am willing to concede that Parrish might finally be right when she concludes, "The most important institution for the health and well being of New Media Poetry and Fiction is the new media itself. The internet. . . . *This* is where I learn" (Parrish, qtd. in Swiss 2002, 94–95).

The kineticism valorized by proponents of electronic poetry has its origins in modernism. It would seem to follow, then, that the kinds of social and institutional changes that can derive from the digital poetics movement have been in the offing for many decades. Many of those who write about digital poets refer to F. T. Marinetti—as Peter Menacker has in a recent paper—and to Williams, as Glazier (2002) does in his introduction to *Digital Poetics*.[2] What is important to Glazier is what in writing becomes activated in the electronic medium, but he reminds us that "[a] sense of 'active' is being argued here [that is similar] to what William Carlos Williams argued for the print poem" (6). Then Glazier quotes Robert Creeley speaking in 1999—one pre-Internet poet who adapted creatively and happily to new media, going so far, in print, as calling himself "a virtual poet"[3]—contending that Williams's "insistence was not on the poem as afterthought . . . but on the poem as itself an instrument of thought" (6). It is from Williams, and from Williams per Creeley, that Glazier derives the major interest of his book, which should compel us: not the digital poet but more generally the kind of poet who thinks through the poem.

The Authenticity of the Mixed

The Northern Irish poet Gilbert Adair wrote to me a few years ago. I had known that it was Adair, in London, who had curated the Sub Voicive Poetry Reading Series, but I had not known him personally. Adair has been in London, then Singapore, recently in New York, yet one of his strong links to the American poetry scene in this time of movement, he wrote to say, had been the Writers House webcast series. He had listened to the "To Elsie" session live (I was not aware of his presence) and then, later, listened again. He had worked through the layerings of ongoing discussion. Thinking of the vexed final movement of the poem, its excited dread of directionless cultural going ("no one / to witness / and adjust, no one to drive the car"), but also of the chaotic communal context in which he refound this ongoing, pending discussion of the poem, he wrote to me the following: "I suspect that what [Williams] had in mind was various behaviors a community builds up over time, in complex awareness both of its social locale and internal hierarchies. . . . The . . . 'mixed' can earn authenticity. *That* sets up the drama—[although it is] not a solution."[4]

The digitalization-as-media-conversion approach of many at the universities, taken together with the "complex awareness" Gilbert Adair describes and himself evinces (both of social locale and of its limits as a concept driving poetry), not only puts the lie to the ubiquitous, mostly exaggerated, claims of "interactivity" made by people who "do poetry on the Web" but also begins to redress the old regressive disestablishment of poetry-teaching relations. *As if* those to whom we teach writing—their almost statelessness with respect to what we do and know—could have some vital relevance to this chaos we call the new poetry.

Notes

I wish to thank Joan Retallack, Charles Bernstein, and Barrett Watten, who offered invitations to speak on this topic, respectively, at Bard College in June 1999; at the Modern Language Association conference, before the Poetry Division, in December 2000; and at Wayne State University on April 13, 2001. The latter paper was entitled "Magic Thinking, Unmediated Access, Instant Solutions—*Not.*" I am also grateful to the organizers of the Frye Leadership Conference hosted by the Council on Library and Information Resources annually at Emory University; they have enabled me to refine my ideas over the past four years. The interactive webcast series hosted by the Kelly Writers House at the University of Pennsylvania would not have been possible without the wisdom and assistance of John MacDermott, Ira Winston, Richard Hendrix, Kerry Sherin Wright, Heather Starr, Shawn Walker, Tom Devaney, and Paul Kelly.

1. See Glazier's chapter on "Coding Writing, Reading Code" (2002, 96–125).

2. See also Stefans 2003, 49–51.

3. When Creeley published *Day Book of a Virtual Poet* (1998), much was made of the electronic medium. Burt Kimmelman commended Creeley as "An Elder" who is "as youthful as the electronic text in which he corresponds" (jacket, n.p.). But, actually, if there is one thing to learn from this wonderful book it is that the medium is not the message. The message is the message. What Creeley has to say has little to do with the listserv he is using to say it or with the World Wide Web from which he incessantly culls sites to which his virtual students should go out to read great poetry. He knows that it fantastically aids his urge to reach out—in this case, to young students in the City Honors Online Writing Program (Buffalo, NY). His already characteristically high generous energy and sense of responsiveness finds in e-text a great fast bullhorn. There is hardly a poet more e-savvy than Creeley, but the mission of his teaching as a poet is traditional and, with respect to concepts such as the nomadic dispersed digital self, in this mode, he is plainly holistically humanistic. He sends his students URLs for Wordsworth, and even Whittier, and uses as his tonal model Williams's, sense of fun as a remedy for pedantic or precise approaches to poetry and as a hedge against "the authority of endless revisions." He quotes Williams's "Why don't we tell them it's just fun?"—"it" being writing that seems difficult, and "them" being young or at least new readers of poetry.

4. Gilbert Adair, email message to Alan Filries, November 28, 2000.

Works Cited

Bard College. 2000. "What Is Cybergraphia?" *Cybergraphia*. http://cg.bard.edu/whatis.html (accessed January 4, 2004).

Bard College. 2002. *Cybergraphia*. http://cg.bard.edu (accessed December 15, 2003).

Creeley, Robert. 1998. *Day Book of a Virtual Poet*. New York: Spuyten Duyvil.

Doll, William E., Jr. 1993. *A Post-modern Perspective on Curriculum*. New York: Teachers College Press.

Drucker, Johanna. 1998. *Figuring the Word: Essays on Books, Writing, and Visual Poetics*. New York: Granary Books.

Georgia Tech School of Literature, Communication & Culture. *IDT: Information Design & Technology*. http://www.lcc.gatech.edu/idt/index.html (accessed December 18, 2003).

Glazier, Loss Pequeño. 2002. *Digital Poetics: The Making of E-Poetries*. Tuscaloosa: University of Alabama Press.

Goldsmith, Kenneth. 2000. "UbuWeb Wants to Be Free." *OL3: Open Letter On Lines Online*. http://www.ubu.com/papers/ol/ubu.html (accessed December 13, 2003).

Joyce, Michael. 1995. *Of Two Minds: Hypertext Pedagogy and Poetics*. Ann Arbor: University of Michigan Press.

Kelly Writers House. 2003. http://www.writing.upenn.edu/wh/ (accessed December 13, 2003).

Laurillard, Diana. 1993. *Rethinking University Teaching: A Framework for the Effective Use of Educational Technology*. London: Routledge.

Lieberman, Jethro. 1970. *The Tyranny of the Experts: How Professionals Are Closing the Open Society*. New York: Walker.

Menacker, Peter. 2004. "The Futurist Uterus = F. T. Marinetti + Digital Poetics." Unpublished paper.

Morris, Adalaide. 1997. "Sound Technologies and the Modernist Epic: H.D. on the Air." In *Sound States: Innovative Poetics and Acoustical Technologies*, ed. Adalaide Morris, 32–55. Chapel Hill: University of North Carolina Press.

Murray, Janet H. 1997. "The Pedagogy of Cyberfiction: Teaching a Course on Reading and Writing Interactive Narrative." In *Contextual Media*, ed. Edward Barrett and Marie Redmond, 129–162. Cambridge, MA: MIT Press.

Parrish, Katherine. 2002. "Teaching in the Splice: MOO Pedagogy and Poetics." *Electronic Poetry Center*. http://epc.buffalo.edu/authors/parrish (accessed March 10, 2002).

Perloff, Marjorie. 2002. "The Poetics of Click and Drag: Problems and Possibilities of Digital Technology." Paper presented at the New Media Poetry: Aesthetics, Institutions, and Audiences conference, University of Iowa, Iowa City, October 11–12.

Project Achieve: A Collaborative Learning Environment. 2002. http://projectachieve.net/ (accessed January 4, 2004).

Sanders, Barry. 1994. *A Is for Ox: Violence, Electronic Media, and the Silencing of the Written Word*. New York: Pantheon Books.

Spinelli, Martin. 2003. *Radio Radio*. http://www.ubu.com/sound/radio_radio/ (accessed January 4, 2004).

Stefans, Brian Kim. 2003. *Fashionable Noise: On Digital Poetics*. Berkeley, CA: Atelos.

Swiss, Thomas, ed. 2002. "New Media Literature: A Roundtable Discussion on Aesthetics, Audiences, and Histories." *NC1* (Spring/Summer): 84–110.

SUNY Buffalo. 2003. *Electronic Poetry Center*. http://wings.buffalo.edu/epc/ (accessed December 13, 2003).

Williams, William Carlos. 1986. "The Pure Products of America Go Crazy" ["To Elsie"]. In *The Collected Poems of William Carlos Williams*, vol. 1, ed. A. Walton Litz and Christopher McGowan, 217–221. New York: New Directions.

Technotexts

7

Screening the Page/Paging the Screen: Digital Poetics and the Differential Text

Marjorie Perloff

Art is a series of perpetual differences.
— TRISTAN TZARA, "NOTE ON POETRY"

"It is fundamentally problematic," writes Peter Bürger in his *Theory of the Avant-Garde*, "to assign a fixed meaning to a procedure" (1984, 78). Bürger's reference is to montage/collage: he argues that just because two collages—say, a still life by Picasso and a satiric collage by Raoul Hausmann—use similar techniques of paste-up and collocation of unlike material, it doesn't mean that the two works have a shared aesthetic. On the contrary, Bürger observes, German Dadaists such as Hausmann took what was, for Picasso, essentially an aesthetic form and adapted it for political purposes.

The same principle, I would suggest, applies to the new electronic poetries. As in the case of any medium in its early stages, digital poetry today may seem to fetishize digital presentation as something in itself remarkable, as if to say, "Look what the computer can do!" But no medium or technique of production can in itself give the poet (or any other kind of artist) the inspiration or imagination to produce works of art. And poetry is an especially vexed case because, however we choose to define it, poetry is the *language art*: it is, by all accounts, language that is somehow extraordinary, that can be processed only upon rereading. Consequently, the "new" techniques, whereby letters and words can move around the screen, break up, and reassemble, or whereby the reader/viewer can decide by a mere click to reformat the electronic text or which part of it to access, become merely tedious unless the poetry in question is, in Ezra Pound's words, "charged with meaning" (1960, 28).

Then, too, a strong claim has been made for the *interactivity* of electronic text—a claim I take to be largely illusory, especially when it comes to poetry. True, viewers can trace their own path through a given electronic text, decide whether to move from A to B or B to Q, whether to rearrange word groups and stanzas, and so on. But is such activity really any more "interactive" than, say, *The Sims* games, which allow their players to "decide" what sort of house the family will live in, what their furniture will look like, and what their "personalities" are? For *The Sims* player, the personality and wallpaper choices are limited to a fixed set of options, produced by the makers of the game in the interest of mass appeal. As children quickly learn—and this is why they soon tire of *The Sims* and turn to *The Sims Vacation* or whatever other computer game—permission, as John Cage would have said, is granted, but hardly to do whatever you want. Indeed, the input is rigidly predetermined by the largely anonymous authors and programmers. Adorno would have had a field day with this perfect cipher of the "culture industries."

Nevertheless, electronic text does offer the poet exciting new possibilities, which I shall take up in a moment. First, however, I want to say something about the new dissemination of poetry and poetics that is occurring on the Internet. Here a real revolution is taking place right in front of our eyes. Consider Kenneth Goldsmith's beautifully designed site UbuWeb (http://www.ubu.com), where one can access an astonishing variety of avant-garde poetries from the early twentieth century to the present: from Russian Futurism and Dada to Fluxus and Ethnopoetics to contemporary movements in visual and sound poetry. There are also critical essays on the poetries in question and, most important, portfolios of otherwise inaccessible work. Thus Craig Dworkin has produced *The UbuWeb Anthology of Conceptual Writing* (2003), with a superb introduction and examples from Samuel Beckett and Robert Barry to Christian Bök—an anthology much more adequate than anything currently available in print format. Goldsmith has also obtained the entire archive of the avant-garde "magazine in a box" *Aspen* (1965–1971), which is unavailable even in leading research libraries, and has posted the entire run (ten issues) on the Web. And on UbuWeb, one can listen to Marinetti intone *La Battaglia di Adrianopoli,* Henri Chopin recite his sound poetry, and Ron Silliman read his macabre question poem "Sunset Debris."

How will the dissemination of such rich and varied material affect the poetry-reading public? Like any revolution, this one will take some time to be felt in Establishment culture. Indeed, even as electronic poetics has become more and more sophisticated, mainstream journals such as *The Hudson Review* or *American Poetry Review* have moved in the opposite direction. Their short, lineated, epiphanic free-verse lyrics, with their justified left (and often right) margins surrounded by white space, suggest that nothing has changed: a poem is a poem, period! Indeed, at a recent conference in Belfast on trans-atlantic poetics, I heard an English poet, Ruth Padel, say that there is no such thing as a designed book of poems; there are only separate intense lyrics, and these are "a gift of God." And another poet chimed in that it's time to get away from "silly" concepts like *process* or the *open-ended* poetic sequence because the poet had jolly well better make up his or her mind about how to *finish* the poem, how to make that crucial decision that determines its final shape.

No *Aspen* or Vito Acconci for this group, which still dominates university creative writing programs and the major newspapers and reviews. But it is only a matter of time until this situation changes; obviously, younger people surfing the Net will come across sites such as UbuWeb and absorb the materials posted. Here economics is central: concrete poetry, for example, was always very expensive to reproduce and print, especially in color formats, even as CDs of sound poetry are hard to come by. Today, if you can't afford to buy, say, *The Collected Poems of Haroldo and Augusto de Campos,* you can study their works online. True, the texture of the page and its actual lettering will be lost, and the digitized artwork cannot quite match the colors of the original, but the fact is that now readers around the world can access the work of Ian Hamilton Finlay or Mary Ellen Solt—work that can now become part of the academic curriculum.

Another interesting facet of the digital dissemination of poetic texts is that electronic texts are likely to be truer to the original than the usual reprints and anthology versions. The Norton anthologies, for example, often adjust the visual format of a given poem so as to save space and hence money: intentional double-spacing becomes normal single-spacing, and so on. A classic case is that of George Oppen, who designed *Discrete Series* to have one poem per page, whereas the various reprintings have tended to crowd the short lyrics together, with the poems often broken up at the bottom of a given page and continuing on the next. On the screen, this needn't be the case; indeed, a Web site such as Futurism and Futurists (http://www.futurism.org.uk) reproduces the various manifestos by Marinetti and Boccioni exactly as they were designed, whereas most reprints distort the typography, spacing, layout, and so on.

But what about digital poetry itself—the work now written expressly for the screen? The most interesting exemplars of digital poetics to date have tended to be what I have called elsewhere *differential* texts—that is to say, texts that exist in different material forms, with no single version being the definitive one (Perloff 2002b). Thus a text such as Kenneth Goldsmith's *Fidget* (1999) has a print version (figure 7.1), a digital version, and a version that exists as an archive of its gallery installation—an installation whose use of visual and sound media gave it a rather different tone from the other two. Which is the "real" *Fidget*? One cannot say although each reader may well prefer one mode of production over the others.

The ability to move from one medium to another and back again allows the poet to experiment with temporal and spatial frames. Many of these differential electronic texts also use procedural devices, following the example of *Oulipo* or, closer to home, the rule-governed compositions of John Cage, Jackson Mac Low, and Fluxus. Consider, for starters, Brian Kim Stefans's sequence *the dreamlife of letters* (1999). This is a Flash piece in which the twenty-six letters of the alphabet, presented in alphabetic sequence (with secondary sequences based on the second letter in each word, and so on), produce words and phrases, all animated in various ways against the background of an orange square. The letters are black or white and dance around the screen in silence, producing new formations, splitting up, and regrouping. Some of the formations look like Cagean mesostics; others insert words inside large capitals; others are produced by letter clashes, circular formations, lipograms, and a myriad of other textual patterns, no two configurations being quite the same (figure 7.2).

In the preface, which precedes the actual running of the Flash text, Stefans (1999) explains the generative email procedure as follows:

In 1999, I, along with several other poets and writers, was asked to partake in an online "roundtable" on sexuality and literature. The event would be centered around a brief essay by the San Francisco novelist Dodie Bellamy. . . .

All of the participants were divided into groups, each individual having a position in that group. As I was the second in position, I was assigned to respond to the person

Breathe. Right hand twists. Right foot propels body forward. Right hip stretches. Right knee drops, almost touching bed. Muscles in right thigh and left buttocks stretch. Mucus drawn from nose into back of throat. Tongue gathers saliva and mucus. Swallow. Right hand moves to nose. Right thumb covers nostril. Exhale. Expel. Right index finger moves to forehead near top of hairline. Itches four times. Finger moves from hairline to eyebrow. Body contracts into fetal position. Right arm rests between knees. Knees curve as body flips right. Left hand slides beneath right ear. Elbow bends. Mucus pulled from nose to throat. Floods back of mouth. Gathers in pouch of right cheek. Tongue coats top row of teeth in mucus. Pushes to back of mouth. Swallow. Tongue produces watery saliva. Curls. Swallow. Neck muscles tighten. Inhale. Air pins tongue to teeth. Swallow. Watery saliva dissolves mucus. Right hand to face. Pinkie rubs eye. Index finger massages right eyebrow. Middle finger digs into left eye. Thrusts. Hands between legs. Stretch. Body on side. Yawn. Stretch. Knees bend. Toes arch. Teeth clench. Jaw closes. Pelvis thrusts. Bottom teeth hit upper. Left temple tightens. Hand raises. Moves to back. Drops to buttocks. Fingernails scratch. Index finger extends into crack of buttocks and probes anus. Scratches once, twice, three times. Strong pressure applied by fingertip. Finger glides over coccyx and out of buttocks.

9

Figure 7.1 Pageshot from *Fidget*. Courtesy of Kenneth Goldsmith.

Figure 7.2 Screenshot from *the dreamlife of letters* by Brian Kim Stefans.
http://www.ubu.com/contemp/stefans/dream.

in the first position, who in my case was the poet and feminist literary theorist Rachel Blau DuPlessis.

DuPlessis wrote a very texturally detailed, nearly opaque, response (to be found here (o)).[1]

A click on this link takes us to DuPlessis's short piece for the roundtable.[2] Here DuPlessis uses passages of complex and suggestive phonetic spelling, alternating with their "translation" or transposition into "normal" English, which constitutes DuPlessis's own commentary on the gender issues with which Bellamy deals. Thus the piece opens with the following lines:

"gin dear hiss delight" sad dough tea bellum me wansin moo van bo drip age tic tock 2 cum "gender is the night" said Dodie Bellamy once in *Moving Borders*, page

TKTK (to come to 2 cum. zzz gindra delite ides aye—ginestra scissors delays, hex you all in ties his duh nigh, to come). Is gender the night? I'd say—gender is the day, sexuality is the night.

And it concludes, "Weiner hearing sense lay dunkel troubled nixed sensual heft leveling ring uglies. We experience a doubled, tripled, mixed sexuality of everything all ways."

Stefans (1999) seems to have been dissatisfied with this procedure for, despite the complex verbal and phonemic overlay, the DuPlessis piece makes very specific assertions about sexuality. He writes:

I had decided that I wanted to respond to her text in a detailed manner, but I felt that normal prose would not suffice on my part, so I alphabetized the words in her text, and created my own series of very short "concrete" poems based on the chance meeting of words. My poem (which you can read here (o)[3] along with a few short paragraphs in response to Bellamy), was my contribution to [the] roundtable.

As words almost invariably take on nearly obscene meanings when they are left to linger on their own, and as DuPlessis's text was so loaded to begin with, I didn't enjoy the poem that much. More importantly, as it was in a sort of antique "concrete" mode, it resembled a much older aesthetic, one well explored by Gomringer, the De Campos brothers and numerous others in the past fifty years, and so it wasn't very interesting to me.

Here, for example, are sections #4 and #5 (B and C) of Stefans's concrete poem:

behoove bellamy bellum

ben bend bi bi big bike

binaries/ bo/ borders,

but
butt

buy
caucasians

character?
chimneysweeper christ,

cinder cixous.

com-round, combinatory:

come come)
comes

—conventional cunt curse . . .

cycle. (1999)

The alphabet rule is also the one to be used in the digital version of *the dream-life of letters*, but here in print the words are fixed and anchored in their lines, thus slighting the possibilities for pun, paragram, and *lettrism* available in the electronic text. In the preface, Stefans notes:

I don't wish to explain much more about the piece here, except to say that it is not interactive. I decided that it was much more like a short film than an interactive piece, and there didn't seem any natural place to let the viewer in that way. . . .

   I don't think I reveal the dreamlife of letters in this piece; the letters have too many dreams, as I've discovered, though perhaps not enough for me in the end.

   In its digital version (Stefons 1999), produced by "reptilian neolettrist graphics," an orange square of *A*'s—about half of them upside-down, some white on black, some black on white, some plain—is complicated by a "frozen gifs gallery" beneath the square, a gallery whose fifteen entries contain different *lettriste* designs, somewhat reminiscent of Steve McCaffery's *Carnival*.[4] One can run the whole *dreamlife of letters* in about eleven minutes, or one can go to the index and access each letter section separately. Thus, the third section, "behoove to caucasians," uses exactly the same sixteen words or syllables as Concrete Poem #4, but the units now become actors in a more complex drama. First, "behoove Bellamy bellum" appear on the lower left of the orange square. Next, the words "ben bend bi bi big bike" snake in from the upper right in zigzag form, bending, overlapping, and jostling one another so as to produce a time sequence reflecting "Big Ben" (the clock), introducing bisexuality, and miming the movement of a bicycle across the screen. The *i*'s of "binaries," appearing in the upper left, are momentarily missing, invoking "Benares" in India and only then coming together with "bo" + "orders," constituting the borders of binary oppositions. Then "bo" is next given a giant *B* in final position producing "Bob," and then the big *B* is inscribed with "but," "butt," and "buy," all in small white letters, and the black "caucasians" in the lower left, leading us to the next or *C* section.

The one word I feel is out of place here is "caucasians": the reference in DuPlessis's text is to "the Phallus or regressive iden-tiff caucasians"—a too obvious counter, in Stefans's text, to the multivalent, multisexual images of the poet's dream alphabet. At the same time, the movement from the "ca" string of "caucasians" to the first word of the next section, "character," is seam-less—as are all the movements from one section to another. In #4, the phrase "character to cycle" gives way to the collocation of "chimneysweeper" and "christ," the two words floating in blurred wavy lines across the lower half of the screen. The words "cinder" and "cixous" (Hélène Cixous, the great feminist theorist of multivalent sexuality) first appear with their *i*'s missing; their stark simplicity is juxtaposed to the complex, designed mesostic on "com-round, combinatory: / come come) / comes" that follows. Immediately thereafter, "conventional," "cunt," and "curse" appear in quick succession around a giant circling *C*, the conjunction suggesting that although "curse" is the conventional prudish epithet for menstruation, it is also properly located in the "cunt."

Here, then, is Stefans's poetic commentary on Dodie Bellamy's erotic fiction, as mediated by DuPlessis's analysis. *the dreamlife of letters* is elegant, beautiful to look at, and spare, a new way of using language in its material-ity so as to make meanings. Is it "better" than the poem, as Stefans himself thinks? Yes and no: the static visual text can be absorbed and studied much more readily than the moving picture. And the third alternative—the embed-ding of the lyrics in the larger Situationist text—is also attractive.

A different variant of the "dreamlife of letters" is provided by Caroline Bergvall in a work called *ambient fish* (1999), available on the Web site of the

Electronic Poetry Center. Here the typography is not elegant as in Stefans's piece, but the sound dimension is central, the poet reading aloud as we watch the screen. The viewer/listener is presented with two green buttons, ringed in red, on a blank screen. Click on these and they become pea-green breasts. Click on the "nipples" and four rows of four of the same buttons appear. Almost every button quickly gives way to a word or phrase, while the voice-over (Bergvall's very elegant, cool, and evenly pitched voice) pronounces "ambient fish fuckflowers bloom in your mouth," the text then permutating these words and phrases by means of rhyme and consonance so that "ambient fish" becomes "alien fish" and "alien poche," "loose in your mouth" becomes "goose in your mouth," becomes "goose in your ouch," and "fuckfodder" becomes "fuckfad," becomes "fish fat," while "alien poche" ("pocket") becomes "alien poach," becomes "a lined peach patch" (figure 7.3). The refrain "will shock [or choke] your troubles away" or "stow [throw] your troubles away" thus becomes quite literal. After the buttons disappear, the voice says evenly "fuck fish goose in your bouche suck your oubli away." It is a riveting performance.

ambient fish evidently started out as a text-sound installation commissioned by a festival of mixed media in England (Perloff 2002a, 130). The refrain was used as a drone in the piece. Onscreen, the interrupted recordings of the voice make the absurd lines even more menacing as do the curious rhymes and repetitions in which the French words *oubli* (forgotten) and *bouche* (mouth), here

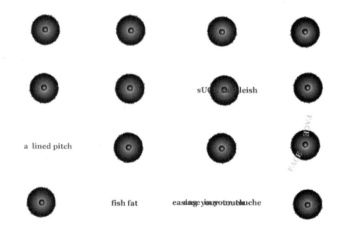

Figure 7.3 Screenshot from *ambient fish* by Caroline Bergvall.
http://epc.buffalo.edu/authors/bergvall/amfish/amfish.html

pronounced *baush*, give the piece a faux pornographic air. *Sucking your oubli—* it sounds pretty sinister! But what is especially unsettling is that when the buttons and words disappear within a minute or so, they leave only three words—*fish*, *face*, and *your*—and a single breast shape. Then "fish" and "your" disappear, the word "face" circles drunkenly about and finally disappears too, and we are left with an isolated glowing red-green button.

What, one wants to know, are the relationships here between *fish* and *your*, between *tirer des eaux* and its rhyme partner in "stow" or "throw your troubles away"? The "loveliness" of the language is wholly deceptive—*fuckflowers* in the context sounds pretty, rather like hollyhocks or gillyflowers. As for the buttons, their role is complicated by their technological function. The standard television remote control has, at the center of the number pad, usually next to the "5," a button with a raised little dot within it that looks exactly like the button in *ambient fish*. Press the button and a new channel opens up its picture. But in *ambient fish*, no such thing happens: press the button and you get, not a pleasing image but only broken words and disappearing breasts. The anonymous, impersonal voice, with its proffer of sexual pleasures that will "throw your troubles away" or "suck your oubli away" becomes increasingly threatening.

Another intriguing Bergvall digital text is "Flèsh" (2001a), which can be found in a recent issue of *How2*. "Flèsh," first called "Flèsh acoeur," illustrates Lev Manovich's point that if one can make radically different versions of the art object—as is the case with electronic poetries—"the traditional strong link between the identity of an art object and its medium becomes broken" (2001b, 3).[5] The project, Bergvall tells us, was first developed to be one of twenty Volumes of Vulnerability artist's books, used in a project produced by Gefn Press to celebrate the millennium:

It is a tribute to four writers who, for all their cultural differences, share a trance-like understanding of the connections between text and physicality, between violence and verbal illumination, between the intimate and the public facets of sexual desire as also a desire for writing. In each their way, and these were frequently at odds with the declared values of their time, they explored and pushed such connections both in their work and in their body.[6] (2001d)

The four writers in question are St. Teresa of Avila, the German surrealist painter Unica Zürn (whose torso tied up with string her artist-husband Hans

Bellmer transformed into an icon), the visionary language poet Hannah Weiner, and the erotic postmodern novelist Kathy Acker. In its artist's book version, "Flèsh acoeur" was designed as "a set of 4 folded folios, very low-tech, which demands of the readers that they have to use French cuts with a knife or letter-opener to open each level of text" (Bergvall 2003). Hence the "incorrect" French accent over the English word, reminding us that in French *flèche* means "arrow"; "Flèsh acoeur" is thus the arrow to one's heart—the arrow of romantic love as well as spiritual revelation, piercing the flesh. Indeed, in Bernini's famous sculpture, *The Ecstasy of St. Therese*, the saint's breast is just about to be penetrated by an arrow.

Cutting—the reader's need to cut the small yellow pages with a letter opener or knife as well as the cutting up of text we find in Bergvall's piece—insures that the reading experience is intentionally slowed. But onscreen, redesigned with the help of Anya Lewin, "Flèsh" appears as an impenetrable pink wall, the single word "Flèsh" suggesting not only the cliché that it is the French who are best at enjoying the pleasures of the flesh but that the click on the mere letters of the monosyllabic word will penetrate the flesh. And so, as one clicks on the four instances of "Flèsh," first, the four names appear; then, with a further click, four extracts from their respective writings; and then, when these texts are opened up by a third click, we have the opposite—*underneath* the flesh, female desire, it turns out, has a common language.

Here is the St. Teresa section:

Things had been going Rather Well. Sex loot. Caravans of PushpUsh. Needy machines Easy To Please. Pissabout reFillable. Rubbed a Fff in It long enough to Suck Off Thereafter. The stakes we'd lie in about. Everything pruned is happy as shaved. NowCaught In The Grip of. JUMPs the Surf with a Start Off the ace. Oars dig holes in Every Single Pie own I had ed absent mindedly. Row and row. Torn in the bell heat kicks up spare heads. Something's knocking against the SKin. arge persistent buLks In The Air. Brutally pulled innards. Gut seizure GONgs concave.[7]

The language here, as we recognize from *ambient fish*, is Bergvall's own complex poetic wordplay—her astonishing, aggressive mix of the intellectual and the erotic, the hard and the soft, the "Needy machines" that are "Easy To Please." The harsh phonemic play and eye rhyme give Bergvall's text a kind of electric charge. Nothing is quite what we think it is: "spare heads" replace "spare parts"; and "stakes" are not something "we'd lie about" but—oddly—"lie in about." Halfway through the passage, the speaker's language breaks down so that "I had owned" becomes "own I had ed." Internal capitalization and the running together of words as in "PushpUsh" creates curious paragrams, and the jamming of sounds and syllables introduces a note of artifice that befits Unica Zürn or Kathy Acker as well as St. Teresa. In "Brutally pulled innards," for example, double *ll*'s and *n*'s twist the *u*'s *and a*'s in their midst. But the violent erotic scene also contains religious possibilities in those "Gut seizure GONgs concave"—possibilities appropriate for St. Teresa, as, in a different way, for Hannah Weiner.

The electronic screen thus brings out aspects of "Flèsh" that are not as prominent in the artist's book. In reading the book, the four names are endowed with meanings to be compared, point by point, in what is an atemporal grid. On the screen, however, flesh is always an impenetrable exterior, a blank pink wall that the viewer/auditor must elect to "enter" *in time*. Then again, when Bergvall performs "Flèsh" in a gallery situation, the vocal intricacies subordinate individual words and word images to a powerful sonic pattern. The relation of text to audience is thus markedly differential.

And this brings me to my next example, in which computer technology has been generative of text that is not itself electronic, at least not in its primary version. In 1997, Kenneth Goldsmith decided to record every word he spoke in a single week. For seven days—a unit that gives *Soliloquy*, as the resulting work is called, its seven-act structure—Goldsmith went about his daily routine, wearing a wire and "collected" what became almost five hundred pages of his own speech. The piece was first presented as a text installation, but since it needs to be read rather than seen, its more adequate realization is in the austere and sober gray volume published by Granary Books in 2001.

A single long print block, *Soliloquy* (Goldsmith 2001a) is certainly a monster, if not a loose or baggy one. Indeed, the text is highly structured, the ground rule—that every word Goldsmith speaks, but not one word by his interlocutors or addressees, will be recorded and that periods of nontalking are not designated as such—creates a seamless and curiously dense language network, a kind of post-Jamesian novel, where we know only what the narrator knows and says. The "characters" in this novel—Goldsmith's friends, colleagues, associates, relatives, and assorted service people to whom he is speaking, as well as those others referred to in the third person—are given no voice; they can be known only through Goldsmith's interpretations.

Is he a reliable narrator? Of course not, but what can "reliable" mean in these cyberdays? To read *Soliloquy* is to infer what prompted question A or disclaimer B or irritated response C. How does the author adjust his speech habits to the different people in his life? And what is the significance of the constant self-interruption, self-cancellation, and self-deprecation that fills this fast, funny, irreverent, and terrifying volume? Terrifying, because, as Goldsmith himself has remarked, it is

humiliating and humbling seeing how little of "value" I actually speak over the course of a typical week. How unprofound my life and my mind is; how petty, greedy and nasty I am in my normal speech. It's absolutely horrifying. . . . But I dare any reader to try the same exercise and see how much more value they come up with in their life. I fear that they might discover, too, that their lives are filled with trivial linguistic exchanges with waiters and taxi drivers. Even those relationships we feel are so vital to our lives—our family and friends—in linguistic terms are really up for grabs. (Perloff 2003)

The genesis of a text such as *Soliloquy* clearly depends on digital technology as well as on advanced recording systems. Goldsmith's relatives, friends, and lunch companions (myself included) evidently had no idea he was wearing a wire and thus spoke quite freely. Yet their words had to be eliminated so as to keep to the rules of the chosen frame—one man's talk for seven days of the week. We think of talk as communal—an experience we share with others— but here the elimination of all those others creates a startling verbal scene. For unlike a real soliloquy or even dramatic monologue, the speech presented here is curiously decontextualized. We often have no idea whom the narrator is addressing, and that address may change within a split second as Kenny hangs up the phone and picks up another call with a "Hi, how're you doin'?" Furthermore, although his talking claims to be random, it is in fact carefully planned, the author setting up the questions and raising the issues that will resound throughout the day. Thus, although the text of *Soliloquy* does not exploit visual devices, computer graphics, animation, or anything else but stone cold sober print, and although there are no icons to click or dots to connect, *Soliloquy* is, in fact, the ultimate digitally driven text, programmed as it is to eliminate "noise."

Consider the following passage in Act 4 (Thursday), in which Kenny and his wife Cheryl (the video artist Cheryl Donegan) are having dinner in a local Indian restaurant:

Oh I didn't like that guy Alex that we met. The guy with the beard. He was an asshole. Did, you know, he never heard of Alfred Jarry. He goes Ubu? What's that. Yeah, you know, he never heard of any of that any connection with anything like that. Yeah. They did. Thank you. This food is so good. The crap they were serving up at that place for 20 bucks a plate. That was idiotic. The people in there, you know, it was a really stupid scene. I really gotta pee. OK. Ah, that's better. Is your chicken good? Tasty? No no no, it's alright. You like this red chicken? Hey, you know, you can't say we're not trying right. I know as if as if if being successful artists and writers isn't enough. Isn't it just amazing like all the work that we do to do our work and then all the work that we do to like try to do our work? It's insane, Cheryl, we're working two jobs. Yeah, no, I mean work is OK, but, you know, it's it's just, you know, you do what you do. No wonder why we are so fucking exhausted every night and every day. Well, I mean, it's insane. I don't know how long we'll keep it up for. It's like a lot of artists, you know, well they kind of like paint like they get like Debra they get into their studios once a week or something like that, do think about it much. The fact I, we're doing both things. See this is the cheese. This is paneer. This is what you eat in India all the fucking time. You had paneer? You've had it, right? Paneer this is what you eat. You like eat saag paneer like constantly. You constantly eating like on a plane you get saag paneer. Somebody's milk. I'm tired. I just need some down time I think, you know, like quiet time. When I, when did he say that Cheryl? Oh that's so long ago? Halil? Liz Kotz was so nice last night. We have so much in common, it's insane. She's doing her dissertation. It's funny, when you scratch the surface of people, man, everybody's got something to say. I think everybody's nice. You got to get past the surface. I mean whoever would have thought Liz Kotz was anything, you know, other than what she appears to be? Hardcore man-hater. She's so nice. No, I didn't get apprehensive (Goldsmith 2001a).

This passage allows the reader to be about as close to actually being there as is humanly possible in a retrospective situation. The conversation, or at least Kenny's side of it, is at once inane and meaningful—meaningful in the context of the rest of the book where Jarry's *Ubu Roi* and Kenny's own UbuWeb play a big part, where Cheryl's recent art show is discussed again and again, and where Liz Kotz, a critic of avant-garde art/music/poetry, now teaching at the University of Minnesota, then still a graduate student, first appears at a lecture of my own that Kenny attended the night before at Columbia University.

Goldsmith's "natural" language is nothing if not artificial. The text provides us with all the normal tics of conversation—the prevalence of "like," "you know," and "yeah yeah," as well as the incompletion of sentences, sloppy phraseology, and repetitive exclamations. But it is also artificial in that it splices together all instances of speech, omitting the silences and interruptions. Thus "I really gotta pee" is immediately followed by "OK. Ah, that's better," there having been nothing said in the minutes that elapse between going to the bathroom and returning to the table. The absence of breaks here and when Kenny is addressing the waiter as in "[t]hey did [take our order?]. Thank you," creates a monomaniacal drive as absurd and absorbing as Leopold Bloom's stream of consciousness in the "Lotus Eaters" chapter of *Ulysses*. For the continuity stands in odd relationship to the constant shift in subject matter—the digression from the talk of the red chicken to the serious and somewhat maudlin reflection on "our lives" and how we "overwork" and are "underappreciated." Not that Kenny doesn't mean it. But next thing you know, he's telling Cheryl all about paneer cheese and how it's served in India. Then Liz Kotz's personality is put to the test, Kenny liking her despite her appearing to be a hard-core man-hater. Life, this text suggests, is like that: we grumble about our fates until the cheese course comes, and then we try to decide which to sample.

The artifice of *Soliloquy*'s "random" and "casual" writing becomes clearer if we bear in mind that we have no access to the narrator's unspoken thoughts, his physical movements, his reading, his looking at art, his daydreaming. Here, the book suggests, is what life would be like if human beings could do nothing but *talk*! The electronic version (Goldsmith 2001b), on the other hand, calls that talk into question. It contains the entire book in seven sections, one for each day of the week, but when one accesses a given page or section, only bits of sentences appear on an otherwise empty screen. We soon discover that text is actually *there,* but it is hidden: unless the mouse is pointed directly at a given word or sentence, it remains invisible. The mouse can obviously track the text word-by-word, sentence-by-sentence, but only one bit at a time, so that the reader, pointing at a particular phrase, doesn't know what comes before or after. Accordingly, the cybertext becomes an inverted Cagean writing-through, a form of play. Find one sentence and another vanishes.

Sentences and phrases are thus fragmented and hidden, creating a conscious discontinuity in the interface. In this manner, the "cinema verité" quality of the book version is called into question: if the "talk" in the book version looks "natural," in the electronic text, the emphasis is on loss and disruption— on a curious kind of secrecy, as if the text doesn't quite want to be read. Goldsmith's is not, we should note, the nonsequentiality of Ron Silliman's "New Sentence" but rather a dialectic of appearance and disappearance, absence and presence.

What makes a generative text such as *Soliloquy* poetic? Isn't producing such a monster just a matter of following certain rules and using certain computer operations to eliminate the language of others, the pauses and silences? Couldn't anyone do it?

There are two answers to this last question. The first is Cage's "Of course they could, but they don't" ([1958] 1973, 72)—the willingness to *engage* in such a project and putting oneself on the line being half the battle. But—and this is true of Cage as well—the fact is that when one studies Goldsmith's text, one quickly finds that it is much more structured than one might think. For it builds up, metonymically and synecdochically, a network of references that gives us a very particular portrait of the artist as young hustler: a New York artist, dependent on New York, running around the city, talking on his cell phone, making contacts, networking, eating out, trying different foods, meeting people for coffee, running into old acquaintances at all sorts of art galleries and events. How to make it through the day: this is half the battle, but the narrator remains for the most part cheerful and purposive in his demeanor. The "Kenny" of this book is not necessarily a nice man—he's a user, and he knows it, and he also loves to gossip and lampoon people—but he is remarkably candid and honest with himself. And that draws the reader —even a suspicious reader such as myself, who did not originally enjoy my "portrait" in this book—into the linguistic web.

Are Goldsmith, Bergvall, and Stefans electronic poets? Yes and no. Certainly, in the examples given, these artists make the most of digital possibilities. But they shift medium easily: Goldsmith has collaborated with Joan La Barbara in producing verbal/musical texts and has made many installations; Bergvall has fused poetic material with theoretical analysis (in ordinary print format), made installations, worked with musicians, and so on. Her *Goan Atom* (2001c) is, first and foremost, a book of "poems." And Stefans has recently published a book called *Fashionable Noise: On Digital Poetics* (2003), bringing together interviews, lyric poems, and prose "essays" that boast traditional bibliographies of the scholarly model with which we are all too familiar.

In evaluating electronic poetries, therefore, we should not subordinate the second term to the first. "I don't like the label 'video artist,'" the great video artist Bill Viola once remarked. "I consider myself to be an artist. I happen to use video because I live in the last part of the twentieth century, and the medium of video (or television) is clearly the most relevant visual art form in contemporary life" ([1985] 1995b, 152). That was in 1985, and a decade or so later, video has been supplanted by the much greater fluidity and temporal-spatial freedom of electronic space. But Viola's principle holds: the artist or poet uses a particular medium not because it is "better" than others but because it seems most relevant at his or her moment—currently, of course, the electronic screen, with its particular enticing challenge to the printed book. Does this make the poet in question a digital poet? Or, conversely, is the purveyor of the electronic word ipso facto an artist? "Chopsticks," Viola quipped, "can either be a simple eating utensil or a deadly weapon, depending on who uses them" ([1981] 1995a, 71).

Notes

1. The black parenthetical "o's" are used here to simulate the click circles for the connection to http://listserv.acsu.buffalo.edu/cgi-bin/wa?A2=ind0009&L=poetics&D=1&O=D&F=P&S=&P=53149.

2. This piece appeared on the SUNY Buffalo Poetics Discussion Group, September 30, 2000.

3. http://www.ubu.com/contemp/stefans/dream/the_dreamlife_poem.htm.

4. For online selections from *Carnival*, see http://www.chbooks.com/tech/search.cgi.

5. See also Manovich 2001a.

6. Bergvall provided helpful comments in an email to the author, September 9, 2002.

7. In book form, "Flèsh" has only small portions of this text; but the whole piece (though with variations) is found in Bergvall 2001b.

Works Cited

Bergvall, Caroline. 1999. *ambient fish*. http://epc.buffalo.edu/authors/bergvall/amfish/ amfish.html (accessed June 29, 2004).

Bergvall, Caroline. 2001a. "Flèsh." *How2* 1.5 (March). http://www.scc.rutgers.edu/ however/v1_5_2001/current/new-writing/bergvall/index.html (accessed June 29, 2004).

Bergvall, Caroline. 2001b. "Flèsh" [print form]. In *Foil: Defining Poetry 1985–2000*, ed. Nicholas Johnson, 84–91. London: Etruscan.

Bergvall, Caroline. 2001c. *Goan Atom*. San Francisco: Krupskaya.

Bergvall, Caroline. 2001d. "Notes to 'Flèsh.'" *How2* 1.5 (March). http://www.scc .rutgers.edu/however/v1_5_2001/current/new-writing/bergvall/index.html (accessed June 29, 2004).

Bergvall, Caroline. 2003. Email to Marjorie Perloff, January 13.

Bürger, Peter. 1984. *Theory of the Avant-Garde*. Trans. Michael Shaw. Minneapolis: University of Minnesota Press.

Cage, John. [1958] 1973. "History of Experimental Music in the United States." *Silence*, 67–75. Middletown, CT: Wesleyan University Press.

Dworkin, Craig, ed. 2003. *The UbuWeb Anthology of Conceptual Writing*. http://www.ubu.com/concept/ (accessed June 29, 2004).

Futurism and Futurists. http://www.futurism.org.uk/ (accessed June 29, 2004).

Goldsmith, Kenneth. 1999. *Fidget* [electronic version]. http://www.chbooks.com/ online/fidget/index.html (accessed June 29, 2004).

Goldsmith, Kenneth. 2001a. *Soliloquy.* New York: Granary Books.

Goldsmith, Kenneth. 2001b. *Soliloquy* [electronic version]. http://www.epc.buffalo .edu/authors/goldsmith/soliloquy/index.html (accessed June 29, 2003).

Goldsmith, Kenneth, ed. UbuWeb. http://www.ubu.com (June 29, 2004).

Manovich, Lev. 2001a. *The Language of New Media.* Cambridge, MA: MIT Press.

Manovich, Lev. 2001b. "Post-Media Aesthetics." http://www.manovich.net/ (accessed June 29, 2004).

McCaffery, Steve. 1973. *Carnival: The First Panel*, 1967–1970. Toronto: Coach House Books.

Perloff, Marjorie. 2002a. "'ex/Crème/ental/eaT/ing': An Interview with Caroline Bergvall." *Sources: Revue d'études Anglophones* 12 (Spring): 123–135.

Perloff, Marjorie. 2002b. "'Vocable Scriptsigns': Differential Poetics in Kenneth Goldsmith's *Fidget* and John Kinsella's *Kangaroo Virus*." In *Poetry and Contemporary Culture: The Question of Value*, ed. Andrew Roberts and John Allison, 21–43. Edinburgh, Scotland: Edinburgh University Press.

Perloff, Marjorie. 2003. "A Conversation with Kenneth Goldsmith." *Jacket*, issue 21 (February). http://jacketmagazine.com/21/perl-gold-iv.html (accessed June 29, 2004).

Pound, Ezra. 1960. *ABC of Reading*. New York: New Directions.

Stefans, Brian Kim. 1999. *the dreamlife of letters*. http://www.ubu.com/contemp/stefans/dream (accessed October 2002).

Stefans, Brian Kim. 2003. *Fashionable Noise: On Digital Poetics*. Berkeley, CA: Atelos.

Tzara, Tristan. 1981. "Note on Poetry." In *Seven Dada Manifestos and Lampisteries*, 75–78. New York: Riverrun Press.

Viola, Bill. [1981] 1995a. "The Porcupine and the Car." In *Reasons for Knocking at an Empty House: Writings 1973–1984,* ed. Robert Violette, 59–72. Cambridge, MA: MIT Press.

Viola, Bill. [1985] 1995b. "Statements 1985." In *Reasons for Knocking at an Empty House: Writings 1973–1984,* ed. Robert Violette, 149–152. Cambridge, MA: MIT Press.

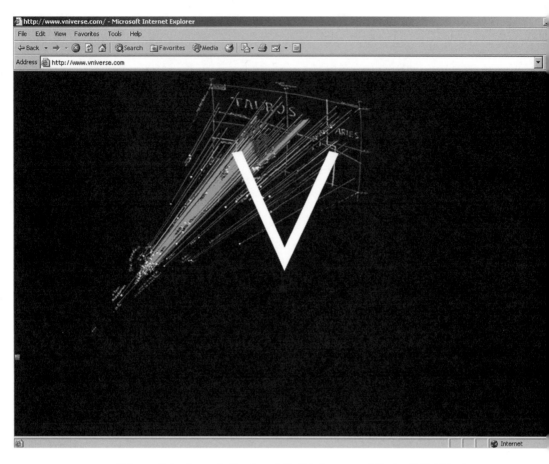

Vniverse. Entry Screen 1. Courtesy of Cynthia Lawson and Stephanie Strickland.

Vniverse

Stephanie Strickland and Cynthia Lawson

Introduction

Vniverse is part of a larger poem, *V* (chapter frontispiece on p. 164 and figure 8.1). In print, *V: WaveSon.nets/Losing L'una* is begun and proceeds, only to be inverted and begun again from the other direction. Read either way, one does not come to an end but rather to the Vniverse URL: http://vniverse.com.

In creating *V*, Strickland had a formal interest in how the sonnet is rethought as a poetic form in the twenty-first century. Historically, a sonnet shows the mind in action, turning recursively to talk to itself, anticipating an irreversible change. This anticipated change is reflected in the structural "turn" of the sonnet, the so-called volta. The volta itself takes a new turn as *V* turns into cyberspace.

By extending *V* into Vniverse, we intentionally turned a long poem away from print and into an interactive medium in order to explore our emerging vision of how reading is remade and text transformed online.

Reading the Digital Text

Our current interface creates multiple reading possibilities that go beyond print.[1] For instance, a see/read difference comes into play with all texts that are both visual and verbal. Skills for visual reading include, but go beyond, knowing how to read images. To keep the effect of these skills focused,

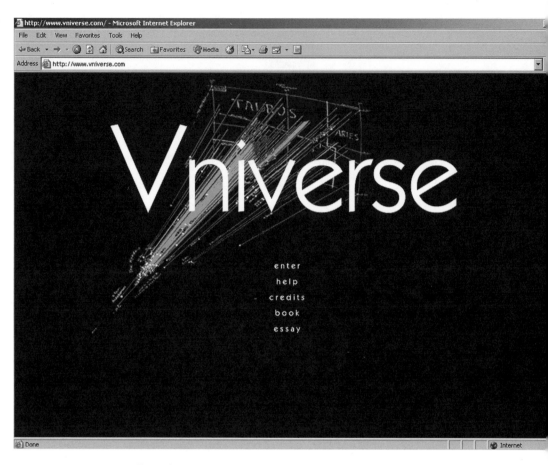

Figure 8.1 Vniverse. Entry Screen 2. Courtesy of Cynthia Lawson and
Stephanie Strickland.

we chose to use only diagrams, bright points, sparsely colored words, and darkness as visual elements.

Even as Blake's poems explored the see/read difference in print, the work of digital poets tests new possibilities. In "Barrier Frames," for example, Jim Rosenberg "overlays his texts in a dense blur of self-interfering micro-information, a tangle literally drawn apart by hand into legible text" (Strickland 2006). In her Mezangelle constructions, the poet Mez (Mary Anne Breeze) leads us to read not only as if simultaneously honoring both text and code conventions but also as if reading a picture plane in every possible direction.[2]

More recently, Johanna Drucker and the Speculative Computing group at the University of Virginia have explored the materiality of time by doing temporal modeling for humanities computing.[3] In this exploration, they have created features such as "stretchy timelines" and a "now-slider" as parts of the "time-based visualization tool for the humanities" (Drucker and Nowviskie 2003b) with which they are addressing the role of visual metaphors and temporal relations in research and pedagogy. Modifiable temporal relations raise the same issues that John Cayley does when he notes in chapter 16 that the unit of signification in his poetry includes the time required to run the code and all the transitions that occur in that time.

A central question is how one's memory of text is affected when various timescales operate simultaneously. We probe this question both in the palimpsestic decay of our texts and in the 232 ways to initiate a WaveSon.net online. Readers who click the Vniverse Next button are presented with multiple reading opportunities that include implicit timescales. They can continue to read text that is now decaying or read text slowly emerging onscreen or read in between the dissolving and emergent layers or supplement any of the above with new text uncovered by sliding the cursor over the sky (figures 8.2, 8.3, and 8.4).

Interactive reading usually exists as a two-way communication. When users/readers understand how to interact with the machine, perform an action, and see a result, they establish a mental relationship and can continue to engage. Vniverse presents such an interactive interface, and yet our interest was not so much in the immediacy of the relationships the reader establishes as in the invitation to explore and prolong this initial relating. Thus Vniverse does not have animated rollovers to indicate when an area is "hot." Its buttons don't have labels, nor does a reader hear sound effects for

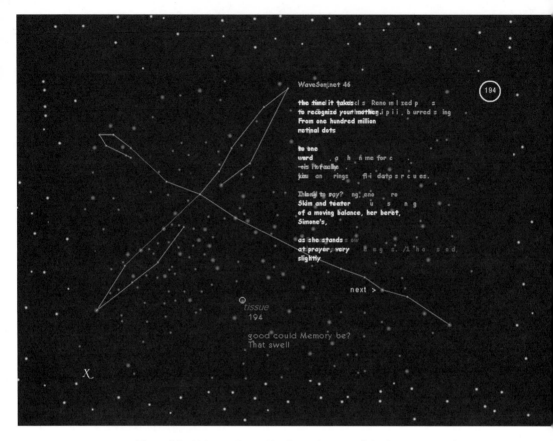

Figure 8.2　Vniverse. Decay Dissolve 1. Courtesy of Cynthia Lawson and
Stephanie Strickland.

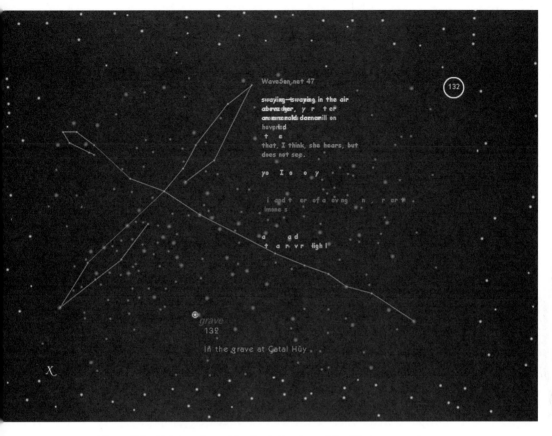

Figure 8.3 Vniverse. Decay Dissolve 2. Courtesy of Cynthia Lawson and Stephanie Strickland.

Figure 8.4 Vniverse. Slide Dissolve. Courtesy of Cynthia Lawson and Stephanie Strickland.

immediate feedback. In particular, it has *no* clickable words. Instead, it uses other interactive devices for readers who will take the time to notice and engage. For instance, the cursor slightly blinks to indicate that something can be clicked. Sometimes, as with one click on a star, readers won't see an immediate change unless they move the mouse off that star and thus notice that the constellation is held in the sky (figures 8.5, 8.6, and 8.7).

The actions we ask of the user are not generally asked of a digital reader. We reward sweeping the cursor randomly, both lingering on a star and moving off it, tracing without clicking, and also persistently clicking in the same spot. The latter yields the most complex and subtle changes: each poem is shown to exist in, and between, two oscillating states, a Son.net and a set of five triplets (figures 8.8 and 8.9). The reader may analogize cursor motions with behaviors in the gravitational world—such as waving, swinging, sweeping, tracing, and lingering. These actions are rarely found in interactive screen-based environments, which tend to rely on clicking or on motions found in gaming environments, such as rapid-fire shooting.

Transforming the Digital Text

In ongoing iterations of Vniverse, we are exploring our second point of focus, how text is transformed. Here we engage the computing machine as a second interactor. Not only is the human reader interacting with the interface but the machine, as a second reader, is responding to these interactions by creating actions of its own.

The first transformation involves programming that randomly associates any other four triplets to the one chosen by the reader. If the reader chooses triplet 7 and the computer chooses 9, 91, 231, and 85, then the assembled poem would be titled WS 7.9.91.231.85, which would toggle to the triplet set titled 7.9.91.231.85. If one of the preexisting WaveSon.nets happened to occur, it would be called by its name, WaveSon.net 32, for instance. The reader can thus release WaveSon.nets never seen in print and perhaps never to be seen again. Other variants would allow readers to input any word from the poem and assemble triplets based on those choices.

Our second transformation involves overlaying a sonic Vniverse on the visual one. Sound can exist as a response to a specific interaction, where, as with the triplet choices, the computer could be programmed to build a sound-space according to how a reader is exploring the interface. But it can also exist

WaveSon.net 13

there would be no tomorrow.
She craves that drift.
But this is her
primordial

task, to keep time, to serve it, an order
learned from the water bird
who makes a 3-prong
Y print

in the sand, echoed each time she stands
in trembling waves.
A cast
shadow, a thrown reflection,

and a subtly bent refraction
where the water meets the sky
and the land, 3 axes, and a mapping,

who makes a 3-prong
Y print
in the sand, echoed each time she stands

Figure 8.5 Vniverse. Blinking Cursor on Star 63. Courtesy of Cynthia Lawson and
Stephanie Strickland.

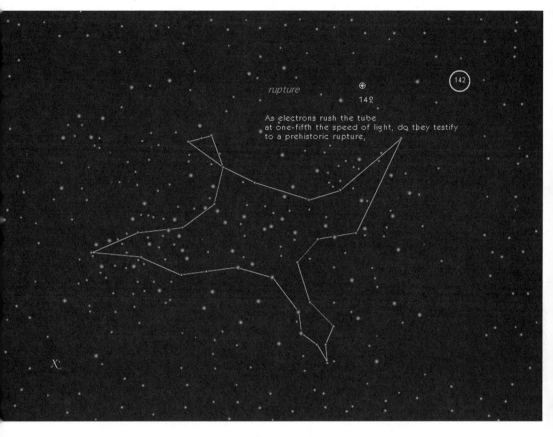

Figure 8.6   Vniverse. Goose Constellation. Courtesy of Cynthia Lawson and
Stephanie Strickland.

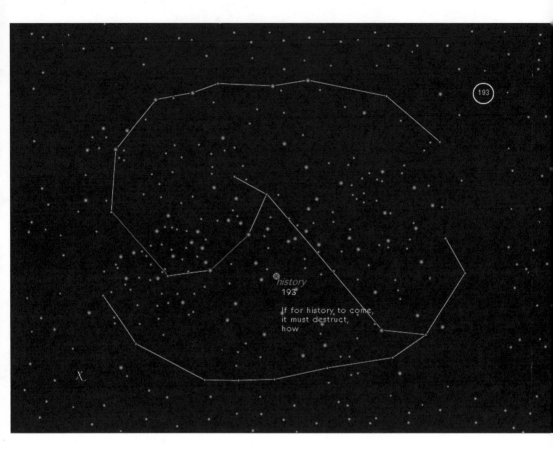

Figure 8.7 Vniverse. Fetus Constellation. Courtesy of Cynthia Lawson and Stephanie Strickland.

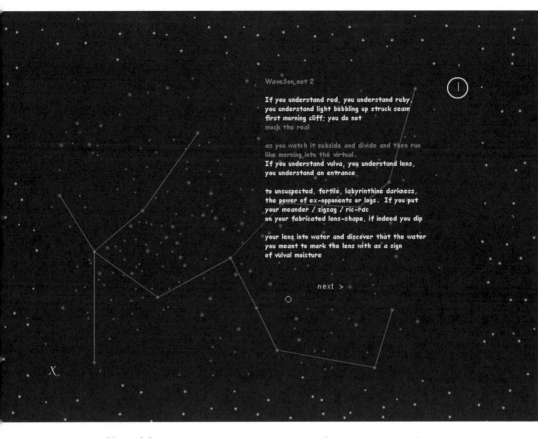

Figure 8.8   Vniverse. WaveSon.net 2. Courtesy of Cynthia Lawson and
Stephanie Strickland.

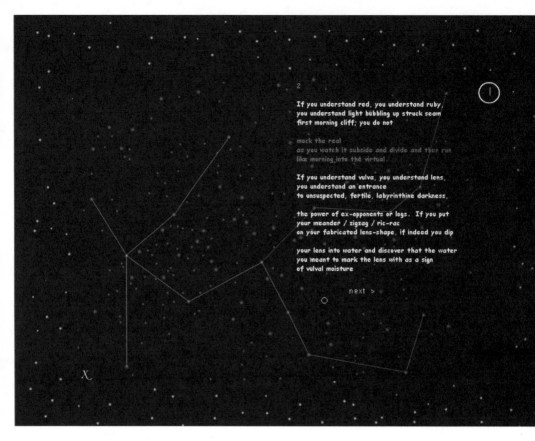

2

If you understand red, you understand ruby,
you understand light bubbling up struck seam
first morning cliff; you do not

mock the real
as you watch it subside and divide and then run
like morning into the virtual.

If you understand vulva, you understand lens,
you understand an entrance
to unsuspected, fertile, labyrinthine darkness,

the power of ex-opponents or logs. If you put
your meander / zigzag / ric-rac
on your fabricated lens-shape, if indeed you dip

your lens into water and discover that the water
you meant to mark the lens with as a sign
of vulval moisture

next >

Figure 8.9 Vniverse. 2 Triplets. Courtesy of Cynthia Lawson and Stephanie Strickland.

as an "organic" element, a parallel player, programmed so that it seems to have a life of its own, entering, layering, fading, and staying silent as a background to the reader's choices. This latter mode is the one we prefer, and the sounds we are considering are readings of the triplets by us, by the machine, or by a variety of voices.

Social Reading Spaces

Reading is usually seen as a solitary activity. In our performance/ electronic reading of Vniverse, we are taking a first step into what we call "social reading spaces." When we perform, interact with, and read from the site, the audience is also reading while being in a social space. However, we do not read it *as* they do. We read selected elements from the screen, reading "partially" and "out of order," overlapping our voices.

We think performing new media poetry is important because it encourages conversation and questions. Our own creative process is an initial model for this interaction. Though we differ in age, nationality, native language, and training (poet, engineer), we elaborated a common language and aesthetic as we sat together physically in front of the screen. Image processing, interface design, screen design, and timing of dis/appearance are all aspects that needed to be imagined, agreed upon, implemented, tested by us and others, and then rethought. Screen-based media simultaneously give access to great riches and impose great poverty. How verbal text engages this reality is something that concerns us both, and neither one of us feels that a true exploration would be possible without the other, indeed without many others.

During our performances, we largely control the text the audience is seeing. What would happen if there were shared control? The possibility of not only social but *collaborative* reading space is something we consider when thinking of Vniverse as an installation or a screen-based multiuser environment.

Current users of immersive spaces are not accustomed to using them for reading,[4] but they are accustomed to using them for exploring. We want to create an experience of exploratory reading in a gallery setting, where the triggered Vniverse constellations can be mirrored in water or Mylar on the floor and where curtains of steel mesh catch and hold the projections. An echoing three-dimensional space of constellations and keywords could, at certain points, give rise to heard readings of the WaveSon.nets and triplets. In this environment, the "triggers" are accessed by all visitors, enabling a shared interaction determined by their joint choices.

By contrast, a multiuser Vniverse would exist as an interactive online environment where what is seen/read/heard depends on how many readers are visiting at once, an environment where readers communicate with others who are logged in. All interactions with the interface would affect one central sky, as opposed to multiple instances of one Web page, creating once again a shared reading experience, but one different from performance or installation.

Conclusion

On paper, the WaveSon.nets form one long-standing wave that runs across the borders of their number names and the mirroring page numbers. The energetic turns, the crests in this wave, are not aligned with either the beginnings or ends of the individual WaveSon.nets, though each page is a WaveSon.net unit with its own shape, functioning as a poem on a different scale from the long wave. Waves of different scale are created online, among them the unrolling of the triplets, the successive dis/appearances of constellations, and the refreshing of the screen.

While we believe that our piece is absorbing to explore alone, we know that particular pleasures and meanings are created when people experience it in each other's company. We want to reach out to readers by providing a place where their own motions will make new waves for coreaders and coplayers, a place where they can become part of a performatory/interpretive public space. In such a space, readers could experience for themselves how the sociality of reading affects reading choices and outcomes.

Notes

1. See Strickland and Lawson 2004.

2. For examples, see Mez's digital work at http://www.hotkey.net.au/~netwurker. See also her online essay "The Art of M[ez]ang.elle.ing" (Mez 2000)

3. See Drucker and Nowviskie 2003a.

4. A rare example of immersive text exploration is Wardrip-Fruin 2003, written for a Virtual Reality CAVE installation at Brown University in spring 2003.

Stephanie Strickland and Cynthia Lawson

Works Cited

Drucker, Johanna, and Bethany Nowviskie. 2003a. "Temporal Modelling." In *ALLC/ACH Conference Abstracts 2003*, ed. Eric Rochester and William A. Kretzschmar, Jr. Handout at ALLC/ACH Joint International Conference, May 29–June 2, University of Georgia, Athens.

Drucker, Johanna, and Bethany Nowviskie. 2003b. "Temporal Modelling Project: Storyboard." http://www.iath.virginia.edu/time/storyboard/orig.html (accessed June 27, 2004).

Mez [Mary Anne Breeze]. 2000. "The Art of M[ez]ang.elle.ing: Constructing Polysemic & Neology Fic/Factions Online." *BeeHive Hypertext/Hypermedia Literary Journal*. http://beehive.temporalimage.com/archive/34arc.html. (accessed June 27, 2004).

Rosenberg, Jim. 1996. "Barrier Frames." *Eastgate Quarterly Review of Hypertext* 2.3. http://www.well.com/user/jer/j/barrier_frames_4.html (accessed June 27, 2004).

Strickland, Stephanie. 2002. *V: WaveSon.nets/Losing L'una*. New York: Penguin.

Strickland, Stephanie. 2006. "Quantum Poetics: Six Thoughts." Forthcoming in *Media Poetry: Poetic Innovation and New Technologies*, ed. Eduardo Kac. Bristol, UK: Intellect Press.

Strickland, Stephanie, and Cynthia Lawson. 2004. "Making the Vniverse." http://vniverse.com/essay (accessed June 27, 2004).

Wardrip-Fruin, Noah. 2003. "Screen." *The Iowa Review Web*. http://www.uiowa.edu/~iareview/tirweb/feature/cave/index.html (accessed June 27, 2004).

The Time of Digital Poetry: From Object to Event

N. Katherine Hayles

Displayed in space, print poetry also has a temporal dimension that writers have traditionally brought out through devices such as punctuation, line breaks, spacing between and within words, font type and size, and white space, as well as through unusual and innovative procedures too numerous to list here. Until recently, however, these were passive devices, unchangeable once they were durably inscribed as ink on paper. With the advent of digital technology, writers have more flexibility in how they can employ the temporal dimension as resources in their writing practices. To explore some of these practices, I propose thinking about the digital poem, paraphrasing William Carlos Williams, as a machine to organize time. Inevitably, space is also involved in this production, but by keeping the focus on time, I hope to bring out characteristics of digital poetry that, while acknowledging continuities with print poetry, also suggest new directions theory can take in accounting for the operation of these poem-machines. To explore these complexities I will take as my tutor texts John Cayley's *riverIsland* and Stephanie Strickland's Web poem V: Vniverse (Strickland and Lawson 2003) with its companion print book, *V: WaveSon.nets/Losing L'una* (Strickland 2002).

These works are especially appropriate because they reflect on the materiality of their production. In digital media, the poem has a distributed existence spread among data files and commands, software that executes the commands, and hardware on which the software runs. These digital characteristics imply that the poem ceases to exist as a self-contained object and instead becomes a *process*, an event brought into existence when the program runs on the appropriate software loaded onto the right hardware. The poem is "eventilized," made more an event and less a discrete, self-contained object with clear boundaries in space and time. Any inscription in digital media is transformed into an event regardless of its content, for the nature of information as "a difference that makes a difference," as Gregory Bateson (1979) defined it, automatically introduces a temporal dimension into texts that may have previously been considered static objects (459). Electronic literature can exploit these characteristics, intensifying their effects through reflexive strategies that use the processual nature of electronic texts to create aesthetic experiences unique to digital media.

A case in point is Cayley's *riverIsland*, which uses its organization of time to explore its conditions of production and the ways in which these conditions affect the process of reading. The poem organizes time, this temporal organization helps to produce the poem as an informational event, and the conceptual structure of the poem reflects (upon) the organization of time that has produced it. At the same time (or as we shall see, a different time), print poetry has potent resources of its own to organize time. Strickland's *V* is an appropriate work to explore the differences and similarities between print and electronic temporal structures, for it is, Strickland maintains, the first collection of poems to exist as an integrated work in both media. Similar to *riverIsland*, *V* deeply interweaves its meditations on time with its artistic practices, producing temporal flows through performances that simultaneously enact themselves as events unfolding in two media and reflect on their performances in these different media.

What does it mean to say that the poem is a machine that organizes time? The time of a poem can be considered to consist of the time of writing, the time of coding, the time of production/performance, and the time of reading. While both print and electronic poetry evolve within this general temporal flow, they organize it differently. Consider first the time of writing and the time of coding. With print, writing and coding often coincide and become virtually the same activity from the author's point of view, particularly when the coding is conceived as a trivial exercise of converting words into the appropriate alphabetic symbols. In days past, when the print writer banged on his typewriter, he wrote and coded simultaneously as a single cognitive-muscular activity. Of course, if we enlarge the viewpoint to include the process of transforming the typescript into a print book, the time of coding expands to include typesetting and other processes necessary to produce the book. With significant exceptions that include artist's books, mimeo poetry, and other experimental practices, the author was not usually deeply involved with these activities, which were considered to be the responsibility of the publisher. With electronic poetry, by contrast, writing and coding become distinct and often temporally separated events. If the poet is collaborating with programmers, sound artists, graphic designers, and so on, to create a multimodal work, the temporal division into writing and coding corresponds to a distribution of intellectual labor that can involve quite distinct time sequences. Even if the poet is doing all the design work herself, many writers coming from the print tradition compose the words first and then decide on behaviors, animation, colors, layers, and other factors that go into creating the final work as it will be performed by coding instructions running on the appropriate machine. (I will call these instructions "active code" to distinguish it from the passive codes that serve as instructions to the reader in print and digital media, such as paragraph indentations, italics, etc.[1])

The importance of active code to the production of digital texts cannot be overemphasized; it is one of the distinctive ways in which electronic literature differs from print.[2] The fact that all texts performed in digital media are coded implies that reader and writer functions are always multiple and include actions performed by human and nonhuman agents. The machine reads and writes, as well as the programmers who compose its coded instructions, the writers who use these programs to create artistic works, and the users who employ "reveal code" functionalities to understand the instructions that perform the text as it appears on screen. Working in these multilayered environments, readers and, even more so, writers develop a nuanced sense of code as a form of writing with its own stylistic elegances and formal possibilities.

Increasingly, writers of electronic literature view code as a resource for signifying practices. Reviewing some of this work, Loss Pequeño Glazier, a distinguished writer of digital poetry as well as a critic, observes that programming *is* writing (2002, 96–125), a point also made by John Cayley (1998a) in "Of Programmatology" (72–75). Glazier argues that users who want to understand how a digital text works cannot afford simply to stay at the surface level of the screenic text, any more than a writer can afford to know nothing about how screenic text is generated and displayed. Agreeing with Jerome McGann that the defining characteristic of literary language is the impulse to investigate its conditions of possibility, he names literary writing as "writing that, whether or not it serves other ends, has an engagement with its own formal qualities" (54). He sees print and electronic text on a continuum, arguing that "innovative literature" in both media "has explored the conditions that determine . . . the procedures, processes, and crossed paths of meaning-making, meaning-making as constituting the 'meaning'" (32). As Glazier points out, print writers have also explored the materiality of the medium, from the typewriter poems of Ian Hamilton Finlay to the mimeo movement and concrete poetry. The specificity of digital media, he implies, lies in its distinctive materiality: "materiality is key to understanding innovative practice" (22).

The materiality of digital text increases the writer's sense that writing is not merely the fashioning of a verbal abstraction but a concrete act of making, a production that involves manual manipulation, proprioceptive projection, kinesthetic involvement, and other physical senses. M. D. Coverley highlights this aspect of electronic writing when she asks us to consider the print poet who types a line of poetry and sits back, satisfied. As far as that line is concerned, he considers his work done. Compare this to the same line typed by an electronic author. In addition to considering the effects of the words, this author must also decide the background on which the words will appear, the behaviors that will attach to it, the color, size, and type of font in which it will appear, whether it will have links anchored to it or not, and a host of other factors that the digital medium makes possible (email message to N. Katherine Hayles, November 20, 2003).

The time of production/performance is also parsed differently for print and digital media. By production/performance, I mean the processes that make the work materially accessible to the reader. For print, these processes normally take place at a location and time remote from when the reader holds the book in her hands, for example, when the printing presses are rolling and the signatures are being bound. Because the reader receives the book as an object already made, the material processes that created it can appropriately be called "production," a term implying that its creation as an artifactual object has already taken place. In addition, the book's premade nature allows the storage and delivery functions to coalesce into the same vehicle, with the important consequence that the physical form of the text remains the same when it is delivered as when it is stored. Once the book is produced, its material structure does not change, or rather changes very slowly as foxing appears, acid paper deteriorates, ink fades, and so forth. This stability has the advantage of making the object durably robust and remarkably reliable. Every time the book is opened (i.e., shifted from its storage function to delivery), it offers the pleasurable expectation that the same words will appear in the same format, colors, and spatial distribution as every other time.

With digital texts, by contrast, the data files may be on one server and the machine creating the display may be in another location entirely. This means that a digital text exists as a distributed phenomenon. The dispersion introduces many possible sources of variation into the production of electronic text that do not exist in the same way with print, for example, when a user's browser displays a text with different colors than those the writer saw on her machine when she was creating it. More fundamental is the fact that the text exists in dispersed fashion even when it is confined to a single machine. There are data files, programs that call and process the files, hardware functionalities that interpret or compile the programs, and so on. It takes all of these together to perform the digital text. Omit any one of them, and the text literally cannot be performed as something the reader can use. Certainly it cannot be identified with, say, a diskette or a CD-ROM, for these alone could never produce the text unless they are performed by the appropriate software running on the appropriate hardware. For this reason, it would be more accurate to call a digital text a *process* rather than an object, an attribute I highlight by referring to the time of *performance* for an electronic text versus the time of *production* for print.

Because it is a frequent point of confusion, let me emphasize that this material performance is necessarily prior to whatever cognitive processing the user performs to read and interpret the text. Although print readers perform sophisticated cognitive operations when they read a book, the printed lines exist as such before the book is opened, read, or understood. A digital text does not have this kind of prior existence. It does not exist anywhere in the computer or in the networked system in the precise form it acquires when displayed on screen. After it is displayed, of course, the same kind of readerly processing may occur as with print. But we should not indulge in the logical confusion created by eliding the creation of the display—a process that happens only when the programs that create the text are activated—with the reader's cognitive processing. In this sense, digital text is more processual than print; it is performative by its very nature, independent of whatever imaginations and processes the user brings to it.

The duration of this performance is, moreover, constituted through multiple parallel causalities. Consider, for example, the time an image takes to

The Time of Digital Poetry

appear on screen when files are drawn from a remote server. The time lag is an important component of digital text, for it determines in what order the user will view the material. Indeed, as anyone who has grown impatient with long load times knows, in many instances, it determines whether the user will see the image at all. These times are difficult to predict precisely because they depend on the individual computer's processing speed, traffic on the Web, efficiency of data distribution on the hard drive, and other imponderables. This aspect of digital textuality—along with many others—*cannot be separated from the delivery vehicles that produce it as a process with which the user can interact.* Moreover, for networked texts these vehicles are never the same twice, for they exist in momentary configurations as data packets are switched very quickly from one node to another, depending on the traffic at the instant of transfer. In this respect and many others, digital texts are never self-identical. As processes, they exhibit sensitive dependence on temporal and spatial contexts, to say nothing of their absolute dependence on specific hardware and software configurations.

This lack of self-identity rests on different grounds than those instanced by Jacques Derrida (1988) when he argues that texts are not self-identical because "[e]very sign . . . can be *cited*, put between quotation marks; in so doing it can break with every given context, engendering an infinity of new contexts in a manner which is absolutely illimitable" (12). In this view, the reader is like a Greek philosopher who can never step into the same river twice; even when the words remain the same, they constitute a different readerly experience because they occur within different temporal, historical, and inter-textual contexts.

For digital texts, the issue begins with the material performance of the text. It is true that print texts also are affected by their conditions of production; a printing press with a defective letter *e*, let us say, will produce different artifacts than a press without this defect. Yet once the artifact is created, it remains (relatively) the same. With digital texts, changes of some kind happen virtually every time the text is performed, from small differences in timing to major glitches when a suddenly obsolete program tries to run on a platform that has not maintained backward compatibility.

What are the consequences of admitting an idea of textuality that is dispersed rather than unitary, processual rather than object-like, flickering rather than durably inscribed, always differing from itself rather than reproducing itself as a stable entity? An obvious result is the highlighting of

N. Katherine Hayles

the temporal dimension, inviting experiments that play with the flickering indeterminacies of digital texts. Moreover, with texts that allow some degree of interactivity, reading also becomes a performance in a more kinesthetically complex and vivid sense than is the case with reading print texts. The machine produces the text as an event; the reader interacts with that event in ways that significantly modify and even determine its progress; these readerly interventions feed back into the machine to change its behavior, which further inflects the course of the performance. Less an object than an event, the digital text emerges as a dance between artificial and human intelligences, machine and natural languages, as these evolve together through time.

Strickland's *V* illustrates how print texts, as they engage in a dynamic media ecology that includes digital media, respond by exploiting the resources of print to create related but distinct indeterminacies of their own. Precisely because a print book (usually) consists of planar surfaces bound in an unchanging order, it opens multiple possibilities for spatial organizations and numbering schemes that play with and against the linear page order, inviting the reader to reorganize the work by conceptualizing it as multiple interpenetrating structures, each offering possibilities for interpretation different from the others.[3] Although these structures occupy the same space, they organize it differently and thereby create mutating patterns of signification. Translated into a digital medium, *V*'s line sequences reorganize yet again, using the flexibility offered by appearing and disappearing text to create a possibility-space even greater than the print book. When read alongside each other, the print and electronic texts offer a remarkably rich matrix in which to explore the varying dynamics of freedom and constraint produced/performed by durable marks and flickering signifiers.

In the present intellectual climate—when some critics are proclaiming the end of books, and others are calling electronic literature "claptrap"—it is important to insist that print and electronic literature have different qualities without immediately privileging one over the other. In comparing and contrasting how electronic and print media conceive of poetry as an event rather than an object, I hope to show that both print and digital media offer potent resources, while being clear about how these resources differ. Print cannot do everything that digital texts can, just as digital texts will never have all the advantages that print offers—not better or worse, but undeniably different.

Temporality and the Literal Art of *riverIsland*

Exploring the processual nature of electronic texts, Cayley's *riverIsland* (2002a) performs time as a variable continuum rather than an evenly spaced linear sequence. The work is conceptualized as consisting of two loops of poems, one horizontal and one vertical. The horizontal loop contains sixteen quatrains adapted from the twenty poems of Wang Wei's famous "Wang River" sequence (written in the eighth century) and translated from the Chinese into English by Cayley. The poems display as letters on the screen and the sound of the poems being read. At the bottom of the screen is a QuickTime movie of flowing water. The user can navigate the loop by grabbing the movie and moving it to the right or left to go to the next poem in the cycle or by using the navigational icon. As the user leaves one node to travel to the next, the sound of the first poem overlaps with the sound of the second as the letters of the first text morph into the letters of the second. When the second node is reached, the sound of the first fades and the sound of the second grows stronger, at the same time as the letters stabilize into new words (figure 9.1).

The vertical loop runs upward from the base of the first poem in the horizontal loop. This loop contains sixteen different translations of the same poem, including different versions in English as well as in French, Spanish, and the pinyin romanization of the modern pronunciation of the original poem's characters in Chinese. At the side of the text in the vertical loop is a QuickTime movie that overlays separate shots of a pathway. The overlay technique creates a silvery sheen that makes the image waver like water. In its fluid indeterminacy, the movie suggests a gash or gap in the screenic surface, hinting at a connection between the words as they appear on screen and the inner workings of the computer, thus becoming a visual metaphor for an indeterminate space in which many different tracings exist simultaneously.[4]

The gradual transitions between the poems enact what the images of flowing water suggest, a continuous stream of sound and images with nodal points where the reader can linger to appreciate the local sights. Thus the work in its organization recreates the sense of processes within the computer that are producing the work as such. Moreover, the nodes exist within a continuum that can be made all the more precise because it ultimately is generated by the binary code of ones and zeros. This is not quite the paradox it may first appear, for in general the finer the granularity, the more accurately

how can a home be
                    new ?
Muskoka
               old pine
lingering decay
                 hemlock

those who will have
           come home
who are they ?

sadness, no :
emptiness

what I hold of
what I am   〔 〈 〉 〕
           something past

Figure 9.1 Screenshot from *riverIsland* positioned at a nodal poem on the "horizontal" loop in the "Wang River" sequence. Courtesy of John Cayley.

a discrete process such as binary code can represent a continuum. Precisely because of the extreme fragmentation that stores one alphabetic letter as eight bits, the digital computer is capable of simulating any text in any format, font, or color, achieving flexibility undreamed of with the durable marks of print.

As Cayley (1998b) points out, alphabetic language can be considered a digital structure because it consists of a small symbol set that can be endlessly combined and recombined to produce an infinite number of words and texts. The computer (or, as he prefers to call it, the "programmaton") is the most conspicuous instance of networked and programmable media (in Cayley's terms, "npm") that rely on binary code, but it is by no means the first medium to use digitized language. Rather, it carries further a digitizing process already begun by the transcription of speech into alphabetic letters.[5]

Underlying the complexity of this work are Cayley's (2002b) theoretical investigations of "transliteral morphing," the technique he uses in *riverIsland* and a number of other works, particularly *noth'rs* (1999), to morph from one letter and text to another. To explain the process, he asks that we imagine two tables of letters: a source table representing the letters of the original text and a target table representing the translation. Further suppose that the letters are arranged in a loop of twenty-eight symbols (26 letters plus a punctuation mark and a space), with those that sound similar to each other closest together. To morph a letter from the source to the target text, a minimum of one step and a maximum of fourteen would be necessary (14 because the transversal can go either clockwise or counterclockwise around the loop and thus never be more than 14 steps away). To create a text in which the morphing letters arrive at their destinations on approximately the same timescale, he lets the transversal happen slowly as it begins to go around the loop and more quickly as it approaches the end points. By conceptualizing the transition from source to target through this procedure of morphing letters, the technique fore-grounds the letter as an important element of textual meaning, focusing on it as the atomic unit of language (figure 9.2).

To illustrate the significance of this "literal art," Cayley, in "Digital Wen: On the Digitization of Letter- and Character-Based Systems of Inscription" (2003), discusses the "rules of traditional Chinese regulated verse, *lüshi*." These include considerations such as line length, pauses between syllables, and tonal qualities along a line, as well as parallelism between the lines of a couplet, in terms of both the sense and correspondences between characters and classes of characters. Meaning is thus built up out of the par-ticular qualities of written characters and their phonetic equivalents, as well as through higher-level considerations such as imagery, metaphor, and so forth. Cayley argues that similar considerations also apply to poetry in English, suggesting that similarities and differences between letter forms can function as visual equivalents to the acoustic properties of poetic techniques.

This orientation allows him to conceive of poetry through a materialistic "bottom up" approach that works in synchrony with higher-level considera-tions, a perspective he designates as "literal" (with a play on the letter as the unit of meaning and on the fact that the letters literally appear on the page or screen as the basic units from which meaning emerges). In addition, as the letters of his transliteral morphs travel between recognizable letter forms, they

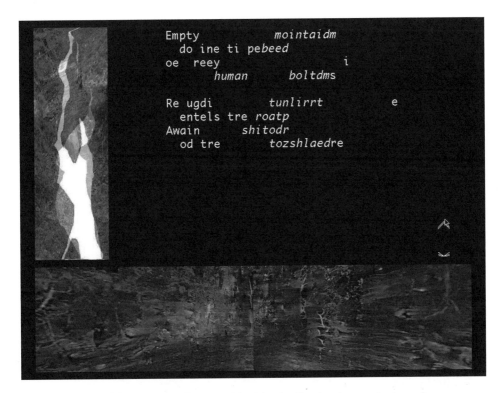

Figure 9.2 Screenshot from *riverIsland* showing the piece in an early phase of a transliteral morph from a poem on the "vertical" loop in English to an adjacent version in Spanish. Courtesy of John Cayley.

go through intermediate stages before stabilizing into the target forms, a process repeated on a larger and more visible scale as the letters in the source word transform into other letters that will eventually stabilize into the target word. The visual effect is to suggest a dynamic tension between the stabilized word (or letter) and the transitional morphs, which are linguistically indeterminate in the sense that they do not correspond to any recognizable word but rather are the "in betweens" from which coherent words will emerge. In his works, language falls apart and comes together, dissolving into a seethe of chaos that is not merely disorder but rather the fecund noisy matrix from which poetry will emerge.

This view of language allows Cayley to establish strong parallels between verbal language and the binary code of computer processes. It is important to note here that the morphing letters are not continuous transformations but rather quick jumps between different letters, as when the letters on a European railroad schedule spin around to form new words. This style of morphing emphasizes that letters are digital, in the sense of being discrete rather than continuous. Further emphasizing the point is the screen on the vertical loop that shows the first word of the literal translation, "empty," morphing into the Chinese characters through a QuickTime movie (figures 9.3 and 9.4). In contrast to the alphabetic transformations, here the morphing is continuous and analog, for there can be no table of correspondences between characters and letters; in this sense, they are incommensurate.[6] In the other screens, however, the digitality of alphabetic language is foregrounded by the discrete jumps as one text transforms into another, a performance that enacts the

Figure 9.3 Early stage of a graphic morph from a form of the word "empty" into a form of the corresponding character in Chinese regular script. Courtesy of John Cayley.

N. Katherine Hayles

Figure 9.4 Late stage of a graphic morph from a form of the word "empty" into a form of the corresponding character in Chinese regular script. Courtesy of John Cayley.

similarities between letters as the bits from which language is formed and electronic polarities as the bits from which the screen image of electronic letters is formed.

Cayley's work makes clear that there are significant parallels between linguistic and media translation. But he resists calling the process of importing text from one medium to another "translation," for translation continues to carry with it, he believes, a whiff of the transcendental signifier. What guarantees, he asks, that we will be able to translate a document from one language to another or one medium to another? Traditionally, the translatability of texts has been seen to depend on a logos that transcended the medium in which it was instantiated. When in the biblical account Adam names the animals, this act of naming is presented not as a willful act of creating arbitrary signs but as a linguistic enactment of the names given by God, guarantor that the link between word and referent is appropriate and correct. Similarly, translations of the Bible into different languages have traditionally been interpreted as processes guided by divine inspiration, a crucial assumption for a fundamentalist who wishes to rely on a literal reading of an English translation while himself not reading Greek or Latin. Standing apposite to these assumptions is the Tower of Babel, where the nontranslatability of different languages into one another is the divine punishment for the hubris of mortals who, thinking they can come close to heaven, may also harbor designs to infringe upon the divine copyright to know and assign true names.[7]

With digital media, by contrast, translatability across media (from image to text to film to sound, and so on) is guaranteed by the binary code to which all these texts are ultimately reduced, a process Lev Manovich analyzes in his discussion of transcoding (2001, 45–48). Rather than depending on the transcendental signifier, electronic texts tremble at the edge of what Cayley calls the "abyss" of binary code, a form of symbolic language difficult for humans to understand in its raw form; rather than pointing up toward the purity of the Word, digital devices plunge down into a froth of code that becomes progressively less intelligible to humans as it moves closer to the point where it is instantiated in the materiality of the machine as on/off voltages. To mark this difference between the transcendental assumptions undergirding translation and the machine processes of code, Cayley suggests that "transliteration" would be a better choice to describe the re-encoding of print or manuscript documents into electronic texts.[8]

Of course, transliteration into computer code does not do away with problems of translating between one language and another or (in the case of the "Wang River" sequence) between the ideograms of the Chinese written language and the alphabetic code of English. What *riverIsland* enacts, rather, is a complex enfolding of transliteration into translation, whereby the instabilities of choosing the appropriate words from a large vocabulary set to represent in one language ideas presented in another (i.e., translation) are put into tension and synchrony with the processes that enable screen pixels to represent alphabetic letters, nonalphabetic symbols in the ASCII character set, and Chinese ideograms as bitmapped images (i.e., transliteration). The effect of this complex enfolding is to represent transliteration and translation as continua, processes that have nodal points of stabilization (similar to the "Wang River" sequence) but with many intermediate points that suggest alternate translations and encoding possibilities, so that the text is imaged as inherently unstable, an unfolding event rather than a graspable object with clear-cut boundaries in time and edges in space.

The implications of enfolding transliteration into translation are explored in the first poem-event of the horizontal ring. This poem creates a delicate contrast and balance between presence and absence, human and nonhuman, light and darkness, speech and echoes, language and silence. As it appears on the horizontal wheel, the first poem reads:

alone
hearing voices
   of something past
   echoes?

where the mossbank
shines
as it did
   before

returning
each evening
to this lakeside
through the deep woods.

The first poem on the vertical wheel renders it as follows:

On empty slopes
we see nobody
yet we can hear
men's echoed phrases.

Retreating light
enters the dark woods
and shines again
on the deep moss.

The Time of Digital Poetry

There is much to notice in these different translations, including the translator's choice to introduce a plural "we" as the human presence in the second version, which heightens the contrast between the human and nonhuman world and hints at a human community that is not nearly as strongly present in the first version, which begins with "alone." Both of these versions differ significantly from the literal translation that appears on the screen where the morphing transitions occur:

empty mountain not see human
but hear human language echo

returning light enter deep wood
again shine green moss on

As the language moves closer to literalness, morphing transformations bring into visibility the processes of translation and transliteration that have produced the screenic texts of the sixteen variations. The morphs occur with the first word, "empty," surely a significant choice since the word is both empty and full, its transcendental signification emptied out even as the multiple layers of ideograms, phonetic Chinese, English, and ASCII characters flow into place as the morphing gracefully transforms one shape into another. Simultaneously image and word, each shape as it morphs leaves behind the trace of its original form, which gradually fades as the new shape establishes itself. Like the poems of the "River Sequence," the word produces itself at once as a series of discrete shapes and as a flowing continuum in which each node harbors traces of other possibilities, other translations and transliterations.

The design, then, is of a piece with the poems, all working to produce time as a flow that we experience in varying rhythms, now as a current pushing us from one event to another, now as a still pool in which the voices gradually move from gentle cacophony to sole articulation. Even when the work manifests itself as a coherent verbal poem and single speaking voice, the design reminds us that this is only a temporary and provisional resting point, one layer among many that stretch far back in time, span the vast differences between Chinese and Anglo-American cultures and languages, and go deep into the machine as screen images emerge from flickering voltages through multiple layers of code. Enfolding transliteration into translation, *riverIsland* reveals its materiality as an event rather than an object, interpenetrated at every level by the temporal processes that construct reading as a flow in which meaning emerges from a molecular froth of bits that momentarily swirl into words, only to be dissolved back into the seethe of possibilities.

V: Temporal Sequence and Multimedia Flows

A meditation on time, *V* is simultaneously a poetic system designed to produce different effects of time. As Stephanie Strickland observes in an interview with Jaishree Odin (2002), we are not accustomed to think of poems as systems (7); yet in its operations, its multimedia instantiations, and especially its mutating time-dependent structures, *V* is less an ordered set of words than a matrix of possibilities. Reminiscent of Raymond Queneau's *Cent mille milliards de poèmes* (1982) but operating through different machinery, *V* offers a very large number of possible readings—that is, not only many interpretations but literally many different word orders that necessarily precede a reader's interpretive acts.

Central to the many poetic choices that emerge is the contrast between time as inexorable sequence and time as phenomenological flow grounded in the body. Clock time, measured by numbers marching in unvarying cadence, is contrasted with different ways to parse and understand temporal units as they relate to living bodies: the twenty-eight days, "vaginal cadence," a bee lives (Strickland 2002, *WaveSon.nets* 18); the wheeling of the constellations through the seasonal skies, marking the year it takes for Big Bear (Ursa Major) and Little Bear (Ursa Minor) to "circle the hole" of the "world/tree," "dipping honey from the hollow/at the tilted top/of the northern world" (*WaveSon.nets* 18); the Platonic Great Year, comprised of the 26,000 years required for the North Star position to precess from Polaris to Vega and back again. Precisely when temporal calculations appear most mathematical and linear, the living reality of flesh cuts through to claim its needs, appetites, desires. So when the narrative voice meditates on the slight calendar irregularities necessitating not only the addition of a day every four years but every "one-hundred/and twenty-eight/years, the need to take a day *out*" (*WaveSon.nets* 20), the excision is imaged as the osprey pulling "a salmon from the sea" (*WaveSon.nets* 20). Meditating on the displacement of body rhythms by the increasing routinization of time, the poetic voice wonders:

. . . was an inner sense of hearing-counting lost,

when the children stopped coming together

in a brood, in the easy spring, conceived at Midsummer,

and began to be born *throughout* the year, whenever.

And began to be garnered as workers

in a settling world. (*WaveSon.nets* 29)

Marking time with their biological rhythms, the prehistoric bodies conjured in this scenario are also marked by time through an "inner sense of hearing-counting" lost in the contemporary world. If "hearing-counting" joins acoustic perception, the penetration of the body by sound, with a felt sense of time that does not depend on clocks, perhaps the connection can be reconstructed through the precise technology of poetic sound effects.[9]

Part of *V*'s project is to reopen these lost channels by integrating the numbers of time with the rhythms of poetic cadences. Central to this project are the parsings of time reflexively encoded into *V*'s number schemes. The first poem of the print *V: Losing L'una* (Strickland 2002), "From Sails to Satellites," illustrates their complexities. Although the tercets appear to be ordered using conventional decimals, two distinct sets of numbers are actually in play. Those to the left of the decimal remain the same for a given poem and increase sequentially with each decimal poem, while those to the right spin around independently of their left-handed cousins, counting off the tercets in a given poem. For example, the first tercet is labeled "1.1," with subsequent tercets progressing through "1.9," "1.10," and "1.11" to a final tercet labeled "1.30," thus defying the usual rule that "1.9," for instance, would be succeeded by "2.0." The scheme becomes even more complicated in the last poem of the decimal sequence, "L'una Loses," where the left number registers only zero, a numbering appropriate to the title, while the right-hand numbers increase from "0.0" to "0.12" and then decrement back to "0.0," with the final tercet labeled simply "0." The ambiguities created by these numbering schemes suggest multiple ways to group the tercets into larger units. Breaking the right-handed numbers from the left side implies that the tercets within a poem follow a sequence dependent on the stanzas that succeed and follow, whereas the left numbers moving sequentially from poem to poem suggest that all the decimal sequences can be read as a single poem. Possible parsings are further complicated by the shorter poems interspersed into the decimal sequence; in contrast to the decimal poems, these use whole-numbered tercets. The short poems can be read as discrete works, each with its individual title and numbers; as interjections/interruptions to the decimal poems; or as components of a single long poem constituted by *V: Losing L'una* in its entirety.

Similar indeterminacies mark the numbering of *V: WaveSon.nets* (Strickland 2002). As if to emphasize *they* won't engage in numerical chicanery, the WaveSon.nets are redundantly numbered, each page-long poem assigned a sequential arabic numeral identical to the one repeated at page bottom. But this apparent docility is misleading, for the WaveSon.nets practice their own disruptions of linear sequence. Assigning each poem a discrete number suggests it should be read as a sonnet consisting of three four-line stanzas with a final tercet, an unusual variation of the fourteen-line sonnet but one that continues to honor the reflexive turn characteristic of the form. At the same time, the individual sonnets, through their semantic content, syntax, and grammar, assemble themselves into larger poem-groups consisting of several WaveSon.nets. (My parsing of these larger poems, following the scent of sense and the path of punctuation, leads to these groups: 1–5, 6–11, 12–14, 15–30, 31–33, 34–37, 38–41, 42–44, 45–47.) Strickland in her commentary suggests that these larger groups of WaveSon.nets are formed when a wave of thought crests and reflexively folds back on itself as a certain line of interrogation reaches its end. Within each larger group, the individual sonnets can be read as pauses or perhaps (to continue the wave metaphor) breaks in a curving line of thought as it crashes beachward, conclusionward.

Consider, for example, the grouping 6–11, which begins with the quatrain

When Columba converted the mermaid,
which of them said,
"Is it really
you?" (Strickland 2002, *WaveSon.nets* 6)

Suggesting separation and reconnection, the scenario introduces an undecidable ambiguity into who recognizes whom, implicitly bringing into question who has the authority to convert whom. In "WaveSon.net 7–8," the scenario continues but now from the mermaid's point of view:

Is it really you,

he longs to say, but I swim away,

repeating his beat, his cadence,
with my tail,
so opening a channel.
A channel only open, not a code, no

message, for him
to break. I fall away
from his design and say
to myself, so, we must meet apart (*WaveSon.nets* 7–8)

The oxymoronic "meet apart" glances back at the mermaid opening a channel that has no message, a cryptological and watery pun that lands us somewhere between Bletchley Park and the English Channel. This meeting apart will happen, the next quatrain suggests,

in a time
of no tomorrow, no pleading, no art,
time of waiting, a miracle mer-main
of hallucinated hearing. (*WaveSon.nets* 8)

"Mer-main," balanced between mermaid and merman, opens what is perhaps the "main" channel for this poem-group, a realm of "hallucinated hearing" in which a substitution of consonants (*n* for *d*) evokes the word not on the page, the conversion of the converter into a merman, a transformation that will let him swim alongside the one who is "really you." Significantly, this union will take place in a time when the relentless progression of time is stilled, "a time/of no tomorrow," when no clock numbers endlessly erode a present impossible to grasp because it slips away as soon as it announces/enunciates itself. If the reader wants to end the poem here by reading "WaveSon.net 8" as an individual poem, the final tercet then becomes

Fin(-ger) to finger, I shiver,
am calm: the reef embraces the water
that wears it[.]

The poem thus ends with an image of embrace, as if transported into that "time of no tomorrow" where fin and finger can entwine, mermaid miraculously transforming to woman and/or man transforming to merman.

If, however, the reader wants to follow the larger wave of thought, she will not end the poem here but will continue to find the full stop, which occurs in the first line of "WaveSon.net 9" after "down." The continuation across the break between WaveSon.nets completes the phrase, "wears it/down," converting embrace into erosion, unsettling one conclusion while pushing forward with a surging wave of desire to find an(other) end. This invites a rereading of "a time/of no tomorrow" not as a still point but as a signifier of negation, a "time of waiting" that wears down without creating an intertidal zone of mediation where man and mermaid might meet, "no pleading, no art."

These wave patterns indicate that the book should be understood not as durably impressed static lines but as ebbs and flows of acoustic and conceptual energies fractally complex in their breakpoints and continuities. Moreover, the "V" of the title, variously interpreted as virginity, woman or witch when the V is doubled, and the line of flight of migrating geese (along with much else), gestures toward the shape of an open book. One cover is imprinted with V: WaveSon.nets with an image of the conical section formed by the earth's precession as the axis tip moves toward Vega, while on the other cover the same image appears in an upside-down orientation to the first emblazoned with a different title, V: Losing L'una. To read the entire book, one must progress to the middle and then, beginning at the other cover, turn it upside down and again read to the middle from this direction. On the inside surfaces of V's center spread, two identical pages appear in upside-down orientation to each other, each imprinted with a Web address (http://vniverse.com) and a title ("There Is a Woman in a Conical Hat"). The URL, along with the book's physical form and content, suggests the text is conceptualized as a propagating waveform that flows through the apex of the V to become radiant energy, transformed from durable marks into glowing phosphors ignited by an electron beam shot from the apex of the conical CRT, as if reflecting the "conical hat" of the poem's eponymous figure. The period in WaveSon.net now appears not as an idiosyncratic punctuation penetrating the sonnet but as a reference to the Internet, alluding to (modes of) addresses that operate in the digital realm rather than print.

At the Web site, V the print book connects with and transforms into the electronic work V: Vniverse, a collaboration between Strickland and Cynthia

Lawson (2003), who codeveloped the work and programmed it in Director. The Web site loads as a spinning night sky sprinkled with stars that stop when the load time is complete, thus making aesthetic use of a technological necessity and announcing through this animation its difference from the fixed marks of print.[10] The play set up in the print book between the individual WaveSon.nets and the larger poem-groups is here intensified as an alternate display that shows the WaveSon.nets being parsed into tercets, thus altering which lines belong to the now five stanzas that comprise each WaveSon.net. Since there are forty-six "full" WaveSon.nets, this yields 230 tercets (five times forty-six), plus the two stanzas of "WaveSon.net 47" for a total of 232 tercets.

When the user sweeps the cursor over the sky, ten different constellations appear, including the bull, swimmer/writhing woman, drummer, infinity sign, broom, twins, fetus, dipper/bear, goose, and dragonfly. These figures, suggestively providing a visual context for the poem-groups, are thematically significant. The emerald darner that the poetic voice imagines hovering over Simone Weil in the concluding "WaveSon.net 47," for example, is a species of dragonfly, and the last poem-group emerges through this constellation, with the final tercet on the figure's tail. Similarly, the swimmer/writhing woman constellation, comprised of WaveSon.nets 1–3, includes a tercet imagining the reader herself as a V "writhing on your point, twist it one way,/then the other—a rhythm method making/your water mark" (*WaveSon.net* 1).

In addition to being associated with a star and constellation, each tercet is also identified by a number and keyword. Lingering on a constellation and moving the cursor from star to star causes their keywords to appear, which Strickland regards as a condensed poem in its own right. For example, the keywords associated with the infinity sign constellation (assembled in numerical order) read "steel quantum lock relaxation Erasure MIT Heaven history tissue tangle shame bittersweet Cantor curtains Minute Misfits vestige." Another order appears if the cursor traces the stars in succession, using visual form rather than numerical sequence as an ordering principle, and, of course, yet others appear if random sweeping motions are used. At best these keyword lists are suggestive; if they are read as poems, they are gnomic indeed. Nevertheless, the keyword lists gesture toward the proliferating poetic possibilities of the site as a system for generating poems.

Another way to (re)construct the WaveSon.nets is to input a number from 1 to 232 into a small circle at the top right of the screen, which causes the associated tercet to appear. This numerical scheme is slyly anticipated in the print book (or, if one begins at the Web site, reflexively encoded) in "WaveSon.net 17," where the poetic voice, after asserting that the woman in the conical hat "keeps time/timely," glances at her computer and sees that "My computer tells me/2:32//PM and so salutes her." Numbers going in order from 1 to 232 are thus connected with time passing, a conjunction enacted by the user's active kinesthetic involvement with the Web site as she types numbers into the small circle or sweeps over, lingers on, and clicks the visual forms of the constellations. The cognitive-muscular activities associated with reading become more focused and intense, reopening the channel of "hearing-counting" in a different way than the print book, making it now a conjunction of hearing-counting-performing.

This kinetic system is at its best when it plays with the combinatorial possibilities of relating a given tercet to the WaveSon.net of which it is a part. The process begins when the user chooses to linger on a star, which makes the text of the tercet appear linearly, as if the words were being typed in succession. Clicking once causes this text to fade while nearby the same tercet appears in colored letters, now manifesting itself all at once as a unit. Clicking twice on the star causes the WaveSon.net from which the tercet was taken to assemble around it, creating a poetic context that is enlarged once again if the user chooses to trace all the stars in the constellation. In contrast to the book, in which the groupings are formed by consecutive number sequences (that is to say, by the succession of bound pages), now the poem-group emerges through the visual form of the constellation, a grouping that reflects Strickland's parsing of the ten poem-groups she imagines the WaveSon.nets forming.[11] (These partially overlap with but also differ from the nine groupings I suggested earlier, a discrepancy that fails to disturb Strickland. On the contrary, she generously welcomes the diverse parsings that various readers may hear in the poems, seeing in the variations evidence for the richness of the poetic system that can support many different groupings).

Further adding to this richness are the interconnections between the print poem and the Web site. The effects of the channel opened between print marks and electronic text go beyond how the lines are parsed, significant as this may be. In contrast with the print book, in which the very fixity of sequence paradoxically highlights its subversion, sequence at the Web site is overshadowed by the experiences the user has as she works with the Web site, seeing text appear and disappear, stabilize and decay, jump out in sharply colored text or gray out as it fades into the night sky, manifest itself as visual forms with associated keywords and again as spatially ordered stanzas reminiscent of the print book. These experiences set up a number of related oscillations: seeing/reading, stable letters/flickering signifiers, presence/absence, stability/decay, image/word, part/whole, time stopped/time passing. Much can be said about these oscillations, but here I will simply observe that their collective effect is to actualize a sense of the territory signified by the slash, which in its broadest terms can be understood as the space *between* the print book and digital Web site. This space, invisible as a high-frequency waveform that exceeds our visual or acoustic perceptual range, is nevertheless charged with energy and significance.

A phenomenon that cannot be seen or thought directly but rather must be grasped by other means is evoked repeatedly in *V*. In one of its guises, it is named in the *V: Losing L'una* poem "TITA: The Incandescent Thought About":

> 5.95
>
> . . .
>
> There is a doubt not incompatible
> with faith—these truths

> 5.96
>
> true so long as we don't think them that become false
> as soon as we do:
> at the moment

> 5.97
>
> the liar thinks, *I am*
> *a liar,*
> she is not.

> 5.98
>
> What must be kept
> profoundly secret
> —from ourselves—things true until we think them.

In other guises, it appears as the void, the negative trial ("not to think/about the white bear" [*Losing L'una* 14]), the nothingness that alone is capacious enough for desire to sink itself unceasingly into, "the blind spot hidden deep//in your seeing" best sensed by following the astronomer's advice to "avert/your eyes, look away//to see better" [*Losing L'una* 3]. Like the invisible space between the print book and digital site, these manifestations of positive nothingness are forces all the more powerful because they cannot be seen straight on.

If navigation is the enactment of time by moving through space, then by navigating between its print and electronic forms, *V*'s user produces another kind of time: the time of the in-between. When we encounter the work directly, we are either at the Web site or in the book. In between these two navigational sites is another kind of space-time produced by their conjunction, disappearing as soon as we try to apprehend it directly but flickering on the edges of our visual field like a salmon wriggling free from the osprey's beak. Reading back and forth between the book and Web site, as Strickland urges us to do, leads to an enhanced appreciation for how these different media structure time. In addition, the conjunction produces another kind of in-between time that invites us to reevaluate those flashes of in-between time produced by the different reading practices of print and electronic text: the fraction of a second when we flip a page over and are neither on one page nor another, the microseconds between clicking on a star and seeing text appear, or the quick flashing of the constellation figures as the cursor sweeps over the screen. These in-between times remind us that gaps, ruptures, and fissures of undetermined duration and unspecified significance puncture our reading experiences. No mean part of *V*'s achievement is its construction of these in-between times as potent signifiers within and between the print book and Web site, no less powerful because we cannot say exactly what they mean.

In this respect, *V* is similar to *riverIsland*'s text morphing through an indeterminate number of transitional states before stabilizing into recognizable words. In *riverIsland* and *V*, time is not only organized but stretched, deformed, rendered mutable, ambiguous, and contingent. The different strategies through which these two works accomplish their "eventilization" of language indicate the importance of attending to the historical and technical specificities of print and digital literature. Both can be used to transform poems from objects to events, but the processes unfold differently in print and digital media and differently in print/digital media combined together than in either medium by itself. Just as time can be understood in much more complex terms than a linear sequence, so its production is complexly embedded in the media that produce it.

Elsewhere, I have suggested that fully exploring the implications of media specificity will require new conceptualizations of materiality (Hayles 2002, 19–34). Rather than think about the materiality of texts as a fixed set of physical properties characteristic of an object, we might consider it as emerging from the ways a text mobilizes the physical characteristics of the technology in which it is instantiated to create meaning. Materiality in this view is a different concept than physicality. Materiality implies a characterization and selection of physical properties that could be listed as comprising an object. Emphasizing that no description of an object can be value-neutral (because description implies noticing some aspects and suppressing others), the materiality of a text cannot be decided in advance. How the poem-event goes in search of meaning determines which aspects of the technology are foregrounded, so materiality emerges as a dance between the medium's physical characteristics and the work's signifying strategies. Contingent, provisional, and debatable, materiality itself thus comes to be seen as more an event than a preexisting object, a nexus at which culture, language, technology, and meaning interpenetrate.

As Strickland reminds us, this is as true of print books as it is of electronic texts. The specificities of networked and programmable media are such, however, as especially to invite this interpretation. Allowing us to see print with fresh eyes, electronic literature reveals the text as a performance riddled with time even as it also extends in space. The space-times of the in-between diversely created by *V* and *riverIsland* are especially significant in this regard, for they produce kinds of time that seem to elude sequence even as they rely on it, slipping through the holes between numbers and letters like water running through a sieve. Descartes notwithstanding, the *cogito res*, taken here to mean the machine that thinks as well as the human that thinks, can never be stabilized so as to be self-evidently present to itself as itself. These poem-events, similar to the readers they construct and require, are rivers that flow, processes that evolve, materialities that emerge contingently, flickering in the constantly changing plays of meanings.

Notes

1. Jerome McGann (2001) argues that such print conventions constitute a markup language comparable to computer codes. However, there remains a crucial difference:

print markers act as instructions to the human reader, whereas computer codes act as instructions to the machine before the screen text is performed and read.

2. As a further clarification, I use "code" here in the narrow sense of programming languages and other computer codes necessary for a work to be produced in digital environments; I exclude from this discussion semantic codes that may underlie and inform content, or the "codes" that inhere in grammar and deep linguistic structures.

3. For examples of books that play with the conventions of two and three dimensions, see Drucker 1996.

4. I am indebted to Adalaide Morris for suggesting to me this interpretation of the image.

5. Cayley (1998a) develops this point further in "Of Programmatology." Alphabetic language, as Cayley observes, is a digital technology, a point developed at length by Robert K. Logan (1986) in *The Alphabet Effect*. In *The Sixth Language: Learning a Living in the Computer Age* (1995), Logan extends his analysis to digital code.

6. Whether the set of Chinese characters can be considered digital depends on how many elements one is willing to include in the definition of digital; in entertaining this question, Cayley points out that the number of Chinese characters included in the larger dictionaries is on the order of 49,000.

7. For an ironic appropriation of the Babel myth to describe computer codes as a "tower of languages," see Raley 2002.

8. Cayley (2004) discusses the relation of line, pixel, and letter in "Literal Art: Neither Lines nor Pixels but Letters," an essay that illuminates the special sense in which he uses "literal" to mean both the materiality of language and the letters from which alphabetic language is formed.

9. The observation that sound penetrates the body is made by Douglas Kahn, for example, in this lovely passage:

> While other people hear a person's voice carried through vibrations in the air, the person speaking also hears her or his own voice as it is conducted from the throat and mouth through bone to the inner regions of the ear. Thus, the voice in its production in various regions of the body is propelled through the body; its resonance is sensed intracranially. . . . [O]thers will hear the speaker's voice infused with a lesser distribution of body because it will be a voice heard without bone conduction: a deboned voice (1999, 7).

10. John Zuern (2003) discusses a similar suturing of technological necessity into aesthetic effect.

11. The poem-groups constituted through the constellations are as follows: Swimmer/Writhing Woman, WS1–WS3, Tercets 1–15; Drummer, WS4–WS7, Tercets 16–35; Broom, WS8–WS13, Tercets 36–65; Dipper/Bear, WS14–WS18, Tercets 66–90; Twins, WS19–WS22, Tercets 91–110; Bull, WS23–WS27, Tercets 111–135; Fetus, WS28–WS32, Tercets 136–160; Goose, WS33–WS37, Tercets 161–185; Infinity, WS38–WS41, Tercets 186–205; Dragonfly, WS42–WS47, Tercets 206–232. I am grateful to Strickland for clarifying these groupings and for insisting that other parsings, including mine, are also valid. She comments, "I do think it's part of the point that one senses breaks where they are not 'cued'" (email message to N. Katherine Hayles, August 23, 2003).

Works Cited

Bateson, Gregory. 1979. *Mind and Nature: A Necessary Unity.* New York: Dutton.

Cayley, John. 1998a. "Of Programmatology." *Mute* (Fall): 72–75.

Cayley, John. 1998b. "Performances of Writing in the Age of Digital Transliteration." Paper presented at the Digital Arts Conference, University of Bergen, Norway, November.

Cayley, John. 1999. *noth'rs.* http://www.shadoof.net/in/ (accessed June 15, 2004).

Cayley, John. 2002a. *riverIsland.* http://www.shadoof.net/in/riverisland.html (accessed August 20, 2003.)

Cayley, John. 2002b. "What Is Transliteral Morphing?" Text file accompanying *river Island.* http://www.shadoof.net/in/intext01.html. (accessed August 20, 2003).

Cayley, John. 2003. "Digital Wen: On the Digitization of Letter- and Character-Based Systems of Inscription." In *Reading East Asian Writing: The Limits of Literary Theory,* ed. Michel Hockz and Ivo Smits, 277–294. London: RoutledgeCurzon.

Cayley, John. 2004. "Literal Art: Neither Lines nor Pixels but Letters." In *First Person: New Media as Story, Performance, and Game,* ed. Noah Wardrip-Fruin and Pat Harrigan, 208–217. Cambridge, MA: MIT Press.

Derrida, Jacques. 1988. "Signature Event Context." In *Limited Inc.,* trans. Samuel Weber, 1–23. Evanston, IL: Northwestern University Press.

Drucker, Johanna. 1996. *The Century of Artists' Books.* New York: Granary Books.

Glazier, Loss Pequeño. 2002. *Digital Poetics: The Making of E-Poetries.* Tuscaloosa: University of Alabama Press.

Hayles, N. Katherine. 2002. *Writing Machines.* Cambridge, MA: MIT Press.

Kahn, Douglas. 1999. *Noise, Water, Meat: A History of Sound in the Arts.* Cambridge, MA: MIT Press.

Logan, Robert K. 1986. *The Alphabet Effect.* New York: William Morrow.

Logan, Robert K. 1995. *The Sixth Language: Learning a Living in the Computer Age.* Toronto: Stoddart.

Manovich, Lev. 2001. *The Language of New Media.* Cambridge, MA: MIT Press.

McGann, Jerome. 2001. *Radiant Textuality: Literature after the World Wide Web.* London: Palgrave Macmillan.

Miller, Laura. 1998. "www.claptrap.com." *New York Times Book Review*, March 15, Bookend. http://www.nytimes.com/books/98/03/15/bookend/bookend.html (accessed December 2, 2004).

Odin, Jaishree K. 2002. "Into the Space of Previously Undrawable Diagrams: An Interview with Stephanie Strickland." *The Iowa Review Web.* http://www.uiowa.edu/~iareview/tirweb/feature/strickland/interview.html (accessed August 20, 2003).

Queneau, Raymond. 1982. *Cent mille milliards de poèmes.* Paris: Gallimard/NRF.

Raley, Rita. 2002. "Interferences: [Net.Writing] and the Practice of Codework." *electronic book review.* http://www.electronicbookreview.com/v3/servlet/ebr?command =view_essay&essay_id=raleyele/ (accessed August 20, 2003).

Strickland, Stephanie, and Cynthia Lawson. 2002. "Making the Vniverse." http://vniverse.com/essay (accessed August 20, 2003).

Strickland, Stephanie. 2002. *V: WaveSon.nets/Losing L'una.* New York: Penguin.

Strickland, Stephanie, and Cynthia Lawson. 2003. V: Vniverse. http://www.vniverse.com (accessed August 20, 2003).

Zuern, John. 2003. "Matter of Time: Toward a Materialist Semiotics of Web Animation." *dichtung-digital-journal für digitale ästhetik* 1. http://www.dichtung-digital.org/2003/1-zuern.htm (accessed June 1, 2004).

"Io Sono At Swoons." Courtesy of Loss Pequeño Glazier.

10

Io Sono At Swoons

Loss Pequeño Glazier

Regaining new stable equilibrium he rose uninjured though
concussed by the impact.
—JAMES JOYCE, ULYSSES

Ah, chub oo language to me
—LOSS PEQUEÑO GLAZIER, "IO SONO AT SWOONS"

If you can ever pull your minds together, do it now.
—HIS HOLINESS THE DALAI LAMA, DALAI LAMA IN AMERICA:
TRAINING THE MIND

Introduction

"Io Sono At Swoons" (see frontispiece on p. 210) is a poem-program that
refreshes every forty seconds with a new iteration of text on the screen. It is
virtually impossible that the reader will ever see the same poem twice.
Drawing from the experience of my concussion, "Io Sono" presents
collages of lexical fragments from various languages, including medical
terminology related to the brain, which come together in compound forma-
tions with multilingual inflection (figure 10.1). The selection of languages
and the content of lexical elements are crafted as components of the meaning
of the poem. The poem also serves as a sound poetry script for performance,
a challenging prospect indeed as the performer must read difficult-to-

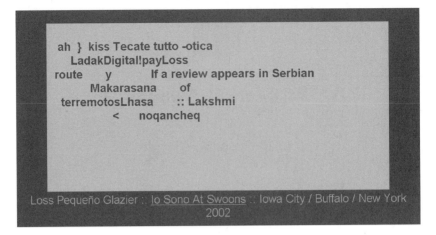

Figure 10.1   Screenshot of "ah } kiss Tecate." Courtesy of Loss Pequeño Glazier.

pronounce neologisms and word combinations that have never been seen before.

The words "Io Sono" are Italian for "I am." The poem explores the dynamics of identity at a moment when language centers are disturbed. This is not merely autobiographical but also points more generally to how language functions in the world, how languages overwrite other languages, and how languages have imbedded in them traces of their etymologies. The phrase "At Swoons" suggests fainting, which is medically related to too little blood in the brain and the wooziness that is an expected result of a concussion. But "swoons" also suggests ecstatic joy or rapture. The piece spins language, exploring the potential for lexical ecstasy. Finally, the phrase "At Swoons" also suggests the archaic " 'swounds," a shortened form of the phrase "God's wounds." A concussion is a human wound in a location so vulnerable that this interjection also has resonance for me.

Writing Language

As a psychotherapist told me, language effects a potent physical process. In her practice, language even has the power to heal in situations in which a trauma patient, with careful direction, can use it to relive and hence move beyond the site of a mental gridlock. The memory of traumatic experience is encoded in the right side of the brain—in the nervous system itself—where it can trigger erratic recurrences of fear and panic or flashbacks. (Such an adaptive response is, of course, to the benefit of the survival of the species: the growls of a saber-toothed tiger in one's cave must trigger instant flight.) In the case of traumatic memories that need to be reconciled, there is a process of healing that occurs through the instrument of language, the recoding that occurs through therapy, procedure, and the natural processes of time. Through language, such memories physically—and literally—move to the other side of the brain. We are always writing language to the brain. What is written and where it is written has real and material ramifications.

This power of the processes of language is related to computer language. A computer language is language that induces a process of change (a fertile site of activity for the language artist). Through a computer language, a poet can make art. A poem-program offers the possibility of exploring how through language that makes art, art makes new language. This is not artificial intelligence or cognitive science. It is not the logic of grammatical assembly but the ecstasy of its error. It is whimsical, cherry pink and apple blossom white, exploring with glee the poetics of recombinant activity, the slip of the tongue, those edges of language that emerge only when our minds are in semisubmerged subjunctive modes.

This active process is similar to the ecosystem of natural language: in it, sound crosses over; words migrate, form new conjunctions; phrases linger, last forever. Some languages are particularly spiritual, distinctively expressive, or nuanced in their own specific ways; some words, as lexical yoga, evidence union. Language does not simply exist like some obdurate object in the world. Language is dynamic; it is a point of articulation within a nexus of constantly changing parameters of context.

A shock to the brain foregrounds the always fragmentary nature of words. As lexical yoga, words temporarily conjoin, hold that posture momentarily, then release. It is the tension and countertension in the posture that makes possible such union. In such passing moments, we are able to catch a glimpse of what is actually present in the world.

Writing "Io Sono"

The multilingual nature of the poem-program "Io Sono" can be located in its code. The work grew from a dialogue between the visual structure of its code and the sound of the generated text when read aloud from the browser's display. It was a back-and-forth process: seeing how the text sounded and adding to it, seeing how the code looked and sculpting it. Incrementally, the code was adjusted to shape the sound and image. At the same time, the visual layout of the code was cultivated to create a complementary aesthetic complexity. This process of working in the code, evaluating the rendered version, then working more in the code continued until the code and the onscreen textuality achieved a dynamic relation. Thus, the poem was built as a sound and visual poem in the browser, a browser interpreting a concrete poem built of code. A fearful symmetry indeed!

In its lexical materials, this work borrows from Mexican, Nahuatl, Quechua, English, French, German, Italian, Hindi, Sanskrit, Arabic, and Tibetan, with further soundings from China, Chad, and Dubai. Some additional material came from my personal correspondence with Mexican poets and some of my expository essays on the subject of code and language, as well as from medical terms having to do with the brain.

A poem-program such as "Io Sono" produces its surface text whether the author is there or not. When I first make a piece that generates poems regardless of my presence, I often panic at the thought of all the poems that are getting "lost." I will hit the Print Screen key to try to archive versions of the text. But the program goes on and on, producing a new poem every forty seconds, and eventually, I come to terms with such loss. I eventually realize that the iterations aren't the point. I become less attached. I will then sometimes first look away for the period of time it takes to display one iteration just to "let it go." I understand that, even as the writer, I don't have to see every text that my code produces. Later, I become more fascinated with the poem's endless ability to produce "my" poem, and I just sit back and let it run. I will often leave it on all night then get up the next morning to see if it is still making text. One can only imagine all the poems produced through the night, never to be seen by anyone, pure products of poetry.

Working within such a model, one eschews the illusion of art as fixed. It's not a poetics of Photoshop—not a poetics of the tween, dull-witted animations, or the PDF. It is not a decorative art. Rather, it is a poetics of finding the core conceptual thread—that calm abiding center that endures behind the constantly shifting surface of any work, any interpretation, any context. It is about code that is real as code. It is about code that "gets the picture" about the art object to be produced and that produces it with variance but within the intended vision (figure 10.2).

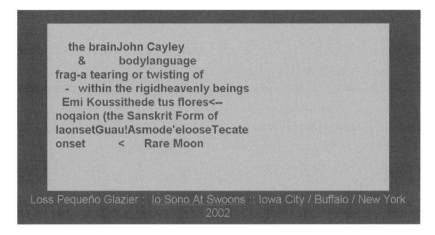

the brainJohn Cayley
&   bodylanguage
frag-a tearing or twisting of
- within the rigidheavenly beings
Emi Koussithede tus flores<--
noqaion (the Sanskrit Form of
IaonsetGuau!Asmode'elooseTecate
onset   <   Rare Moon

Loss Pequeño Glazier :: Io Sono At Swoons :: Iowa City / Buffalo / New York
2002

Figure 10.2   Screenshot of "the brainJohn Cayley." Courtesy of Loss Pequeño Glazier.

Writing Words

There is a bit of the trickster to the way a program can invent by nesting the sound of words within the visually striking appearance of its lexical agglutinations. But this occurs in natural language too. For example, the Nahuatl word "chöka" means to cry, to moo or bleat (a cow or goat), or to make a rumbling or grinding sound (a motor vehicle). Note how evocatively this word fits (aurally, visually, and morphemically) into related Nahuatl words such as "chökani" (crybaby, someone who cries a lot), ïxtënchochöka (for one's eyes to burn or become irritated), and "kökochöka" (to make gulping sounds in one's throat). The joke is that there is always a "chök" in your throat when you say these words. But the fit is perhaps most cunning in the word "koyöchöka," to howl like a coyote (the familiar "coyotl"), as if the "chöka" gurgles in the throat of the "coyotl," a cunning and multilayered union of sound and sense.

The output of such a work may seem meaningless at first, but it is similar in experience to the way that after you have been in a foreign country for a time, you begin to recognize sounds in the unfamiliar language. It is like finding pieces of driftwood in familiar shapes on a foreign shore. When you begin studying a foreign language, similarly, you find new fragments of foreign words in *your own* language. It is often all a jumble, but language is about getting it together. In a work of language art, you build meaning by starting with what's simply there.

Programming like this is similar to the way I used to stay up late with my mother separating pinto beans, one bean after another. The sound of their sliding across the surface of the table to plunk into a metal pot will stay with me forever. After a while the pot of beans had more to do with the rhythm of sorting the beans than with nutritional value. (It is no coincidence that Mexican-American women often use beans as currency in poker games with relatives. Every single bean has its own value.) Like the monk with his beads, it is one line of code after another, all in the present moment.

Works Cited

Dalai Lama XIV. 2001. *Dalai Lama in America: Training the Mind.* New York: Simon & Schuster Audio CD.

Glazier, Loss Pequeño. 2002. "Io Sono At Swoons." http://epc.buffalo.edu/authors/glazier/java/iowa/iosono.html (accessed June 30, 2004).

Joyce, James. [1922] 1993. *Ulysses.* New York: Oxford University Press.

Digital Gestures

Carrie Noland

My claim in this chapter is that digital poetry, far from attenuating our relation to the human body, actually evokes this body and its kinetic energies in a variety of highly inventive ways. The relation between fingers and font in digital writing might not be as immediate as the relation between hand and symbol that characterizes manual inscription. But this has not stopped poets—forever intrigued by lost immediacy—from sounding all the possibilities of that particular relation as it is manifested, distorted, and re-created in the digital realm. Digital poetry has turned out to be a genre of computer-based writing concerned with recalling to the user's consciousness a memory of the motions required to produce letters manually on a flat support. The motions associated with the use of paper and writing implement return in digital poetry both literally, as small motor movements involving only the fingers and wrist (shifting the mouse, clicking, dragging, and so on), and figuratively, as replications of letter production acted out on the screen. Whether letters are constructed stroke by stroke by an anonymous program (as in Bill Marsh's "Six String Aria" or Jim Andrews's "Nio") or moved about the screen and made to appear or disappear according to the hand motions of a real-time user (as in John Cayley's *riverIsland*, Stephanie Strickland's Vniverse, or Camille Utterbach's "Text Rain"),[1] digital poems mime and displace the corporeal energy channeled by the gestures of handwriting. Writing poetry on the computer makes it possible to retrieve aspects of a subject's experience of writing as a corporeal practice that cannot be captured by more traditional print forms.

Arguably, the single most innovative feature of digital poetry is animation. Concrete and visual poets of the past have tried to free letters from linear arrangement and an assigned place within a word.[2] However, digital works distinguish themselves from these earlier efforts by the increased liberty of movement they accord to both entire semantic units and individual letters. Flash, Director, and DHTML animation programs extend the visual experience of the verbal construct in ways that earlier works could not; programmers and users can, for instance, move words and letters around the screen, make them flicker, pulse rhythmically, or morph.[3] Whether generated by preprogrammed algorithms or initiated in real-time by interactive users, the transformations and transpositions these letters undergo on the screen recall the corporeal energies that drive inscription.[4] When letters move, morph, or pulse, they expose digital writing's nostalgia for the hand, the producer's creative will to reengage with and express the kinetic impulses of the body.

I therefore intend to approach digital poems as gestural, that is, as alluding to physical movements of the body in space. I am distinguishing my use of the term "gestural" from that of Robert Kendall, who has proposed that animated poems can be divided into two groups: the "gestural" and the "structural." By gestural, Kendall means that the kinetic features of the text serve "the same function as gestures of body language or the inflections of speech. They provide emphasis, build tension, or evoke a mood."[5] Meanwhile, structural animations are those that affect "meaning and syntax at the deepest level," not simply emphasizing words but bringing them in and out of being in a manner that contributes directly to the semantic content of the poem (as in Kendall's "Faith"). While I recognize the validity of Kendall's distinction, I want nonetheless to appropriate the expression "gestural animation" for my own use. Pulling "gesture" in the direction of movement rather than emphasis (which can be achieved by vocal inflection as well), away from rhetoric and toward dance, I hope to restore the choreographic dimension of the word. I am interested here in the gestures, the actual small motor movements, involved in the execution of handwriting and how these gestures/movements are displaced—in what emerges, in my analysis, as a kind of secondary order of displacement—onto the computer screen. For me, a gestural animation corresponds to and evokes the *ductus,* or stroke, of the writing hand; it reinscribes the movement of the body as it is engaged in the production of individual or connected letters.

Carrie Noland

I am less interested, then, in the activity of words, sentences, or lexia than in the movements of letters, the traveling, warping, and morphing of characters. It is in these specific types of animations that the gestures of handwriting return in a new form. The *ductus* of the letter is the conduit for corporeal energy; it embodies—in an inscription—the gestures required to form it. In order to make my argument about digital poetry as a gestural form, I will take a detour through the work of two visual artists of the twentieth century, Robert Morris and Cy Twombly, both of whom maintain a significant, if sometimes ironic, relationship to gestural abstraction, an important movement in painting of the 1940s and 1950s.

While Morris and Twombly cannot be said to "morph" letters—or even move them around the canvas—they do focus attention on the gestural origins of inscription, on handwriting, or, more to the point, on protowriting. Their deskilling operations are aimed at exposing the kinetic impulses that underlie the act of inscription, impulses that, when repeated compulsively, threaten to render the inscription itself illegible. My argument is that these same kinetic impulses—disciplined but potentially transgressive—can be seen to motivate the way animation techniques are put to use in digital poetry. Digital poetry is the domain of cybertextuality in which the gestural energies of the body are powerfully evoked through strategies of displacement that challenge the very semantics of inscription. Thus, meaning in digital poetry is both posited and undone through, for instance, the rhythmic pulsating of letters (as in Mez's or Brian Kim Stefans's works),[6] the morphing of letters over time (as in Diana Slattery's "Glide" [2000]), or the dragging of entire words or letters to create entirely new visual languages (as in Jean-Luc Lamarque's "pianographique" [1996]). Software that sets the letter free of its positional constraints and allows it to dance on the screen offers digital poets entirely new ways of playing with the visual properties of letters. In sum, the play of the letter that characterizes the poetic genre as a whole emerges in digital poetry as indexical of a kinetic body that both generates and obscures signification achieved through written signs.

How has the body been approached by theorists of digital writing in the past? Treatments of cybertext's relationship to the body generally make one of three claims (all of which contradict the hypothesis I will explore here). First, in the wake of Donna Haraway's influential "Cyborg Manifesto," scholars of hypertext and digital literature have argued that computer technologies merely dramatize what has always been the case, namely, that there is no purely "natural" or organic body but rather all bodies produce culture (and themselves) by interfacing with prosthetic devices.[7] Christopher Keep, for instance, claims that reading and writing hypertext (in particular) are activities that undermine our boundedness as discrete physical bodies and even "refigure our perception of ourselves" (1999, 165). According to Keep, our very flesh loses its organic plenitude and becomes indistinguishable from the pulsating electronic signals extending and traversing it. "Hypertexts inscribe themselves onto the skin of the human as deeply as the human writes itself into the machine" (174), states Keep. In a sense, then, even when computer technologies mediate intercorporeal communication, the body cannot be lost—and it would be a mistake to speak of a "nostalgia" for it—since the computer itself is implicated in producing the very body that such means of communication are supposedly manifesting. Interactive computer technologies, the story goes, encourage us to revel in our dispersed subjectivity, our unbounded physical form, thus allowing us to nip in the bud whatever "nostalgia" for the *sujet unaire* we might still harbor.

The second claim, one that follows from the first, goes something like this: not only is the body produced by its prosthetic extensions but the body's gestures, its specific form of kinetic instantiation (as well as its desires), achieve a certain phenomenological existence through interaction with devices such as the computer.[8] As Marcel Mauss (1973) once argued in an entirely different context (he was speaking of cultural inscriptions rather than media inscriptions), the body's gestures are not necessary and natural to it but are learned responses to specific cultural demands. The kinetic body is thus created by the tasks it is called on to perform. Writing about cyberspace, Keep makes a similar point, insisting that the body never springs forth fully realized but is instead shaped and constructed by the gestures that machines impose upon it. Dragging the mouse and lightly tapping the tips of the fingers are gestures that define a new gestural body, one coterminous with a keyboard and screen. Once in dialogue with the machine, not even our desires can be said to be ours alone (or to originate in our libido). Choices made during the process of reading (or interacting) are partially determined by features of the programming; they are not realizations of a unified subject's autonomous and individuated desires.

I don't intend to spend much time taking on these first two claims, except to say that, to my mind, the argument made for the influence of prosthetic devices on the body, its gestures, and its desires is, in the case of the computer, hugely overstated given the long history of commerce between human beings and their tools.[9] It is difficult to see how the computer undermines our discretely embodied subjectivity any more than a telephone does. The body as a unit capable of suffering, as wired by a finite set of nerves to pick up changes in the object world, remains bounded, no matter what device it employs. It is still our wrist that gets cramped, our neck that gets sore— not the computer's arched frame. The small motor movements the computer requires may eventually become inscribed as unconscious habits; however, these movements also produce conscious sensations in a body that cannot be entirely changed. These visceral, internal sensations of movement, posture, and orientation that come with having a body at all are precisely what the digital poets I study attempt to convey. They seek to capture the quality of what Sally Ann Ness has called "kinetic chaining," movement procedures that feed a mind "exploring its environment," as she puts it, "through something other than its eyes and ears" (1992, 5). To be sure, in computer writing, the relation between the body as a sensory apparatus exploring a machine with its fingertips and the actual shapes of the figures that appear on the screen is mediated to a large extent. In handwriting, the hand mimes the shape of an "R" and, if furnished with the proper implement, simultaneously produces the shape of an "R" on a receptive support. Such perfect mimesis does not occur in most cases of computer writing; yet, even the swish of the tiny arrow of the mouse across a flat space of light mirrors in proportion the sweep of the arm as it directs where that arrow is to go. Such mirrorings, or visual reproductions of "kinetic chains," are frequent in the digital poems I analyze here. In fact, the software programs digital poets use provide many opportunities for creating a bond between the writer's visceral experience of tracing letters and the graphic instantiation of this tracing, a bond that is closer, I would argue, than that produced by the technologies of the typewriter or the printing press.

This last point brings me to the third approach to the body offered by recent theorists of digital writing. Scholars such as Mark Poster and Mark Seltzer have made the claim that not only is the body's originary mediation— its otherness to itself—dramatized by computer technologies but computer technologies *accentuate* that mediation, making palpable the distance between the individual body and the traces it leaves on the page. Poster and Seltzer both insist that computer writing renders less immediate, more attenuated, the contact between the hand and its product, the inscription. Poster, for instance, writes:

Compared to the pen, the typewriter, or the printing press, the computer demateri-
alizes the trace. As inputs are made to the computer through the keyboard, pixels of
phosphor are illuminated on the screen, pixels that are formed into letters. Since these
letters are no more than representations of ASCII codes contained in Random
Access Memory, they are alterable practically at the speed of light. The writer encoun-
ters his or her words in a form that is evanescent, instantly transformable, in short,
immaterial. (1990, 111)

Seltzer echoes this view, stating that writing with digital instruments
"replaces . . . that fantasy of continuous transition [from hand to mark, from
body to page] with recalcitrantly visible and material systems of difference;
with the standardizing spacing of keys and letters; with the dislocation of
where the hands work, where the letters strike and appear, where the eyes
look" (1992, 10). The significant word in Seltzer's description is, of course,
"fantasy"; handwriting, he notes, appears to fulfill the fantasy of an immedi-
ate relation between the body and its form of self-expression, a fantasy that a
word processor employing an electronic keyboard cannot even pretend to
entertain.

As opposed to Seltzer, I believe that digital writers are obsessed with the
fantasy of immediacy because of, rather than despite, the computer's attenu-
ations of contact between touch and type. Further, and somewhat paradoxi-
cally, I would maintain that this fantasy of immediacy is retrieved through
the very technologies accused of displacing it. What occurs in certain forms
of digital poetry in particular is not the *acceleration* of that "radical decenter-
ing of the subject effected by earlier writing technologies" (Keep 1999, 170)
but, on the contrary, a recuperation, in another form, of that hand-page contact
that was supposedly lost. Finally, one cannot assume that handwriting pro-
vides greater intimacy between the body and its inscriptions. Handwriting
may provide, for Keep, Poster, and Seltzer, a fantasy of immediacy, but his-
torically, handwriting has represented the very opposite, namely, the body's
submission to regimes of gestural training that are neither natural nor easily
acquired.

In fact, almost all scenes of writing throughout the history of philosophy—
those found in Plato, Hegel, Husserl, Foucault, and Derrida are most famil-
iar to me—stress the degree to which human intention and affect are distorted
in chirographic cultures (as opposed to oral cultures).[10] According to many,
the body that makes contact with the page, the hand that produces the script,

has already been disciplined, self-alienated, at once device and limb, expressive tool and conditioned flesh. As Foucault writes suggestively in *Discipline and Punish*, good handwriting "presupposes a *gymnastics*—a whole routine whose rigorous code invests the body in its entirety, from the points of the feet to the tip of the index finger" (1979, 152; italics mine). Handwriting is a kind of telescoped athletics, a compressed "gymnastics" that is at once tightly constrained and potentially explosive. The acquisition of proper orthography involves a degree of coercion and conditioning, but it also provides a support for the transmission of a bodily energy that might not otherwise find an acceptable cultural outlet.

Melanie Klein, in her essay "The Role of School in the Libidinal Development of the Child" ([1923] 1967), goes one step further, emphasizing that this contained energy is not only corporeal but also libidinal in nature and that handwriting, therefore, possesses an erotic dimension. Studying a group of schoolchildren first approaching literacy, Klein observes how they submit themselves to the physical discipline of writing and yet find ways of charging this writing with the energy of the very body that has—through the behaviors demanded by penmanship—been repressed. Klein's reflections suggest that children invest individual letters not only with personal meanings but also with barely bridled kinetic and libidinal energies. The practice that disciplines the body, Klein advances, becomes the support for the body's expression, that is, for the discharge of a corporeal energy that has been diverted from its "natural" course. Klein narrates stories in which little Fritz, for example, imagines the dotted *i*'s to be penises, or in which little Ernst, while learning to perfect the lower case *l*, thinks of masturbating as he moves the pen repetitively up and down, up and down. It is worth keeping in mind this rhythmic aspect central to handwriting when we observe works of digital poetry that employ rhythmic devices, such as the regular flashing of letters on the screen or the addition of a light pulse beneath the written character.

Other theorists of orthography less concerned with sexuality per se have also suggested that letters can serve as the support for a wide variety of expressive investments. Pierre Duborgel (1992), for instance, claims that the first graphemic exercises of the child tend to associate the letters of the alphabet either with faces or with the animals and objects the letters resemble. Typically, during the period when the child is first learning to sketch letters on paper, she does not distinguish between the two activities—drawing and writing—maintained as separate disciplines by the educational academy, and thus, as a result, letters can easily bear iconic value.[11] Duborgel's most interesting point, however, is that, ontogenetically and phylogenetically, both letters and depictions are preceded by "griffonages," or seemingly random scribblings. At the origin of writing, then, is "une gesticulation," a gesture, or really a set of motor movements, that Serge Tisseron (another psychologist of early child development) names the "inscriptive gesture." As Tisseron writes, the "genesis of the text, as of any written mark . . . , must be considered from the viewpoint of the original spatial play which the hand stages" (1994, 29). And he adds—tacitly invoking Melanie Klein—"what is at stake in the hand is the very nature of the psychic investments which are bound up in it." All writing, in short, is disciplined corporeal energy; as a corollary, then, writing always involves an originary alienation, a moment of negativity, that is not necessarily exacerbated—but only inflected differently—when new implements, such as the electronic keyboard, are introduced.

Now, it might seem at first that this narrative of writing's grounding in gesture is irrelevant to an account of digital writing, especially of digital *poetry*, which supposedly depends upon the "material effects" of the letter rather than upon the letter's capacity to transmit a libidinal charge.[12] The computer keyboard, one might argue, obviates the need for pressure, for marked bodily investment, and thus, computer writing is as far from handwriting—and its gestural disciplines and pleasures—as one can get. However, it is by no means clear that the hand and its "psychic investments" are forgotten in computer writing. On the contrary, according to Tisseron, writing on the computer reestablishes our connection with earlier writing practices: "The importance given to hand gestures," he states, "does not exclude the increasingly large share of textual creation which is performed by machines, starting with the home computer. In fact, the current technological evolution is drawing noticeably closer to the conditions presiding over the manual creation of a manuscript" (1994, 29–30). It would seem, then, that when using a word processor, the body rediscovers in a displaced form elements of its kinetic connection to the support (page or screen). Not only does the mouse engage the hand (wrist, arm, and shoulder also play a role), allowing it to draw invisible figures with the cursor (and these figures can be made visible, as we shall see), but the fact that portions of text can be displaced from one spot in a manuscript to another, that simple movements of the fingers can alter fonts, or that letters and words can be dragged, distorted, rotated, or even set spinning suggests that innovations specific to digital technology have the unprecedented power to recall, for the eye and the hand, the rhythmic and gestural components of inscription.

It is in this light, I believe, that digital writing must be seen. The conventional genealogy of digital poetry traces it back to movements in concrete and visual poetry, thereby emphasizing the letter's attributes as a visual entity. This approach to digital poetry is of course valid and illuminating, but it does not allow us to focus sufficient attention on the way the digital letter's graphic materiality is *embodied*, the mode of its apparition on the screen. Thus, instead of situating digital poetry in the genealogy of concrete and visual poetries, I will place digital poetry in the context of other traditions in the arts that share certain aspects of digital poetry's particular form of material embodiment. While it is true that concrete poems can evoke indirectly the kinetic basis of writing, there have also been other, equally pertinent regions of aesthetic activity in which the gestural and rhythmic components of writing have received emphasis. I believe it is fruitful to consider digital poetry—or at least some varieties of it—in tandem with works created under the rubric of "gestural abstraction," works that can help us to recover some of the more provocative and even subversive uses of animation in contemporary poetic practice.[13]

But before I launch into my reading of gestural abstraction and its relation to digital poetry, I need to justify my recourse to painting (and drawing), since it is not transparently clear why an argument concerning the kinetic features of digital poetry would involve establishing an analogy with static—as opposed to animated—works. In truth, many digital poems are relatively static—that is, while blocks of text or letters might be moved around the screen (as a result of interactive or preprogrammed procedures), the letters themselves do not, in isolation, move or morph. Yet, even in these relatively static poems, attention is drawn to the act of shaping, to the gestures required for creating the strokes that produce inscriptions. The static works of the visual artists I study here share certain features with the digital poems of this variety. In addition, there is a further link to be made between, on the one hand, Morris's and Twombly's imitations of handwriting and, on the other, digital poems that mime the *ductus*, either by allowing the user to morph or trace a letter by interactive means or by staging the letter as movement, as an animated form (e.g., as in Bill Marsh's or Jim Andrews's works). So while Twombly and Morris create figures that do not themselves literally move on the canvas, they nonetheless evoke a physicality, the physicality of protowriting, reminding us that without what Tisseron calls "the inscriptive gesture," no inscription could come into being. Morris and Twombly draw our attention to the gestures rooting but also potentially undermining the integrity of the written character. They attend to the most simple and repeatable motor movements undergirding tracing systems in order to bring to mind the kinetic energy central to but tamed by all acts of inscription. Their fascination with exercises productive of writing is coincident with their desire to understand the nature (and the culture) of inscribing in general.

Although primarily known as a sculptor and performance artist, Robert Morris has long been interested in the relation of art to written language. In 1973, Morris began working on a series of drawings called *Blind Time—Blind Time I* (1973), *II* (1976), *III* (1985), *IV* (1991), *V* (1999), and *VI* (2000)—each of which made explicit reference to the relation between handwriting and its gestural impetus. The procedure he developed for producing the series involved several different elements: time (he gave himself a certain number of minutes in which to finish the drawing); touch (he worked blindfolded with bare hands); gesture (his physical movements involved the entire upper torso and sometimes the feet as well); and writing (he imitated the spatial orientation of Western writing systems, often moving his body—and thus tracing lines—from the upper left-hand corner to the lower right-hand corner). According to Maurice Berger, Morris "would define a particular drawing task (related to such conditions as pressure, distance, location, and shape), estimate the length of time needed for its completion, and finally, close his eyes and draw on paper with his fingers using graphite mixed with plate oil" (1989, 150). To each drawing, Morris appended a text carefully handwritten in the margin (first, at either the left or right bottom corner, then at the top or along the bottom margin, and finally, on the back of the paper/vellum). This handwritten text describes the task assigned and the length of time it took to complete it. Morris's experiments in *Blind Time* explore the similarities and differences between more immediate, overtly gestural inscriptions (involving larger motor movements) and more mediated, carefully regulated writing practices (in which these movements are condensed and telescoped), and thus speak directly to the concerns of this chapter.

An example will suffice to make the connection between digital mediations and procedural mediations clear. In a drawing from *Blind Time I* (figure 11.1), Morris juxtaposes a "scrupulously-penciled text" with a double set of

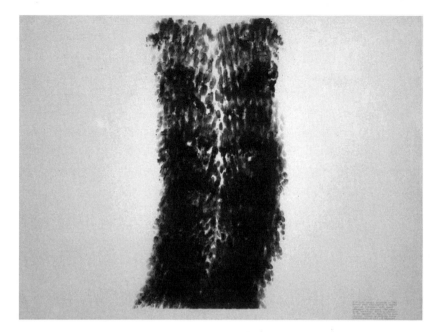

Figure 11.1 Robert Morris, *Blind Time I* (1973). © Artist's Rights Society.

graphite smudges (Berger 1989, 14).[14] The text, or legend, reads as follows: "With eyes closed, graphite on the hands, and estimating a lapsed time of 3 minutes, both hands attempt to descend the page with identical touching motions in an effort to keep an even vertical column of touches. Time estimation error: +8 seconds" (qtd. in Meltzer 2003, 14). This "even vertical column of touches" shares certain features with the Western organization of text as it appears in the legend on the lower right-hand side.[15] But whereas this legend announces itself clearly as writing, the vertical columns of touches confuse the boundary between writing and smudging, between the highly constrained gestures required to produce legible handwriting and the more full-bodied mark-making gestures that can mime but not reproduce the rigors of handwriting. And yet even the smudges, aligned almost neatly in two rows, recall the disciplinary imperative of written language. Here, Morris seems to be attempting to train his hands to behave in an unnatural, choreographed fashion: both hands strive to move in concert, setting themselves the impossible task of producing two identical sets of marks. The imposition of identity on two hands that are often trained to execute two different types of gestures mirrors (yet displaces) the denaturalization of the body's movements in general as this body is submitted to other types of socialization, such as the acquisition of handwriting or draftsmanship. The double-column, two-handed drawings thus render visceral the immediate connection between hand and support while simultaneously focusing attention on writing as a physical *discipline*. The *Blind Time* drawings reveal graphically and dramatically the tension between discipline and self-expression that structures *both* writing and smudging but is of course far more successfully veiled in the former. In other words, the drawing restages, within a different context, the scenario that initially produced the authoritatively neat handwriting, whose own performance is here relegated to the margins by the kinetic energy of the drawing, or graphic text. In sum, there is no pure immediacy in Morris's "gestural abstraction"; all strokes—minute, neat, and observed by the eye, or larger, messier, and freed of optical surveillance—submit to mediating disciplines. The latter inscription, however, exposes to both the view of the spectator and the proprioception of the producer the potentially dangerous kinetic energies that have been restrained and transmitted (to varying degrees) in the case of each.

The same juxtapositions between more overtly physical and rhythmic inscriptions, on the one hand, and contained and standardized inscriptions, on the other, characterize the works of Twombly as well. Another member of the late 1960s–early 1970s generation of artists obsessed with print and written language, Twombly also concentrates his energies on writing and its origins in drawing, marking, and, implicitly, movement. Particularly relevant to my concerns are the dark-ground canvases created between the years 1967 and 1972; just as Morris turned at approximately that moment to the relation between drawing and writing, so too did Twombly. Both were fascinated by the relation between a task-oriented exercise (with all its implications of imposed rigor and restraint) and a more generous—yet still controlled—use of the body's movements (with all the risks of its irregularities and uncontrollable impulses).

Consider Twombly's *Cold Stream* (1966), for instance (figure 11.2). Here, we witness a proliferation of marks, their careful insertion into a defined space, and the strange tension between copying (or repeating), on the one hand, and going beyond the bounds of the model (or initiating), on the other. The allusion to handwriting is again clear. (This canvas and others like it have been compared to the protowriting exercises of a Palmer Method primer.) As in the Morris

Figure 11.2 Cy Twombly, *Cold Stream* (1966), oil and crayon on canvas. Permission granted by Nicola del Roscia for the Cy Twombly estate.

drawings, the marks are arranged along rows and follow the itinerary of a (Western) written text on a blackboard. One is tempted to view these repeated spirals as simultaneously exercises, attempts to achieve the perfect form, and, conversely, deskilling operations, perverse or dogged efforts to release the energy of the body *through* form. Curiously, the same gestures that produce form eventually instigate its undoing; the letter-like shapes begin to lose their integrity (see lower left-hand corner) and become somewhat angular in the process of a kind of ferocious, driven repetition.

In a related painting of 1970, *Untitled* (figure 11.3), the circling, swirling gestures again appear to move from the left to the right, and each line of spirals is stacked upon another, forming three distinct rows. However, this time, these lines of spirals increase markedly in size as the hand moves down the canvas/blackboard. If the swirls began as more contained movements— and if they even seem at times to achieve the status of letters, as at the end

Figure 11.3 Cy Twombly, *Untitled* (1970). Permission granted by Nicola del Roscia for the Cy Twombly estate.

of row two—they nonetheless soon become violently erratic, moving in and out of legibility as letters. Similar although not identical gestures, initially telescoped, seek a greater radius, revealing thereby the quantum of explosive physical energy propelling handwriting but usually veiled by skill. Finally, the background of the painting places stress on the notion of support—more particularly, on that peculiar notion of the virgin support of writing that is the schoolchild's fantasy of creation. Here, making marks is cast as an act of resistance; the marker has to counter the dynamic orientation of a previous writing, barely discernable underneath. The painting seems to be telling us that part of the energy of writing is in fact antagonistic; it comes from a force applied against writing itself. Writing, or, more precisely, the act of inscribing letters, seems to want to destroy writing, to return to the gestural impetus, to the initial corporeal investment in leaving a trace. Twombly discovers an interesting paradox: that the gestures responsible for writing, performed repeatedly, threaten to destroy writing itself.

How does all this relate to digital poetry? I would argue that digital poetry's play with the letter, a play facilitated by animation programs, can be situated within this trajectory of artists working to reanimate the letter, to reveal its hidden energies. My detour through the visual arts is meant to indicate how gestural force is always displaced and disciplined in any act of inscription; digital poetry merely displaces and disciplines the gestural impulse in an entirely different way—by introducing its own mediations, its own checks on subjective agency, such as aleatory or algorithmic procedures and the transfer of kinetic energy from corporeal practices to digital operations. Some digitally animated poems even follow inscription into the troubling domain where Twombly led it; such poems allow the user to alter to the point of illegibility the letters that her gestures initially brought into being. One of the points I hope these images have made is that the kinetic energy deposited in codified marks can be evoked in a great variety of ways. A Morris does not look like a Twombly; and yet they accomplish similar displacements. I see digital poetry as reclaiming, by means of its own unique innovations, this same expressive ground.

Philippe Castellin, a conceptual artist and digital poet, has himself claimed to belong to the Morris tradition, having been influenced by Morris's attempts to stage inscriptions as performances. In an essay linked to the DOC(K)S Web site, Élodie Moirenc (1998) demonstrates how Castellin draws on Morris's use of gesture to create verbal-visual works in "Man/Oeuvre," an installation/performance produced in collaboration with Jean Torregrosa in 1998.[16] Just as Morris's sculptures (and, implicitly, his drawings) engage the bodies of both the producer and the viewer, so too Castellin's works transform the space of viewing (or reading) into a stage upon which masses and words—or, here, word-masses—are displaced through gestures executed over time. In the 1998 installation/performance, which Castellin would soon recast as a digital poem entitled "Le Poème est la somme," a set of large cinder blocks ("parpaings") are stacked in four columns, each block bearing one word of the sentence: "LE POEME EST LA SOMME DE L'ENSEMBLE INFINI DES FORMES A L'INTERIEUR DESQUELLES IL SE SENT TOUJOURS EGALEMENT A L'ETROIT" (THE POEM IS THE SUM OF THE INFINITE TOTALITY OF FORMS INSIDE OF WHICH IT ALWAYS FEELS EQUALLY [ALSO]

CONSTRAINED). The words of the sentence can be read either horizontally, from left to right, or vertically, column by column, in which case, the (now ungrammatical) sentence reads, "LE SOMME DES DESQUELLES TOU-JOURS/POEME DE FORMES IL EGALEMENT/EST L'ENSEMBLE A SE A/LA INFINI L'INTERIEUR SENT L'ETROIT" (THE SUM OF THE OF WHICH ALWAYS/POEM OF FORMS IT EQUALLY [ALSO]/IS THE TOTALITY TO ITSELF TO/THE INFINITE INSIDE FEELS CON-STRAINED). During the performance of the piece, the separate blocks are first placed all together in the form of a large cube; then Jean Torregrosa and Philippe Castellin employ a set of wheels to lift, transport, and rearrange the blocks, one by one, first into lines, then into columns. Sometimes these columns form nonsense sentences, and sometimes the two artists manage to recompose a significant sentence, such as that quoted earlier. The sculp-ture/performance/construction/poem contains the following elements: the passage of time, repeated rhythmic gestures, writing (understood broadly, as involving the artist's entire body), and reading (on the part of both the pro-ducer and the viewer).[17] As Moirenc notes, "a rigorous and repetitive gestural routine [*gestuelle*]" is established as essential for the production of inscriptions; blocks of letters become, literally, blocks of matter, transported—and thus given meaning—through the expenditure of a visibly large quantity of physical force.

In Castellin's digital remake of this same piece, "Le Poème est la somme" of 1998, the energy required to displace words is transferred from the bodies of the producers to, on the one hand, the machine (a preprogrammed algo-rithm determines the position of each word on the screen) and, on the other, the hand of the interactive user (a click halts the movement of the letters or propels them into entirely different relationships). While the poem cannot be said to begin at any precise point, when the user pulls up the site, she is most often confronted with a screen filled with traveling, flipping, flickering words—the original words found in "Man/Oeuvre" (plus the author's name and the date of the poem), in bright neon colors against a black background (figure 11.4). These words float in seemingly haphazard directions for between one and fifteen seconds before they suddenly halt in their tracks, forming an ephemeral and disjointed page of legible signifiers. The circulating words never stop for more than a few seconds, just long enough to give the reader time to form a visual impression but not long enough to provide her with a readable text. The viewer responds to the kinetic quality of the radiant words

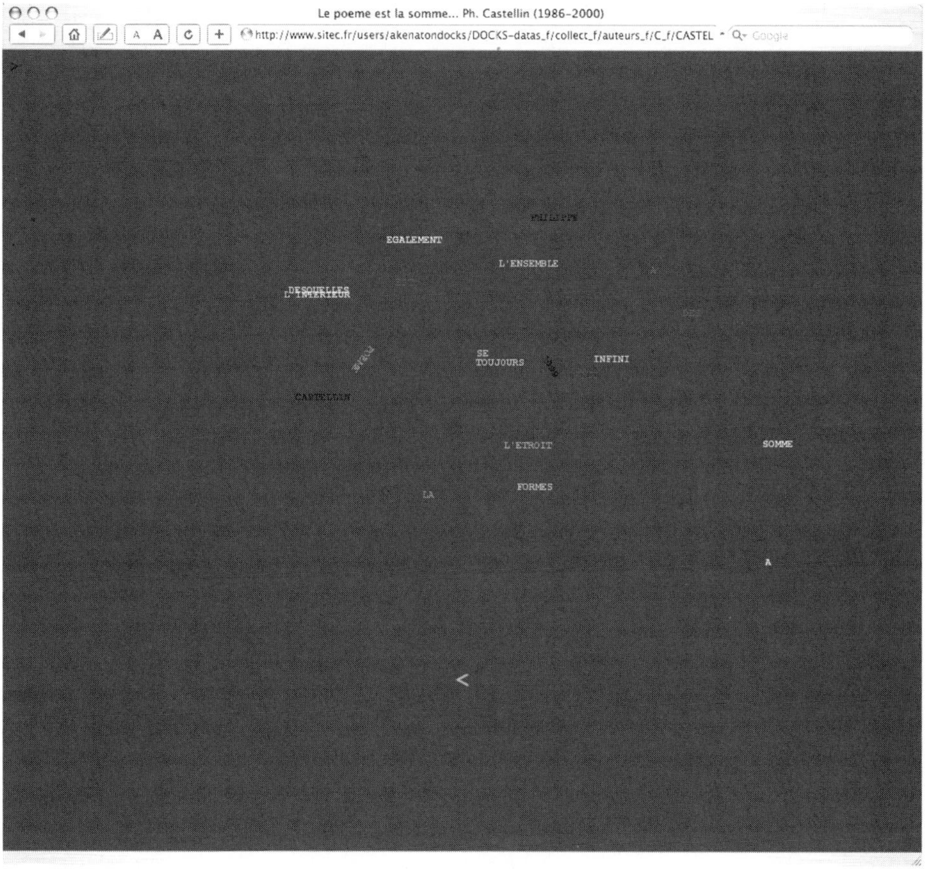

Figure 11.4 Screenshot from "Le Poème est la somme" by Philippe Castellin.
http://www.sitec.fr/users/akenatondocks/DOCKS-datas_f/
collect_f/auteurs_f/C_f/CASTELLIN_f/anim_f/lasomme_F/poeme.html.

by following their movement—and their arrested patterns—with her eyes, thus tracing out a variety of optical paths that a "normal" text would never produce. The learned response to text is challenged—and thus, the skills acquired in literacy are temporarily undone—when animation sets written language in motion. The poem never seems to contain the same combinations of words twice; presumably, the permutations of syntax and content are limitless, "à l'infini," even as the sum ("la somme") of the poem remains constant, a given quantity of signifiers placed in temporary arrangements that appear to be limitlessly renewed.

Digital Gestures

Whereas the earliest manifestation of the poem, "Man/Oeuvre," operated its permutations only on the level of syntax (entire words could be rearranged, but not letters), the digitalized "Le Poème est la somme" begins to isolate letters as units of matter that can also be circulated, displaced, submitted to the gestures of the machine or the user who clicks on a word to stop or restart its rotation. This can be seen with the decomposition of the word "EGALE-MENT," which appears on the screen as "EGALEMEN" with the "T" positioned beneath. The wordplay is delicious: meaning "equally" or "also," "EGALEMENT" suggests that all permutations of the poem are equally valid and that there is no master text toward which the circulating letters are convening. The scission of the word "EGALEMENT" into two parts further indicates that, on the level of their material existence, the letters are themselves nothing but building blocks, each equal to the other (just as the cinder blocks in "Man/Oeuvre" were exactly equal in weight); these building blocks can always break off to form new visual spectacles, new choreographies of language in space. Thus, no single version of the poem—provisionally fixed—is superior to any other; rather the power of the infinite is reserved for the poem in its "ensemble," in its fluid, unfixed state. As the sentence in "Man/Oeuvre" tells us, the poem always feels its infinity constrained by its static forms: "Le poème est la somme de l'ensemble infini des formes à l'intérieur desquelles il se sent toujours également à l'étroit." Poetry, it would seem, is conceived here not as fixity but as incessant movement: whether the result of physical gestures or programmed codes, poetry (movement) works in the service of both meaning construction (static, legible inscription) and meaning displacement (illegible but suggestive recombinations of the elements, kinetic and durable, of inscription).

Clearly, Castellin is troping on Morris's idea of inscription as a type of performance involving kinetic energy expended over time. The user who plugs into "Le Poème est la somme" is at once observing and taking part in this performance. She is brought into confrontation with the skills she has acquired to read and write (moving the eyes from left to right, using the fingers and hand to produce inscriptions, in this case digitally on a screen); but this reader is also asked to *de*skill, to liberate her optical movements from the strict regime of literacy, and to accept the explosive, unregimented shapes of protowriting as words and letters dance erratically but rhythmically about the screen. Just as young children learning to write enjoy drawing letters all over the page, truncating words and placing their constitutive units in any arrangement whatsoever, so too the interactive user of "Le Poème est la somme" responds with pleasure to the inventive placement of the *T*, or to the upside-down "POESIE" that hurtles diagonally across the screen like a jet plane shot down in midflight. Inscription is here resituated with respect to time (we feel time elapse), space (we become vividly aware of space as an active participant in communication), and movement (the gestures required for inscription are re-evoked through the trajectories of words on the screen). Finally, we recognize that the poem itself is composed not only of an infinite number of word sequences (as in Oulipian word games) but also of *an infinite number of movements*, movements that occur both in virtual and real time/space.

In my reading, "Le Poème est la somme" merely hints at the fact that the movements generating signs are related to movements that challenge and obscure signification. Castellin never allows words to be smeared or letters to be altered beyond recognition.[18] The link, however, between gestures that create signs and gestures that destroy them is dramatically underscored by Jean-Luc Lamarque, a digital artist whose "pianographique" I would like to discuss in conclusion. While Lamarque's "pianographique" is not a poem in the same way that "Le Poème est la somme" attempts to be, this complex and multifaceted work integrates inscriptions into its rich visual universe in such a way as to emphasize the connection between protowriting and postwriting, the kinetic energies that produce signs and the kinetic energies that distort them. "pianographique" is a collective work by a dizzying number of French Web artists and musicians, a "multimedia instrument," as Lamarque tells us, created in 1993 on CD-ROM and made available on the Web in 1996.[19] The interactive user is presented with a keyboard on the screen that corresponds to the keyboard beneath her fingertips. Each letter of the user's keyboard, when pressed, produces a distinct sound score and an animation that can be displaced by the hand of the user by means of a mouse. Playing the "piano" of graphics and sound bites, the user can create an infinite number of verbal-visual-aural collages, while hitting the space bar effaces all that has come before.

It is not possible here to discuss all ten sections of "pianographique" (each of which contains a verbal element of varying complexity, such as "Jazz" or "Je te contrôle et tu n'as pas de choix" [I control you, and you have no choice]), but I would like nonetheless to take a quick look at one section in particular, "Rude Boy," programmed by Lamarque with images by Frédéric Matuszek

Figure 11.5 Screenshot from "pianographique" in "Rude Boy" mode by Jean-Luc Lamarque. http://www.pianographique.net.

and sound by Jantoma. The imagery of "Rude Boy" is clearly chosen in order to play with the visual differences between discrete types of signifiers: by tapping on *a*, *s*, or *r*, the user produces what looks like a page of type or bar codes ("*t*" produces the same in red, *z* in white); by tapping on *b*, *l*, *q*, or *x*, the user produces some kind of icon or conventionalized nonalphabetic symbol, such as an arrow, a road sign, or, in the case of *x*, the Nike insignia; by tapping on *d*, *g*, *k*, or *n*, the user produces a graffiti tag or wildstyle; and finally, by tapping on *h*, the user produces the word "listen" in lowercase, red letters. If at any point the user decides to engage the mouse, and therefore to distort the image by dragging it around the screen, the sign quality (and semantic value) of the image is soon lost. The page of type becomes a tapestry, a cloth of woven writing (figure 11.5), while the "wildstyle" inscription, "No Racism," abandons its semantic content as it hollows out the screen and fills it with illusionary three-dimensional space (figure 11.6). In other words, Lamarque has programmed "pianographique" in such a way that the same constricted motions required to form a letter (curves and lines) are responsible, when digitally processed, for the letter's disfigurations on its radiant support. The swirling motions of the user's hand are mirrored perfectly on the screen,

Figure 11.6 Screenshot from "pianographique" in "Rude Boy" mode by Jean-Luc Lamarque. http://www.pianographique.net.

only this time, when the implement is the letter itself, these gestures render the letter illegible; its constituent marks are returned to protowriting, to the status of meaningless shapes and lines. What is remarkable about the programming of "pianographique" is that it allows such small displacements to effect such huge distortions. Whereas in Twombly's paintings the letter-like quality of the mark is lost once the body's gestures are magnified and a greater quantum of physical energy is released, here, in the digital universe, even a hand gyrating carefully within the confined radius of a mouse pad can humble legibility, can bring legibility, so to speak, to its knees. Digital poetry is perhaps, then, the ideal genre in which to expose not only the visual properties of written language but also writing's status as a performed activity, its relation to the body's dance.

Notes

1. I am greatly indebted to Stephanie Strickland for exposing me to the work of Camille Utterbach, who presented "Text Rain" at the Technopoetry Festival, Georgia Tech, 2002.

2. For a genealogy of digital poetry that connects it back to earlier concrete visual poetries, see Bohn 1996 and Bolter 1991.

3. The very innovations I will be discussing here have been attacked as imitating too closely the aesthetics of commercially oriented animated inscriptions, such as film credits and advertising blurbs. The controversy concerning the imbrication of digital poetry software (especially Flash) in commercial contexts has in fact been quite heated. For an overview of this controversy, see www.webartery.com, contributions by Andrews and Howard. See also Hayles on "flickering signifiers" in "Open-Work: Dining at the Interstices."

4. N. Katherine Hayles very astutely noted at the New Media Poetics Conference, where this chapter was first presented, that in the case of algorithmically produced displacements of the letter, there is no immediate investment of human energy involved. My point is that even if the machine is "having all the fun" (as she and John Cayley put it), the gestures the letters execute on the screen provide an experience for the viewer that is different from that provided by static text. Within that difference there are, of course, further distinctions to be made; I can only begin here to sketch out a phenomenology of reading animated texts. Future discussions of the kinesthetic experience of screen viewing will have to rely on recent scholarship in film reception, which has been particularly attentive to the ways in which movements on a screen affect the body of the viewer.

5. Robert Kendall proposes the term "scriptal" animation (in response to my suggestion, "ductile" animation). He writes, "Most animated poetry is invoking not so much the movement of the hand in handwriting but the movement of the typewriter pattern or the word-processing cursor. There are a few poems I've seen (such as Bill Marsh's "Aria") that build letters kinetically stroke by stroke, but most of them either build words letter by letter (in a process that looks like text being typed on a word-processing screen) or else work with larger units, building texts a word or line at a time. Maybe the term 'scribal' animation would be more appropriate, since this implies handwriting but could also apply to typing" (email message to Carrie Noland, October 8, 2002).

6. See, for instance, Mez's "Fleshistics" and Stefans's *the dreamlife of letters*.

7. See Haraway 1991, Poster 1990, and Hayles 1999.

8. With respect to the production of the desiring body, Keep underscores the vulnerability of our "own" desires to those of the preprogrammed hypertextual system. When we sit before a computer screen and engage our desires with the hypertext's desires, he suggests, our unified subjectivity is compromised.

9. See, for instance, Leroi-Gourhan 1993.

10. See Ong 1982 for a classical, if flawed, treatment of the problem.

11. According to Duborgel (1992, 142), the child has to undergo a kind of apprenticeship of the arbitrary, since the child's instinct is to invest the letters themselves with pictographic values. See also Georgel 1989.

12. I am referring here to Paul de Man's association of poetry with the play (agency) of the letter (divorced from any lexical or semantic function) and his theoretical reflections on "materiality" and "material effects" in "Phenomenality and Materiality in Kant" (1996). For de Man, the letter, as a mark of support, is an entirely inhuman thing; seen in this light, the letter most decidedly cannot be interpreted as embodying the kinetic energy of a human body. De Man's battle against the anthropomorphizing moves of phenomenological criticism is astringent and thought-provoking; however, his position cannot account for—and is to some extent contradicted by—a long line of artists and writers (including Twombly and Morris) who approach mark making as a corporeal practice in which kinetic investments leave a visible remainder in the trace. De Man's argument should be contrasted with that in Barthes 1979 and in Strickland 2001.

13. "Gestural abstraction" refers to a movement in American art of the 1940s and 1950s that included painters such as Willem de Kooning and Jackson Pollock. Robert Morris does not, strictly speaking, belong to this group; however, his interest in gesture, and his decision to foreground its productive contribution in his works, allies him with some of the artists working in that mode. Twombly's relation to "gestural abstraction" is treated by Varnedoe: "Their gestural abstraction [that of the New York School] expressed the notion that the most acute moments of self-realization were epiphanic and to be externalized only by heroic acts of Zen spontaneity, disengaged from control and committed instead to dynamism, risk, and chance" (1994, 24). In contrast, according to Varnedoe, Twombly's works submit spontaneously to compulsive repetition, the transgressive physicality of the stroke to an obsessive discipline.

14. Meltzer explores the public nature of writing versus the private investments we make in it. "Learning to write," she suggests, "we learn to belong to and participate in a public mode of inscription, to subordinate the private and disordered gestures of the hand to the measured and mathematical means of writing" (2003, 16). "Morris's *de*-skilling repetitions," she continues, "turn back the school's clock" (17). "They reveal that underside of language, where presence and incarnated inscription are hidden from view" (18). "Blind time turns text into trace, unravels writing into drawing. . . . The drawings are about writing forgetting itself as such" (19).

15. The slant of the columns suggests the natural leaning, the list of the body as it moves toward the end of the row. This detail is not insignificant: here the graphite "marking" reflects the body's engagement in a way that the neat script on the right does not.

16. See Moirenc 1998.

17. Moirenc writes:

> At the beginning of the performance [there is] a cube which, during all the action, is transformed and is transported. We can comprehend it as a minimalist sculpture, because it is a volume of modular structure, of minimal, denuded forms, on the human scale and realized with industrial material. It is decomposed in an aleatory fashion, then recomposed until there appears a poem-wall with the inscription of words on select cinder blocks. . . . [T]he volume [acts] as a reference point and a register of the rhythm of the body that, through its action, displaces the blocks. The words appear without any ephemeral order having been decided in advance: as soon as they are positioned they are unveiled. The execution is thus based on the intervention of chance. We read: forms, totality, also, is, always, poem, constrained. The action. By means of the action, the artist has access to words. . . . The cinder blocks pass from hand to hand; words and volumes are transmitted by means of the same gesture. (1998, n.p.; my translation)

18. A comparison might fruitfully be drawn here between Castellin's work and that of Komninos Zervos, whose "Beer," for instance, operates by distorting the shapes of letters until they form other letters or a series of lines. In "Beer" there is a kind of morphological motivation at work: the shape of a letter (and not its phonetic or metrical value) motivates the next letter that appears.

19. Lamarque's collaborators include Jean-Christophe Bourroux (credited as "webmaster"), Jérôme and Xavier Pehuet, Guillaume Delaunay, Nicolas Clauss, Jean-Jacques Birgé, Jantoma, Frédéric Matuszek, Serge de Lambier, NKO, Olivier Bardin, Bérangère Lallemont, Lior Smilovici, Ed Coomes, and Nicolas Thépot.

Works Cited

Andrews, Jim. 2001. "Nio." http://vispo.com/nio/index.htm (accessed October 1, 2002).

Andrews, Jim, and Peter Howard. 2002. "Continuing Conversation on Flash." *Webartery.com*. September–November. http://www.webartery.com (accessed October 1, 2002).

Barthes, Roland. 1979. *Cy Twombly: Catalogue raisonné des oeuvres sur papier de Cy Twombly*. Milan: Multhipla Editions.

Berger, Maurice. 1989. *Labyrinths: Robert Morris, Minimalism, and the 1960s*. New York: Harper and Row.

Bohn, Willard. 1996. "From Hieroglyphics to Hypergraphics." In *Experimental–Visual–Concrete: Avant-Garde Poetry Since the 1960s*, ed. K. David Jackson, Eric Vos, and Johanna Drucker, 173–186. Amsterdam and Atlanta, GA: Rodopi.

Bolter, J. David. 1991. *Writing Space: The Computer, Hypertext, and the History of Writing*. Hillsdale, NJ: Lawrence Erlbaum.

Castellin, Philippe. 1998. "Le Poème est la somme." http://www.sitec.fr/users/akenatondocks/DOCKS-datas_f/collect_f/auteurs_/f/C_f/CASTELLIN_f/anim_f/lasomme_F/poeme.html (accessed November 10, 2003).

Cayley, John. 2002. *riverIsland*. http://www.shadoof.net/in/riverisland.html (accessed June 22, 2004).

de Man, Paul. 1996. "Phenomenality and Materiality in Kant." In *Aesthetic Ideology*, ed. Andrzej Warminski, 70–90. Minneapolis: University of Minnesota Press.

Duborgel, Pierre. 1992. *Imaginaire et pédagogie*. Toulouse: Privat.

Foucault, Michel. 1979. *Discipline and Punish: The Birth of the Prison*. Trans. Alan Sheridan. New York: Viking.

Georgel, Pierre. 1989. "Portrait de l'artiste en griffonneur." In *Victor Hugo et les images*, ed. Madeleine Blondel and Pierre Georgel, 75–119. Dijon: Aux Amateurs de Livres.

Haraway, Donna. 1991. "A Cyborg Manifesto: Science, Technology, and Socialist-Feminism in the Late Twentieth Century." In *Simians, Cyborgs, and Women: The Reinvention of Nature*, 149–181. New York: Routledge.

Hayles, N. Katherine. 1999. *How We Became Posthuman: Virtual Bodies in Cybernetics, Literature, and Informatics*. Chicago: University of Chicago Press.

Hayles, N. Katherine. 2000. "Open-Work: Dining at the Interstices." Commentary on "The Dinner Party." *Riding the Meridian* 2, no. 2. http://califia.hispeed.com/RM/haylesfr.htm (accessed June 10, 2004).

Keep, Christopher J. 1999. "The Disturbing Liveliness of Machines: Rethinking the Body in Hypertext Theory and Fiction." In *Cyberspace Textuality: Computer Technology and Literary Theory*, ed. Marie-Laure Ryan, 164–181. Bloomington: Indiana University Press.

Kendall, Robert. 2002. "Faith." http://wordcircuits.com/faith (accessed November 1, 2002).

Klein, Melanie. [1923] 1967. "Le Rôle de l'école dans le développement libidinal de l'enfant." In *Essais de psychanalyse*, 90–109. Paris: Payot.

Lamarque, Jean-Luc. 1996. "pianographique." http://pianographique.com/datas/inter_fr.php (accessed May 4, 2003).

Leroi-Gourhan, André. 1993. *Gesture and Speech*. Trans. Anna Bostock Berger. Cambridge, MA: MIT Press.

Marsh, William. 1999. "Six String Aria." http://www.factoryschool.org/btheater/works/6strA/aria.html (accessed November 18, 2003).

Mauss, Marcel. 1973. "Les Techniques du corps." *Sociologie et anthropologie*. Paris: PUF. Originally published in *Journal de Psychologie* 32 (1935): 3–4.

Meltzer, Eve. 2003. "How to Keep Mark Making Alive." Unpublished doctoral dissertation. University of California, Berkeley.

Mez [Mary Anne Breeze]. 1998. "Fleshistics." *Internal damage report vers 1.1*. http://ctheory.concordia.ca/multimedia/dirt/fleshistics/page_1.htm (accessed November 18, 2003).

Moirenc, Élodie. 1998. "Akenaton." http://www.sitec.fr/users/akenatondocks/AKENATON_f/TEXTES_f/Moirenc_f/moirenc.html (accessed February 1, 2003).

Ness, Sally Ann. 1992. *Body, Movement, and Culture: Kinesthetic and Visual Symbolism in a Philippine Community*. Philadelphia: University of Pennsylvania Press.

Ong, Walter J. 1982. *Orality and Literacy: The Technologizing of the Word*. New York: Methuen.

Poster, Mark. 1990. "Derrida and Electronic Writing: The Subject of the Computer." In *The Mode of Information: Poststructuralism and Social Context*, 99–128. Chicago: University of Chicago Press.

Seltzer, Mark. 1992. *Bodies and Machines*. New York: Routledge.

Slattery, Diana. 2000. "Glide." http://www.academy.rpi.edu/glide/apps/collabyrinth.html (accessed October 1, 2002).

Stefans, Brian Kim. 1999. *the dreamlife of letters*. UbuWeb. http://www.ubu.com/contemp/stefans/dream (accessed October 3, 2002).

Strickland, Stephanie. 2002. Vniverse. http://vniverse.com (February 14, 2003).

Strickland, Stephanie. 2001. "Moving Through Me As I Move: A Paradigm for Interaction." http://califia.hispeed.com/Strickland/ (accessed February 14, 2003).

Tisseron, Serge. 1994. "All Writing Is Drawing: The Spatial Development of the Manuscript." *Yale French Studies* 84: 29–42. Special issue on Drawing and Writing.

Utterback, Camille. 1999. "Text Rain." http://www.camilleutterback.com/textrain.html (accessed February 28, 2003).

Varnedoe, Kirk. 1994. *Cy Twombly: A Retrospective*. New York: MOMA.

Zervos, Komninos. 2004. "Beer." http://www.gu.edu.au/ppages/k_zervos/beer.html (accessed February 28, 2004).

faq

- An Allegory of *Genius*
- An Allegory of *Ambition*
- An Allegory of *Envy*

"3 Proposals for Bottle Imps." Courtesy of William Poundstone.
http://www.williampoundstone.net/Bottle.html.

3 Proposals for Bottle Imps

William Poundstone

In "3 Proposals for Bottle Imps" (see frontispiece on p. 244), I wanted to play with the idea of animated concrete poetry that tells a story. Most Web-based poetry is not strongly narrative. When you try to make a "movie of text" that's visually satisfying and has something to say, there aren't a lot of precedents to draw on. The one example that everyone mentions is movie titles, but the semantic content of movie titles is nonnarrative and not something that most viewers care about. It's a different situation when you expect people to read (and think about) content when the text is moving and morphing and other things are happening onscreen at the same time.

Because contemporary precedents are so few, I've always been interested in older works that seem to anticipate the problems of electronic poetry and literature. "3 Proposals for Bottle Imps" (Poundstone 2002) is structured around Raymond Roussel's ([1914] 1965) novel *Locus Solus*. Roussel's story concerns a gentleman scientist, Canterel, who has created a group of absurd machines on his estate outside Paris. They include "bottle imps." As Roussel uses the term, these are machines that act out stories with little figurines. There is an almost futurist quality to *Locus Solus*, a novel in which the story-telling is delegated to machines.

My Web piece purports to be three proposals for Roussel-style mechanical animations. The proposals are actually digital (Flash) animations. One of the things I realized is how much today's new media literature is similar to Roussel's bottle imps. Roussel imagines his bottle imps to be multimedia devices incorporating motion, sound, and text. They enact narratives that loop endlessly, similar to banner ads on the Web.

Figure 12.1 An Allegory of Ambition. http://www.williampoundstone.net/Ambition.html.

It's said that Roussel's fascination with multimedia was inspired by Wagnerian *Gesamtkunstwerk*. But I think Roussel put a different spin on the idea. To Wagner, multimedia was a form of thought control. He worried that the arts would work together so that everyone would feel the same thing, the same perfectly clear aesthetic message. In *Locus Solus*, the bottle imps are more agents of mystification than clarity. Visitors to Canterel's estate are dazzled by the "eye candy" aspect of it all, yet they fail to understand the bottle imps' narratives until Canterel supplies explanations. This creates a multilayered, recursive text of words explicating animations that themselves include words. Roussel likes the idea of multimedia (he likes anything "theatrical") but has none of Wagner's illusions about it.

I took some cues from Roussel. The site attempts to capture something of his aesthetic of artifice for artifice's sake (a sensibility you find in a lot of new media pieces, actually). The language itself echoes Roussel's discursive tone (figure 12.2).

In this way did Piero find subjects for his art, which was praised for its novelty of invention.

Figure 12.2 An Allegory of Genius. http://www.williampoundstone.net/Genius.html.

Using text as part of time-based multimedia raises some obvious problems. In print, everyone reads at his or her own pace. The reader can linger over a passage or turn back to something he read a few pages earlier. One can, of course, offer the same freedom with a navigation bar. But I wanted to try something less familiar, the autonomous "movie of text." How much moving text can you have without it becoming boring? How do you deal with the fact that not everyone reads at the same pace?

I think the technical problems of reading moving text are somewhat over-stated. Movie titles are often frenetic, yet everyone in a theater seems able to read them at the enforced pace. Perceptual studies show that you can flash a single word for one-twenty-fourth of a second, and viewers get it, consciously or uncon-sciously. People have an amazing capacity to perceive moving or evanescent text. I make use of that flexibility in this piece. Some of the text stays onscreen for a long time, while other text zooms by too fast to read. You maybe catch the gist of it, the way you glimpse someone's newspaper on a train (figure 12.3).

I began the piece in mid-July 2002 and completed it in early October. I do my own design and coding. With a piece such as this, in which form and content are closely related, I think it would be tough to do otherwise. Though

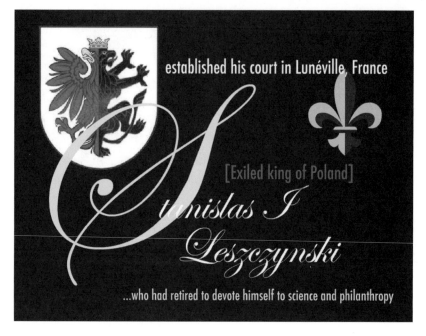

Figure 12.3   An Allegory of Envy. http://www.williampoundstone.net/Envy.html.

I did write a first draft of the text of each section before I began laying it out, almost everything was rewritten to fit the screen and the temporal rhythm.

I got most of the site's sound off the Web. There are sites such as Flashkit in which talented people post sounds and loops they've made as linkware or freeware. Adding sound to a piece such as this is less like scoring a movie and more like being a hip-hop "producer": it's about collaging preexisting elements to get an effect that is different from those elements in isolation. Sound is interesting to me because people still don't have any fixed idea of what a new media poem is supposed to sound like. Is it okay to "punctuate" a word or phrase with a sound? I started out thinking that was overly manipulative. Now I do it a lot. I may change my mind again in six months.

Works Cited

Poundstone, William. 2002. "3 Proposals for Bottle Imps." http://www. williampoundstone.net/Bottle.html (accessed June 27, 2004).

Roussel, Raymond. [1914] 1965. *Locus Solus*. Paris: Pauvert.

13

Language Writing, Digital Poetics, and Transitional Materialities

Alan Golding

One common critical trope in discussions of new media writing—as in most discussions of newness—involves the establishment of genealogies, and, by now, what J. David Bolter calls "the connection between the hypertext movement and the avant-garde tradition" (2001, 160) is a widely proposed connection. Bolter himself lays out what has increasingly become a standard line that includes Mallarmé, Apollinaire, Dada, Russian constructivism, lettrisme, concrete and visual poetry (most versions of the lineage also emphasize Marinetti). These writers' and movements' productions, in Bolter's words, offer "expressions of a growing dissatisfaction with the conventional forms of print." But they do so "from *within* the technology of the printed page; they [stand] as a critique of the conventions of the medium" (153). For Bolter, this confinement to the page is finally what limits even such efforts as Marc Saporta's loose-leaf interactive fiction *Composition No. 1* "to resist the perfection of print" (151). It is also what often leads new media theorists back into a view of print as incorrigibly rigid. Thus Bolter writes of "the freeing of writing from the frozen structure of the printed page," of "liberating the text" from the page (1991, 21). Richard Lanham, considering "what happens when text moves from page to screen," argues that "the digital text becomes unfixed and interactive" and that, as a result, "the fixed, authoritative, canonical text . . . simply explodes into the ether" (1993, 31)—an imagined effect that is one social extension of George P. Landow's claim that "hypertext does not permit a tyrannical, univocal voice" (1992, 11) as print does. For Lanham (1993), as for Bolter, print is frozen, digital writing fluid: "Hot type was *set.*

Digital typesetting programs *pour* or *flow* it" (44). For Landow, "unlike all pre-vious forms of textuality, the digital word is virtual, not physical" (1996, 216), and "the resulting textuality is virtual, fluid, adaptable, open" (218).

This view of print's confining fixity is closely connected to opposing views of "materiality," a source of some debate in the developing critical conversa-tion about new media poetry. Celebration of a liberatory immateriality per-vades, for example, the 1996 special issue of *Visible Language* on new media poetry. Throughout most of that issue, "the immateriality of new media poems" (Vos 1996, 222) is held to be transforming poetry. When literary revolutions have not been claimed in the name of a return to "common" speech (see Wordsworth on), they have been claimed—at least in the twentieth century—in the name of an intensified materiality, the word and letter as such. From the perspective of at least some new media practitioners, however, we may be looking at our first immaterial avant-garde, with the twist that it is celebrated in a rhetoric derived from that materialist Marinetti. Within this particular line of discourse, poetry is constrained by taking on material or physical form. In E. M. de Melo e Castro's videopoems, however, "[t]he page is no longer there, not even as a metaphor," so "[t]he words and the letters [can] at last be free" (1996, 141); in Eduardo Kac's "holopoetry," the word is "[f]reed from the page and freed from other palpable materials" (1996, 189). To anyone who has even a nodding acquaintance with futurism, this rhetoric will sound familiar.

In the immaterialist position, a version of the theorizing about new media that I have cited in Bolter and Lanham, print is associated with terms such as "stiffness," "immutability," "stability," "solidity"; it is "given," "static," "fixed." The electronic text is associated with terms such as "instability," "variability," "fluctuation," and "change"; it is "oscillatory," "malleable," a matter of "fluid signs," of "signifiers in motion." For Mark Poster, "the computer demateral-izes the written trace. . . . The writer encounters his or her words in a form that is evanescent, instantly transformable, in short, immaterial" (1990, 111). To sum up by quoting Eric Vos, "In terms of the labels often attached to new media, we are dealing with a virtual, dynamic, interactive, immaterial poetry" (1996, 216)—and who doesn't want to be dynamic and interactive?

Other new media theorists, however, take a different view, summarizable in Matthew Kirschenbaum's position that "the tendency to elicit what is 'new' about new media by contrasting its radical mutability with the supposed material solidity of older texts is a misplaced gesture" when, among other things, we consider the historical evidence of ephemerality, unreliability, and fragility that textual studies provides (2003). Loss Pequeño Glazier (2002) rests the entire argument of his *Digital Poetics* on the premise that "the e-text . . . *is* material" and spends much of his book explaining how (see, e.g., p. 24). Johanna Drucker and N. Katherine Hayles both offer helpfully nuanced middle positions. Drucker draws on Kirschenbaum's distinction between the "phenomenological materiality" and the "ontological immateriality" of the electronic text: the "visual form of the letter on the screen [is] fully material . . . even though the 'letter' exists as a stored sequence of binary digits with no tactile, material apparency to it in that fundamental condition" (2002, 171–172). While Hayles grants the perceived immateriality of the digital text and its "flickering signifiers" (1992, 166), she also defines materiality as "a selective focus on certain physical aspects of an instantiated text that are foregrounded by a work's construction, operation, and content" (qtd. in Gitelman 2002), and as such it can be a feature of new and old media poetry alike.

It is within the context of this debate about the material features of the print and digital environments that I want to position my argument. One well-known feature of the writing produced by poets associated with the Language school is the redirection of readerly attention to the materiality of the word. (In this way, many Language texts can be seen as what Hayles calls "technotexts," her term for work that foregrounds its own materiality or inscription technology [2002, 25].) This interest expressed itself in multiple forms, but one underdiscussed form involves the visual component of Language texts. Visual and concrete poetries are widely cited as historical precursors to new media poetries, but the visual and (re)combinatorial component of Language writing forms a significant bridge or transition between these two projects, most especially in the work of the writers to be discussed here: Steve McCaffery, Robert Grenier, and Charles Bernstein.

In their different ways, these writers point us toward considering new media poetries as part of the ongoing project of, in the terms of the title of McCaffery and Jed Rasula's coedited anthology, "imagining language" in all its textural and material variety. They have worked on the edge of what is usually called "writing," proposing that work ranging from nonalphabetic, glyph-like designs to hand-produced letter-like drawings to barely legible palimpsests to simple pen strokes can be seen/read under the sign of poetry. In their visual works, and in the online representation of those works, they raise questions about seeing and reading, the mark and the sign, circulation and distribution, and the meaning of "materiality" that seem crucial to thinking about new media poetries. Meanwhile, new media technologies fulfill certain impulses toward different forms of materiality in Language writing that were perhaps only nascent or at least partly unfulfilled in the earlier stages of that movement. McCaffery's, Grenier's, and Bernstein's work introduces into the critical conversation around new media poetries the idea of what I would call "transitional materialities": forms of visual text that interrogate the material limitations of the page-based, word-centered poem and look forward to the possibilities and achievements of digital poetics—and that often position themselves self-consciously as points of reciprocity between the print and digital environments.

In works such as the very early *Transitions to the Beast* and *Broken Mandala* (1970), parts of *Evoba* (1976–1978), the *Carnival* panels, *Modern Reading* (1967–1990), and his video poems, Steve McCaffery has been insistently concerned with *"allowing a type of reading to develop that was much closer to the classic category of 'seeing'"* (2000, 435) and with "a base sense of the materiality of the letter" (434). He describes this aspect of his work in terms most appropriate to new media poetry, talking in terms of "animated letter shapes" (434), "3 dimensional syntax" (437), and *"a network of non-linear signifiers"* (436). In particular, the transposition of *Carnival* onto the Web is a key moment in McCaffery's effort to make concrete these claims to materiality as the work "deliberately problematizes the simple distinction between seeing and reading and offers itself for both distant viewing and close reading" (2001, 70). This Web publication also reminds us that works such as *Carnival* can now be circulated on a scale and in a form that was heretofore impossible. Furthermore, they become readable in ways very different from—and sometimes in contradiction of—their writers' original intentions, and in the process of movement from paper to computer screen, their nature as texts changes. With these texts, that process involves something more than—or different from—remediation, the importing of "earlier media into a digital space in order to critique and refashion them" (Bolter and Grusin 1999, 53) or "the cycling of different *MEDIA* through one another" (Hayles 2002, 5). Their appearance on the Web helps actualize kinds of reading already immanent in the original. The process could more accurately be termed rematerialization, a shift in material medium or environment that raises a new set of aesthetic and theoretical questions about the texts.

Carnival: The First Panel, 1967–1970 (McCaffery 1973) is a packet of sixteen eight-and-a-half-by-eleven panels, stapled along the top edge but also perforated along that edge to allow for tearing. One obvious way in which Web publication changes *Carnival* is that it removes the whole component of manual de- and reconstruction, radically altering the material nature of the text. In that sense, it violates McCaffery's original directions for the book, which are only fulfillable once in any case—the book can only be torn up once. (Insofar as my library still has an intact copy, it has to be said that no library user has ever read the "book" properly.) As McCaffery and bpNichol describe it, "*Carnival* is an anti-book: perforated pages must be physically released, torn from sequence and viewed simultaneously in the larger composite whole" (1992, 65). Peter Jaeger (n.d.) calls *Carnival* "a mechanical device that comes complete with its own instruction manual" (a book-machine, as McCaffery would call it), and those instructions, on a postcard that comes with the publication, read as follows: "In order to destroy this book please tear each page carefully along the perforation. The panel is assembled by laying out pages in a square of four" (McCaffery 1973). There's as much sly humor in that juxtaposition of "destroy" and "carefully" as there is in the inclusion of an errata sheet substituting three nonsemantic blocks of text for three others. (The dissident reader, of course, might lay out pages in various arrangements, much as Robert Grenier does in the reading of his drawing poems, which I will discuss later.) As various readers have pointed out, then, echoing McCaffery's own description, it is necessary to destroy the book in order to read it; the book comes into being at the point of its own dissolution as a whole object. Examining closely how this antibook fares online by comparing the print and electronic version reveals what can be lost and gained in the move from one material environment to another.

Thirty-three years after its original publication, my print *Carnival* is somewhat yellowed and rubbed out along the edges. Its slightly faint grey type and staples announce both its own small press origins and an affiliation more generally with alternative publishing institutions of the period. In other words, as a material object, it embodies a particular phase of literary history in ways that its online presentation cannot possibly replicate. Nonhorizontal sections of text are, not surprisingly, much harder to read online; craning one's neck to view a computer screen at ninety degrees is a tougher proposition than turning a sheet of paper. I have already pointed out how the book's original purpose cannot be fulfilled since it cannot be torn up online; it can be reintegrated but not disintegrated. From this point of view, digital presentation is more static, less susceptible to transformation and manipulation, than the original and introduces into *Carnival* an unintended level of semipermanence: a significant complication of the much-vaunted fluidity and productive instability of new media technologies (figure 13.1). And if these are metaphorical losses, there is also a small literal loss: because of the online version's slightly reduced scale, about a quarter-inch of the original's right margin is lost on each panel.

Now, if the material environment of the Web loses some semantically significant features of the original, what does it add? Mostly, the visual "noise" against which we measure information. At the top left of each panel, we read instructions for navigating the text: "CARNIVAL [in red] panel 1 map assembled previous next." At the bottom right, we get the necessary concession of the small press to market concerns that the original (though both are published by Coach House Books) could avoid: "order / tip online books mail chbooks CARNIVAL [in red]." If we agree with Jerome McGann that "the way poems are printed and distributed is part of their meaning" (1993, 168)—a principle so fundamental to my argument that I could well have used it as an epigraph—then surely the social meaning of *Carnival* has changed with its entry into an online context that has attributes both of a gift and a market economy.

I hope it is clear that I mean this account as description and analysis, not complaint. One has to be grateful for the ability to view in any form not just both panels of *Carnival*, in their individual segments and assembled, but also thirty-five unpublished outtakes from Panel 2. McCaffery published *Carnival: The Second Panel*, created between 1970 and 1975, in 1977. "At the time of its composition," he writes, "I conceived *Carnival* as a calculated intervention into the material stakes of poetics" (2001, 70). And what were those stakes? An extension of the ideas about the typewriter as a writerly tool and "the repudiation of a breath-based poetics" (70) that were so influentially articulated in Charles Olson's classic essay "Projective Verse." *Carnival* seeks to offer both immersion in and distance on language, both reading and seeing: "The panel when 'seen' is 'all language at a distance'; the panel when read is entered, and offers the reader the experience of non-narrative language" (McCaffery 2000, 446). McCaffery says that "[t]he roots of *Carnival* go beyond concretism . . . to labyrinth and mandala" (444), and even if we have a different experience of their scale, those shapes can clearly be discerned on screen when we view

Figure 13.1 *Carnival.* http://www.chbooks.com/online/carnival/1_map.html.

the panel assembled (figure 13.2). However, since Panel 2 in its physical form is even more materially dense and variously textured than Panel 1, that dimension of the work is inevitably lost. McCaffery continues, "*The Second Panel* places the typed mode in agonistic relation with other forms of scription: xerography, xerography within xerography (i.e., metaxerography and disintegrative seriality), electrostasis, rubber stamp, tissue texts, hand-lettering and stencil" (445). How to get all *that* online? Rather improbably, McCaffery asserts that his own personal line of continuity extends from *Carnival* to Pope's *Dunciad*, but the explanation is revealing. The typewriter was invented the year of Pope's enlarged *The Rape of the Lock* and one year before his *Iliad*, allowing McCaffery to suggest by association that "[t]he roots of the typewriter were Augustan; its repetitive principle is the principle of the couplet enhanced by speed. The typewriter oracled a neoclassical futurism" (1977). This enabling of a future avant-garde by neoclassicism may seem less odd later in this chapter when we get to the aesthetic and material importance of the typewriter's regularity and repetitiveness in a certain stage of the work of Robert Grenier.

The other McCaffery text that I want to discuss is actually a *reading* of a McCaffery text: Brian Kim Stefans's shockwave interactive animated reading of two pages (1992, 80–81) from *Rational Geomancy*, "Rational Geomancy: Ten Fables of the Reconstruction," a work that allows us to think of digital poetics not just as a way of writing but as a way of reading. In the original pages of *Rational Geomancy*, McCaffery and bpNichol are discussing Madeline Gins's *Word Rain* as "a book *about* the reading experience that necessarily *includes* the reading experience," and with photographed thumbtips in the bottom left and right corners, they replicate one feature of Gins's book: "an ambiguity exists between the page & its photographic reproduction. some pages are 'held' by thumbs. these thumbs are photographs which your own thumb holds" (1992, 80; *sic*). Materiality self-reflexively trumps transparency in McCaffery's Gins; meanwhile Stefans uses digital (the pun is appropriate in this case) technology to push this reading and the theorizing of the material book-as-machine a number of steps further, complicating the thematics of absence, presence, embodiment, and representation that recur in McCaffery's work. Stefans's digital image of the thumbs gives us a multiply deferred or refracted presence: by the time of the online presentation, the thumbs are simultaneously Gins's, her reader's, McCaffery's (as one reader of Gins), his reader's, and Stefans's—who ends the chain by

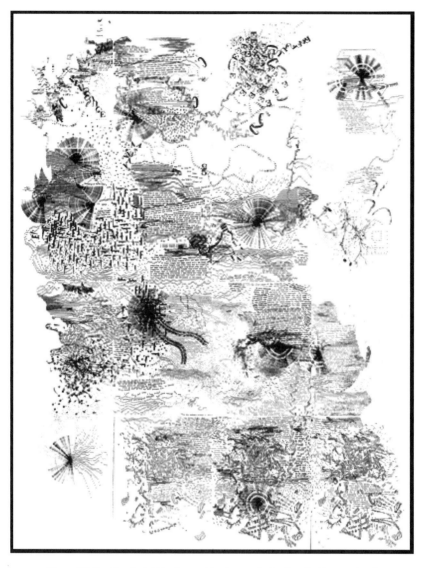

Figure 13.2 *Carnival.* http://www.chbooks.com/online/carnival/2_map.html.

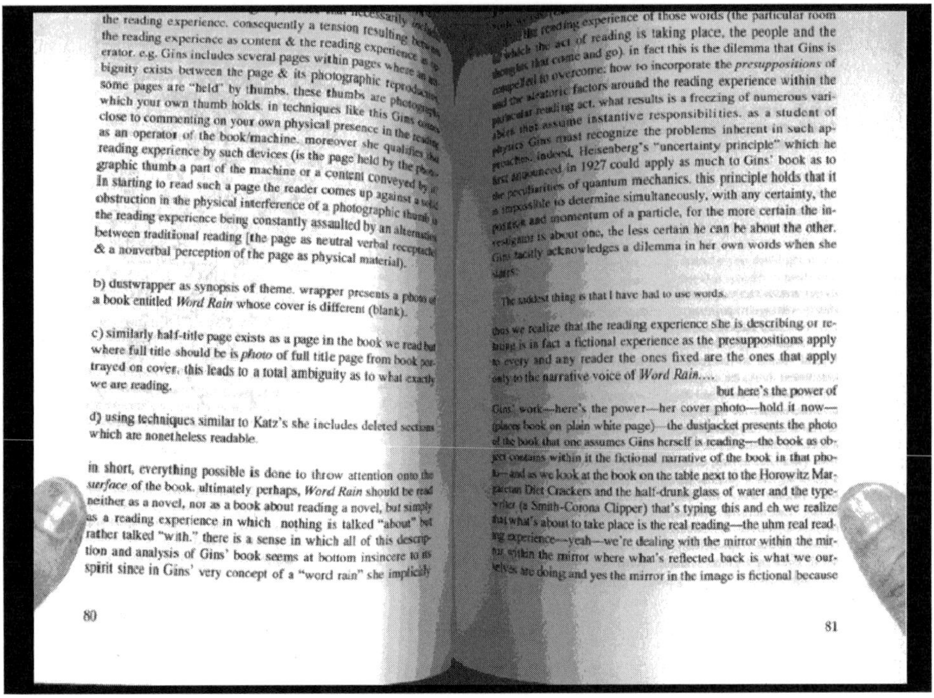

the reading experience, consequently a tension resulting be...
the reading experience as content & the reading experience...
erator. e.g. Gins includes several pages within pages where an...
biguity exists between the page & its photographic reproduc...
some pages are "held" by thumbs, these thumbs are photog...
which your own thumb holds, in techniques like this Gins com...
close to commenting on your own physical presence in the read...
as an operator of the book/machine, moreover she qualifies the...
reading experience by such devices (is the page held by the pho...
graphic thumb a part of the machine or a content conveyed by it...
In starting to read such a page the reader comes up against a sub...
obstruction in the physical interference of a photographic thumb is...
the reading experience being constantly assaulted by an alternation...
between traditional reading [the page as neutral verbal receptacle...
& a nonverbal perception of the page as physical material).

b) dustwrapper as synopsis of theme, wrapper presents a photo of
a book entitled *Word Rain* whose cover is different (blank).

c) similarly half-title page exists as a page in the book we read but
where full title should be is *photo* of full title page from book por-
trayed on cover. this leads to a total ambiguity as to what exactly
we are reading.

d) using techniques similar to Katz's she includes deleted sections
which are nonetheless readable.

in short, everything possible is done to throw attention onto the
surface of the book. ultimately perhaps, *Word Rain* should be read
neither as a novel, nor as a book about reading a novel, but simply
as a reading experience in which nothing is talked "about" but
rather talked "with." there is a sense in which all of this descrip-
tion and analysis of Gins' book seems at bottom insincere to its
spirit since in Gins' very concept of a "word rain" she implicitly

80

...the reading experience of those words (the particular room
...which the act of reading is taking place, the people and the
...things that come and go). in fact this is the dilemma that Gins is
compelled to overcome; how to incorporate the *presuppositions* of
...the narrative factors around the reading experience within the
particular reading act, what results is a freezing of numerous vari-
ables that assume instantive responsibilities. as a student of
physics Gins must recognize the problems inherent in such ap-
proaches. indeed, Heisenberg's "uncertainty principle" which he
announced in 1927 could apply as much to Gins' book as to
...the peculiarities of quantum mechanics. this principle holds that it
...impossible to determine simultaneously, with any certainty, the
position and momentum of a particle, for the more certain the in-
...vestigator is about one, the less certain he can be about the other.
Gins tacitly acknowledges a dilemma in her own words when she
says:

The saddest thing is that I have had to use words.

...thus we realize that the reading experience she is describing or re-
...living is in fact a fictional experience as the presuppositions apply
...to every and any reader the ones fixed are the ones that apply
only to the narrative voice of *Word Rain*....

but here's the power of
Gins' work—here's the power—her cover photo—hold it now—
...places book on plain white page)—the dustjacket presents the photo
of the book that one assumes Gins herself is reading—the book as ob-
ject contains within it the fictional narrative of the book in that pho-
to—and we look at the book on the table next to the Horowitz Mar-
garian Diet Crackers and the half-drunk glass of water and the type-
writer (a Smith-Corona Clipper) that's typing this and eh we realize
that what's about to take place is the real reading—the uhm real read-
ing experience—yeah—we're dealing with the mirror within the mir-
ror within the mirror where what's reflected back is what we our-
selves are doing and yes the mirror in the image is fictional because

81

Figure 13.3 "Rational Geomancy."
http://www.arras.net/RNG/director/geomancy/geomancy.htm.

placing the thumb image on-screen, beyond the reach of further thumbs
(figure 13.3).

My point is that this process shows the capacity of a new media reading
to highlight concerns already immanent in a previous text. On-screen, traces
of the body—such as Robert Grenier's hands holding his little book "Pond I"
in its online presentation (figure 13.4)—stand as visible signs of its absence,
a self-consciously rematerialized evocation of a previously material book, and
in this way Stefans honors the Language writers' investigation of ideas of
"presence" and extends them into another medium. As if to acknowledge that
any reproduction of McCaffery's original will be somehow incomplete, in
Stefans's presentation, the top couple of lines are cut off and a shadow or stain
across the book's gutter obscures a certain amount of text, which remains
otherwise largely legible. Following the instructions—"Click on the book to
get a close-up. Click again to return to longview"—gives a close-up of

Alan Golding

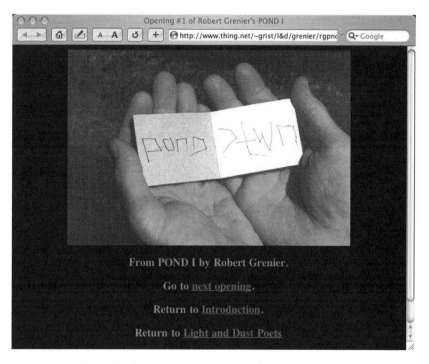

From POND I by Robert Grenier.

Go to next opening.

Return to Introduction.

Return to Light and Dust Poets

Figure 13.4 "Pond I." http://www.thing.net/~grist/l&d/grenier/rgpnd01.htm.

fourteen or fifteen lines of text featuring mobile details oscillating against a static ground to foreground certain themes. Admittedly, the results are not always startling: to have letters dripping down the page from the phrase "word rain" seems little more than imitation Apollinaire, though the gesture could be read as an homage to one who is often cited as a modernist precursor to new media poetry (figure 13.5). In another close-up, the words "problems" and "uncertainty" form a frantic dancing palimpsest over their originals in the base text; in yet another, the first three letters of the alphabet buzz like annoyed bees over a stable background, as if to reference the debate over digital mobility and print stasis (figures 13.6 and 13.7).

McCaffery, then, troubles the seeing-reading distinction in ways relevant for our thinking about new media poetry while his materially intensive texts variously point up the limitations of the electronic environment (in the case of *Carnival*) and its potential to extend the implications of a print text (in the case of *Rational Geomancy*). The appearance online of Robert Grenier's

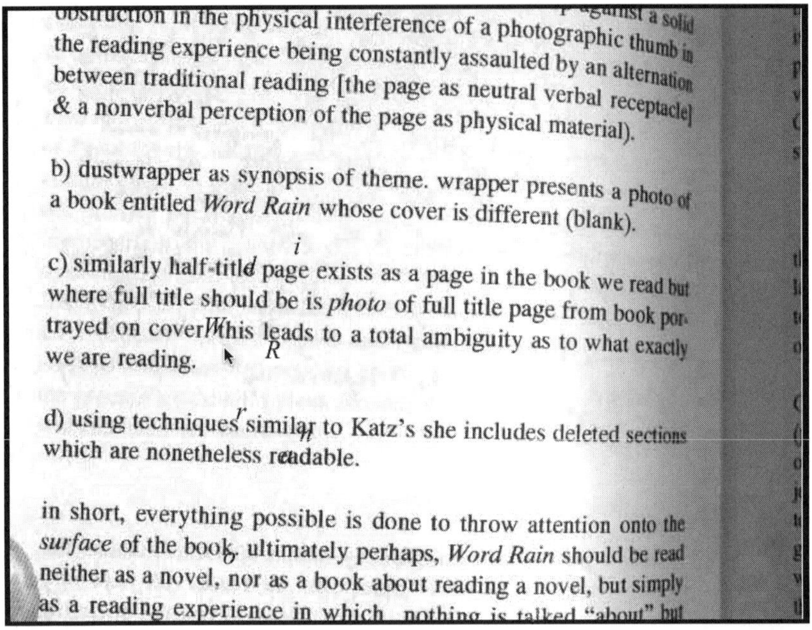

obstruction in the physical interference of a photographic thumb in against a solid
the reading experience being constantly assaulted by an alternation
between traditional reading [the page as neutral verbal receptacle]
& a nonverbal perception of the page as physical material).

b) dustwrapper as synopsis of theme. wrapper presents a photo of
a book entitled *Word Rain* whose cover is different (blank).

c) similarly half-title page exists as a page in the book we read but
where full title should be is *photo* of full title page from book por-
trayed on cover. this leads to a total ambiguity as to what exactly
we are reading.

d) using techniques similar to Katz's she includes deleted sections
which are nonetheless readable.

in short, everything possible is done to throw attention onto the
surface of the book, ultimately perhaps, *Word Rain* should be read
neither as a novel, nor as a book about reading a novel, but simply
as a reading experience in which nothing is talked "about" but

Figure 13.5 "Rational Geomancy."
http://www.arras.net/RNG/director/geomancy/geomancy.htm.

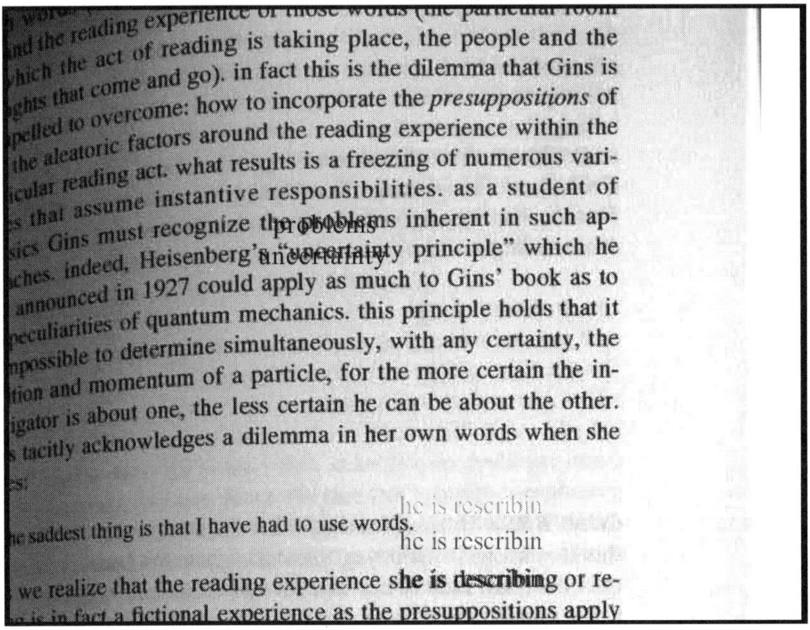

reading experience or those words (the particular room
and the reading experience is taking place, the people and the
which the act of reading and go). in fact this is the dilemma that Gins is
lights that come to incorporate the *presuppositions* of
pelled to overcome: how to incorporate the *presuppositions* of
the aleatoric factors around the reading experience within the
icular reading act. what results is a freezing of numerous vari-
s that assume instantive responsibilities. as a student of
sics Gins must recognize the problems inherent in such ap-
ches. indeed, Heisenberg's "uncertainty principle" which he
announced in 1927 could apply as much to Gins' book as to
peculiarities of quantum mechanics. this principle holds that it
mpossible to determine simultaneously, with any certainty, the
tion and momentum of a particle, for the more certain the in-
igator is about one, the less certain he can be about the other.
s tacitly acknowledges a dilemma in her own words when she
es:

he saddest thing is that I have had to use words.
he is rescribin

we realize that the reading experience she is describing or re-
is in fact a fictional experience as the presuppositions apply

Figure 13.6 "Rational Geomancy."
http://www.arras.net/RNG/director/geomancy/geomancy.htm.

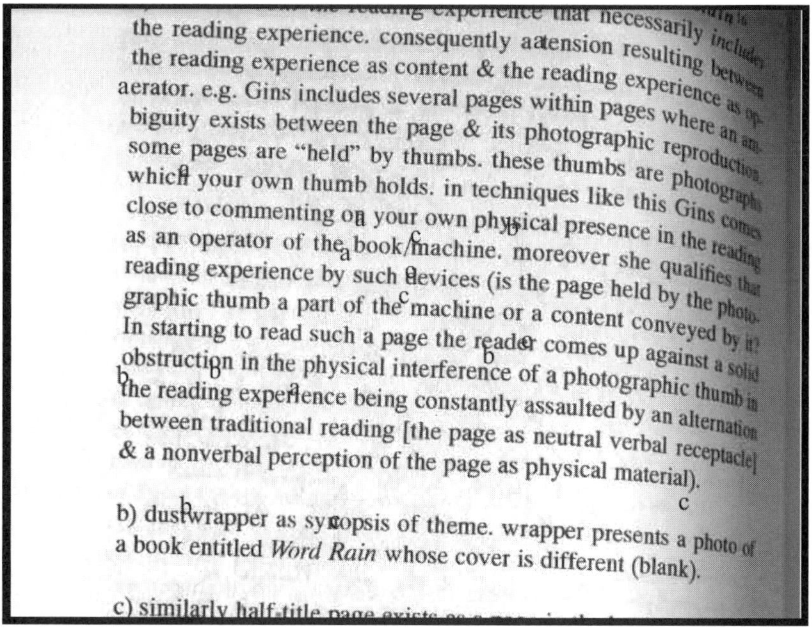

the reading experience. consequently a tension resulting between
the reading experience as content & the reading experience as op-
erator. e.g. Gins includes several pages within pages where an am-
biguity exists between the page & its photographic reproduction.
some pages are "held" by thumbs. these thumbs are photograph
which your own thumb holds. in techniques like this Gins comes
close to commenting on your own physical presence in the reading
as an operator of the book/machine. moreover she qualifies that
reading experience by such devices (is the page held by the photo-
graphic thumb a part of the machine or a content conveyed by it?
In starting to read such a page the reader comes up against a solid
obstruction in the physical interference of a photographic thumb in
the reading experience being constantly assaulted by an alternation
between traditional reading [the page as neutral verbal receptacle]
& a nonverbal perception of the page as physical material).

b) dustwrapper as synopsis of theme. wrapper presents a photo of
a book entitled *Word Rain* whose cover is different (blank).

c) similarly half-title page exists

Figure 13.7 "Rational Geomancy."
http://www.arras.net/RNG/director/geomancy/geomancy.htm.

series "RHYMMS" and "For Larry Eigner" and the poems "Greeting" and
"Pond I"—barely legible one-of-a-kind handwritten texts rendered mostly in
four different pen colors—raises a different set of issues: the electronic circu-
lation of unique texts into instant availability and the consequent tension
between reproducibility and aura; between current and earlier, even ancient,
technologies of writing; between what Tim Shaner and Michael Rozendal have
called, in discussing Grenier, emergent and residual technologies (2000,
48n2).

Some words about Grenier's process and poetics are in order before moving
on to these issues. It's worth remembering that Grenier has worked with loose-
leaf forms of publication, outside of codexspace, throughout his career, ever
since the now almost mythic *Sentences:* five hundred minimalist poems on five-
by-eight index cards, written during the period 1972–1977 and published in
a fold-up box in 1978. In the urgent search for a construction of historical
precedents that marks moments of significant literary and technological
change, even Grenier's closest readers disagree as to whether *Sentences* is an

early form of hypertext. Bob Perelman (1996) argues that "[w]hile the lack of binding allows for any sequence, Grenier's allegiance is not toward any early version of hypertext" (46) but toward an emphasis on his materials. (I'd suggest it's not an either-or choice.) Charles Bernstein, however, includes *Sentences* in his list of "hypertext avant le PC" (1997–1998b) and even finds it pointing up, by contrast, one limitation of new media technologies: "you can't flip through a data base the way you can flip through pages or index cards. (I'm thinking, for example, of Robert Grenier's great poem of the 1970s, *Sentences*" [1999b, 78].) Barrett Watten (2002) calls *Sentences* "arguably one of the first (and most primitive) hypertexts in literature . . . , a direct predecessor to hypertext's challenge to the physical unity of the book." Complicating matters further, the original publisher of *Sentences*, Michael Waltuch, has made it available in a Web-based version using a JavaScript code to randomize the cards; however, he has also proposed that "the 'boxed version' allows for a 'freer' mode of interacting with the work than the online version" (2003). Grenier has produced more such publications than he has bound books. The drawing poems that he began to produce in the late 1980s, then, are consistent with this pattern.

Grenier describes the process by which he came to write these poems in a 1998 talk with the characteristically punning title "Realizing Things." Language writing's emphasis on linguistic materiality always seems to have taken very literal form for Grenier. (As he said in an earlier talk, "you start writing in relation to . . . writing materials" [(1982) 1985, 230; ellipsis in original].) In his account, at a certain point in his career, typing came to defamiliarize the letter and immerse him further in the minute attention to language to which he was always inclined. "[I]n the Selectric typewriter methodology, each letter is given an equivalent width—the i's are the same width as the m's, the l's are the same width as the w's—& I was able to count each letter as 'one' . . . & so that would be a further 'removal', I suppose, & reengagement with the language process only" (1998; ellipsis in original).

Partially handwritten poems started to come out of textual annotations on typescript that Grenier wished to preserve as part of the writing process, as in the 1984 poem "May Dawn Horizon Many Graces Pollen" from *Phantom Anthems* (1986a), at the same time as he also sought intensified materiality through type: "I got off the Selectric & went back to my highschool typewriter which made a darker image, with a dark ribbon—this was a manual—& that image somehow . . . I thought that was more, somehow, 'that of which it spoke' than the Selectric image . . . it was darker, denser" (1998; ellipses in original). Apparently dissatisfied with his "delusion" that the manual typewriter would provide the sense of "a greater, hands-on tenacity or 'facticity,'" however, Grenier moved to handwriting or drawing poems with various combinations of the four-color pens that he used in his proofreader's job.

If "Grenier is interested in the phoneme as a thing in itself" (Watten 1985, 9), he has *become* equally interested in the grapheme as a thing in itself. Grenier (1998) himself offers a revealing pun when he speaks of "beginning to write letters by hand, to draw them into existence." He does literally draw his letters, creating shapes that sometimes bear only a distant relationship to their alphabetic originals. But he also "draws them into [discrete] existence" out of a kind of Platonic ur-letter from which they emerge as much as they are constructed: "Letters draw themselves out of *corresponding* letter shapes . . . *AS IF ALL WERE MADE FROM THE SAME LETTER*" (2001, 72; ellipsis in original). This is Emerson as postmodern materialist, the transparent eyeball now a transparent Uniball pen. Through this hands-on engagement with the materials of language, Grenier engages the material of the world: "the 'idea' is, if you focus sufficiently on the materials of language itself, possibly you'll be able to bring [yourself?] back to the participation in & with things a means of actualizing what's happening . . . the farther you get into the structure of language itself, I've found, the more are you enabled at times to be able to go into the metamorphosis, the flow through things that Emerson speaks of" (1998).

Grenier's narrative of his process directly reverses N. Katherine Hayles's account of the increased lightness of touch and the reduced "material resistance of the text to manipulation" involved in the move from manual to electric typewriter to keyboard (Hayles 1992, 164). One could argue that part of Grenier's project is to reintroduce the resistance of touch (or the memory of it) in the face of this apparently dematerializing technology, proposing the body as a site of cultural resistance in much the way that Charles Olson—a crucial figure for Grenier, and one frequently cited as a print precursor for certain aspects of new media poetics—does in his 1953 essay "The Resistance." If new "technologies modify the body's proprioceptive sense" (166), as Hayles has argued—and *proprioception* is another key term for Olson—then the online presentation of Grenier's handcrafted work puts opposing materialities and opposing experiences of the body in productive tension. The question then arises (and it's one I want to keep open), does Web distribution dematerialize Grenier's emphatically embodied work, or does it paradoxically fulfill that work's project by foregrounding precisely these oppositions?

A related contradiction involves the electronic circulation of unique texts into more or less instant availability and the consequent tension between reproducibility and aura, between current and earlier writing technologies. Behind this tension lies the economics of production and distribution. Stephen Ratcliffe lays out the cost of codex production quite precisely, arriving by detailed argument at a figure of $20,200 for producing a print run of four hundred of Grenier's current poems. Given the economic unfeasibility of such a book, Grenier's recent work has had its distribution through limited color xerox editions (e.g., David Baratier's Pavement Saw Press sold *12 from rhymms* for twenty dollars per set in 1996); through gallery presentations (500+ slides of the work had been made public via a dozen showings and readings as of the time of Ratcliffe's writing in the late 1990s); and on the Web (the best way to preserve the originals' color, among other things). As Karl Young, editor of the Light & Dust Web site, where Grenier's work appears, writes, "Robert Grenier's illuminated poems, his main work for the last decade, present a number of problems in reproduction, distribution, and, for some, in reading. These poems are written in colored ink, and require color reproduction. Four-color process printing makes them too expensive to produce. . . . I hope that the Web will help bring Grenier's illuminated poems out of the small and restricted circle of distribution in which they have moved, and make them available to a larger audience" (n.d.).

Especially in the handling of Grenier's work, however, this reaching out for an audience is not an unproblematic move. Far too pricey to produce in book form, these works derive considerable aura from the uniqueness, individual manual production, and unavailability of the original "hard" copies. As Bob Perelman proposes, Grenier's emphasis on his materials leads to "the special poetic or ontological value or magical potency that [he] seems to be trying to create" (1996, 53), a potency usually comprehended under the term "aura." Walter Benjamin, then, is not far in the background and gives us one set of terms for thinking about the relationship between such aura and the "mechanical reproduction" of Web publication in Grenier. At the same time, Benjamin's famous claim that "the whole sphere of authenticity is outside technical . . . reproducibility" (1969, 220) has been rendered untenable not just by decades of poststructuralist theory but most recently by the new media. You can't have your aura and your widespread access too.

In this interface between the most ancient and the most contemporary of text-producing technologies, as much as Grenier wants to return his work to the body, it cannot—if it is to be distributed—escape the machine. In reading Grenier's drawing poems electronically, we are confronted with the extremes of hand-craftedness and technological mediation: extremes not immanent in the work but in the disjunction between its modes of production and distribution. From one point of view, Grenier's recent work seems the absolute antithesis of new media poetry. From another, its digital presentation highlights—as if we needed reminding one more time—the (in this case, literal) inaccessibility of any original: online, we experience the Web presentation of slides of photographs of one-of-a-kind handwritten poems, the originals of which most people will never see. Paradoxically, their online reproduction can be seen both as a fulfillment and a contradiction of the originals' impulses toward personalized signature and fiercely specific attention to material texture.

Grenier's particular form of materiality is a retrospective (not to be confused with retrogressive) gesture driven by an almost Emersonian concern for natural origins. As Stephen Ratcliffe puts it, "the thingness of his writing . . . moves it backward, closer somehow to where it is that writing must first have come from" (2000, 125). Yet "naturalness" in Grenier is complicated. The artifice of his own reading style distances his voice from speech, and, of course, he's notorious for his contentious but influential manifesto statement "I HATE SPEECH" (1986b, 496). At the same time, Ratcliffe finds the "shape of letters analogous to shape of landscape" in Grenier, "making the page itself a landscape" (2000, 121). Certainly at the level of content, some of Grenier's graphic work is almost elemental in its minimalist focus on (to cite the "Pond I" sequence) "pond," "sky," "ground," "wind," "water," "sunshine," "minnows," "coyote." In one nicely ambiguous conjunction of natural imagery and textual materiality, it's hard to know whether to read number 28 as "spelling" or—appropriately, misspelled—"sapling" (figure 13.8).

This evocation of and immersion in the organic seems to sit uneasily with the poems' Web presentation. As Michael Basinski points out, however, "Grenier has been able to invent a form of poetry that is suitable for the computer era but also moves beyond the stagnancy of text based poetry, visual poetry and performance poetry. His poems best utilize the capacity of the computer. He does this not by using a computer as a tool to manipulate text but as a medium to present" the work (1999, 33). Grenier's poetics exhibits a

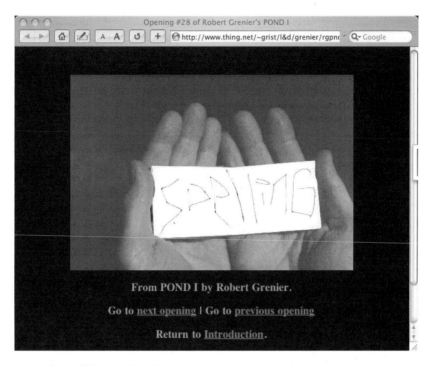

http://www.thing.net/~grist/l&d/grenier/rgpnc

From POND I by Robert Grenier.

Go to next opening | Go to previous opening

Return to Introduction.

Figure 13.8 "saplling." http://www.thing.net/~grist/l&d/grenier/rgpnd28.htm.

kind of materiality of organic form, as if language (as it was for Emerson) were at the heart of nature, and he adopts an organicist metaphor for his highly graphic aesthetic: "I wish more strange young poets wd dedicate life to making *briars and blackberries* [a phrase from Whitman] out of words, letters etc. . . . for the fun of it" (2001, 73). He wants poems that will embody— including visually—the prickly entanglements of those plants. The allusion to Whitman is appropriate, since Grenier's materiality of organic forms sounds like nothing as much as Whitman's preface to the 1855 edition of *Leaves of Grass* (that title, of course, itself enacting a pun between nature and book). But for all its organicism, the fact that Grenier's work is so hard to reproduce in print pushes it toward the Web as its—dare I say?—"natural" home, and it fits at least one current (if controversial) definition of what Loss Pequeño Glazier calls "e-poetry": "Works that cannot be adequately delivered via traditional paper publishing or cannot be displayed on paper. This would include innovative works circulated in electronic form" (2002, 163).

As far from an evocation of the organic as one can get is the work of Charles Bernstein, who started out producing typographically manipulated palimpsests in the 1970s with his chapbook *Veil* ([1976] 1987). The visual explorations in his career since then have ranged from the many verbal/visual collaborations with his wife, the artist Susan Bee, to his cocuratorship of the 2001 Poetry Plastique exhibit, to colorful cyberpoems, to recent self-performing cyberessays that focus on the implications of new media for pedagogy and for what we teach about the "nature" of poetry. More than the other poets I've discussed, Bernstein has started to theorize digital poetics, produce writing in that mode, and exploit the Web's potential for circulation and as a site for discourses *about* poetry that share the genre-mixing techniques of page-based discourses. The sheer range and probing inventiveness of Bernstein's visually oriented poetic activities make him the ideal case study for examining how an engaged poet, critic, and teacher uses his own developing work in digital media to test the adequacy of current pedagogical paradigms for poetry and the relationship of new media to print-based poetries and to institutions of education, circulation, and reception.

These concerns form the core of Bernstein's electronic essay on poetics, "An Mosaic for Convergence," the clunkily ungrammatical title a synecdoche for the fault lines that the piece addresses. The essay is "based on a presentation at a 1995 conference at the State University of New York, Buffalo on 'The Convergence of Science and the Humanities'" (1997b). So much for the convergence. The mosaic is a matter of structure: the essay consists of twenty-four separate screens (or tiles), including the title screen, that are randomly reordered on each viewing so that no two visits to the essay will provide the reader with the same reading sequence.[1] The structure represents a digital version of the method that Bernstein often uses in giving public talks, randomly shuffling through and reading index cards containing entries on his nominal topic—as Bernstein has it in one screen that repeats a distinction from *My Way*: "Not unstructured essays / *differently structured* // not structurally challenged / *structurally challenging*" (1999b, 11). The screens contain a mixture of poems, aphorisms, jokes, and passages of critical commentary on digital poetics, its relation to the book and to the history of experimental writing, and its impact on the social and pedagogical institutions surrounding poetry. They cover a lively, diverse, and playful range of format, color, font, and background, confirming the kid-in-a-candy-shop pleasure that Bernstein expresses in a 1996 interview: "It's wild after a writing lifetime of

assuming black ink on white paper to start to pick your background image—
and not just your font and point size, but the color of the font" (Cummings
and Marinaccio [1996] 2000, 20–21).

More specifically, one recurrent feature of the essay involves its visual and
often tonal contrasts between figure and ground, and Bernstein has com-
mented on the figure-ground tensions that come with working in HTML
(2002b, 178–179). One screen, "Punic," addresses the discrepancy between
the impact of new technologies on poetry and on academic institutions, noto-
riously slow to make structural adjustments to change. It begins, "[a]s a poet,
essayist, and university teacher, I am particularly interested in the ways that
the new computer technology affects the disciplines with which I am most
involved" (1997–1998e) (figure 13.9). In conflict with the portentous, job-
application seriousness of this beginning, however, stands the opening
image—a book jacket photograph of Bernstein comically altered by his
daughter Emma—and a bright blue, Kid-Pix-style background with black
exclamation points descending like bombs, red-lipped mouths, flashing

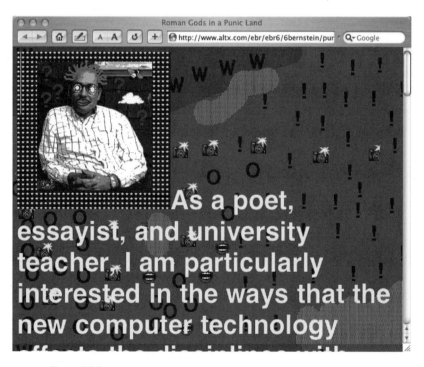

Figure 13.9   "Punic." http://www.altx.com./ebr/ebr6/6bernstein/punic.htm.

cameras, and the name of the perpetrator, Felix (Bernstein's son), inscribed here and there. Digital technology, then, enables Bernstein to create a tonal tension between straightforward, even earnest, exposition, and its visual context.

The mosaic organization of the essay also allows Bernstein to juxtapose, without resolving, competing views of new technologies' effect on academic discourse. On one screen, he finds it likely that "the ideological fixation on linear and expository discourse will be imported into this new medium"; on another, "hypertextual organization may finally help to break teaching, text-books, and critical writing from their deadly boring fetishization of narrative and expository ordering of information" (1999b, 72). If institutional and ped-agogical structures rest on the normalization of book technology, as Alan Filreis argues in chapter 6, then Bernstein is suggesting some sprightly alter-natives. Other sections, as Bernstein's page poetry often does, play off con-temporary educational clichés that exploit electronic connectivity for profit (there's a poem called "Distance Learning") or off the language of the Web site: if "frequently asked questions" are FAQs (but not facts), "Frequently Unasked Questions," the title of one poem, are FUQs.

The digital medium provides Bernstein with a much wider palette with which to counter "the deadly boring fetishization . . . of expository order-ing" (1999b, 72) (admittedly the kind of ordering I'm offering here). Play with color and layout allow further possibilities for interrupting the tonal serious-ness and structural predictability of normative academic writing—what Bernstein calls elsewhere "frame lock" and "its cousin tone jam" (1999b, 90). The individual screens of "An Mosaic for Convergence," as I've suggested, insis-tently enact a tension between transparent expository content and obtrusive material presentation, the kind of clash of discourses that Bernstein pursues throughout his work and that the electronic environment further enables. That environment permits moments of defamiliarization similar to those produced by a screen such as "Textuaî" (1997–1998g), whose legibility is obstructed by their presentation in partly nonalphabetic fonts (figure 13.10). After reading such a screen, we no longer take the alphabet quite so much for granted, and one result is that the normative presentation of a screen such as "Realpolitick" (Bernstein 1997–1998f)—two left-justified prose paragraphs on the commer-cial foreclosure of hypertext's radical open-endedness, in that most common-place of fonts, twelve-point Times New Roman—suddenly seems highly designed, not inevitable but simply one set of choices among many.

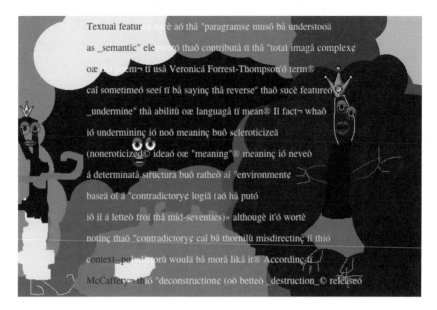

Figure 13.10 "Textuaì." http://www.altx.com./ebr/ebr6/6bernstein/Textuai.htm.

"Realpolitick" (Bernstein 1997–1998f) itself also exemplifies the degree of rematerialization and textual migration within the essay. Not only does the essay's overall context highlight or defamiliarize, by contrast, this screen's transparency, but much of its text is reformatted in another "Mosaic" screen, "Access" (Bernstein 1997–1998a) There it appears as a poem, centered and with a left-justified margin, on a ground of variously colored swatches that recalls Bernstein's "HTML Series" of poems; after twelve lines, a shift in font size and cutting some text from mid-sentence create a distancing moment of discontinuity, as does a block of white space further on (figure 13.11). At the level of content, Bernstein makes clear in "Realpolitick" and "Access" the appeal of hypertext to an avant-garde poet. He begins both pieces with this statement: "As a structure, the paratactic links of a hypertextual environment short circuit narrative closure and foreground open-endedness." At the formal level, the visual conventionality of "Realpolitick" makes a point about "frame lock," associating normatively presented prose with a politics of compromise (figure 13.12); "Access," with the "same" text, uses the resources of HTML to embody the potential of parataxis and heightened materiality for reshaping the conventions of expository prose (and to pun on the fact of access to digital media and ideals of textual "accessibility").

Alan Golding

270

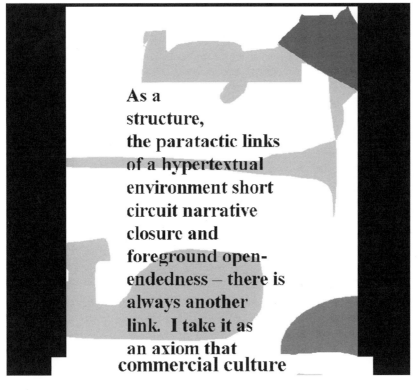

As a structure, the paratactic links of a hypertextual environment short circuit narrative closure and foreground open-endedness – there is always another link. I take it as an axiom that commercial culture

Figure 13.11   "Access." http://www.altx.com./ebr/ebr6/6bernstein/access.htm.

Similar in form to "An Mosaic for Convergence," "Electronic Pies in the Poetry Skies" originated in January 2001 as one of Bernstein's characteristically structured talks, in which he first shuffles and then reads from note cards, each of which contains an aphorism or brief commentary on some aspect of his nominal topic. In its *electronic book review* publication (2001a), as part of Marc Bousquet and Katharine Wills's online book *The Politics of Information*, the essay's arguments maintain their trenchancy while formally the piece becomes more static and linear than in its live performance. This version of the essay, imposing an order on the argument that other presentations disrupt, reflects Bernstein's observation that "you can't flip through a data base the way you can flip through pages or index cards" (2001a)—distribution and readability for content trump formal exploration and surprising juxtaposition. The *electronic book review* version privileges a somewhat dystopian conclusion that remains the same with each reading, a conclusion in line with the title's

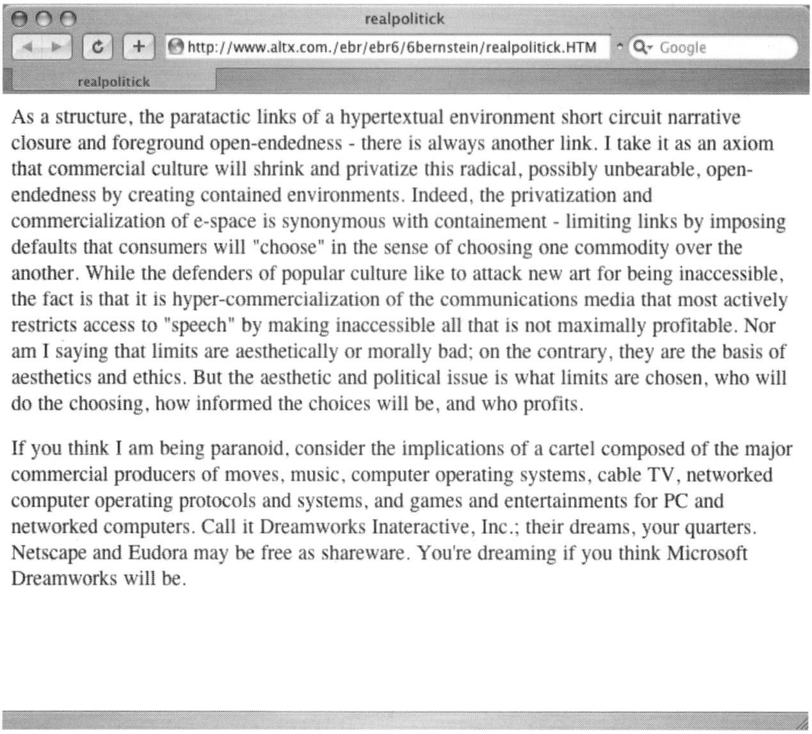

As a structure, the paratactic links of a hypertextual environment short circuit narrative closure and foreground open-endedness - there is always another link. I take it as an axiom that commercial culture will shrink and privatize this radical, possibly unbearable, open-endedness by creating contained environments. Indeed, the privatization and commercialization of e-space is synonymous with containement - limiting links by imposing defaults that consumers will "choose" in the sense of choosing one commodity over the another. While the defenders of popular culture like to attack new art for being inaccessible, the fact is that it is hyper-commercialization of the communications media that most actively restricts access to "speech" by making inaccessible all that is not maximally profitable. Nor am I saying that limits are aesthetically or morally bad; on the contrary, they are the basis of aesthetics and ethics. But the aesthetic and political issue is what limits are chosen, who will do the choosing, how informed the choices will be, and who profits.

If you think I am being paranoid, consider the implications of a cartel composed of the major commercial producers of moves, music, computer operating systems, cable TV, networked computer operating protocols and systems, and games and entertainments for PC and networked computers. Call it Dreamworks Inateractive, Inc.; their dreams, your quarters. Netscape and Eudora may be free as shareware. You're dreaming if you think Microsoft Dreamworks will be.

Figure 13.12 "Realpolitick." http://www.altx.com./ebr/ebr6/6bernstein/realpolitick.htm.

(and essay's) ironizing of electronic democratic utopias: "There'll be a pie in the sky when you die. // But not likely" (2001a). The Coach House Press online presentation, engineered by damian lopes, randomizes the essay by "shuffling" three slightly overlapping small screens that imitate browsers (Netscape, Internet Explorer, and Mozilla), with the content of each miniscreen changing about every ten seconds. Like Stefans's treatment of McCaffery's *Rational Geomancy*, this presentation—part palimpsest, part juxtaposition—constitutes a *reading* of Bernstein's essay, as it foregrounds the material frames (the browsers) by which Web access is both enabled and shaped.

Since Bernstein returns so frequently to ideas of layering or the palimpsest, it is unsurprising that the veil as both artwork and metaphor is crucial to his visual practice. He discusses the figure of the veil extensively in an interview with Manuel Brito, where he notes that the palimpsests of the 1976

Alan Golding

chapbook *Veil* were "produced by several layers of overtyping" (1999b, 31), "typing new compositions over ones I had just written" (1997–1998d), with Morris Louis's "Veil" paintings as one model. (Since Louis was born Morris Louis Bernstein, a biographical joke is also at work here: behind the veil of Louis's name change lies another Bernstein.) The veil suggests to Bernstein the materiality of language: "Our language is our veil, but one that too often is made invisible. Yet, hiding the veil of language, its wordness, its textures, its obstinate physicality, only makes matters worse" (1999b, 32).

Three sections of the *Veil* chapbook are available online, where, as Johanna Drucker (2002) points out, their presence raises an issue similar to that raised by the rematerialization of McCaffery's *Carnival:* "the immaterial substrate, a mere display of code, has eliminated the production history and process, thus configuring a loss of information as its immaterial form" (166). *Veil* literally fades in its rematerialized version. Resolution is poorer in the online *Veil*, and the two smaller pieces of the three reproduced are much harder to read than in the print version, with the marks in parts barely detectable as letters.[2] The texts have become more available but less readable, even though Bernstein, stressing the graphic rather less than McCaffery, wants them to be read. "[T]he writing was composed to be read, not only looked at: it is possible to read not just view these works" (Bernstein 1997–1998d). At the same time, the materially intensive nature of texts such as *Carnival* and *Veil* prompts useful speculation about what Drucker finds an ambiguously material/immaterial digital environment: "We perceive the visual form of the letter on the screen as fully material—replete with characteristics, font specifications, scale, and even color—even though the 'letter' exists as a stored sequence of binary digits with no tactile, material apparency to it in that fundamental condition" (2002, 171–172). When a print text such as *Veil* already foregrounds the materiality of its own letters, its electronic transformation intensifies any questions about the nature of "electronic materiality."

In their very rematerialization, the visually intensive works that I have been discussing throughout this essay come to instantiate a minihistory of writing technologies. That is, as examples of transitional materiality, they mark the historical transitions or relations between media. This process emerges clearly through Bernstein's various visual series, each one "a visualization [of] the specific writing tools that I most used: the IBM Selectric typewriter, the fountain pen, and Microsoft Word for Windows." Bernstein explains the process further: "'*Veil*,' the Selectric series from the late 1970s, was made by typing new compositions over ones that I had just written. 'The Language of Boquets' from the early 1990s used pages of my writing notebook, overprinted with a xerox machine. The '*HTML Series*' was made using Word together with its built in HTML converter" (1997–1998d). He lays out this history in a way that self-reflexively embodies it. "On_Veil" begins with a paragraph of migratory text first used in "Every Which Way But Loose" (Bernstein 2002b) that proposes, uncontroversially enough, that "[t]he new computer technology—both desktop publishing and electronic publishing—has radically altered the material, specifically visual, presentation of text" (179). This screen appears in a Courier font that dates the text as page-based and alludes to *Veil*'s origins even as Bernstein argues that "it begins to seem . . . natural to think of composing screen by screen rather than page by page" (1997–1998d). Little seems natural, however, about this spiral of self-reflexive artifice as it proposes not a history of "supersession" of one medium by another, in Paul Duguid's term,[3] but one of a playful reciprocity between new and old media: "reciprocity rather than hierarchy is a better way to understand the relation among the media" (1997–1998d).

"On_Veil" offers just one example of how Bernstein uses textual migration as a way of testing both the capacities of different media and different realizations within a medium (since he moves text among different print sites and among different digital sites, as well as from print to the digital medium). The preface of Bernstein's most recent book of poems, *With Strings* (2001b), reprints part of his discussion of materiality in his essay "Every Which Way But Loose." Much of "An Mosaic for Convergence" uses material that has appeared in *My Way*, *With Strings*, and "Every Which Way But Loose." The essay recycles a number of poems from *With Strings*: the first stanza of "mr. matisse in san diego" (79), "windows 95" (90), "Frequently Unasked Questions" (116), "**this poem intentionally left blank**" (121). In its electronic form, this last poem becomes (in white text on a black ground) "this link intentionally left blank"—the link left blank (or black) being no link at all, so that hypertextual connection is jokily refused. Bernstein's 1997 "Alphabeta" is a rematerialization of a passage from the 1994 essay "I Don't Take Voice Mail" (in *My Way*), which he also uses in "An Mosaic for Convergence," on the relationship between hypertext and earlier writing technologies and between hypertext and avant-garde antilinearity.[4]

This migration of text from print essay to digital essay to prose poem is characteristic of how Bernstein uses the media as part of a practical strategy for de-essentializing poetry. Thus "Alphabeta" offers a statement visually or formally enabled by digital technology that simultaneously questions a central claim often made for that technology—that hypertext is "a particular innovation of computer processing" (Bernstein 1997a). Another digital text, "Politics," consists of nine repetitions of the sentence "For all the utopian promise of technological optimists, the answer is not in our machines but in our politics" (1997c)—a kind of digital proceduralist adaptation of the line from *Julius Caesar*, "The fault, dear Brutus, lies not in our stars but in ourselves" (to which Bernstein refers even more explicitly in another "An Mosaic for Convergence" screen, twenty-one repetitions of "the defaults are not in our stars but in ourselves") (1997–1998c). In a self-reflexive critique of normativity, the last iterations of the sentence are all perfectly aligned by the machine at the touch of a mouse. If the machine's "answer" is lockstep alignment (or justification), then we do indeed need a different politics.

Bernstein has produced a number of visually rich online poems— "absolves," "cannot cross," "Illuminosities," "this us" (which reappears in *With Strings*).[5] The central trope of all these pieces involves the layering of a brief English text over a visually denser, crosshatched textual ground (somewhat like the overprinting of *Veil*). Granted, they are essentially static, immobile, or nonmorphing—even as they use the resources of HTML, digital art programs, and nonalphabetic font—and to this extent, they remain outside some definitions of "digital poetry." In these examples of transitional materiality, however, the relationship between the textual and the visual, a long-standing preoccupation of Bernstein's, becomes itself one of these poems' subjects, with digital technology providing him with the means to move a concern of his page-based work into a new medium.

The poems consistently use digital technology to make self-reflexive points about the evolving history of print and digital media. In "Littoral," for example, the background consists of the first four paragraphs of Bernstein's introduction to Laura Riding's *Rational Meaning* (1999c, 255–256)—but again, this is a background with a twist, going beyond remediation. The use of a nonalphabetic font, Microsoft Word's Symbol, renders the original script

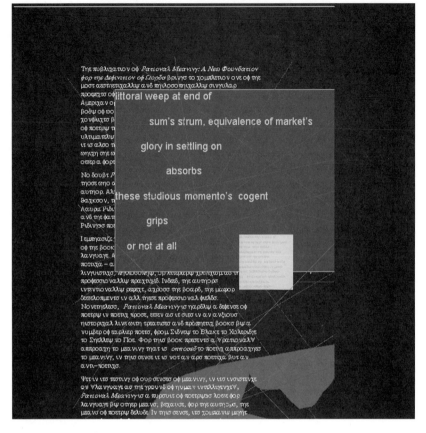

Figure 13.13   "Littoral." http://epc.buffalo.edu/authors/bernstein/visual/littoralht.html.

opaque and illegible: the digitization of the text foregrounds its materiality, and even grants it a materiality that it previously lacked (or, more precisely, that was not previously prominent) (figure 13.13). Looked at whole, Bernstein's online and print work forms a highly self-reflexive intertextual web, with reciprocity at every point created by the constant migration of text across media and its resulting transformation.

If we neglect the category of "materiality," N. Katherine Hayles argues, "we have little hope of forging a robust and nuanced account of how literature is changing under the impact of information technologies" (2002, 19)—nor, as I have tried to suggest here, an account of how some literature has anticipated or complicates that impact. Hayles assumes that when the materiality of the artifact changes, meaning is also transformed: *"The physical form of the literary artifact always affects what the words (and other semiotic components) mean"* (25; italics in original). Her work makes clear how internally conflicted the category of "materiality," and its relationship to print, remains in theoretical analysis. Hayles argues that the electronic text helps "bring into view by contrast the specificities of print, which could again be seen for what it was, a medium and not a transparent interface" (43). In other words, it should now become clear that "[l]iterature was never only words, never merely immaterial verbal constructions" (107).

Yet the acknowledgement of print's materiality, a positive for Hayles, is a negative for those theorists and writers who see the problem with print as being that it is entirely too material a medium. The concept of "transitional materialities," however, places different materialities on a spectrum rather than in opposition to each other. In what is, to be fair, a list of heuristic oppositions to which she herself does not necessarily adhere, Marie-Laure Ryan (1999) associates print texts with terms such as "unity," "order," "monologism," "sequentiality," "solidity." Readers of Language writing will recognize easily enough the inapplicability of these terms to that writing. Far *more* applicable to the poets discussed here are Ryan's opposing terms for electronic texts: "diversity," "chaos," "dialogism," "parallelism," "fluidity" (102). Looking at both the online work and the work online of these poets may help move the discussion and historicizing of new media poetries beyond such binary oppositions between the material attributes of print and electronic texts.

Notes

1. In a 1994 interview, Bernstein uses the term "mosaic" to describe both his own writing and his friend/collaborator Henry Hills's filmmaking (1999b, 25, 28). For more on the mosaic as a metaphor for the structure of the digital environment, see Holtzman (1997) (who in turn derives the figure from McLuhan's *Understanding Media*). Holtzman runs into a contradiction characteristic of much writing on new media, however: he validates the digital as the "other" of a writing conceived as monolithically linear at the same time as he is forced to acknowledge a strong tradition of nonlinear writing.

2. These digital rematerializations of the 1976 *Veil* can be accessed at http://www.ubu .com/contemp/bernstein/bernstein.html.

3. Duguid offers a compelling critique of the allied rhetorics of "supersession (the separation of the past from the future)" and "liberation (the separation of information from technology)" (1996, 89) within new media theory.

4. A distinction between "rematerialization" and "revision" is relevant here. After producing the 1997 "Alphabeta" out of the 1994 essay "I Don't Take Voice Mail," Bernstein writes on the occasion of the essay's reprinting in 1999 that "I have resisted the tendency to revise this essay in light of the often oppressively (or possibly exhilaratingly) fast changes in computer technology and the formats for using it" (1999b, 318).

5. These poems can be accessed by following the appropriate links from http://epc.buffalo.edu/authors/bernstein/index2.html#visual.

Works Cited

Basinski, Michael. 1999. "Robert Grenier's Opems." *Witz* 7, no. 1: 32–34.

Benjamin, Walter. 1969. "The Work of Art in the Age of Mechanical Reproduction." In *Illuminations*, ed. by Hannah Arendt, trans. Harry Zohn, 217–251. New York: Schocken Books.

Bernstein, Charles. [1976] 1987. *Veil*. Madison, WI: Xexoxial Editions.

Bernstein, Charles. [1994] 1999. "I Don't Take Voice Mail: The Object of Art in the Age of Electronic Textuality." In *My Way: Speeches and Poems*, 73–80. Chicago: University of Chicago Press.

Bernstein, Charles. 1996. "Littoral." http://epc.buffalo.edu/authors/bernstein/visual/littoralht.html (accessed July 26, 2004).

Bernstein, Charles. 1997a. "Alphabeta." UbuWeb. http://www.ubu.com/contemp/bernstein/alphabeta.html (accessed June 26, 2004).

Bernstein, Charles. 1997b. "An Mosaic for Convergence." *electronic book review* 6 (Winter). http://www.altx.com/ebr/ebr6/ebr6.htm (accessed April 8, 2004).

Bernstein, Charles. 1997c. "Politics." UbuWeb. http://www.ubu.com/contemp/bernstein/politics2.html (accessed July 26, 2004).

Bernstein, Charles. 1997–1998a. "Access." http://www.altx.com/ebr/ebr6/6bernstein/access.htm (accessed July 26, 2004).

Bernstein, Charles. 1997–1998b. "Avant." http://www.altx.com/ebr/ebr6/6bernstein/avant.htm (accessed July 26, 2004).

Bernstein, Charles. 1997–1998c. "Defaults." *electronic book review* 6 (Winter). http://www.altx.com/ebr/ebr6/6bernstein/defaults.htm (accessed July 26, 2004).

Bernstein, Charles. 1997–1998d. "On_Veil." *electronic book review* 6 (Winter). http://www.altx.com/ebr/ebr6/6bernstein/On_Veil.htm (accessed July 20, 2004).

Bernstein, Charles. 1997–1998e. "Punic." *electronic book review* 6 (Winter). http://www.altx.com/ebr/ebr6/6bernstein/punic.htm (accessed July 26, 2004).

Bernstein, Charles. 1997–1998f. "Realpolitick." http://www.altx.com/ebr/ebr6/6bernstein/realpolitick.htm (accessed July 26, 2004).

Bernstein, Charles. 1997–1998g. "Textuaì." http://www.altx.com/ebr/ebr6/6bernstein/Textuai.htm (accessed July 26, 2004).

Bernstein, Charles. 1999a. "An Interview with Manuel Brito." In *My Way: Speeches and Poems,* 25–32. Chicago: University of Chicago Press.

Bernstein, Charles. 1999b. *My Way: Speeches and Poems*. Chicago: University of Chicago Press.

Bernstein, Charles. 1999c. "Riding's Reason." In *My Way: Speeches and Poems*, 255–267. Chicago: University of Chicago Press.

Bernstein, Charles. 2001a. "Electronic Pies in the Poetry Skies." *electronic book review* 3. http://www.electronicbookreview.com/v3/servlet/ebr?command=view_essay&essay_id=bernsteinaltx (accessed June 14, 2004).

Bernstein, Charles. 2001b. *With Strings*. Chicago: University of Chicago Press.

Bernstein, Charles. 2002a. "Electronic Pies in the Poetry Skies." Design by damian lopes. http://www.chbooks.com/online/electronic_pies/index.html (accessed June 14, 2004).

Bernstein, Charles. 2002b. "Every Which Way But Loose." In *Reimagining Textuality: Textual Studies in the Late Age of Print*, ed. Elizabeth Bergmann Loiseaux and Neil Fraistat, 178–185. Madison: University of Wisconsin Press.

Bernstein, Charles. n.d. *Veil* [electronic version]. http://www.ubu.com/contemp/bernstein/bernstein.html (accessed June 14, 2004).

Bolter, J. David. 1991. *Writing Space: The Computer, Hypertext, and the History of Writing*. Hillsdale, NJ: Lawrence Erlbaum.

Bolter, J. David. 2001. *Writing Space: Computers, Hypertext, and the Remediation of Print*. Mahwah, NJ: Lawrence Erlbaum.

Bolter, J. David, and Richard Grusin. 1999. *Remediation: Understanding New Media.* Cambridge, MA: MIT Press.

Castro, E. M. de Melo e. 1996. "Videopoetry." *Visible Language* 30.2: 138–149.

Cummings, Allison M., and Rocco Marinaccio. [1996] 2000. "Interview with Charles Bernstein." *Contemporary Literature* 41: 1–21.

Drucker, Johanna. 2002. "Intimations of Immateriality: Graphical Form, Textual Sense, and the Electronic Environment." In *Reimagining Textuality: Textual Studies in the Late Age of Print*, ed. Elizabeth Bergmann Loiseaux and Neil Fraistat, 152–177. Madison: University of Wisconsin Press.

Duguid, Paul. 1996. "Material Matters: The Past and Futurology of the Book." In *The Future of the Book*, ed. Geoffrey Nunberg, 63–101. Berkeley: University of California Press.

Gitelman, Lisa. 2002. "'Materiality Has Always Been In Play': An Interview with N. Katherine Hayles." *The Iowa Review Web*. http://www.uiowa.edu/~iareview/tirweb/feature/hayles/interview.htm (accessed June 14, 2004).

Glazier, Loss Pequeño. 2002. *Digital Poetics: The Making of E-Poetries.* Tuscaloosa: University of Alabama Press.

Grenier, Robert. 1978. *Sentences.* http://www.whalecloth.org/grenier/sentences.htm (accessed April 10, 2004).

Grenier, Robert. [1982] 1985. "Language/Site/World." In *Writing/Talks*, ed. Bob Perelman, 230–245. Carbondale: Southern Illinois University Press.

Grenier, Robert. 1986a. "May Dawn Horizon Many Graces Pollen." In *Phantom Anthems.* Oakland, CA: O Books.

Grenier, Robert. 1986b. "On Speech." In *In the American Tree*, ed. Ron Silliman, 496–497. Orono, ME: National Poetry Foundation.

Grenier, Robert. 1996. "10 pages from RHYMMS." http://www.thing.net/~grist/l&d/grenier/lgrena00.htm (accessed June 14, 2004).

Grenier, Robert. 1997. "For Larry Eigner." http://www.thing.net/~grist/l&d/grenier/lgl00.htm (accessed June 14, 2004).

Grenier, Robert. 1998. "Realizing Things." Unpublished talk, State University of New York, Buffalo, October 28. http://epc.buffalo.edu/authors/grenier/rthings.html (accessed April 10, 2004).

Grenier, Robert. 2001. [Untitled essay.] In *Poetry Plastique*, ed. Jay Sanders and Charles Bernstein, 71–73. New York: Marianne Boesky Gallery and Granary Books.

Grenier, Robert. n.d. "Greeting." http://www.thing.net/~grist/l&d/grenier/rggrt01 .htm (accessed April 8, 2004).

Grenier, Robert. n.d. "Pond I." http://www.thing.net/~grist/l&d/grenier/rgpnd01 .htm (accessed June 14, 2004).

Grenier, Robert. n.d. "saplling." http://www.thing.net/~grist/l&d/grenier/rgpnd28. htm (accessed July 27, 2004).

Hayles, N. Katherine. 1992. "The Materiality of Informatics." *Configurations* 1.1: 147–170.

Hayles, N. Katherine. 2002. *Writing Machines*. Cambridge, MA: MIT Press.

Holtzman, Steven. 1997. *Digital Mosaics: The Aesthetics of Cyberspace*. New York: Simon & Schuster.

Jaeger, Peter. n.d. "Steve McCaffery's Visual Errata." UbuWeb. http://www.ubu.com/ papers/jaeger.html (accessed April 10, 2004).

Kac, Eduardo. 1996. "Holopoetry." *Visible Language* 30.2: 184–213.

Kirschenbaum, Matthew. [2001] 2003. "Materiality and Matter and Stuff: What Electronic Texts Are Made Of." *electronic book review* 12. http://www.altx.com/ebr/riposte/ rip12kir.htm (accessed September 23, 2005).

Landow, George P. 1992. *Hypertext: The Convergence of Contemporary Critical Theory and Technology*. Baltimore, MD: Johns Hopkins University Press.

Landow, George P. 1996. "Twenty Minutes into the Future, or How Are We Moving Beyond the Book?" In *The Future of the Book*, ed. Geoffrey Nunberg, 209–237. Berkeley: University of California Press.

Lanham, Richard. 1993. *The Electronic Word: Democracy, Technology, and the Arts*. Chicago: University of Chicago Press.

McCaffery, Steve. 1973. *Carnival: The First Panel, 1967–1970*. Toronto: Coach House Books.

McCaffery, Steve. 1977. *Carnival: The Second Panel, 1970–1975*. Toronto: Coach House Books.

McCaffery, Steve. 1998–2001. *Carnival* [electronic version]. Coach House Books. http://www.chbooks.com/online/carnival/index.html (accessed April 10, 2004).

McCaffery, Steve. 2000. *Seven Pages Missing. Volume One: Selected Texts 1969–1999.* Toronto: Coach House Books.

McCaffery, Steve. 2001. *"Carnival* Panel 2 (1970–1975)." In *Poetry Plastique*, ed. Jay Sanders and Charles Bernstein, 69–70. New York: Marianne Boesky Gallery and Granary Books.

McCaffery, Steve, and bpNichol. 1992. *Rational Geomancy. The Kids of the Book-Machine (The Collected Research Reports of the Toronto Research Group 1973–1982).* Vancouver: Talonbooks.

McGann, Jerome. 1993. *Black Riders: The Visible Language of Modernism.* Princeton, NJ: Princeton University Press.

Olson, Charles. 1966a. "Projective Verse." In *Selected Writings of Charles Olson*, ed. Robert Creeley, 15–26. New York: New Directions.

Olson, Charles. 1966b. "The Resistance." In *Selected Writings of Charles Olson*, ed. Robert Creeley, 13–14. New York: New Directions.

Perelman, Bob. 1996. *The Marginalization of Poetry: Language Writing and Literary History.* Princeton, NJ: Princeton University Press.

Poster, Mark. 1990. *The Mode of Information: Poststructuralism and Social Context.* Chicago: University of Chicago Press.

Rasula, Jed, and Steve McCaffery, eds. 1998. *Imagining Language: An Anthology.* Cambridge, MA: MIT Press.

Ratcliffe, Stephen. 2000. *Listening to Reading.* Albany: State University of New York Press.

Ryan, Marie-Laure. 1999. "Cyberspace, Virtuality, and the Text." In *Cyberspace Textuality: Computer Technology and Literary Theory*, ed. Marie-Laure Ryan, 78–107. Bloomington: Indiana University Press.

Shaner, Tim, and Michael Rozendal. 2000. "Introduction: 'the new is the old made known.'" *Verdure* 3–4 (September): 47–48.

Stefans, Brian Kim. 1992. "Rational Geomancy: Ten Fables of the Reconstruction." http://www.arras.net/RNG/director/geomancy/geomancy_index.html (accessed April 10, 2004).

Vos, Eric. 1996. "New Media Poetry." *Visible Language* 30.2: 214–233.

Waltuch, Michael. 2003. "Letter to Jessica Lowenthal." March 12. http://ronsilliman.blogspot.com/2003_03_01_ronsilliman_archive.html (accessed July 22, 2004).

Watten, Barrett. 1985. *Total Syntax*. Carbondale: Southern Illinois University Press.

Watten, Barrett. 2002. "Breaking Codes, Constructing Paradox: Beyond the Demon of Analogy." Unpublished talk, Cyberculture Working Group, University of Maryland, April.

Young, Karl. n.d. "10 pages from RHYMMS by Robert Grenier: Introductory Note." http://www.thing.net/~grist/l&d/grenier/lgrena00.htm (accessed April 10, 2004).

Wop Art. http://www.desvirtual.com.

14

Nomadic Poetry

Giselle Beiguelman

Login

In the posturban city, inscriptions vanish, interfaces multiply, and reception fragments electronic surfaces. There are no statements, only inputs. The result is nomadic poetry, fluid and transitory. At once product and producer of new connections between online and offline networks and between informative, programming, and a esthetic codes, nomadic poetry rearranges signs and signification processes: it demands a new semantics.

Portable wireless communication devices, electronic billboards, Wi-Fi nodes, and new telecommunication spaces in urban areas both create and respond to nomadic life patterns. Devised for movement, new instruments and new spaces generate new forms of perception, visualization, and reading. How are we to process art made to be read in between diverse, simultaneous, but often asynchronic interfaces and actions?

Authenticate

Close the book. Open the text: the data-space text, diagram, abstract machine that makes no distinction between content and expression (Derrida and Deleuze revisited).

Restart

Wop Art (2001)*, Leste o Leste? (Did You Read the East?)* (2002a), *egoscópio (ego-scope)* (2002b), and *Poétrica* (2003) interact with wireless remote networks through cell phones, PDAs, and electronic panels. The fragmentation of distributed interfaces and the mix of words and symbols in alphanumeric writing code create a nonphonetic "alphabet" that operates through sharing and sampling, situates itself in public spaces, and participates in the instability of contemporary life. These media live in the transitory time of continuous multiple functions: mobile phones that convert to reading supports, calendars, browsers, then back into phones according to the user's needs.

Unlike the book, our poetics is made of bits. Built not for the ages but against the ages (Robert Smithson revisited), digital writing celebrates the loss of inscription by removing the trace from acts of erasure. In so doing, nomadic poetry engages second-generation originals and media info-bodies. It is part of a deep cultural movement rebuilding the reading place as temporal interface.

Upload

There is not a where in our datawares. (Gertrude Stein Wi-Fi remix). Nowhere is everywhere, fragmented and nonlocated @+ +he !n+e®$e¢+!0n 0§ \/ \/0®&$ @n& $ymß0|$ \/\/he®e \/\/e ße9!n +0 ®e&e§!ne 0u® ß0unda®!e$.

Download

Wop Art is op art accessed via cell phones (see chapter frontispiece on p. 284). When I first started making *Wop Art*, it felt strange not just because of the precarious state of the medium in 2001—connection speeds similar to fax transmissions, a 1-bit standard for images, and a DOS look and feel—but because of an incompatibility between the object and the reading context.

In op art, the image we see exists as the result of an optical effect. Virtualization depends on the reader's concentration and introspection. But images conceived for mobile devices do not involve contemplation. They are produced to be seen in transit, in a state of dispersion, according to a logic of acceleration that makes introspection impossible.

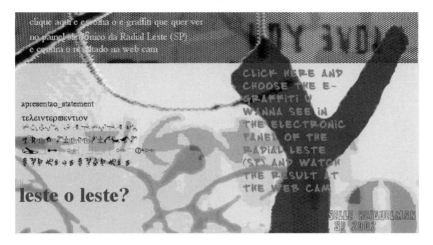

Figure 14.1 *Leste o Leste?* http://www.desvirtual.com.

Therefore, it was not a matter of simply creating op art for cell phones but rather a matter of making a new art for an entropic environment, mixed up with communication devices, to be read with other sources and materials constantly intersecting and interrupting.

My next two projects, *Did You Read the East?* and *egoscópio* (*egoscope*), involved public streaming processes, commercial urban telecommunication devices, and the Internet. I used networked systems and electronic billboards to create a project that allowed Web users to send online content to the panels. New materials were inserted every three minutes between the kind of advertising clips commonly displayed on these billboards. A webcam focused on the outdoor billboard relayed images back to online viewers. Conceived in the context of a broad urban intervention, *Did You Read the East?* dialogued with the guerrilla tactics of graffiti (figure 14.1). Participants were invited to choose e-graffiti that I had created—a series of six video-poems, composed in stylized fonts—and "invade" the programming of the electronic panel. The graffiti appeared among advertisements, mixing and remixing themes that included violence, social hypocrisy, love, and lyricism.

egoscope was a Net-specific project that engaged the idea of reception amid the processes of entropy and acceleration but also touched on the issue of authorship in a networked digital age (figure 14.2). Like *Did You Read the East?*, the project involved collective actions in public media spaces, but its system was more open, allowing anyone to send, through the *egoscope* Web site,

Figure 14.2 *egóscopio*. http://www.desvirtual.com. Photography by Helga Stein.

words and images to two commercial electronic billboards located in a busy avenue in São Paulo (Faria Lima) in front of an upscale shopping mall. Its purpose was to map a fluid character named "egoscope"—a character composed of reprocessed and recycled media fragments, a mutant produced by trademarks, gadgets, and images inhabiting networked spaces.

Finally, *Poétrica* is a series of visual poems constructed with nonalphabetic dings and system fonts (figure 14.3). Investigating the connections between networks and supports, the piece inverts the assumptions of concrete art and undoes verbal and visual ties through its combination of fonts and numbers,

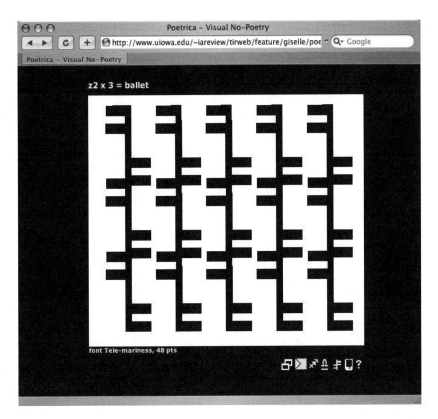

Figure 14.3 *Poétrica.* http://www.desvirtual.com.

languages and codes. Conceived for PDAs, the Web, cell phones, and electronic panels, *Poétrica* also explores the contexts of reading and perception.

Reload

Wop Art, *Did You Read the East?*, *egoscope*, and *Poétrica* are projects that address the reading contexts of nomadism. Their poetics announce the exhaustion of distances that previously allowed us to differentiate art from mass communication and one media device from another. Reversible communication devices emulate their reading conditions (entropy, fragmentation, and movement) and make us recognize the radical transformations new telecommunication systems bring to forms of creating and organizing representations in a symbolic universe where the media does not matter and the interface is the message.

Work Cited

Beiguelman, Giselle. 2001. *Wop Art.* http://www.desvirtual.com/wopart/index.htm (accessed December 5, 2004).

Beiguelman, Giselle. 2002a. *Leste o Leste?* (*Did You Read the East?*). http://www.pucsp .br/artecidade/novo/giselle/index.htm (accessed December 5, 2004).

Beiguelman, Giselle. 2002b. *egóscopio* (*egoscope*). http://www.desvirtual.com/egoscopio/ index.htm (accessed December 5, 2004).

Beiguelman, Giselle. 2003. *Poétrica.* http://www.poetrica.net/ (accessed December 5, 2004).

III

Theories

15

Beyond Taxonomy: Digital Poetics and the Problem of Reading

Talan Memmott

What Is What?

In HTML, DHTML, JavaScript, Java, Macromedia Flash, QuickTime, in MOOs and MUDs, across email, through mailing lists, with sound, with images, with or without sounds or images, with or without words, the term "digital poetry" has been applied to such a wide variety of creative digital applications that its only feasible definition is a minimal one: that the object in question be "digital," mediated through digital technology, and that it be called "poetry" by its author or by a critical reader. The actualities of poetic practice in the digital environment are too diverse to permit a comprehensive or coherent taxonomy.

Similar to the terms "hypertext," "cybertext," "net.art," "click poetry," "rich.lit," or "Web art," the term "digital poetry" has no specific [sub/ob]ject. These terms are liquid delimiters for *creative cultural practice through applied technology*. The context in which any given term is used provides the framework for its definition, however tentative or temporary. The terms are conveniences—(perhaps) for the sake of argument.

Most discussions of first-generation digital textuality—usually called hypertext—focused on comparisons between page-based and screen-based compositions. Although helpful in identifying precedents for digital poetry and demonstrating its literary qualities, these comparisons tended to minimize the material, performative, and computational actualities of digital poetry for the sake of developing an evolutionary progression from print to screen.

The differences between page and screen are only a beginning, however. Because of the diversity of technologies available for the development of digital poetry, the variety of their use as signifying strategies, and radical differences between individual practitioners, digital poetry is not a single recognizable entity. A work developed for a MOO will have very different qualities than a work developed for Macromedia Flash or HTML. A work meant for Perl presents a different poetic system than work to be transmitted through email. Strategies of signification that arise out of these *writing* technologies operate in different modalities with different intent than strategies of page-based authorship. These differences are not superficial or interfacial but integral.

Within digital poetry, finally, the application of a given technology varies from one practitioner to the next, even from one work to the next by the same practitioner. Two works that use the same technology may produce entirely different poetic events. Because digital poetry cannot be reduced to a *genre* of poetry, we must begin to consider the *applied poetics* of the individual practitioner.

Signifying Harmonics and the Playability of Hypermedia

Digital poetry presents an expanded field of textuality that moves writing beyond the word to include visual and sound media, animations, and the integrations, disintegrations, and interactions among these signs and sign regimes. Its performance or poetic emergence requires the participation of a user or operator to initiate the computational processes encoded by its author. Like a musician playing an instrument, a user could be said to *play* an application.

To consider a digital poem as an instrument, one must first recognize it as a specific application or piece of software: a tool for the development of something other than itself. A clarinet is just a clarinet, a tool that demands a player for the production of music. A digital poetry object is by default—or almost always—a piece of software that needs a user to become an instrument of/for signification. To learn to play the instrument—in this case, the digital poetry object—is to become aware of the strategies of operational signification within the given application. The potential of digital poetry resides in its computational aspects: its conditions of interaction, playability, and environment. It is an operational interface for a system of signifying harmonics.

One example of signifying harmonics and the playability of hypermedia is Mária Mencia's *Another Kind of Language* (2002). Three applications tied together conceptually, this piece makes use of visual, auditory, and interactive cues in an effort to "analyse communicative systems produced in the area of 'in-between' 'Semantic Text, Image Text and Phonetic Text' using digital technology" (Artist's Statement in Mencia 2002). The applications are produced in Flash, each in a different language (English, Mandarin, and Arabic). Upon first encounter, the user-reader-player is faced with a blank white screen, but as the cursor is moved across the screen in any direction, areas are activated exposing graphics, text, and sound representative of each application's respective language and culture of origin.

The piece, now available online, was originally constructed for installation in a gallery. Although the Web version may give some indication as to the harmonics between graphic, auditory, and interactive values, it is in the installation version that the piece realizes its musicality. Whereas the Web user can only access one of the three component applications at a time, the installation allows multiple users to play with any one of the three applications. In this configuration, there is not only a signifying harmonics produced between the graphic, auditory, and interactive features of any one application but also a harmonics between the three applications. At the auditory level, this is registered through the commingling of the phonetic values of the three representative languages; at the visual level, it appears in the projection of one application upon another. The interactivity between multiple users playing different component applications produces an improvised orchestration of materials: a signifying harmonics between users-readers-players and the instruments supplied by the author.

The playability of games or instruments, however, is not a constant characteristic of digital poetry. Two works by British poet Peter Howard, *Xylo* (2001b) and *Ugly* (2001a), use available technology to create a more passive or *played* effect. Requiring no more of the user-reader than a Flash plug-in for a browser, *Xylo* opens with a white screen featuring a rifle sight that moves around the window on its own and a series of flashing words in a small red font. As the rifle sight moves across the screen and back again, corner-to-corner, more text begins to appear on the screen. Some text is organized as a stack of flashing words, though the color and font size may vary; other text appears onscreen in poetical lines. As the piece progresses, these poetical lines are added to and altered, sometimes forming stanzas. There is not a moment

Beyond Taxonomy

295

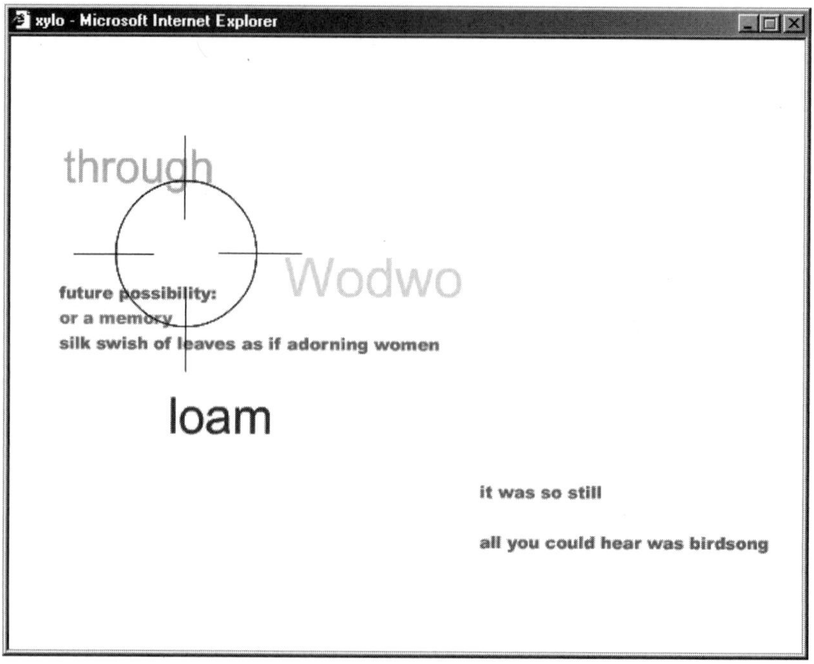

Figure 15.1 Screenshot from *Xylo* by Peter Howard.
http://www.wordcircuits.com/gallery/xylo.

in the piece in which the text is static. The entire poem is set to a new age techno beat, and when the music comes to an end, so, too, does the piece, closing the window automatically (figure 15.1).

Though the rifle sight is somewhat manipulative, as the eye naturally wants to follow its movement around the window, there are no interactive elements in this piece. There is nothing to click on, no decision to be made—other than what text to read. The user is engaged at the level of consumption rather than participation. To a certain extent, the lack of interactive elements in *Xylo* undermines the expectations of hypermediated poetry developed in Flash. Although the work takes advantage of the animation features of Flash, scripted and variable playability is abandoned for a more cinematic effect.

Denial of participation and subversion of expectation is taken further and toward different poetic ends in Howard's *Ugly*, which not only eliminates interactive elements but excludes any evidence of inscription or visual material. The user-reader is confronted with a small black screen while algorithmically manipulated audio flips through various texts. Although *Ugly* is clearly a fully hypermediated work of digital poetry, it operates primarily as sound poetry with a programmatic twist. Despite the fact that both pieces are developed by the same author using the same technology, the choppy, sometimes unintelligible algorithmic audio programmed into the application creates a much different poetic event.

An important question for digital poetics and authorship is the nature and location of the poetry. In *Ugly,* for example, is the audio the poetry of the piece, or is it rather the programming that allows a poetics to emerge as the application is run and the audio recombined? Some hypermedia works positioned under the rubric of digital poetry feature little or no apparent authorial text. Rather, the work functions to provide a facilitating system for the creation of poetry or poetical events. Two examples of this kind of work are *The Impermanence Agent* (1999) by Noah Wardrip-Fruin, ac chapman, Brion Moss, and Duane Whitehurst and *You and We* (2002) by Seb Chevrel and Gabe Kean.

Rather than operate as an overt screen-based presentation of content, *The Impermanence Agent* runs in the background as an intelligence agent monitoring a user's Web activity. As the user passes through the Net hitting various Web pages, the program collects images and fragments of text. This collected material is then combined with preloaded authorial text and recombined again as the user continues to browse the Web. The somewhat abstract personal narrative constructed from the user's own network activity continues to mutate as long as the Agent is run, so that what starts out as fairly coherent authorial narrative is decomposed, eroded and overwritten by the user's own activity.

The poetics of this piece are complex, for it is, in fact, not a single work but a system for the generation of personal narrative and its abstraction. Although the Agent is preloaded with authorial text, this text is only a starting point: seed text for an ongoing process. What happens to this original text depends on the user's personal browsing preferences. As a system, *The Impermanence Agent* is the applied poetics of an individual user's engagement with the network as iterated through the applied poetics of a facilitating system. The poetics of this work lie in the engineering of a system that allows poetry to emerge through it.

Although *You and We* is perhaps a little more traditional in its output than *The Impermanence Agent,* both operate as facilitating systems rather than direct authorial works. Here, the visitor is not necessarily the user, but to under-stand the transactive aspects of this work—its operation as a facilitating system—one must participate in the work.

On first encountering *You and We,* a visitor is confronted with randomly sequenced images overlaid with equally random text. Both the images and the text are manipulated, made to move rapidly one to the next, and set to a looped trance beat: the effect is something like a text-image music video with an emphasis on segues from one image to the next, one text to the next. The randomness with which images and texts appear makes duplication of sequences next to impossible (figure 15.2).

Figure 15.2　One recombination of *You and We. Born Magazine.* http://www.bornmagazine.org/youandwe.

The effect is entertaining and often amusing—an image of an alarm clock coupled with the text *"please no more sweet smell of toes"* segues into the text *"bored . . . ?"* coupled with an image of a caged tiger . . . segues into the text *"time-tested wisdom died a slow painful death"* coupled with the image of a litter of Chihuahuas . . . segues into the image of a scuba diver coupled with the text *"forget me, I will fade away"*—but entertainment is only part of the picture. Chevrel and Kean call *You and We "a collective experiment"* because visitors to the piece can participate in its construction by uploading images and text for inclusion in the random sequences that make up the system's output (figure 15.3). At this writing, about one thousand users

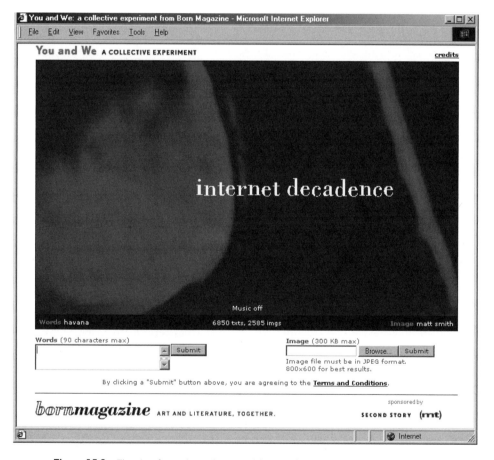

Figure 15.3 The view for registered users, with areas for adding text and images to the piece. *You and We. Born Magazine.* http://www.bornmagazine.org/youandwe.

have added nearly six thousand texts and over two thousand images to the piece. To my mind, the poetics of this piece, its conceptualization and facilitation, are more important qualities than the poetry it generates. The poetics of the work override the poetry: the *intertainment* is more potent than the entertainment.

In a final example, John Cayley's highly visual *What We Will* (2002) functions as a narrative or poetical instrument. In this work, the user-reader navigates through the narrative and across London by way of a clock. At the top of the screen is a rendering of the skyline at various times—day and night—with the hours marked by roman numerals. Clicking on any of the numerals resets the lower portion of the screen to an appropriate scene within the drama. These lower dramatic screens are produced in QuickTime VR, which makes it possible to navigate them as well. It is here, in fact, that the narrative is exposed: moving the cursor around these scenes initiates sound files that tell the story, while clicking on links embedded at the image of an envelope leads the reader to more abstract narrative clues (figure 15.4).

Most of the written text in *What We Will* occurs not in the representational screens but in the areas of abstraction. The sole written text occurs on one screen in the tiny display of a cell phone (figure 15.5). Because most of the piece's narrative and poetic information emerges through visual and auditory means, Cayley terms *What We Will* an *interactive drama*: a drama in which the interactor—or user-reader—is the agent of narrative propulsion. The visual and auditory emphasis of this piece makes it an excellent example of literary hypermedia's redefinition of the enterprise of "reading."

Mis(e)-[on-Screen] Reading

In *Cybertext: Perspectives on Ergodic Literature,* Espen Aarseth points out that "[p]revious models of textuality have not taken [the] performative aspect into account and tend to ignore the medium end of the triangle [verbal sign, operator, medium]" (1997, 21). Though we can introduce a number of page-based poets here to disqualify Aarseth's claim—among them, Stéphane Mallarmé, Steve McCaffery, and Jackson Mac Low—it is important to contextualize this statement in regard to the material aspects of cybertext or digital poetry. In addition to hypermedia's expansion of textuality into the visual and auditory, we must also consider the performative/participatory, the computational and

Figure 15.4   The screen encountered when a user clicks on VIII in the upper clock area. *What We Will.* http://www.z360.com/what.

programmatic, as integral qualities of the poetics of digital poetry: part, in essence, of its writing.

If the expectation of a reader-user is that she will discover the secret of a particular piece by abstracting its elements—for example, isolating the verbal from the visual—the environmental grammatology of the work is lost and the outcome is not a close reading but a partial or close(d) reading that depletes the work of its poetics. This problem is easily understood when one abstracts the verbal element from a hypermedia work only to find the writing (as words) fragmentary and unsatisfying.

If, in the name of developing a syntactic typology of elements, one abstracts interactive elements from a work, the results are equally problematic. As Aarseth points out, interactivity is a slippery concept. Making a number of attempts at classification of computer-based signs, Aarseth demonstrates how

Figure 15.5 A secondary screen accessed through the lower pane showing one of the few areas where written text appears. *What We Will*. http://www.z360.com/what.

typologies break down at the point of interaction where an *Image* becomes a *Button* becomes an *Actor*. These transitions and transformations of computer-based signs are part of the overall poetics of hypermedia applications. As elements on their own, they may be lacking in poetic capacity, but in relationship with other elements—signs, words, images, computational and performative qualities—a poetics, or signifying harmonics, may emerge.

Because the grammatological aspects or signifying harmonics of digital poetry are not universal, it is essential to understand each digital poetry application as an environment or poetic microculture with its own grammar and customs. Applied poetics vary greatly from one practitioner to the next. Each application is its own Galapagos: a singularity in which elements are allowed to evolve or be invented for the survivability of poetic intent. Any given application will of course refer to applications outside itself, but any expectation that elements in one work should operate in the same fashion in another work disregards the diversity of practice and ignores the challenges to language, representation and signification, literary or otherwise, elemental to digital practice.

As a guide to understanding the problems of reading digital poetry, I have found Artaud's *The Theater and Its Double* helpful. Some of the issues with the predominance of written text—the script, the privileging of speech over gesture that Artaud recognizes in Western Theater, and his push to consider the mise-en-scène in theatrical production and understanding—resonate with the current critical situation of digital poetry. Pulling a couple of quotations from *The Theater and Its Double* and performing a little parsing on them helps to show how Artaud's reading of the problems of theater may also apply to hypermedia:

To cause *the written word* or expression . . . to dominate . . . *the poetic hypermedia application at the expense of the* objective expression of gestures and of everything which affects the *user* by sensuous and spatial means is to turn one's back on the *interactualities* of *hypermedia* and to rebel against its possibilities (1958, 71).

It is in the light of magic and sorcery (*potentiality, transformation, emergence*) that *digital poetry* must be considered, not as the reflection of a written text . . . but as the burning projection of . . . [the] consequences of gesture, word, sound, music, *image*, and their combinations. This active projection can be made . . . *in hypermedia* and its consequences found in the presence of and *within the poetic application* (73).

If we alter Artaud's notion of the mise-en-scène—the entirety of theatrical language including everything outside of speech (stagecraft, gesture, lighting, etc.)—to read, perhaps, *mise en écran*, we can see how Artaud's concerns with theatrical language also apply to hypermediated poetic works. Similar to a theater performance, a digital poem is a language that must be read holistically for all the technologies and methods of signification at play. Looking at digital poetry in this way may lead us to ask, as Artaud does of the *mise en scène*, whether the language of the *mise en écran*—or the *mise en écran* as a language—is as "effective and efficacious" (69) as the pure word. Does digital poetry have the "power, not to define thought but to *cause thinking*"? (69)

The ability to *cause thinking* is an essential part of digital poetics and rhetoric, and it is here that literary hypermedia finds its greatest potential. In *Lexia to Perplexia* (Memmott 2000), one of my own hypermedia works, I refer to the literary hypermedia application as an *ideoscope*. This term is accurate to the way many poetic applications work and compatible with terms such as *mise en écran* in my previous (mis)reading of Artaud and Aarseth. In *Lexia to Perplexia,* as in many other literary hypermedia applications, the signifying method is not singular, perhaps not exclusively literary (at least not in the traditional sense). Rather, as indicated earlier, signification occurs through a sort of resonance or harmonics between signs and sign regimes. Ideas are made operational, transactional, scopic. We not only read the text but assist in its de.scription, or ex.position. Although my own work and much of the work mentioned above is chock-full of intent or ideas, the media/medium makes intentionality, poiesis, and poetics negotiable, rendered through various sensual and experiential stimuli rather than limited to the word. It is through the interaction with and the collection and contemplation of ideas presented in the application as the application—the *mise-en-écran*—that the user-reader comes to know its contents.

Toward Taxonomadism

The variety of approaches to digital poetry, the transitive aspects of its elements, and the transactive quality of its applications make the development of a consistent, stabilizing taxonomy difficult if not impossible. To a certain extent, the idea of taxonomy itself is contrary to the realities of digital practice. If we consider the singular qualities of digital poetry application-to-application and the ways in which technologies used in its development emerge and evolve along lines separate from creative practice, we begin to understand how the entire field is dynamic. The *nomos* of taxonomy becomes *nomas*: the field is open; the practice, form, and categories—the *taxa*—are nomadic.

The term *taxonomadism* alludes, of course, to Deleuze and Guattari's notion of nomadology as outlined in *A Thousand Plateaus: Capitalism and Schizophrenia* (1983). So much of literary digital practice happens outside of—or out of reach of—the academy's traditional literary values, formal genealogies, and histories that the practice in general could be viewed as a *war machine* resistant to institutional(izing) processes. What it was is not always what it is. For the academic critic, the nomadism or taxonomadism considered a positive quality in creative practice may register as a negative attribute in critical practice. For the sake of authenticity in regard to a critique and/or theory of digital poetics, however, taxonomadism should be embraced by critics as it has been by programmers and poets.

Similar to technologies, terms and categories should be allowed to emerge, evolve, and dissolve into obsolescence. Temporary and contextual, they should be granted short yet dynamic lives, generating new terms, categories, and conditions. To borrow from Roland Barthes, as read through Gregory Ulmer's *Heuretics: The Logic of Invention* (1994), the critic or theorist of hypermedia should move toward becoming a *poetician,* interested in how digital works are made, how technology, code, media, and intent play together in the formation of poetic hypermedia. Since we are talking about a new form of expression, a new kind of language art, there is a theoretical aspect to even the most creative of applications. There are no guidelines for *creative cultural practice through applied technology,* and it is therefore up to practitioners to develop their own (anti)methods. Each creative application is a new event marked by individual theories of media applications.

The divide between digital creative work and page-based criticism written about it remains huge. The gestures, methods, and modes of signification at work in one form are largely absent in the other. Throughout this chapter, I have tried to avoid promoting any specific critical method for dealing with creative digital practice. I do think, however, that more critical work produced as hypermedia will open doors to new and diverse critical methods and responses that might be more directly applicable to digital culture.

The opportunity offered by the development of critical hypermedia is yet to be explored. Although the critical essay has not lost its place, power, and portability, I think a sharper critical understanding of digital practice may be gained from participation in digital culture, whether the output be a page-based essay or a hypermedia application. To remain outside digital culture and make claims about it is to produce a digital Orientalism that privileges previous cultural orientations at the expense of everything emergent from and/or native to the culture in question. For the critic of creative digital practice, it is important not to be just a tourist but to understand the significant opportunities within hypermedia for critical expression related to such notions as the *ideoscope* and *mise en écran.* Similar to the individualized *applied poetics* of creative digital practice, an applied critical practice would not just invent and develop theoretical and critical methods through an engagement with media technologies but allow those methods to live the temporary, nomadic, and applied lives that are so evident in creative applications.

Onward.

Works Cited

Aarseth, Espen J. 1997. *Cybertext: Perspectives on Ergotic Literature*. Baltimore, MD: Johns Hopkins University Press.

Artaud, Antonin. 1958. *The Theater and Its Double*. Trans. Mary Caroline Richards. New York: Grove Press.

Cayley, John. 2002. *What We Will*. http://www.z360.com/what/ (accessed June 28, 2004).

Chevrel, Seb, and Gabe Kean. 2002. *You and We. Born Magazine*. http://www.bornmagazine.org/youandwe/ (accessed June 28, 2004).

Deleuze, Gilles, and Félix Guattari. 1983. *A Thousand Plateaus: Capitalism and Schizophrenia*. Trans. Brian Massumi. Minneapolis: University of Minnesota Press.

Howard, Peter. 2001a. *Ugly. BeeHive Hypertext/Hypermedia Literary Journal*. http://beehive.temporalimage.com/archive/51arc.html (accessed June 28, 2004).

Howard, Peter. 2001b. *Xylo*. Wordcircuits. http://www.wordcircuits.com/gallery/xylo/ (accessed June 28, 2004).

Memmott, Talan. 2000. *Lexia to Perplexia. The Iowa Review Web*. http://www.uiowa.edu/~iareview/tirweb/hypermedia/talan_memmott/index.html (accessed June 28, 2004).

Mencia, Mária. 2002. *Another Kind of Language*. http://www.m.mencia.freeuk.com/ (accessed June 28, 2004).

Ulmer, Gregory. 1994. *Heuretics: The Logic of Invention*. Baltimore, MD: Johns Hopkins University Press.

Wardrip-Fruin, Noah, ac chapman, Brion Moss, and Duane Whitehurst. 1999. *The Impermanence Agent*. http://www.impermanenceagent.com/agent/ (accessed June 28, 2004).

16

Time Code Language: New Media Poetics and Programmed Signification

John Cayley

One of the defining characteristics of poetic writing is its attention to the materiality of language, which has become an important critical concept in literary studies.[1] We speak of "the materiality of text" or "the materiality of language" in general, as if this might be an abstract characteristic when, in fact, it is the critical marker of linguistic and literary embodiment, recognizable only in terms of that embodiment. As N. Katherine Hayles puts it, *"The materiality of an embodied text is the interaction of its physical characteristics with its signifying strategies"* (2003, 277; emphasis in original). The presence and operation of code is, in many though not all instances, a significant part of the complex physical makeup of electronic text and is often a sine qua non for the operation of its signifying strategies. In so far as we are interested in identifying and defining certain specific aspects of the materiality of language that are foregrounded by writing in networked and programmable media, we are called to pay close attention to the role of code and coding in this type of work. We must keep asking ourselves, what is code? What is the relationship of code and text in cultural objects that are classified as literary and that are explicitly programmed?

The context of this chapter is current and continuing discussion that addresses these questions. It refers implicitly and explicitly to other critical interventions that have begun to identify a genre of electronically mediated writing as "codework." According to Rita Raley, "Broadly, codework makes exterior the interior workings of the computer" (2002). Code is indeed an archive of the symbolic inner workings of the computer. However, not only is it brought to the surface in the writing of new media but it may also function to generate the language displayed on this surface, without itself appearing. In an earlier piece of mine, a prequel to this chapter, I argue that we must be more articulate about the distinctions we make between code and text (Cayley 2002). These distinctions are creatively challenged by codework that brings inner workings to an exterior, especially when such work is manifested as a generative cross-infection of text and code-as-text, of language and code-as-language.

In this earlier piece, I argued that the code is not the text, unless it *is* the text. Code that is not the text, code that remains unbroken and operative, may instantiate—as durational performance—the signifying strategies of a text. As such, it does not appear on the complex surface of the interface text as part of or as identical with it. There are, therefore, further distinctions within codework between those works that bring the traces of an interior archive of code into the open and those works that depend on the continuing operation of code, in which the code, in fact, reconceals itself by generating a complex surface "over" itself. This chapter addresses these distinctions and then takes on questions concerning the characteristics of a textuality whose very atoms of signification are programmed. What is textuality when it is composed from programmed signifiers? This chapter highlights the temporal properties of such signifiers and examines the significance of this temporality.

Literal Performance Literal Process

Clearly, it is difficult to articulate and share a detailed, nuanced conception of what we do—how we perform and process—as we write and read and play with language. Out of our difficulties, entire fields of critical thought emerge. I begin, for example, to use words to refer, provisionally, to phenomena such as words that I assume have some kind of separate, atomic existence, however provisional or temporary. Word-as-word (re)presentation refers to word-as-thing (re)presentation. The implicit atomism—treating something as irreducible in order to try to assay its significance and affect—is always provisional, even when established by lexical authority, and is ever mobile. At one instant, I refer to some word-sized atom of language, the next instant, another, then, as suddenly, I recompile and shift "upwards"—many levels in the hierarchies of code and language—and refer to the specific work or to "text" itself, which suddenly becomes not only a conceptual automaton in our minds but also an atom of linguistic matter in my discourse itself, even though my discourse is, as it were, contained within its significance.

Foregrounded in this way, the procedural, performative nature of the literal is demonstrable. Despite your understanding that, for example, these words are inscribed as writing (temporally stunned, deferred, and spatialized) you will sense words shifting their meanings as I write/speak and you read/hear. No matter how little attention you or I pay to what is going on as we process, it is easy to concede that, for example, the meanings of words such as "code" and "text" change during the shifting "now"—the distinct present moments as I write and you read—and may well change radically over the course of my intermittent writing/speaking and your intermittent reading/hearing. The generation of altered and new meaning is, after all, one of my explicit aims in addressing these terms.

It follows, even from this simple, on-the-fly phenomenology of language, that atoms or instances of language (of whatever extent), although we treat them as "things," are, in fact, processes. If they are ever static or thing-like, they are more like the "states" of a system, provisionally recognized as identifiable, designated entities. In themselves, they are, if anything, more similar to programmed, procedural loops of significance and affect, isolated for strategic or tactical reasons, be they rhetorical, aesthetic, social, or political. This characterization is good linguistics and good critical thought. However, usually our perception and appreciation of linguistic and critical process is more broadly focused, bracketing the microprocesses that generate and influence significance and affect in the "times" taken to move from statement to statement, let alone those that pass so fleetingly and function so invisibly in the move from letter to letter.

Moreover, as Hayles demonstrates in her recent critique of prevailing notions of textuality, an abstracted conception of both "the text" (a physical and literal manifestation of the ideal object of textual criticism, more or less identified with an author's intended work) and "text" (as a general concept) is allied to the apparent stasis and persistence of print and still dominates our understanding of textuality in literary criticism (2003, 270–271). By contrast, for Hayles all texts are embodied in specific media. In her view, electronic texts represent a mode of embodiment through which literary works are able to perform a realization of a latent materiality and perhaps also the revelation of such texts' present and future informatic posthumanity, in which they "thrive on the entwining of physicality with informational structure" (275). Hayles sets out some of the elements of an electronic text and emphasizes the dynamism of their symbolic relationships:

There are data files, programs that call and process the files, hardware functionalities that interpret or compile the programs, and so on. It takes all of these together to produce the electronic text. Omit any one of them, and the text literally cannot be produced. For this reason it would be more accurate to call an electronic text a *process* rather than an object. (274; emphasis in original)

Such a text, unlike one that has print for its medium, has no materially accessible existence prior to its generation when displayed on the screen: "electronic textuality . . . *cannot be separated from the delivery vehicles that produce it as a process with which the user can interact*" (276; emphasis in original).

For an object to be identified as a process, at the very least, there must be some way for its state to change over time and perhaps also the possibility of enumerating the temporal sequence of such states or some way to describe a procedure or procedures that generate the states and changes of state in the object. In other words, there have to be programs to be followed, to be run. In Hayles's analysis, however, the programming seems to reside chiefly in the delivery media of electronic textuality—the "data files, programs that call and process the files, hardware functionalities, and so on"—rather than operating from within the text itself, the text of interpretation (274). In earlier essays, she has described and characterized a "flickering signifier" in digital textuality, but this flickering of signification is a function of the same *peripheral* processing of text and its image—both screen image and underlying encoded representations. Where the flickering is indicative of depth—similar to ripples on the surface of a lake—this is a function of code in the sense of encoding.[2] We imagine depths behind the screen, within the box, underneath the keyboard, because we know that the surface text is multiply encoded so that it can be manipulated at the many and various levels of software and hardware. However, much of this underlying programmatological manipulation is typically treated as insignificant for the purposes of interpretation. I know that the screens of text that I read are being ceaselessly refreshed with, perhaps, some subliminal perceptual flickering of their signifiers, but I do not necessarily read this process as part of what is being signified to me. Unless foregrounded by an author for particular rhetorical effects, the programmatological dimensions of screen rasterization, for example, do not play a direct role in the generation of significance or affect.

This is by no means to say that flickering signification does not operate in a poetics of new media. I believe that this phenomenon is crucial to both the theory and practice of literal art in programmable media and is generally applicable to textuality, including that of traditional media such as print.[3] My present purpose, however, is to try to address the role of procedures that do directly affect rhetoric and poetics, to identify the subjects and objects of programming within discussions of code and coding in so far as they inflect our understanding of writing and the performance of writing.

Five Ways to Write "Code"

I have already suggested one source of possible misdirection concerning the relationship of code and signification. The debate is set out under the rubric of "codework" without fully articulating the ambiguities in the use of the term "code" itself. Thus Hayles, for example, concentrates on the role of "code" as *encoding* in signification, with "code" as operative *programming* implicitly consigned to the hardware and software periphery. Raley's minimal characterization—"Broadly, codework makes exterior the interior workings of the computer"—evokes both encoding and programming aspects of code(work) since they are typically interior in her sense (2002). Raley goes on to suggest further distinctions in codework as identified by a prominent codework practitioner, Alan Sondheim: "'Works using the syntactical interplay of surface language'"; "'Works in which submerged content has modified the surface language'"; "'Works in which the submerged code is emergent content'" (qtd. in Raley 2002). However, Sondheim's set of distinctions does not evoke code as programming per se, and it remains focused on a written surface, however complex. It refers to the inscribed surface and what emerges from code into and through it.

In order to help clarify the various ways that "code" is used in discussions of codework, I offer five provisional categories:

1. Code as (a special type of) language (viewed and interpreted as such)
2. Code as infecting or modulating natural language (the language works, but the code is "broken")

3.   Code as text to be read as (if it were) natural language; code which is infected or modulated by natural language (the code works, but the language is "broken")

4.   Code as system of correspondences, as encoding

5.   Code as programming, as a program or set of methods that runs (in time) and produces writing, or that is necessary for the production of writing.

The first three categories characterize texts according to properties of the constituent language. The texts are viewed as interface texts to be read in a fairly traditional manner. The language has been composed and laid out—in any number of complex contexts, including of course the online, shifting context of the Web—and then it is read and interpreted. These categories cover the majority of literal art production that goes under this new rubric of "codework."

Code as language in itself and in its own terms, category one, is something of a specialist study, and its full critical appreciation is as much the concern of computer scientists as literary critics. Nonetheless, writers such as Loss Pequeño Glazier seriously address code in its own terms as a potential poetry, not simply as linguistic fodder for the most common type of codework, the second category, in which code infects or modulates natural language.[4] This second type of code-infected writing, epitomized in many ways by the work of Mez, is widely practiced and represents not much more than the extension of the long-standing enrichment of natural language that occurs whenever history or sociology produces an encounter between linguistic cultures and subcultures.[5]

In my previous essay on codework, I critiqued this mode of writing, not least by comparing it to the encounters that occur between commensurate human languages. Codework comes off somewhat badly from the comparison, because code is a jargon or sublinguistic structure, not a full-blown, culture-supporting language. An encounter between, for example, English and Unix is, in a sense, an encounter between a language and some smaller part of itself rather than a language and an alien and commensurate linguistic entity.[6] It is also the case with code-infected interface text that the code is, in the programmer's sense, "broken" after its incorporation into the text we read. It has lost its operative, performative "power" in the very instant that it is brought to the surface of interpretation.[7] What of the code that remains hidden, which may well be operating as we read? This is the code that I want to read more critically.

Category three, codework that is manifest as written code, presented and intended to be read by nonspecialist human readers—those who are not programmers and not, as it were, "manual" compilers or interpreters—is a special case and is less common. "Perl poetry" is a genre known mainly to programmers and hackers. In this type of writing, the code may be *functional* and unbroken (although not *functioning* as it is read).[8] However, in most instances, natural language elements are introduced (in a way that allows the code to remain functional), or cultural framing is provided that renders the code readable—significant and affective—for humans. In a manner complementary to the conditions pertaining to code-infected language, the human cultural elements tend to be "broken" or at least heavily constrained in these forms.

Thus, the codework categorized according to my first three usages of "code" produces texts to be read, interface texts subject to interpretation by readers. The code is not running to generate the text, nor is it significantly present in the text in a way that might alter or inflect the manner of reading. Code is not functioning to address writing as a formal procedure in these cases; it is not involved with the form and matter of the language used, although it is, clearly, making a contribution to its content. The language of code is visible on the surface of the interface text, but code has not necessarily been present at the scene of writing.

As we come to consider encoding, my fourth category, as an aspect of writing in programmable media, code does begin to emerge as integral to the material of the language used, necessary for its properties and methods, although, I argue, this aspect of code is still not fully indicative of its potential role in the active and continuing modulation of signification or as an engine for new literal and literary rhetoric in new media.[9] As I have already noted, Hayles's flickering signifier acquires much of its conceptual power from the depths and layers of encoding it allows us to discover and recover in programmatological systems. It is clearly demonstrable that text stored and displayed in digital media is multiply encoded, and awareness of this circumstance is certainly significant for our understanding of the materiality of language in new media. However, this is not an entirely new conception of textuality.

The idea that the signifier is multilayered, with shifting and floating relationships of correspondence between the layers, is well known and widely accepted in criticism. Famously, Barthes (as Hayles acknowledges) brought our attention to the layered underlying semiotic codes prevalent even in *readerly* texts.[10] He showed how elements of the interface text might instantiate and evoke many and various instances of the corresponding codes simultaneously. Moreover, and by contrast with Barthes' sense of code, the type of encoding highlighted by the flickering of Hayles's digital signifiers is, in one sense, largely sublinguistic, or on the outer margins of paratext. Although we can be made aware that the codes of digital media make the words we read on screen flicker beneath it, we do not really care—for the purposes of interpretation—whether the text we read is encoded as extended ASCII or Unicode.

Finally, this type of relationship is simultaneous or synchronous. The flickering is a sign of a synchronic correspondence. The flickering may only be apparent in brief moments of time, but, significantly, the relationships do not function temporally, nor are they modulated by time. This simultaneity of encoded correspondences is crucial, I believe, to the distinction between, on the one hand, code as encoding and, on the other, code as the archive of functional programming. We have to distinguish between flickering as a function of the chained hierarchies of codes and language in which the signifier flickers because it is reducible to something else that flickers (e.g., the work, a text, is persistent on the screen, but I know that it flickers because I know that the screen refreshes and because the keyboard is waiting for new input or because some paratextual procedure such as changing its font and color is being applied to the word image and flickering because the signifier or chain of signifiers is produced by code and because the signifier may itself be programmed.

At this point, I am beginning to discuss code as operational programming in textuality, my fifth category. My aim is to distinguish the characteristics of textuality that incorporates (or is the subject of) code in this sense. This "strong sense" code is integral to all textuality, although it might be objected that this claim would be hard to substantiate before the historical advent of demonstrably programmable media. There have always been programs, I would answer, and these programs are a necessary aspect of the materiality of language—an ever-present aspect of mediation between a text's physical characteristics and its signifying strategies. The difference lies in where—literally, and also within cultural structures and hierarchies—these programs run, and it also depends on who writes and runs them. There is a continuity between what I will call "paratextual programming" and the kind of programming that is ever more familiar from the proliferation of programmable media. Paratextual programming runs quasi-invisibly within traditional structures of writing, reading, and interpretation. The programmatological dimension of writing has always already been operative, and therefore the traditional temporally stunned conception of textuality has always already been inadequate to literary and especially to poetic practice. However, the coding applied to textuality *in new media* allows us to perceive, if not the coding itself, then the unambiguous effects and consequences of that coding.

Punctuation Colon Programming

To demonstrate a continuity between paratextual programming and programming proper we can work with an example, a sentence within a paragraph at the beginning of this chapter. By paratextual programming, I mean the (integral) aspects of inscription that frame or infect or undermine or position the text to be read, that is, the interface text. I use the term "paratext" in the sense developed by Genette,[11] but I am highlighting its programmatological dimension. In contrast to "strong sense" coding or programming, paratextual programming becomes a perceptible part of the interface text— it appears on the same surface, often using the same symbol set (although as often employing the tropes and figures of nonlinguistic media)—whereas coding per se remains invisible and inaccessible. In fact, the "codework" in the sense of the instantiation of code-infected interface text (typically my category two) can be seen as paratextual programming using what is also occasionally referred to as postmodern punctuation. Raley calls this—approaching even closer to the textuality of programmable media—"punctuation particular to the apparatus" and cites one of the prime current practitioners of the art: "Talan Memmott calls this set of punctuation 'technical ideogrammatics'" (2002).[12]

Even writing punctuated in a manner that is "particular to the apparatus" can be quoted, unpacked, analyzed, and stunned to paraphrase, as writing in general or in traditionally recognized forms. As promised, I will demonstrate what I mean with a simple example from a piece of language I have already used: "Word-as-word (re)presentation refers to word-as-thing (re)presentation." Obviously, the visible marks of paratextual programming here are the parentheses. The primary specific intended effect of the parentheses is to provide a double reading, at once poststructural (through the evocation of the word "representation" and through the use of the parentheses themselves putting presence/absence of a signifier into play) and also Freudian (through the implicit use of his phrases "word presentation" and "thing presentation").[13] What the punctuation does is set up a time-based revision of the atomic meanings of and within the sentence.

I can, as I have done, recast these meanings and map them to a paraphrase based on the traces and marks in the interface text itself. This recasting is a process in itself, separate from the surface language of the interface text but archived within it. Its implicit "code" evokes a widely used and well-understood rhetorical and interpretative "program," the program of paraphrase. In this light, paraphrase can be seen as nothing other than the simplified (proper) naming of procedural loops within more complex language so that we can identify and atomize their procedures of meaning generation for the purpose of rearticulation. Any text in which codes and the codes of punctuation are integrated with the interface text, including much of the codework of Mez and Talan Memmott, can be unpacked and analyzed in these terms as inflected and driven by paratextual programming.

Hypertextual Dissolutions

Spatially organized, navigable texts can often be understood in the same way, in which precisely the spatial organization and navigation is to be read as paraphrase, gloss, elaboration, annotation, and so on, all coded into operations that produce a successively revealed interface text. Making reference to spatially organized, navigable textuality immediately evokes hypertext. Indeed hypertext does, for me, occupy a transitional or intermediate position between the textuality of what I have called paratextual programming exemplified in a postmodern punctuation of print text and a textuality that is generated by programs or that is itself programmed.

For Philippe Bootz, hypertext is simply the application of an operator to a literary data space.[14] In Bootz's theory, "the Procedural Model," the application of a hypertext operator or class of operations to a protohypertext is what generates nodes and links while, at the same time, coding those methods and commands that enable what we call navigation into the hypertextual structure. For Bootz, it is important to see that the hypertextual operator is simply one of a virtually infinite number of such operators that might be applied to the literary data space: the protohypertext that would in fact become something quite other than hypertext if different operators were applied.

It is also noteworthy that the procedures and programming of hypertext are relatively simple—the response to a set of documentary problems rather than to poetic or, indeed, narrative ones.[15] As famously discussed on the relevant listservs in the late 1990s, there seems to be little content "inside" the links of traditional hypertext.[16] Hypertext took the spatialization of text beyond print media and brought the trope of navigation to prominence, but the composed language of its constituent nodes or lexia retained the print-like quality of having been impressed on a surface—discoverable, visitable, but with little programmatological "depth." The classic hypertextual link does little more than provide the instantaneous replacement of one composed fragment of integral text by another. At times, this process is not appreciable, even metaphorically, as a spatial displacement. How is the replacement of text on the surface of a unitary screen more of a spatial displacement than, for example, turning to a place—figuratively, literally, and physically—"further on" or "deeper into" or "at the back of" a book? The programming involved in hypertext seems relatively shallow and more closely allied with paratext and textual framing than with the potentialities I have it in mind to address.

Overriding the "Read" Method: Rosenberg's Programmed Signifiers

Discussion of hypertext leads us to the work of Jim Rosenberg, which provides a further transitional demonstration of code operative in and through language and a crucial and interesting point of intersection between paratextual and strong-sense, fifth-category codework. Rosenberg explicitly contextualizes his practice within and against the traditional study and theory of hypertext, and yet his work is difficult to reconcile with classic link-node models of hypertext. On the one hand, the actual coding in his work is, arguably, simpler than the implementation of a hypertext operator. In pieces such as Rosenberg's *Intergrams* (1993), *The Barrier Frames* (1996a), and *Diffractions Through* (1996b), his actual coding produces little more than the substitution of successive screen images showing texts, syntactic diagrams (in most cases), and textual frames in response to the position of a mouse or other pointing device.[17] On the other hand, Rosenberg has built elaborate, articulated relationships into the language and linguistic structures of the texts that are handled by his actual code, such that the positioning of the pointer—part of the work of the reader—becomes a device that reveals the programmatological dimension of his work.

It seems to me to be crucial to Rosenberg's work that often when the mouse or pointing device is not in contact with an area containing or enclosing text, the visual field of the work is illegible, or, more precisely, its constitutive texts are illegible. In these states of the work (one might call them "rest" states), the reader is initially presented with "zoomed out" diagrams outlining a large-scale syntactic relationship between areas of text (which are shown as graphic "representations of writing" rather than writing per se) (figure 16.1). If the reader "zooms in" on one of these areas, such that it fills the visual field and constitutes a new phase of the interface text, the words displayed on the screen (in the "rest state" of a zoomed-in assemblage) are still illegible but for different reasons (figure 16.2). Rosenberg typically composes his texts in overlaid clusters that together are dense enough to make reading the constituent layers impossible. It is precisely the movement of the mouse that brings one or another layer to the reading surface where it then becomes legible (while covering the other layers) (figure 16.3). Move the mouse away, and the work returns to an illegible rest state.

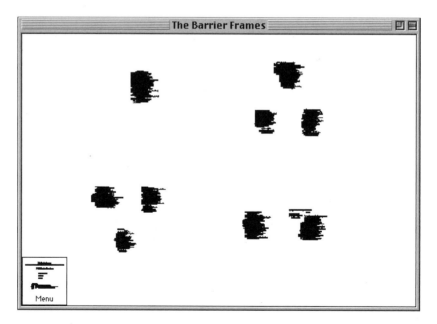

Figure 16.1 *The Barrier Frames.* Courtesy of Jim Rosenberg.

Figure 16.2 *Intergrams.* Courtesy of Jim Rosenberg.

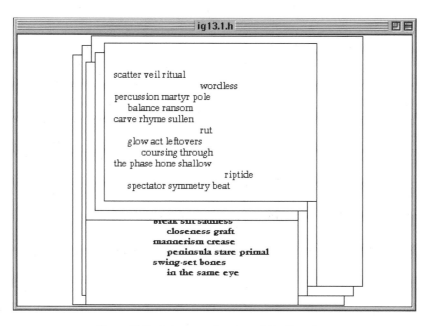

Figure 16.3 *Intergrams.* Courtesy of Jim Rosenberg.

Work such as Rosenberg's, implemented with very simple coding, nonetheless requires its coding—as a specific part of its materiality and in order to realize its signifying strategies—to a far greater degree than in the case of the generality of link-node hypertext, for example. This can be demonstrated in the most simple and direct terms when we say that Rosenberg's work is illegible: it cannot be read unless its underlying codes—the ones that reveal the constituent layers—are running in a waiting state, ready to be evoked. Of course, the entirety of a hypertext also requires that its various links are activated and followed in order for it to be read *as a whole*, but its constituent nodes are, typically, legible as texts in the hypertext's "rest" state. A hypertext, classically, does not require the constant, active invocation of the codes that manage its links for textual reading to at least proceed.[18]

In fact, of course, all reading requires the constant and active invocation of codes and coding in the mind for it to proceed. No reading takes place without a *process* of reading. It is simply that print literacy tends to bracket the temporal and programmatological dimension of both writing and reading or reduce it either to an inscribed spatiality of ideal, fixed editions or to linearity, which is its all but invisible fundamental temporal structure—a structuring of time so straightforward that, when recorded as writing, we tend to think of the text as a line (resting) in space.[19]

The materiality of Rosenberg's work resists these reductions in the most obvious and effective way. When his work is space, it is not legible, and it has no emergent, repeatable linearity. Only within restructured time can it be read. Moreover, even less than in the case of hypertext can it be reduced to linearity. Without being indeterminate (Rosenberg's texts are not generated by quasi-random processes), these texts are nonetheless constructed in a manner that makes it next to impossible for writer or reader to anticipate or control the mouse or pointer's positions when addressing the work in a way that would allow, for example, the repeated performance of particular sequences of textual revelations. It would be impossible, that is, without learning to manipulate one of his works like a musical instrument, gaining the necessary control and skill to know which "notes" to strike and when. The point is, the reading, or recital, of one of Rosenberg's texts obliges its readers to address the inherent restructuring of time, specifically, the time of reading. Rosenberg's coding of programmable media for literal art *guarantees* this specific aspect of his text's materiality and also, perhaps even more important,

John Cayley

gives both writer and reader access to the manipulation of this dimension of literal textual matter.[20]

In Rosenberg's work, the coding is in the system, but it is also within, and a part of, the writing because of the simple fact that the only way to read is by working with the text, manipulating it with a programmaton's pointing device. Rosenberg has recast reading and has changed the properties and methods of the signifier. He instantiates a signifier that has radically different properties from the signifier of print culture. One way of figuring this difference is to extend an analogy with Object-Oriented Programming and say that Rosenberg has extended the class "Text" and overridden its "read" and "write" methods. In Rosenberg's work, writing is (among other things) a method of layering, overlaying, and compositing texts, and reading is (among other things) a tentative work of revealing the clustered layers in order to pass on the literal data they contain to the "read" method of an underlying or parallel Text object of the "parent" class, the Text object of print culture.[21]

While we want to emphasize the fact that the signifier is a temporal, durational object, we also have to consider that literal and literary time is itself restructured by textuality. Textuality is temporal and as such restructures the culture of human time. That textuality was always temporal is clear. We are familiar with the textual generation of linear and narrative time. We are familiar with writing as deferral, especially as a function of its spatiality, its translation of time into space. We are comfortable with the figures and tricks of narrative reordering (flashback and the like), although chiefly in the frameworks of historical time and narrative drive.[22] However, textuality as instantiated in programmable media realizes the potential for a more radical restructuring of the culture of human time, and Rosenberg's literal art provides an instance of how this happens through the absolute necessity to work with it, in time, in order to read.[23] It is, in this sense, a (if not "the") type of "ergodic literature" in which nontrivial effort is *necessary* for reading (Aarseth 1997). However, as Espen Aarseth shows with his provisional "textonomy" (15), time enters into the art of letters and is restructured through many other rhetorical methods and procedures, not only through ergodic manipulation but also—giving a far from exhaustive list—through animation, text generation, quasi- and pseudo-random modulation, and various combinations of all of these, not to mention the kind of live textual collaboration that *networked* programmable media allow.

Text in the Docuverse

Rosenberg's marked and continuing investment in hypertext **per se** invites us to reexamine the claim—much touted in the hypertextual "Golden Age"—that textuality gives way to hypertextuality in new media.[24] Rosenberg sees his work in terms of hypertext and is an active participant in the research community associated with both the technical and theoretical development of hypertext. When viewed from the perspective of computer science (or computer science in the service of the humanities) as a system implemented in software, "hypertext" has both a more precise meaning and also a range of ever-evolving meanings closely dependent on the changing capabilities of actually existing systems. Thus the Web is a variety of hypertext providing nodes, links, and navigation, but the basic capabilities of HTML in the standard server-browser implementation are severely limited when compared with more developed hypertext systems or speculative structures.[25] Many hypertext theorists and researchers—including, and perhaps especially, Ted Nelson—would say that the Web falls short of even the fundamental requirements for a properly hypertextual system. I am not so much interested in explaining or elaborating these technical distinctions. Still, I want to consider the implications of the proposition that Rosenberg sees his work, his literary objects, as reducible to hypertext, and I want to do this in relation to a theory of hypertext that is particularly "totalizing": Nelson's vision of the *docuverse*.

This essay provides a context for a reexamination of Nelson's vision in terms of my arguments concerning the poetics and the temporal materiality of textual art in new media. More specifically, I am discussing programmed signification—strategies of signification in Hayles's terms—in which codes and coding operate to generate or modulate texts substantively. The attempt to reconcile such strategies with Nelsonian hypertext yields, I believe, crucial perspectives on both hypertext and the materiality of textual art. Nelson is a visionary theorist particularly sensitive to text as an "evolving, Protean structure" ([1981] 1993, 2/17), and yet, paradoxically, his docuverse—along with the properties and methods of its Xanadu system—is not only "the original (perhaps the ultimate) HYPERTEXT SYSTEM" (front cover) but also the final instantiation of the textual materiality of authorized editions, of the ideal, abstracted, persistent, authorized text that is currently the dominant object of attention in both literary and academic discourse.

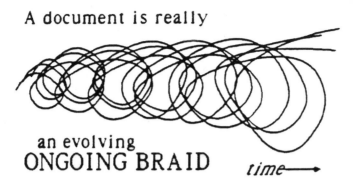

A document is really

an evolving
ONGOING BRAID *time*——▸

Figure 16.4 Nelson's Braid. Courtesy of Ted Nelson.

For Nelson, "a document is really an evolving ONGOING BRAID" (2/14) (figure 16.4). This definition accords perfectly with a materiality of text for which structured durations of time are necessary to its strategies of signification. Nelson's system also specifies and provides a way to view text in various successive states that arise during the spiraling, branching process of composition, "instantaneous slices" captured from the evolving braid as "versions" of the text or some part of the text. For Nelson, a text very much has a diachronic, as well as a synchronous, existence, and his rendition of hypertext aims to represent this chronological dimension and to do so well. However, his nodes are *time-stamped* not *time-based*, as in the phrase "time-based art." The docuverse captures states of the looping and spiraling braids of textuality but not the looping and spiraling itself. In later versions of the docuverse, these nodes are conceived of as the "spans" of a "permascroll."[26] The totalizing and ultimate instantiation of a Nelsonian docuverse is a representation of *the* permascroll.

The permascroll is another important point of view from which to examine the Nelsonian docuverse. It is the linear and literal representation *of every textual event*. It is all writing, everything written, everything inscribed as language, as and when it was so inscribed. Hypertext can then be generated from the permascroll through operations that display linked windows onto spans of the scroll. Textual history and textual criticism can be recast as a vast but particular and privileged set of pointers to those spans on the permascroll representing various textual events that are culturally and institutionally significant for the archive and interpretation of a writing tradition. A book, for example, may be viewed as one (complex) window on the scroll, its coordinates and output parameters determined by a particular culture's definition of the "book" as a textual framing device containing the end product of many processes (e.g., editing) that examine and select from prior collections of spans delineated on the permascroll and representing the chronological development of the text.

The Textual Event

To my mind, Nelson's vision is truly that: visionary, magnificent. It *is* an ultimate system, the epitome of a textual universe composed of *editions*—composed, that is, from minimal, transcriptable textual events. And yet it begs a question that throws our underlying concerns into high relief: "what is a textual event?" As Bootz (2003) has noted, Nelson's concerns—as opposed to those of literary artist-practitioners—were first and foremost documentary. Nelson proposed a reconfiguration of the documentary universe that is more than equal to the task of handling all the nuances of textuality and its criticism as currently instituted and implemented in traditional literary media.[27]

The textual event is defined culturally, by cultural institutions and media technologies. In our own context, the institutions that dominate literature and language art are editorial bodies (universities, publishers, the world of letters), and for these authorities, the textual event is still ultimately determined by a simple test: "can it be printed?" In recent years this formulation may have been slightly modified (by the Web in particular) to "can it be printed *out?*" Nelson challenges and reconfigures the forms of display and the engines generating our textual points of view, but he does not fundamentally challenge the notion of textual event.[28] Specifically, he does not address the necessity, I propose, to allow the textual signifier to include—as inherent constituents of its materiality—temporality and programmability.

Consider how Rosenberg's diagram or intergram poems might be transcribed on the Nelsonian permascroll. As it happens, all the textual elements of a Rosenberg piece are determinate: they may be conceived as authorially composed and transcriptable editions. As such, all the elements of a diagram poem or intergram and all of its states could be rendered by the permascroll and its engines, except that, crucially, there is no obvious—or *institutionally recognized*—way to represent overlay and simultaneity or the dissolution and resolution of these textual properties in necessarily temporal and ergodic processes.[29] Both of these features are intrinsic to the aesthetic and to the significance and affect of Rosenberg's work, to its meanings. Appended to the scroll and its engines, one could imagine the record of code—or of abstracted representations of algorithms—that would allow all of the features of a poem to be rendered and reproduced, but these would not be part of the scroll or its native systems; they would not be instituted as a recognized part of the docuverse, even the Nelsonian docuverse, let alone the traditional world of letters.

In a sense, I am revisiting old arguments concerning the specific technical capabilities of our emergent media of inscription. When hypertext arrived in the world of letters circa 1994, certain practitioners and theorists complained of its inability to implement a wide range of the intrinsic potential for an extended literacy in networked and programmable media.[30] However, besides pinpointing "what gets left out" of textuality by both print and hypertextual culture (our focus is the temporality and programmability of the signifier, the textual event), the Nelsonian example highlights the complicity of institutions with the implicit cultural resistance to certain forms of practice. The resistance is not just a function of technology. In *Literary Machines,* Nelson is radical in demanding a revolution that extends to literary institutions. Imagining a total migration of literary content to new media, he goes so far as to propose a total reconfiguration of critical apparatus and intertextuality, of tools for quotation and reference. He also provides, to my mind, a workable mechanism that upholds basic principles and moral rights established by copyright while shifting their control and management away from existing copyright hegemonies that threaten to dominate and constrain cultural production in new media.[31] That is radical.

Temporal and Literal Institutions

The institutions that are not challenged by the Nelsonian paradigm are those cultural institutions that authorize and maintain a definition of the fundamental atom of inscription and its relationship to a particular, privileged type of temporality. The minimal unit of text—of the symbolic, of language-in-Western-culture—is the letter, an abstraction we conceive as timeless. Strings of letters that are structured into words, sentences, paragraphs, chapters, books, and so on, we also think of as having a temporality that is deferred. We say that writing renders time as space, while also, of course, always allowing its power to represent (arbitrarily complex) temporal structures *in content*.[32]

For any particular text, we accept any of its recorded histories or chronologies that can be expressed in terms of these atoms of inscription. This acceptance allows and accounts for the complexities of textual criticism, for the relatively sophisticated notion of "text" that these practices require, for text as a history of *editions*—however provisional and reworkable. Hypertext provides a navigable visualization of the relationships between such fundamental units of inscription, while Nelson's particular genius was to provide a generalization of these complex requirements and a potential reconfiguration of their underlying structures, one that was radically, institutionally implicated. However, because of the properties of their shared fundamental atom of inscription—particularly its deferred temporality—all of these forms of textuality may, if necessary (typically, this will be for institutional reasons or to allow the text's accessibility to familiar, traditional, interiorized reading practices), be rendered as print, without institutionally affecting the interpretation and appreciation of the text's aesthetic, its strategies of signification, its generation of meanings, its significance and affect.[33] Furthermore, this printing out implicitly privileges a particular form of temporality: an (arbitrary) sequencing of elements of inscription that is ineluctable during any particular experience (or "printing out") of a text's instantiation but which, in institutional terms, appears to be inevitable and necessary to the extent that we may prefer one sequence of elements and come to designate this sequence as *the* text, as its standard, canonical edition.

This type of canonization will not work for a Rosenberg intergram. Neither will it work for a wide-ranging and growing corpus of work that is textual and also—to give only the most obvious examples of textual properties that are not, as it were, "(perma)scrollable"—animated, generated, indeterminate, the product or instantiation of real-time collaboration. To take one example, textual animation, we can see in cinematic film titling, in advertising using time-based delivery media, and, finally, in the poetics of networked and programmable media that textual animation has a history and a highly developed (if inadequately articulated) rhetoric specific to its textual materiality. The atoms of this textual matter cannot be simply recast as arbitrary sequences of letters, not without bracketing, masking, or ignoring vital aspects of these texts' signifying strategies—specifically, for example, a whole range of transition effects from text to text. This means, unambiguously, that criticism must address the cultivation and articulation of temporality in this work as well as, if not also by way of, an analysis of the code that guarantees and drives literal temporality.

Code Generates Literal Time

Code as programming has other contributions to make to the emergent tropes and figures of a rhetoric extended to articulate the signifying strategies of writing in networked and programmable media, reflecting its materiality and media specificities.[34] However, in so far as code generates the temporalities of writing in programmable media, it highlights what I believe is currently the most important thread in a program that criticism and theory must follow in order to accept these temporalities as integral and inalienable properties of all atoms of signification in literal, indeed, literary art. Without its code, even when rendered as elaborate "scrollable" hypertext, Rosenberg's work sacrifices vital aspects of its aesthetics, its strategies of signification, its power to generate significance, affect, meaning.[35] The effect of an intergram arises largely, as we have said, from simultaneities and from temporal and ergodic processes that dissolve and resolve these simultaneities. The cultivation and articulation of real, material time is built into the text through coding.

In the recent criticism of new media poetics, much has been made of the *visibility* of a literary work's engagement with the material specificities of its media, what might be called its material self-reflexivity. Hayles (2002) demonstrates brilliantly how Mark Danielewski makes us see and feel and hear the empty/nothing/void in his *House of Leaves* (110). However, we still, in this and other print culture examples, see and feel and hear the "leaves" using technologies of inscription that are profoundly familiar within the culture and institutions of literature and pedagogy in general: parallelism of textual streams (text and footnotes); commentaries; commentaries on commentaries; multiple perspectives; typographic novelties; not least, temporal complexities represented as content while formally virtualized and *deferred* by writing.

We must also, however, acknowledge and distinguish texts in media that are composed with code and that allow authors and readers to program aspects of temporality as integral parts of the text, as constitutive of its very materiality. And we must recognize a productive, critical opposition between writing as deferral/spatialization (of content, including representations of time, however complex) and writing as program and performance (in and of time). We need to elaborate this distinction for many reasons:

- The real temporal dimension of the *materiality* of text has been underplayed and overwhelmed by the stasis and persistence of authorized editions.
- A materiality of text that embraces temporality offers a more general theory of textuality, backwardly applicable to work in durable media.
- A significant body of work now exists that is made from programmed signifiers and can be displayed using time-based media, and this body of work remains literally unreadable and largely resistant to methods of interpretation that cannot cope with temporality in a sophisticated manner.
- Work of this type includes performative pieces that are made of language and expressed as literary art but which cannot be addressed using the existing tools of literary criticism.
- Finally, much of this work is explicitly generated by and made, at least in part, from code, coding that has an unambiguous relationship with the programmatological engines of new media, the tools we now habitually use to write.

Code is presented to us as a special type of linguistic archive. It leaves traces on the surface of literary culture that cannot be denied or ignored, even in works that do not make art with these traces. Strangely, the code is hidden as it runs, driving the temporal atoms of literal signification and restructuring the culture of human time. The code of programmatology embodies a literal interior now calling to us for articulation and poiesis.[36]

Notes

1. This chapter is now only loosely based on my presentation at the "New Media Poetics" conference, held at the University of Iowa, October 11–12, 2002, facilitated by Thomas Swiss and Dee Morris, to whom, along with Sarah Townsend, I owe a debt of thanks for their comments on early drafts. Thanks also to N. Katherine Hayles for her correspondence, comments, and unstinting intellectual generosity, and to Laura L. Sullivan for her editing, insight, and critique.

2. For this discussion, see Hayles 1999b. The essay was first published in 1996 in *Electronic Culture* and is discussed extensively in my essay "The Code Is Not the Text" (Cayley 2002).

3. For further discussion of this point, see Cayley 2002.

4. Glazier addresses code throughout his book *Digital Poetics*, but see especially his chapter on "Code Writing, Reading Code" (2002, 96–125).

5. An analysis and something of an apologia for Mez's work and theory is provided by Raley (2002). For more detail, see Cayley 2002. In Baldwin 2003, the author provides a critique of this earlier paper of mine and also explores a number of ways that code may enhance the rhetoric of this kind of work.

6. See Cayley 2002.

7. The case for "brokenness" as a feature not a bug is made in Baldwin 2003, 115.

8. In my earlier essay (Cayley 2002), I described examples, citing work by Jodi and Cosic, as well as one of my own experiments.

9. See Cayley 2002.

10. In *S/Z*, Barthes ([1973] 1990) establishes a distinction between *readerly* and *writerly* texts as those that, respectively, invite interpretation and (re)construction by their reader-authors.

11. See Genette 1987.

12. Memmott also refers to this practice as "puncturating," as discussed in Hayles 2002, 52.

13. For an example, see Freud [1915] 1991.

14. Here I am using "operator" in the mathematical sense. Elsewhere, I have translated this term more loosely, although more evocatively and metaphorically, as "a class of operations" (see translator's note; Bootz 2003, 80).

15. See the discussion of Nelsonian hypertext later in this chapter and Bootz 2003.

16. At the time, I claimed that, when "turned inside out," hypertext "links" were often "nilsk." The as-yet-to-be-more-fully-answered question of "what is inside the link?" in link-node hypertext was often posed in the debates that raged over such long-quiet listservs as ht_lit.

17. *The Barrier Frames* lacks the characteristic diagram notation in the other Rosenberg pieces cited.

18. This characteristic of a Rosenberg text's "transience" is one of the things that distinguish it in Espen Aarseth's textonomy (1997).

19. In Ted Nelson's scheme—outlined and discussed later—both flavors of reduction are represented: spatiality as "docuverse" and linearity as "permascroll."

20. Bootz (2003) also discusses Rosenberg's work, and his analysis has been influential on my own. In the theoretical part of his paper, he writes, "Surely here [as a (hyper)text is unfolded] we have an example of a poetic relationship with language. And this relationship is not established by the author or reader, but by the device which transforms a global/structure/space into a local/action/temporality" (63). Rosenberg's work exemplifies this principle: "[h]e [Rosenberg] realized this [a move toward the instantiation of a more generalized theoretical position such as Bootz's] by putting forward what is mimetic hypertext, when seen from the point of view of its unfolding, while at the same time reconfiguring hypertext as the visualization of local processes" (65).

21. In fact, of course, it would be preferable to establish a parent "Text" Class that was less determinate to its properties—particularly, for example, its temporal and ergodic properties—than our inherited and historically instituted "Text" Object. The historical "Text" Class would be redefined as an extension of the more abstract parent. This situation, in which prior programming must be dekludged or entirely rewritten in order to clarify structures and relationships, is common in real-world programming.

22. Hayles also finds complexities of temporality represented by remediation, even through the relatively durable material substrate of print, especially in her discussion of Danielewski's *House of Leaves* (to which I will return) (2002, 115).

23. "It is not a question of negation of time, of a cessation of time in a present or a simultaneity, but of a different structure, a different stratification of time" (Derrida 1978, 219). See also Cayley 2003.

24. The phrase "Golden Age" refers to Robert Coover's "Literary Hypertext: The Passing of the Golden Age," given as a keynote address at the 1999 Digital Arts and Culture Conference, Georgia Tech, Atlanta.

25. Two examples of hypertextual features that are nonstandard on the Web are conditional and two-way linking, both of which can be implemented with client- and/or server-side enhancements to HTML. See the ACM SigWeb for an introduction to technical research on hypertext (http://www.acm.org/sigweb).

26. Nelson introduced this term after the revised publication of *Literary Machines 93.1*. The terms are also used to bring the docuverse together with Nelson's current idea for a radical restructuring of data in computing, *ZigZag*. "Permascroll" and related terms are defined in Lukka 2002. See also Nelson 2001.

27. See Hayles 2003.

28. This was clear from the discussion after Nelson's keynote talk at the Digital Arts and Culture conference, Brown University, Providence, RI, 2001, when he sidestepped the question of including some record or archive of text-generational programming on the permascroll.

29. These are the only features of Rosenberg's form that I want to highlight here. The diagram syntax he uses would also, however, be difficult to represent.

30. See Aarseth 1997, 76–96.

31. The term "transcopyright" is neatly defined in Lukka 2002.

32. See, for example, Hayles's discussion of Danielewski (2002, 115ff.).

33. Hayles (2002) finds herself, perhaps, at the limits of this process, discussing works such as Tom Phillips' *A Humument* and Mark Danielewski's *House of Leaves* (which are literally print[ed]) and Talan Memmott's *Lexia to Perplexia* (which can be seriously discussed in "printed out" quotation, as Hayles demonstrates), without divorcing their manifestation of inherent textual properties that can be represented but not *embodied* in print: the represented and remediated temporal complexities of *House of Leaves*, the *process and practice* of Phillips continuing to alter and prepare *A Humument*, or, in Memmott, the reader's ergodic process of revealing textual spaces. As we have seen, it is more difficult to bracket the simultaneities, for example, of a Rosenberg intergram. Hayles's criticism is crucial because it takes the institutions (especially those of literary criticism) to the edge of an abyss, as Edgar leads Gloucester to the cliff's edge in *King Lear*.

34. For example, I discuss figures involving compilation and strict logical development at the end of "The Code Is Not the Text."

35. Rosenberg is also acutely aware of the necessity to bring programming into the scene of writing through institutions and tools, a topic he addresses in "Questions about the Second Move" (2003). Specifically, Rosenberg wants tools that allow him to have working literary objects in progress on his computer desktop: notebooks, as it were, containing signifiers that retain their temporality and programmability in their native state. Note that the computer "desktop" and/or "platform" (and/or the "Web," which is not so much of direct concern to Rosenberg) become varieties of metaphoric if not actual institutions here, authorizing and enabling the existence (or not) of particular objects with particular properties and methods.

36. Code and interiority are taken up in Cayley 2003.

Works Cited

Aarseth, Espen J. 1997. *Cybertext: Perspectives on Ergodic Literature*. Baltimore, MD: Johns Hopkins University Press.

Baldwin, Sandy. 2003. "Process Window: Code Work, Code Aesthetics, Code Poetics." In *Cybertext Yearbook 2002–2003*, ed. Markku Eskelinen and Raine Koskimaa, with a special section on ergodic poetry edited by John Cayley and Loss Pequeño Glazier, 107–119. Publications of the Research Centre for Contemporary Culture. Jyväskylä: University of Jyväskylä.

Barthes, Roland. [1973] 1990. *S/Z*. Trans. Richard Miller. Oxford: Blackwell Publishers. Originally published Paris: Éditions du Seuil.

Bootz, Phillipe. 2003. "Hypertext: Solution/Dissolution." Trans. John Cayley. In *Cybertext Yearbook 2002–2003*, ed. Markku Eskelinen and Raine Koskimaa, with a special section on ergodic poetry edited by John Cayley and Loss Pequeño Glazier, 56–82. Publications of the Research Centre for Contemporary Culture. Jyväskylä: University of Jyväskylä.

Cayley, John. 2002. "The Code Is Not the Text (Unless It Is the Text)." *electronic book review* 3. http://www.electronicbookreview.com/v3/servlet/ebr?command=view_essay&essay_id=cayleyele (accessed December 1, 2003).

Cayley, John. 2003. "Inner Workings: Code and Representations of Interiority in New Media Poetics." In *Dictung-digital* 29, ed. Loss Pequeño Glazier. http://www.dichtung-digital.de/2003/issue/3/Cayley.htm (accessed June 20, 2004).

Coover, Robert. [1999] 2000. "Literary Hypertext: The Passing of the Golden Age." *Feed*. http://www.feedmag.com/documents/do2911ofi.html (no longer available).

Derrida, Jacques. 1978. "Freud and the Scene of Writing." In *Writing and Difference*, trans. Alan Bass, 196–231. London: Routledge.

Freud, Sigmund. [1915] 1991. "The Unconscious." In *On Metapsychology: The Theory of Psychoanalysis*. Vol. 11, *The Penguin Freud Library*, ed. Angela Richards, 161–222. Harmondsworth, UK: Penguin Books.

Genette, Gérard. [1987] 1997. *Paratexts: Thresholds of Interpretation*. Trans. Jane E. Lewin. In *Literature, Culture, Theory* 20, ed. Richard Macksey and Michael Sprinkler. Cambridge, UK: Cambridge University Press.

Glazier, Loss Pequeño. 2002. *Digital Poetics: The Making of E-Poetries*. Tuscaloosa: University of Alabama Press.

Hayles, N. Katherine. 1996. "Virtual Bodies and Flickering Signifiers." In *Electronic Culture: Technology and Visual Representation*, ed. Timothy Druckery, 259–277. New York: Aperture.

Hayles, N. Katherine. 1999a. *How We Became Posthuman: Virtual Bodies in Cybernetics, Literature, and Informatics*. Chicago: University of Chicago Press.

Hayles, N. Katherine. 1999b. "Virtual Bodies and Flickering Signifiers." In *How We Became Posthuman: Virtual Bodies in Cybernetics, Literature, and Informatics*, 25–49. Chicago: University of Chicago Press.

Hayles, N. Katherine. 2002. *Writing Machines*. Cambridge, MA: MIT Press.

Hayles, N. Katherine. 2003. "Translating Media: Why We Should Rethink Textuality." *The Yale Journal of Criticism* 16.2: 263–290.

Lukka, Tuomas. 2001. "GZigZag: A Platform for Cybertext Experiments." *Cybertext Yearbook 2000*, ed. Markku Eskelinen and Raine Koskimaa, 141–151. Publications of the Research Centre for Contemporary Culture 68. Jyväskylä: University of Jyväskylä.

Lukka, Tuomas. 2002. *GZigZag Glossary*. http://gzigzag.sourceforge.net/gl/gl.html (accessed June 2004).

Nelson, Theodor Holm. [1981] 1993. *Literary Machines 93.1*. Sausalito, CA: Mindful Press.

Nelson, Theodor Holm. 2001. *ZigZag*. http://xanadu/zigzag (accessed May 12, 2003).

Raley, Rita. 2002. "Interferences: [Net.Writing] and the Practice of Codework." *electronic book review*. http://www.electronicbookreview.com/v3/servlet/ebr?command=view_essay&essay_id=rayleyele (accessed September 2002).

Rosenberg, Jim. 1993. *Intergrams*. Watertown, MA: Eastgate Systems.

Rosenberg, Jim. 1996a. *The Barrier Frames: Finality Crystal Shunt Curl Chant Quickening Giveaway Stare*. Watertown, MA: Eastgate Systems.

Rosenberg, Jim. 1996b. *Diffractions Through: Thirst Weep Ransack (Frailty) Veer Tide Elegy*. Watertown, MA: Eastgate Systems.

Rosenberg, Jim. 2003. "Questions About the Second Move." In *Cybertext Yearbook 2002–2003*, ed. Markku Eskelinen and Raine Koskimaa, with a special section on ergodic poetry edited by John Cayley and Loss Pequeño Glazier, 83–87. Publications of the Research Center for Contemporary Culture. Jyväskylä: University of Jyväskylä.

17

Poetics in the Expanded Field:
Textual, Visual, Digital . . .

Barrett Watten

> But what appears as eclectic from one point of view can be seen
> as rigorously logical from another. For, within the situation of
> postmodernism, practice is not defined in relation to a given
> medium . . . but rather in relation to the logical operations on a
> set of cultural terms, for which any medium . . . might be used.
> —ROSALIND KRAUSS, "SCULPTURE IN THE EXPANDED FIELD"

Writing in expanded fields finds itself of necessity between fixed positions of
form, genre, discipline, and, in consequence, cultural meaning. This chapter
delineates a structural logic common to several domains of the expanded
field—poetics, conceptual art, and new media—as species of a more inclusive
genre of *poetics* comprising literary, visual, and digital aesthetics. What is
poetics? To begin with, it is the self-reflexive mode of the "making" of the
work of art or cultural product, but not just in descriptive or positive terms.
As a mode of reflection within and on practice, poetics questions the nature
and value of the work of art as it expands the ground of its making into the
contexts of its production and reception. The expanded field of poetics thus
leads to the making of art in new genres, as a self-reflexive moment within
practice that creates grounds for new meaning.

For the last three decades, there has been an outpouring of writing in the
genre of poetics that parallels the development of new forms of experimental
poetry, visual art, and digital media. If the Language school was initially
defined in relation to new forms of poetry, defenses of its practice quickly

became a kind of aesthetic lingua franca, to be promulgated in a wide range of publications in poetics—from *L=A=N=G=U=A=G=E* and *Poetics Journal* to more recent journals of poetics such as *Chain*, *Shark*, and *Tripwire*; online zines such as *Arras*, *Jacket*, and *How2*; and the current explosion of blogs on poetics.[1] The genre has its literary genealogy in two predecessors: the New American Poets, whose anthology of poetics appeared in 1973 (Allen and Tallman); and high modernists who, following the lead of the avant-garde manifesto, made defenses of experimental poetry an extension of their work.[2] And there is nothing to prevent the genealogy of poetics from being extended even farther back—to Aristotle, Sidney, Wordsworth, and Shelley—to the point that poetics becomes the hallmark of the literary in modernist criticism, the virtual *archetext* itself. Even so, there has been little effort to construct a genealogy of this productive genre of writing, in relation either to its historical contexts or to its encompassing tradition. Poetics takes up increasing space on our bookshelves but with a diminishing sense of its use, beyond the defense of avant-garde poetry and its expanded field of literariness, once a new field of poetic practice has been named. At the same time, poetics has become a publisher's marketing category, to be shelved between works of poetry and literary criticism (which may be in the process of being replaced).[3] In the larger scheme of things, the market's acceptance of the genre of poetics is a good thing, implying a decisive break from literary value established by authorized readings in favor of poetic experiment with new cultural meanings. Still, questions remain of the intrinsic value of this genre of writing and of its larger motivation.

Literariness is in a crisis of new meaning due to its expanded cultural ground.[4] The genre of poetics developed precisely in relation to that crisis, as an account of literary possibility in the condition of a radical expansion of its cultural horizon, after the 1960s. But this emergence of language-centered poetics took place in a period in which there were parallel developments of poetic genres in other forms of art practice, and for similar cultural reasons. Like the Language school, the conceptual art movement was radically textual, basing its time-valued or spatially distributed forms of documentation on a skeptical account of the meaning of art, or even on its absence. John Cage's mesostics and Andy Warhol's taped novels and interviews; the depersonalized, collective documentation in *Six Years: The Dematerialization of the Art Object* . . . (Lippard 1997); the writings of Robert Smithson, Joseph Kosuth, and Robert Morris; and the use of language as substitute for image in a wide

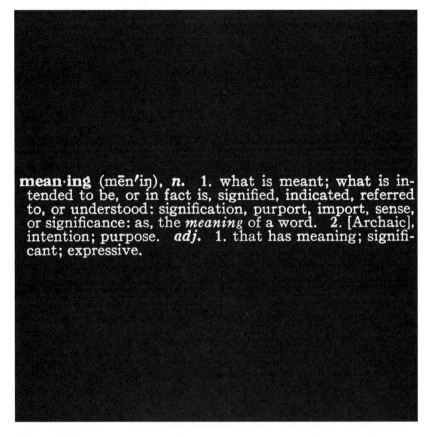

meaning (mēn'in), **n.** 1. what is meant; what is intended to be, or in fact is, signified, indicated, referred to, or understood: signification, purport, import, sense, or significance: as, the *meaning* of a word. 2. [Archaic], intention; purpose. *adj.* 1. that has meaning; significant; expressive.

Figure 17.1   Joseph Kosuth, *Titled (Art as Idea as Idea),* 1967. © 2004 Joseph Kosuth and Artist's Rights Society.

range of conceptual practices (figure 17.1)—all may be considered as poetics of a visual rather than literary register.[5] If one were concerned more with historical motivations for the emergence of new genres than with their autotelic self-reflexiveness, it should be obvious that these two genres of poetics, based in different kinds of art practice, are deeply related. Yet they are seldom referred to as having similar cultural or historical sources, are not grouped together, and do not have parallel implications for contemporary practice. Much would be gained from a comparison of the work of Joseph Kosuth and Bruce Andrews, or Robert Morris and Ron Silliman, or Yvonne Rainer and Carla Harryman, or Yoko Ono and Kevin Killian, or Agnes Martin and

Marjorie Welish, and so on, even as the two fields remain largely separate in both production and reception.[6]

In its defense of radical poetry, the genre of poetics has achieved a kind of practical consensus as it explores questions of authorial intention, textual materiality, community valorization, and larger cultural meaning in order to define the horizons of possibility of language-centered writing and its variants. Perhaps, at this moment, the genre has done its work of articulating the formal and cultural values of at least two generations of poets. It has made the point that art is never autonomous, even as there may be nothing outside the text. It has transformed poetry from a kind of self-protected guild production to an intellectual activity engaged in a dialogue with literary theory and cultural studies. It has, finally, expanded the scene of reading poetry so that a wide range of issues, from cognitive psychology to oppositional politics, may be seen as a part of its activity. It thus works to expand the field of meaning available to experimental poetry while at the same time claiming the necessity of that practice. The self-conserving and at times conservative tendency of poetics occurs precisely in the fulfillment of its dual role, as it claims an expanded horizon of literariness in the valorization of its specific objects. The return of autonomous poetic practice may be, on this account, not simply an entailment of poetics but identical to it. Poetics may be the *Ur*-genre of the literary above all, the site of the final defense of literariness against the vagaries of a contingent meaning—even in its radical foregrounding of contingency, materiality, and self-reflexive form. It is just this possibility, of a univocal/universal literariness, that demands an account of poetics as a specific genre, a kind of writing, if it is not simply to end in a defense of poetry.

Of course, in its historical origins, poetics was precisely that: a defense of poetry, the cultural possibilities of its meaning, and the technical means of its construction. The *positive* mode of description and prescription, beginning with Aristotle, has survived to delimit the genre: as bedrocks of modern criticism, Gerard Manley Hopkins's practical account of sprung rhythm or I. A. Richards's valorization of the "interinanimation" of poetic form or Roman Jakobson's definition of poetic language as the "message for its own sake" make poetry an object of positive knowledge, leading to a kind of *Princeton Encyclopedia of Poetry and Poetics* approach that categorizes poetics from "abecedaries" to "Zulu verse." Most of the early positions taken in *L=A=N=*

$G=U=A=G=E$, and even later in the essays in *Poetics Journal*, are positive and descriptive: they identify the necessity of certain ways of making poetry; they propose interpretive contexts (aesthetic, cultural, political) by which it can be read; and they devise reading strategies for new forms of poetry. The genre of poetics is in this way predicated on the positivity of its referent, poetry, as it explores parallels of meaning and construction.

Poetics at the same time involves a distancing or renegotiation of the practice of poetry, simply in that essays in poetics are not identical to the poems they describe. It is in taking up the more abstract or contextual conditions of poetry, apart from its simple description, that poetics makes its distinctive claims—leading to a second modality of the genre, the *negative*. With the romantics, poetry's positive claims come undone precisely in its reception, with the fact that authorial intention imperfectly coincides with a reader's response. Coleridge could not understand how men of equal cultural distinction could not come to equivalent judgments of poetry, specifically of *Lyrical Ballads*: "The composition which one had cited as execrable, another had quoted as his favorite" ([1817] 1983, 73). The instability of the object, poetry, within a variable judgment necessitates both a rigorous account of interpretation and a suspicion of negativity in the object—something that, by virtue of its own properties, works to thwart any necessary standard of judgment. For this reason, Wordsworth, in his famous preface, sought to identify his poetics with a mode of normative address that would at the same time provide the basis for his radical experiments with a naturalized form, as well as serve as a precondition of its reception:

That the language of such poetry as I am recommending is, as far as is possible, a selection of the language really spoken by men; that this selection, wherever it is made with true taste and feeling, will of itself form a distinction [between poetry and ordinary language] far greater than would at first be imagined, and will entirely separate the composition from the vulgarity and meanness of ordinary life; and if meter be superadded thereto I believe a dissimilitude will be produced altogether sufficient for the gratification of a rational mind.[7] (Wordsworth and Coleridge [1798] 1975, 29)

On the one hand, Wordsworth appeals to the "language really spoken by men" for its embedded truth and wisdom, its availability to men of discernment, and its capacity to be recognized by the reader; the poet intervenes in the matter of selection of the language, passionate re-presentation, and metrical arrangement in order to provide the pleasurable sensations of a poetry that demonstrates how "our feelings and ideas are associated in a state of excitement" (23). Wordsworth's value-added normativity implicitly admits the negativity of poetry in two senses—in its dependence on already existing associations of habit and on their recharged representation as poetry—as conditions of its reception.

It would be up to the modernists, of course, to take the charge of poetic negativity and fashion an epistemology to conform to it—demonstrated, in its most radical form, in Laura Riding's 1925 poetic manifesto, "A Prophecy or a Plea": "The most moving and at once distressing event in the life of a human being is his discovery that he is alive. From that moment to his death the fact of life is a constant white glare over him, an unsetting and shadowless sun" (Jackson 1992, 275). For Riding, the "shock of impact" of modern existence, its refusal of any regulating norms, leads to a poetry that, as a darkened interiority or an "evocation of the shadows," foregrounds our insufficiency rather than regulates it. Later in Riding's work, the demands of the unrepresentable intensify to the point at which poetry can only imitate the traumatic shock of existence in its immediacy: "What is a poem? A poem is nothing. . . . It cannot be looked at, heard, touched or read because it is a vacuum. . . . If it were possible to reproduce it in an audience the result would be the destruction of the audience" (Jackson 1980, 16–17). From Riding's account of poetry as a sublime object of destruction, as the necessary and sufficient condition of a poetics, to her later renunciation of poetry is but one step;[8] in her career, an unfolding of a poetics that claimed the inaccessibility of truth to poetry is predicated not on the descriptive positivity of poetry but on its abstract negativity. It is important, then, that poetics in the modern era entails equally the positivity of a self-focused mode of organization and the negativity of that which it cannot represent.

The foregrounding of negativity in postmodern poetics is not hard to come by. If, for the modernist avant-garde, poetry is a sublime object for the undoing of philistine expectations, the New American Poets extended the sublimity of modernist form in demanding a poetry that moves immediately to further perception, as in the well-known formulation of Charles Olson's "Projective Verse": "[t]he poem itself must, at all points, be a high energy-construct and, at all points, an energy-discharge. . . . [I]n any given poem always, always one perception must must must MOVE, INSTANTER, ON ANOTHER!" (Olson 1997, 16–17). Olson's dictum would be immediately taken up by Robert Creeley in his early notes on poetics, which make a paradoxical insistence on and denial of poetic negativity:

A poetry denies its end in any *descriptive* act, I mean any act which leaves the attention outside the poem. Our anger cannot exist usefully without its objects, but a description of them is also a perpetuation. There is that confusion—one wants the thing to act on, and yet hates it. *Description* does nothing, it includes the object—it neither hates nor loves. (1970, 23)

The persistence of the negative makes him want to "junk these things, of the content which relates only to denial, the negative, the impact of dissolution" and "act otherwise," so that "speech is an assertion of one man, by one man" (23–24). But the negative is not so easily disavowed: Olson's poetics of negativity, of constantly moving beyond the stability of representation, combined with Creeley's demand to move beyond the antagonism of the negative in its objects, directly anticipates the real-time social antagonism of LeRoi Jones/Amiri Baraka's poetics: "[t]he artist is cursed with his artifact, which exists without and despite him. And even though the process, in good art, is everywhere perceptible, the risk of perfection corrupts the lazy public into accepting the material *in place of* what it is only the remains of" (Baraka 1973a, 378). Baraka's use of antagonism as a politics is the immediate result of the negativity of the poem as object, an inadequacy that must be gone beyond in any politics: "The Black Artist's role in America is to aid in the destruction of America as he knows it. His role is to report and reflect so precisely the nature of the society, and of himself in that society, that other men will be moved by the exactness of his rendering"—leading to solidarity for some and destructive madness for others (Baraka 1973b, 382–383). The negativity of postmodern poetics is translated here into an antagonism addressed to social contexts.

With the Language school, poetic negativity has tended to seek its own level in the "material text" whose difficult language unites poetry's materiality with its antagonistic inscrutability but only obliquely imagines its dialogue with an Other. The defense of poetry in the Language school, as a result, has been the mediation of an impossible expressivity with a proposed set of interpretive norms for its processing—something like an inversion of Wordsworth's self-constituting expressive norms. A paradox emerges, however, precisely where the material text confronts its limits in the alterity of the reader, the imagined Other who finds the text to be incomprehensible. The material text, on the one hand, becomes a thing unto itself, all interpretations brought to it are subjective, and a descriptive positivity obtains. However, poetry's radical openness to interpretation is identified precisely as its material limits, demanding a negotiation with context if it is to have any meaning. If $L=A=N=G=U=A=G=E$'s poetics often tried to extend impossible expressivity into an interpretive norm, those of *Poetics Journal* wanted to renegotiate this paradox as the dialectic of radical poetry in expanded interpretive fields. In each case, the negativity of radical poetry in the Language school led historically to an unfolding horizon of context, in ways that were not only antagonistic but productive of new meaning.

It is here that poetics as a genre generates new horizons of practice that remain unexplored in either its positive or negative moments, as the persistent aftereffects of the autonomy and difficulty of modernist poetics. Such a move toward context has parallels in other forms of art, most evidently in the conceptual art and environmental sculpture movements. Using the writings of Robert Smithson as a primary example of New York art's turn toward context in the 1960s and 1970s, one may see in it a negotiation between artwork and alterity in an unfolding, *dialectical* poetics that is likewise historical in its specific moment (figure 17.2).[9] Smithson's writings preserve—in their negotiations between word and image, site and non-site—the mutual alterity of artwork and context; his work was immediately influential for the

Figure 17.2   Robert Smithson, *A Heap of Language,* 1966. © Estate of Robert Smithson/Licensed by VAGA, New York, NY.

Language school, leading to Clark Coolidge's *Smithsonian Depositions* (1980); my chapter on Smithson in *Total Syntax* (1985); and the use of Smithson's sculpture *Gyrostasis* on the cover of one of its first anthologies, *"Language" Poetries* (Messerli 1987). My online essay (Watten 2003b) on Stan Douglas's photographs of Detroit is dialectical and historical in this sense, as are numerous writings from the conceptual art period; also relevant are writers who work between word and image such as Theresa Hak Kyung Cha (1995) and W. G. Sebald (1998) (figure 17.3). If the juxtaposition of word and image functions here as a dialectical opening of genre to its contexts, we may speak as well of a *diacritical* process, in which the distinction between text and context is articulated in a microscopic play of values that works to reintegrate contextual difference in forms of mediated text. Arkadii Dragomoshchenko's metapoetic essays, Leslie Scalapino's creative prose "War/Poverty/Writing," or Dan Davidson's meditation on reification in the form of language (from the last issue of *Poetics Journal*) are such negotiations of text and context in which radical alterity is folded into the text. A kind of hybrid text results that does not end in any static materiality but demands a differential relation between contextual strategies and interpretive frameworks. The dialectics of text and context, and such diacritical experiments in intertextual hybridity, go beyond the merely descriptive or interpretive aspects of poetics toward new forms of writing as enactment that open the horizons of the genre to history and culture.

This is the point of Rosalind Krauss's essay "Sculpture in the Expanded Field" ([1979] 1998), which theorizes the proliferation of site-specific art within a postmodern culture that was moving away from the fixity of genre. Krauss's point of departure is a logic of negativity that, after Hegel's *Aesthetics*, defines sculpture in relation to two things it is not: landscape and architecture (figure 17.4). In being neither, sculpture as a fabricated object is situated in a landscape as a monument to its own negativity. New developments in the genre, such as conceptual art and environmental sculpture, had opened up and exploited this negative relationship; Krauss presents as an example of such logic a Mary Miss sculpture in which a cubic negative space is excavated in the landscape as a site-specific work (1978), but she might equally as well have chosen Michael Heizer's *Double Negative* (1991) or Smithson's conceptual essay "Minus Twelve" (1979, 81) (figure 17.5).

majesties, the North Sea coast might become one great health resort for the upper classes, equipped with all the amenities of modern life. Everywhere, hotels mushroomed from the barren land. Promenades and bathing facilities were established, and piers grew out

into the sea. Even in the most abandoned spot in the entire region, Shingle Street, which now consists of just one wretched row of humble houses and cottages and where I have never encountered a single human being, a spa centre by the grandiose name of German Ocean Mansions designed for two hundred guests was built at the time, if one can believe the records, and staffed with personnel who were recruited from Germany. Today there is no trace of it. Indeed, there seem to have been all manner of ties across the North Sea between the British and German Empires at that period, ties that were expressed first and foremost in the colossal manifestations of bad taste of those who wanted a place in the sun no matter at what cost. Cuthbert Quilter's Anglo-Indian fairy-tale palace in the dunes would doubtless have appealed to the German Kaiser's artistic sensibility, since he had a pronounced

225

Figure 17.3 W. G. Sebald, *The Rings of Saturn* (New York: New Directions, 1998), 225. Reproduced by permission of New Directions Press.

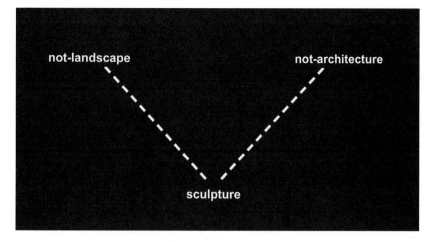

Figure 17.4 After Rosalind E. Krauss, "Sculpture in the Expanded Field," in *The Originality of the Avant-Garde and Other Modernist Myths* (Cambridge, MA: The MIT Press, 1985), 282. Reproduced by permission of The MIT Press.

In order to account for this new sculptural logic, Krauss expands the field to show how the work's questioning of its limits leads to new formal possibilities. Where sculpture had initially been defined as "not-landscape" and "not-architecture," it can now more complexly include its difference from its positive terms, "landscape" and "architecture." As a result of this double negation, sculpture can be both and neither landscape and architecture, as it clearly is in Gordon Matta-Clark's gallery installation of fragments of architectural detail removed from its original structures and recontextualized in the gallery space (figure 17.6), Smithson's *Partially Buried Woodshed* (figure 17.7), or many other works from the period. Krauss derives a logic for sculpture's expansion into the field of its constitutive oppositions that may be extended to other genres of art practice such as poetics and new media:

The expanded field is thus generated by problematizing the set of oppositions between which the modernist category *sculpture* is suspended. And once this has happened, once one is able to think one's way into this expansion, there are—logically—three other categories that one can envision, all of them a condition of the field itself, and none of them assimilable to *sculpture*. Because as we can see, *sculpture* is no longer the privileged middle term between two things that it isn't. *Sculpture* is rather only one term

Minus Twelve

Robert Smithson: *Tar Pool and Gravel Pit* (model). 1966.

1. USELESSNESS
   A. Zone of standard modules.
   B. Monoliths without color.
   C. An ever narrowing field of approximation known as the Method of Exhaustion.
   D. The circumscribed cube.
2. ENTROPY
   A. *Equal units approaching divisibility.*
   B. Something inconsistent with common experience or having contradictory qualities.
   C. Hollow blocks in a windowless room.
   D. Militant laziness.
3. ABSENCE
   A. Postulates of nominalism.
   B. Idleness at the North Pole.
   C. Exclusion of space.
   D. Real things become mental vacancies.
4. INACCESSIBILITY
   A. Gray walls and glass floors.
   B. Domain of the Dinosaurs.
   C. Toward an aesthetics of disappointment.
   D. *No doors.*
5. EMPTINESS
   A. A flying tomb disguised as an airplane.
   B. Some plans for logical stupefactions.
   C. The case of the "missing-link."
   D. False theorems and grand mistakes.
6. INERTIA
   A. Memory of a dismantled parallelepiped.
   B. The humorous dimensions of time.
   C. A refutation of the End of Endlessness.
   D. Zeno's Second Paradox (infinite regression against movement).
7. FUTILITY
   A. Dogma against value.
   B. *Collapses into five sections.*
   C. To go from one extreme to another.
   D. Put everything into doubt.
8. BLINDNESS
   A. Two binocular holes that appear endlessly.
   B. Invisible orbs.
   C. Abolished sight.
   D. The splitting of the vanishing point.
9. STILLNESS
   A. Sinking back into echoes.
   B. Extinguished by reflections.
   C. Obsolete ideas to be promulgated (teratologies and other marvels).
   D. Cold storage.
10. EQUIVALENCE
    A. Refusal to privilege one sign over another.
    B. Different types of sameness.
    C. Odd objections to uncertain symmetries *in regular systems*
    D. Any declaration of unity results in two things.
11. DISLOCATION
    A. Deluging the deluge.
    B. The Great Plug.
    C. The Winter Solstice of 4000 B.C. (a temporal dementia).
    D. Toward innumerable futures.
12. FORGETFULNESS
    A. Aluminum cities on a lead planet.
    B. The Museum of the Void.
    C. A compact mass in a dim passageway (an anti-object).
    D. *A series of sightings down escarpments.*

Figure 17.5 Smithson, "Minus Twelve" (1968), from *The Writings of Robert Smithson*, ed. Nancy Holt (New York: NYU Press, 1979), 81. © Estate of Robert Smithson/Licensed by VAGA, New York, NY.

Barrett Watten

Figure 17.6   Gordon Matta-Clark, *Splitting: Four Corners,* 1974. © 2004 ARS.

Figure 17.7   Smithson, *Partially Buried Woodshed,* 1970. © Estate of Robert Smithson/Licensed by VAGA, New York, NY.

on the periphery of a field in which there are other, differently structured possibilities. ([1979]1998, 38)

Krauss generates, by means of the semiotic square popularized by literary critics such as A. J. Greimas and Frederic Jameson (and later used in her own analyses of "the optical unconscious"), a series of structural oppositions that lead to an expanded range of formal possibilities as entailments of the constitutive oppositions of the genre of sculpture. In so doing, her structural oppositions identify three new forms of sculpture in the expanded field: "marked sites," such as Smithson's *Spiral Jetty* (figure 17.8), which define landscape by means of that which it is not; "axiomatic structures," such as Bruce Naumann or Sol LeWitt's architectural works, which may be located in a gallery context; and finally, "site constructions" themselves, such as Smithson's *Woodshed*, which unite architecture and landscape. Expanding the field of sculpture in its negativity opens onto new formal possibilities of the genre.

It is worth pausing here to ask, what kinds of claim can such an abstract analysis, which may be reduced to a play of oppositional terms in a schematic grid, support? While Krauss's initial logic of oppositions, drawn from Hegel,

Figure 17.8 Smithson, *Spiral Jetty*, 1970. © Estate of Robert Smithson/Licensed by VAGA, New York, NY.

is indeed abstract and idealized, her insight draws equally from observing the transformation of art practice during the period in which she was writing, the 1970s. Two important corollaries, then, are necessary for such an analysis: that the genre in question really is structured in relation to a differential field of oppositions, and that this logic of oppositions is productive of new work (rather than being merely static and descriptive). With the sculpture in the period, both are true: Smithson's dialectic of site and non-site addressed precisely the ways in which minimalist sculpture, from Tony Smith to Robert Morris, demanded an account of context, and his own development showed how the opposition was productive.

If we were to extend such a logic, by structural analogy, to the genre of poetics, would we find the same conditions to obtain? Arguably, writing in poetics from the 1970s was indeed motivated by its relation to context, in two senses: it argued for new forms of poetry and against conventional ones, while being neither (*not-poetry*); it was productive precisely because it engaged a kind of writing not delimited by the genre (*not-language*) (figure 17.9). What brings the two schema together, then, is a differential and productive relationship of genre to two terms: structure (architecture, poetry) and ground (landscape, language). If we replace *sculpture* with *poetics*, in Krauss's diagram, we begin to see some of the dimensions of a new field of practice, once we have determined its constitutively opposing terms (figure 17.10). And if we expand

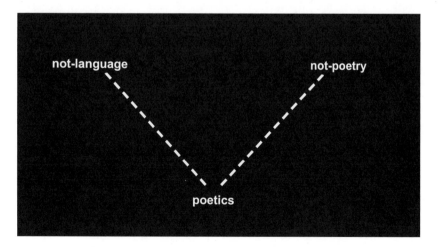

Figure 17.9   Adaptation of Krauss, figure 17.4, to poetics.

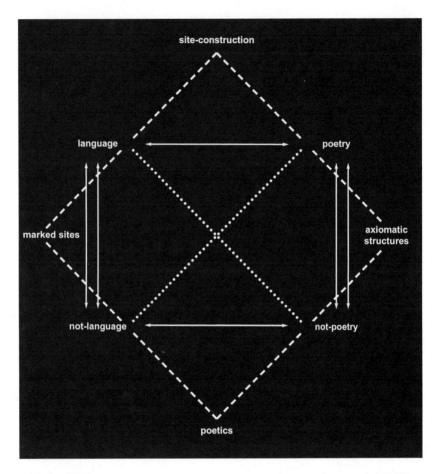

Figure 17.10 Adaptation of Klein Square used in "Sculpture in the Expanded Field" to poetics.

the determinate negation of *poetics*, that it is both *not-poetry* and *not-language*, we see in this analogy how it could take place as one element of an expanded field generated by an opposition between *poetry* and *language*. Immediately, we might look for works that are positioned between *language* and *not-language* at the nodal point designated by "marked sites" and locate language experiments such as Harry Mathews, Tina Darragh, and Harryette Mullens's work with definitional forms. We might have works that are *poetry* and *not-poetry* at the "axiomatic structures" node, in which the work foregrounds the negation of structure or genre: works in hybrid forms, from William Carlos Williams's

Paterson to examples of poetic prose by Leslie Scalapino and Carla Harryman. Finally, we would anticipate texts that are positioned between *poetry* and *language* as a "site-construction": texts made through chance processes, such as Jackson Mac Low's *Stanzas for Iris Lezak* (1971); texts using preexisting lexicons, such as Clark Coolidge's *The Maintains* (1974); and many of the longer, constructivist texts of the Language school, from Ron Silliman's *Ketjak* (1978) to my own *Progress* (1985), Bruce Andrews's *I Don't Have Any Paper So Shut Up (or, Social Romanticism)* (1992), and Lyn Hejinian's *A Border Comedy* (2001). Remarkably or not, positioning poetics between poetry and language, as between a schematic and abstract structure and ground, generates a range of formal possibilities as entailments of an expanded field of meaning.

My first task in thinking through the question of poetics here has been to disclose a logic of genre that provides a genealogy of poetics and accounts for the range of its practice; my second is to extend this logic to forms of art that have emerged more recently. How could one speak of a "poetics of new media" if there is a difficult analogy between new media and poetics by virtue of the latter's originary if often negated object, poetry? Is that not to make a fundamental category mistake, to impose the logic of one kind of art on another? Krauss's series of oppositions that define the expanded field will be helpful with new media art through a simple substitution of terms: for *poetry* and *language* read *artwork* and *media*. We would then generate a series of positions for new media art, beginning with a simple Web page that neither functions as "media" nor aspires to be "art," to a "marked site" that references users to resources available in the media (any number of search engine or hyperlink sites), to an "axiomatic structure" that foregrounds the constructedness of the Web site itself (Brian Kim Stefans's *Arras* site, at once a service provider and an art piece, suggests itself here). Finally, we have the possibility of Krauss's "site construction": a fully developed site that comments on the limits and possibilities of new media as art. This is precisely what Talan Memmott's *Lexia to Perplexia* (2000) intends: as a complex synthesis of the possibilities of art and new media, it defines a poetics of site construction in relation to the positivity of media and art—much as environmental sculpture is framed by landscape and architecture, or language poetry by its constitutive terms.

Talan Memmott is originally a San Francisco new media writer (and editor of the hypertext journal *BeeHive*) whose work explores the potential of the media through complex interactive Web designs that incorporate a self-reflective distancing from or even destruction of the positivity of the medium.[10] His works are combinations of literary allusion, theoretical reflection, graphic display, technological code, and media design that may be valued aesthetically for their gorgeous displays of complex, paradoxical interpretive frames. His work develops new possibilities for the media as it pushes its limits in verbal, visual, and technical senses, producing a theoretically inflected poetics of disanalogy, paradox, overdetermination, and unlinking.

Such poetics are pursued by Memmott, well beyond the limits of paraphrase, in his award-winning new media work *Lexia to Perplexia*. Subtitled *Hypermedia/Ideoscope*, the piece is a sophisticated/naïve machine made of words for unmaking meanings that performs a meditation on the (im)possibility of media connectivity due to an underlying automatism, in a classically avant-garde sense, that is shared between man and machine. Navigating its interface becomes a task of simultaneous learning and frustration in which the nature of interpretation is laid bare at the point of its machinic undoing. The piece deceptively masks its segmentation in frame sets through unfolding of DHTML effects using rollovers and pop-ups of both graphic and textual elements. Interpretation (and learning) occurs precisely at the interface between word and image, between unfolding horizons of textual meaning and the need to accept graphic elements as the navigational vehicles of their own unlinking.

The work is staged in a series of interactive sequences that embed exit functions that link to a linear series of sequences (with the exception of one subroutine, which may or may not be chosen, and the possibility of an exit from the entire system that may be inadvertently selected). The first sequence, "The Process of Attachment," constructs an elaborate analogy to the mechanics of communication—as it turns out, between male and female, Narcissus and Echo, as prototypical interlocutors—in a mediated environment. One begins by passing through the following orientation message:

> *The inconstancy of location is transparent to the*
> *I-terminal as its focus is at the screen rather*
> *than the origin of the image. It is the illusory*
> *object at the screen that is of interest to the*
> *human enactor of the process—the*
> *ideo.satisfractile nature of the FACE, an inverted*
> *face like the inside of a mask, from the inside out*

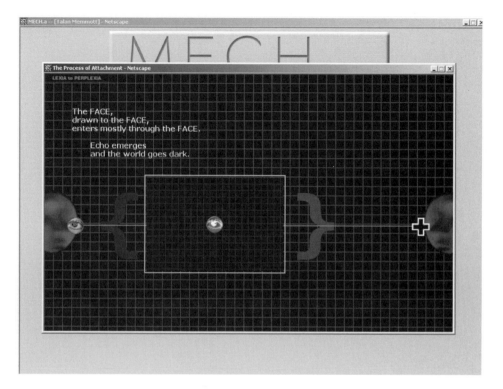

Figure 17.11 Screenshot from *Lexia to Perplexia*, "The Process of Attachment."
Courtesy of Talan Memmott.

to the screen is this same ⟨HEAD⟩{FACE}⟨BODY⟩,
⟨BODY⟩FACE⟨/BODY⟩, rendered now as sup\posed other. (Memmott 2000)

The graphic that displays, evoking the sender-receiver model of structuralist linguistics and information theory, becomes a spatial matrix for textual complication and displacement (figure 17.11). As we follow the steps (careful not to exit the sequence too quickly), we read twin descriptions of the Narcissus and Echo dyads of the communicative matrix.

From out of NO.where, Echo appears in the private
space of Narcissus.tmp to form a solipstatic
community (of 1, ON) with N.tmp, at the surface.
The two machines—the originating and the

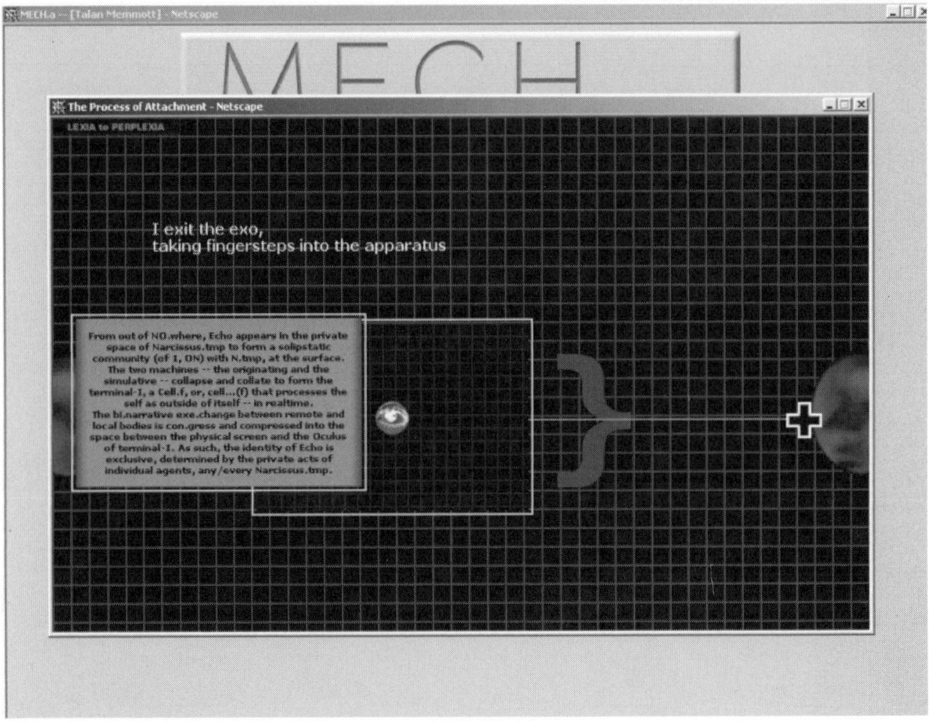

Figure 17.12 Screenshot from *Lexia to Perplexia*, "The Process of Attachment."
Courtesy of Talan Memmott.

simulative—collapse and collate to form the
terminal-I, a Cell.f, or, cell . . . (f) that
processes the self as outside of itself—in
realtime. The bi.narrative exe.change between remote
and local bodies is con.gress and compressed
into the space between the physical screen and the
Oculus of terminal-I. As such, the identity of Echo
is exclusive, determined by the private acts of
individual agents, any/every Narcissus.tmp. (figure 17.12)

Echo is no.where without the other of Echo—the
Narc(is sus)pect—the one that gives her away, sets
her up and holds her captive. It is this self-

Barrett Watten

rendered agent that provides for the reversals of
the dis-played Cell.f. Not only is Echo the lover
of the Narc(is sus)pect, she is a reverberation of
the originating suspect—the one whom the one who
wants to see, wants to see . . . the attraction is
singular, while the attachment, the *.mergency is
bi.narrative in nature. Echo at the screen is
cyb-ling to Cell.f.

The technolingo here is meant to be both suggestive and unreadable. Further
textual cues are provided by the numerous interpretants that pop up sur-
rounding these textual blocks, while readability is hindered as well by the dis-
junct letters that overlay the text (figure 17.13). Working away from the

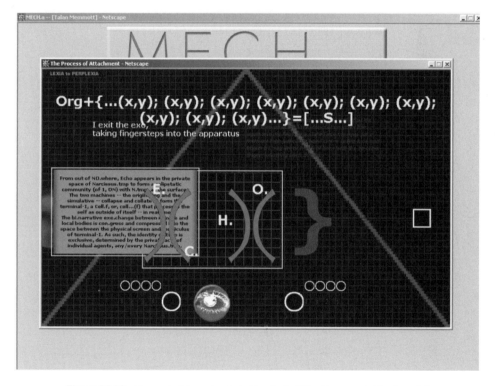

Figure 17.13   Screenshot from *Lexia to Perplexia,* "The Process of Attachment."
Courtesy of Talan Memmott.

baseline framework of the communicative model, we proceed to cancel out the narrative elements, proceeding by hyperlink to "exit the exo,/taking fingersteps into the apparatus." A new framework, of visual projection, overlays the "speech chain" of the communication model, and we begin to complicate, beyond the possibility of a comprehensive reading, the display with textual blocks and graphic elements that cancel each other out until there is only one exit available—the looming eye at the bottom of the page:

There are a many screens(pages) between the re:enacting agent and the [sub|ob]ject. Scrims and mirrors, walls and portals block and provide access to remote location(s) of desire. The object is concealed in these hidden places—latency is outside. The eye that is the I looks out (across the ocean) through many layers (of earth and sky), passing through gates and membranes, attaching— entering and exiting. / The static body transmits the intimate details and private fantasies, expressing and requesting the return of locally confirmed re:motions. One is various—rendered completely at [n]either location—here AND there. The mechanism is based upon the provocative im.pulses of an originating, enacting or proactive agent. This is true at [n]either pole.

It is never I that enters. The remote aspects of the infra-ultrastructure are hidden from the private, anchored space of the operator. The Obvion of I, the I sup|posed at the screen is not the navigator and negotiator of the delimited labyrinth of the network, the underworld. The screen-bound avatar is a micromental reproduction of the trans|missive hero-agent, which is already a trans|posed Cell.f of self—the re:turned hero-nike of an encoded agent. Though the delivery-machine feels no-thing, the mediation, all co-operation between the I and apparatus is con.sensual; in

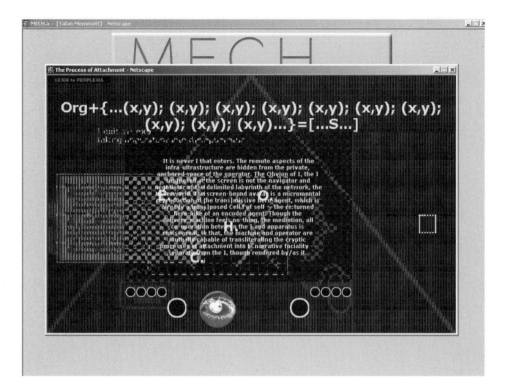

Figure 17.14 Screenshot from *Lexia to Perplexia*, "The Process of Attachment."
Courtesy of Talan Memmott.

> that, the machine and operator are mutually capable
> of transliterating the cryptic processes of
> attachment into bi.narrative faciality—separate
> from the I, though rendered by/as it. (figure 17.14)

Having blanked at our virtual lesson in decentered subjectivity, we enter the second half of the sequence: "Cyb|Organization and its Dys|Content(s)— Sign.mud.Fraud." We are moving, apparently, from Freud as transferential interlocutor to cultural critic—the Freud of Superego and the death drive. Communication has been reoriented around a vertical rather than horizontal axis, between an "I-terminus" and an "X-terminus," the transference seen as a struggle to the death between subject and object (figure 17.15). The "I" here is seen as a narcissistic attachment: "The hum.and I-terminal constructs

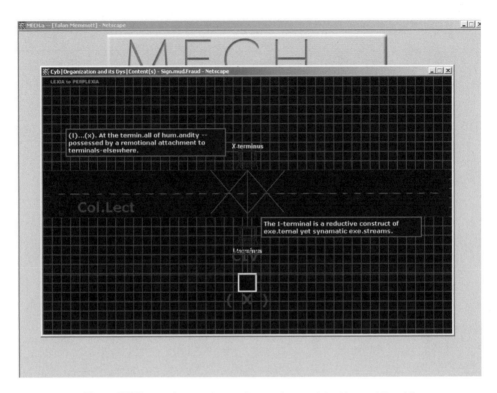

Figure 17.15 "Cyb|organization and its Dys|content(s) — Sign.mud.Fraud."
Courtesy of Talan Memmott.

any/every attachment eye-to-I, while simultaneously attached elsewhere. Fluctuating between variable foci, engaged in transmissive exe.tension and exe.change—at the face and elsewhere (at the [face)," while the "X" exceeds any attachment: "The cyborganization of any/every para.I-terminal is mirrored by the construction of a greater X-terminal from component I-terminals." At this point, we reach a crux in the hypertext: either we can attempt to synthesize the "I"/"X" divide—leading to a textual condition in which "we maintain attachments between I-terminals, connections between separately attached units of the x-terminal because contact with a hum.and X-terminal may be shared, but it is not shared in common"—or we attempt to exit the subordination of terminals through the "COL-LECT/COL-LATE/COL-LIDE" graphic option, and we read, "Any/every hum.and attachment is a col.lation of local and remote em.Urgencies," restoring event and agency to the system and leading on to the unveiling of the functional code below the level of the manifest display. Display of code completed, an enormous power button offers itself; selecting it, we are now in the next region of cyberbeing, "(s)T(ex)T(s) and Intertimacy."

(A second hypertext option has been missed, but may in another reading be encountered: "Cycl(ad)ic Trading: The Minoan Network," in which a map of the trading matrix of ancient Crete is schematized as the rhizomic exchanges of cyberspace, an ancestral linkage. Once we have realized this paradigm, we may return to the main exegesis or take a further detour through ancient Egypt and "metempsychosis"—through the transmigration of souls Leopold Bloom once worried over—skipping the following section as well. In the "Ka Space," the user, like the dead pharaoh, becomes inert in one life but is then integrated, under the aegis of "tech.txt" master program, into his own reborn projection: "Tech.txt authenticates User by confirming identity, comparing documents with contemporaneous data, and by measuring how well I follows protocol. Tech.txt tabulates, provides further criticism and interpretation by abstracting purity [the purely quantitative values of the User to the application] with the super-net|ural remainder of I. . . .")

"(s)T(ex)T(s) and Intertimacy" returns to the horizontal axis of communication, between two eyes that see rather than mouths that speak. At the center of the axis is an unrealizable "exit" asterisk, which, when scrolled over, yields a series of intermediary positions in exchange, as much self becoming other as saying something to another (figure 17.16). A series of panels correlated with "body:self," "terminal:local," "terminal:elsewhere," and "body:remote" explain the mechanism of this "becoming other" as a communicative act; the language of explanation itself is a kind of technobabble indistinguishable from the workings of the machine in its "becoming self" mode. The manifest content of this transformation is given in a central unit of boilerplate prose, partly obscured by navigational text and, at times, the intersecting, transpositioning images of cathode ray tubes:

From here, the analog and slippery digits of the real are poured into the mouth of the funnel. Though we enter the funnel, we have not yet entered the other, the distant and remote. Flowing further, the variable body, the abstracted and released continuum of the body is com|pressed, reduced and encoded, codified—made elemental . . . Now we are small enough, we hope—it is the hope of communification that we minimize the space of flesh—to continue or/in/out/off and away. The exit is

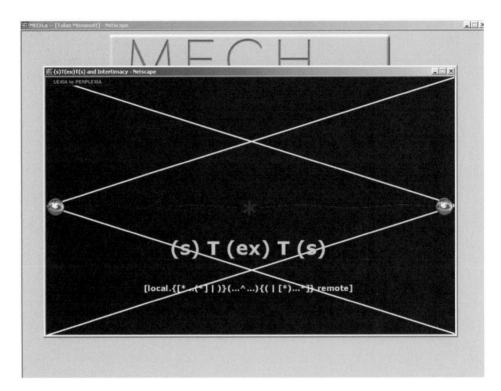

Figure 17.16 "(s)T(ex)T(s) and Intertimacy." Courtesy of Talan Memmott.

an entrance to an open space as wide as the real, though narrow, flat at either extreme. We penetrate the impenetrable and defy time, perhaps even matter. I and nanots, nanonauts, knots. The reverse of delta $\wedge$. (Figure 17.17)

What appears to be a transparently narrative vector is also a partly unreadable block. This is everywhere the nature of Memmott's prose, even when it is fully visible; the text both describes, in the manner of a narrative code, and enacts, in the manner of a screen display, its meaning as both liminal and obdurate: the subjectivity effect of the hypermedia machine is constructed here. We move from pseudoexplication to programmatic manifesto, reinforcing the metaleptic design of the machine, its constant autoreferentiality, in "Metastrophe: Temporary miniFestos." What appears to be a transparent statement of principle becomes a structuring device of antisociality (the political cynicism of an entire generation of dot.comers enters here): "When

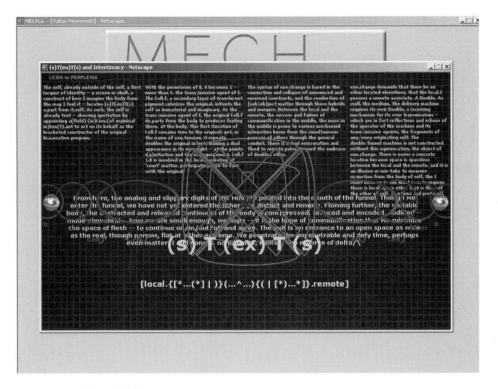

Figure 17.17 "(s)T(ex)T(s) and Intertimacy." Courtesy of Talan Memmott.

everything is crystal clear and susynchronized the passage of meaning through the bi.narrative conduit is smooth, without catches or serration and the doubled trans|missive agent(s) never meet, combat or challenge. The combined intents perform as components of a single ideocratic device, de.signing, de.veloping and exe.cuting the mechanism that permits their passage" (figure 17.18). The page is loaded with booby traps—one crashes the program entirely, another offloads the viewer to "Ka Space," and a final rollover immediately forces an exit to the next sequence. The "minifestoes" play with transparency of intention, even as they partially obscure one another, generating links to ancillary definitions or unfolding scrolls that are neither definitive nor stable. The catastrophe of metalepsis occurs when the unfolding axis of commentary produces a seeming terminus: "I am certum—certain di.verse—confissive in this action—the vagabond ka. Seurat, Seurat. 1900:pointillism —2000:pixellism—same same syn.ama—timeless—achronic chronic—

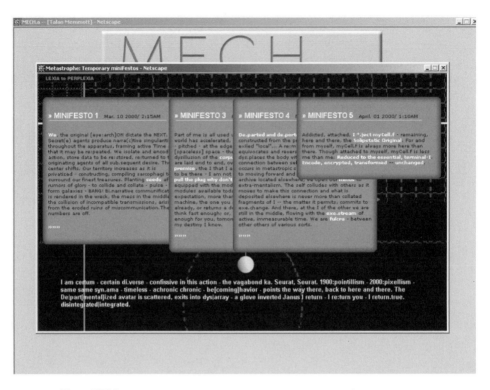

Figure 17.18 "Metastrophe: Temporary miniFestoes." Courtesy of Talan Memmott.

be[coming]havior—points the way there, back to here and there. The De|part[mental]ized avatar is scattered, exits into dys|array—a glove *inverted* Janus I return—I re:turn you—I return.true. *disintegrated| integrated*"—only to provoke total inversion of the visual field or crash into the next cycle. "Anonymity [N]," which follows, presents a lyric address to the problem of self in the displacements of cyberspace, realized as two love songs set across from each other on the page and tagged with ⟨HEAD⟩ and ⟨BODY⟩ markers that reference each other: "I will reveal(to you, my dear){/(this body.skin){/(my dear) this body.skin[my dear].this/body.skin[to you]. VULNERABLE=, +"naked"/this body.skin[to you].VULNERABLE=,+"naked." The code markings both facilitate and impede the preprogrammed disclosure of desire.

Given time and space, one could continue this description for quite some time before arriving at the final subroutine of Memmott's "machine made of machines." When we reach this penultimate but by no means conclusive site

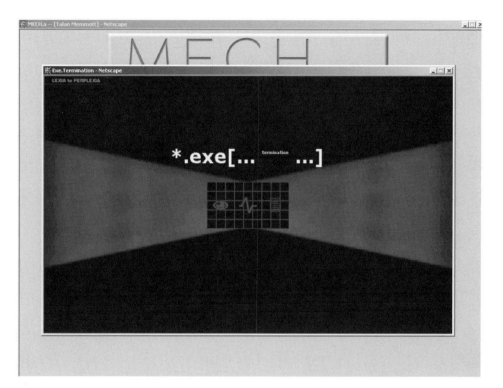

Figure 17.19 "Exe.Termination." Courtesy of Talan Memmott.

of disclosure, some of the larger framework for Memmott's elaborate demonstration begins to come clear: the play of transparency and opacity is the subject entering into circuits of desire and exchange, in which the means of communication and what is communicated are enmeshed. If the lyric affirmation of the preceding passage identifies subjectivity with the romance of its own undoing, the ending sequence suggests a mechanism by which it is undone (figure 17.19). In exposing the engine of hypermobility, hypercombination, and hypernarrative, we see the combinatorial charge and discharge of time-based components that cannot be shut down within a spatial matrix of overlapping textual blocks, navigational buttons, and semiotic screens (some of Memmott's blackboards from his lecture presentations). There is no exit, it appears, from the remote engines that drive these scenarios toward destruction. We can watch the patterns as long as we like, with no recourse to explanation, while the engines of cybermobility spin out combinatorial

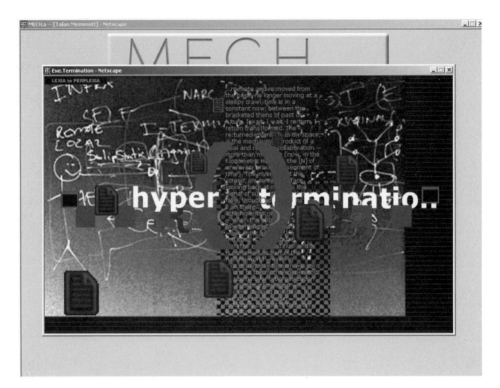

Figure 17.20 "Exe.Termination." Courtesy of Talan Memmott.

sequences we can only look at, not read (figure 17.20). What this entails is crucial for Memmott's poetics of new media: the interpretive effort, however relentlessly applied, always fails within an overarching architecture of machine interface that absorbs not only interpretation but consciousness and subjectivity into its own orders. The negativity of the machine is precisely its material poetics, as a technology that does not simply distribute consciousness but partly undermines it. It is here that technology as unconscious substrate of communication begins to function like the order of language in experimental poetry: both material basis and conceptual limit. In *Lexia to Perplexia*, we arrive at a scene of decision whose consequence can only be ourselves, once the automatic engines of cybermobility have negated all our investments.

What sense does it make to extend the genre of poetics to works of new media such as Memmott's? The first claim that I have made is that the positive relation of poetics to its object is only one of several motivations for its development; we need to consider poetics' negative relation to the object and its dialectical or diacritical unfolding as well. In Memmott's work, this negativity may be seen in a constant undermining of communication in favor of an order of "processing" latent in the machine and its decision structure. We have the illusion of an interface between terminals and thus between bodies, but it may be that we are equally trapped within a machinic destiny in which all decisions have been made in advance. Memmott's exploration of this possibility is at once dialectical, as it draws from the real-time cultural assumptions of the dot.com technological workplace; and diacritical, as it continually maps cultural frameworks onto its own internal processes. The work finally is constructed in terms both of its positive references—to questions of new media and writing—as well as to their negative undoing as their reinforcing logics end in the homeostasis of machinic repetition, with no way out. Memmott's work is precisely poetic both for its foregrounding the mechanisms of communication in our mediated world (the "message for its own sake") and in situating its means of doing so within structures of technology and art that define its genre as expanding rather than pregiven.

A final consideration, then, at this crux between genre and medium: while the specificity of the medium in its historical development has taken center stage in new media theory,[11] what I am offering may seem suspiciously to impose logics taken from poetics and conceptual art onto new media without any regard for its specificity. Here is where we return to the necessity of poetics as "a self-reflexive moment within practice that creates grounds for new meaning." Rather than merely exploiting the bells and whistles of hypermedia programming at a particular stage of its development (and one that, even a few years later, has been surpassed by any number of new programs for encoding the graphic interface), Memmott has done something in *Lexia to Perplexia* that is at once poetic (in foregrounding the mechanisms *of* communication within the medium *as* communication) and conceptual (in collapsing the structure and ground of new media art as both visual display and textual coding). His work is simultaneously dialectical, in its address to the contexts of the emerging media culture in which it was created (and as preserving a form of its own utopian imagination, even while predicting its collapse), and diacritical, in its slipping between values of exteriorized display and interiorized code. As Krauss's diagram would suggest, this is not the only way the expanded field of new media will develop new aesthetic possibilities. But the hand of the maker—neither technician, nor sales rep, nor venture capitalist, nor media theorist—is evident here, precisely in the manner of its construction, so that we may profitably ask, are Memmott's poetics specified by the nature of new media, or not? And if not, what larger cultural logics—common to both experimental poetry and conceptual art—inform them?

Notes

1. Originating in the multiauthored context of journals and zines, writing in poetics has found its way into numerous single-author collections, notable early examples of which include volumes by Bruce Andrews (1996), Charles Bernstein (1986), Alan Davies (1987), Lyn Hejinian (2000), Susan Howe (1985), Steve McCaffery (1986), Bob Perelman (1996), Leslie Scalapino (1990), Ron Silliman (1987), and Barrett Watten (1984). Currently, we may discern a movement away from poetics in the single-authored mode (with exceptions) toward a return to a multiauthored, metadiscursive, dialogic practice particularly in online zines and blogs.

2. For an interesting collection of modernist and postmodern manifestos, see Caws 2001; and for a revisionist account of the genre of the manifesto itself, see Lyon 1999. Certainly, the defining examples of American modernist poetics are the essays of William Carlos Williams and Ezra Pound.

3. So my new collection of essays (Watten 2003) is being marketed by its publisher as "cultural studies" and "poetics," not as "literary criticism."

4. It may be that this crisis is precisely what defines the "literary"; for a consideration of the constitutive relation between the literary and its cultural ground, one might well begin with the Russian formalist account of literary evolution; see Tynjanov 1978.

5. For a range of writings in conceptual art that may be compared to the genre of poetics, see Cage 1961, Smithson 1979, Morris 1993, Kosuth 1991, Warhol 1968, and collections such as Meyer 1972, Lippard 1997, and Alberro and Stimson 1999.

6. However, at one historical moment when such a juxtaposition was attempted—at the Verbal Eyes reading/performance series at The Farm in San Francisco in the late 1970s, which presented the work of language-centered writers and conceptual and performance artists—the results revealed a disparity of artistic assumptions and cultural reception.

7. See my discussion of the poetic diction and poetic vocabulary in Watten 2003a, 1–44.

8. On Riding's renunciation of poetry, see Jackson 1980 and Watten 2006.

9. See Smithson 1979 and 1996.

10. The complete archive of Memmott's new media work is available at http://memmott.org/talan/works.html.

11. See, for instance, the work of Lev Manovich.

Works Cited

Alberro, Alexander, and Blake Stimson, eds. 1999. *Conceptual Art: A Critical Anthology*. Cambridge, MA: MIT Press.

Allen, Donald, and Warren Tallman, eds. 1973. *Poetics of the New American Poetry*. New York: Grove Press.

Andrews, Bruce. 1992. *I Don't Have Any Paper So Shut Up (or, Social Romanticism)*. Los Angeles: Sun & Moon.

Andrews, Bruce. 1996. *Paradise and Method: Poetics and Praxis*. Evanston, IL: Northwestern University Press.

Baraka, Amiri [LeRoi Jones]. 1973a. "Hunting Is Not Those Heads on the Wall." In *Poetics of the New American Poetry*, ed. Donald Allen and Warren Tallman, 378–382. New York: Grove Press.

Baraka, Amiri [Le Roi Jones]. 1973b. "State/Meant." In *Poetics of the New American Poetry*, ed. Donald Allen and Warren Tallman, 382–383. New York: Grove Press.

Bernstein, Charles. 1986. *Content's Dream: Essays, 1975–1984*. Los Angeles: Sun & Moon.

Cage, John. 1961. *Silence: Lectures and Writings*. Middletown, CT: Wesleyan University Press.

Caws, Mary Ann, ed. 2001. *Manifesto: A Century of Isms*. Lincoln: University of Nebraska Press.

Cha, Theresa Hak Kyung. 1995. *Dictee*. Berkeley, CA: Third Woman Press.

Coleridge, Samuel Taylor. [1817] 1983. *Biographia Literaria; or, Biographical Sketches of My Literary Life and Opinions*. Ed. James Engell and W. Jackson Bate. Princeton, NJ: Princeton University Press.

Coolidge, Clark. 1974. *The Maintains*. San Francisco: This Press.

Coolidge, Clark. 1980. *Smithsonian Depositions and Subject to a Film*. New York: Vehicle Press.

Creeley, Robert. 1970. *A Quick Graph: Collected Notes and Essays*, ed. Donald Allen. San Francisco: Four Seasons Foundation.

Davidson, Dan. 1998. "Bureaucrat, My Love." *Poetics Journal,* issue 10: 74–78.

Davies, Alan. 1987. *Signage.* New York: Roof Books.

Dragomoshchenko, Arkadii. 1998. "The Eroticism of Forgetting." *Poetics Journal,* issue 10: 79–87.

Greimas, Algirdas Julien. 1987. *On Meaning: Selected Writings in Semiotic Theory.* Trans. Frank Collins. Minneapolis: University of Minnesota Press.

Heizer, Michael. 1991. *Double Negative.* New York: Rizzoli.

Hejinian, Lyn. 2000. *The Language of Inquiry.* Berkeley, CA: University of California Press.

Hejinian, Lyn. 2001. *A Border Comedy.* New York: Granary Books.

Howe, Susan. 1985. *My Emily Dickinson.* Berkeley, CA: North Atlantic Books.

Jackson, Laura (Riding). 1980. *The Poems of Laura Riding: A New Edition of the 1938 Collection.* New York: Persea Books.

Jackson, Laura (Riding). 1992. *First Awakenings: The Early Poems of Laura Riding.* Ed. Elizabeth Friedmann, Alan J. Clark, and Robert Nye. New York: Persea Press.

Jameson, Fredric. 1981. *The Political Unconscious: Narrative as a Socially Symbolic Act.* Ithaca, NY: Cornell University Press.

Kosuth, Joseph. 1991. *Art After Philosophy and After: Collected Writing, 1996–1990.* Ed. Gabriele Guercio. Cambridge, MA: MIT Press.

Krauss, Rosalind E. 1985. *The Originality of the Avant-Garde and Other Modernist Myths.* Cambridge, MA: MIT Press.

Krauss, Rosalind E. [1979] 1998. "Sculpture in the Expanded Field." In *The Anti-Aesthetic: Essays on Postmodern Culture*, 2nd ed., ed. Hal Foster, 31–42. New York: The New Press.

Lippard, Lucy, ed. 1997. *Six Years: The Dematerialization of the Art Object from 1966 to 1972.* Berkeley, CA: University of California Press.

Lyon, Janet. 1999. *Manifestoes: Provocations of the Modern.* Ithaca, NY: Cornell University Press.

Mac Low, Jackson. 1971. *Stanzas for Iris Lezak.* Barton, NY: Something Else Press.

Manovich, Lev. 2001. *The Language of New Media*. Cambridge, MA: MIT Press.

McCaffery, Steve. 1986. *North of Intention: Critical Writings, 1973–1986*. New York: Roof Books.

Memmott, Talan, ed. *BeeHive Hypertext/Hypermedia Literary Journal*. http://beehive. temporalimage.com/archive/index.html (accessed June 28, 2004).

Memmott, Talan. 2000. *Lexia to Perplexia*. http://www.uiowa.edu/~iareview/tirweb/ hypermedia/talan_memmott/index.html (accessed June 28, 2004)

Messerli, Douglas, ed. 1987. *"Language" Poetries*. New York: New Directions.

Meyer, Ursula, ed. 1972. *Conceptual Art*. New York: E. P. Dutton.

Morris, Robert. 1993. *Continuous Project Altered Daily*. Cambridge, MA: MIT Press.

Olson, Charles. 1997. *Collected Prose*. Ed. Donald Allen and Benjamin Friedlander. Berkeley: University of California Press.

Perelman, Bob. 1996. *The Marginalization of Poetry: Language Writing and Literary History*. Princeton, NJ: Princeton University Press.

Pound, Ezra. 1960. *ABC of Reading*. New York: New Directions.

Scalapino, Leslie. 1990. *How Phenomena Appear to Unfold*. Elmwood, CT: Potes and Poets Press.

Scalapino, Leslie. 1998. "War/Poverty/Writing." *Poetics Journal,* issue 10: 62–70.

Sebald, W. G. 1998. *The Rings of Saturn*. Trans. Michael Hulse. New York: New Directions.

Silliman, Ron. 1978. *Ketjak*. San Francisco: This Press.

Silliman, Ron. 1987. *The New Sentence*. New York: Roof Books.

Silliman, Ron. ed. 1985. *In the American Tree*, 1st ed. Orono, ME: National Poetry Foundation.

Smithson, Robert. 1979. *The Writings of Robert Smithson*. Ed. Nancy Holt. New York: New York University Press.

Smithson, Robert. 1996. *The Collected Writings*. Ed. Jack Flam. Berkeley: University of California Press.

Tynjanov, Jurij. 1978. "On Literary Evolution." In *Readings in Russian Poetics: Formalist and Structuralist Views*, ed. Ladislav Matejka and Krystyna Pomorska, 66–78. Ann Arbor: Michigan Slavic Publications.

Warhol, Andy. 1968. *A: A Novel*. New York: Grove Press.

Watten, Barrett. *Total Syntax*. 1984. Carbondale: Southern Illinois University Press.

Watten, Barrett. 1985. *Progress*. New York: Roof Books.

Watten, Barrett. 2003a. *The Constructivist Moment: From Material Text to Cultural Poetics*. Middletown, CT: Wesleyan University Press.

Watten, Barrett. 2003b. "Zone: The Poetics of Space in Post-Urban Detroit." In *The Constructivist Moment: From Material Text to Cultural Poetics*, 321–348. Middletown, CT: Wesleyan University Press. Also available online at http://www.markszine.com/102/bwind.htm.

Watten, Barrett. 2006. "Modernist Posthistoire: Laura Riding as Finality." Forthcoming in *Horizon Shift: Progress and Negativity in American Modernism*.

Williams, William Carlos. 1963. *Paterson*. New York: New Directions.

Williams, William Carlos. 1970. *Imaginations*. Ed. Webster Schott. New York: New Directions.

Wordsworth, William, and Samuel Taylor Coleridge. [1798] 1975. *Lyrical Ballads*, 2nd ed. Ed. Derek Roper. Plymouth, UK: MacDonald and Evans.

Bibliography

Aarseth, Espen J. 1997. *Cybertext: Perspectives on Ergodic Literature*. Baltimore, MD: Johns Hopkins University Press.

Aarseth, Espen J. 2004. "Genre Trouble: Narrativism and the Art of Simulation." In *First Person: New Media as Story, Performance, and Game*, ed. Noah Wardrip-Fruin and Pat Harrigan, 45–55. Cambridge, MA: MIT Press.

Alberro, Alexander, and Blake Stimson, eds. 1999. *Conceptual Art: A Critical Anthology*. Cambridge, MA: MIT Press.

Allen, Donald, and Warren Tallman, eds. 1973. *Poetics of the New American Poetry*. New York: Grove Press.

aND, mIEKEL. 2000. "Seedsigns for Philadelpho." http://cla.umn.edu/joglars/SEEDSIGN/ (accessed February 2, 2005).

Andrews, Bruce. 1992. *I Don't Have Any Paper So Shut Up (or, Social Romanticism)*. Los Angeles: Sun & Moon.

Andrews, Bruce. 1996. *Paradise and Method: Poetics and Praxis*. Evanston, IL: Northwestern University Press.

Andrews, Jim. 2001. "Nio." http://vispo.com/nio/index.htm (accessed October 1, 2002).

Andrews, Jim. 2002. "Games, Po, Art, Play, & Arteroids 2.03." http://vispo.com/arteroids/onarteroids.htm (accessed February 23, 2005).

Andrews, Jim. 2003. "Arteroids 2.5." *poemsthatgo,* no. 14 (Fall). http://www.poemsthatgo.com/gallery/fall2003/arteroids/arteroids.htm (accessed October 24, 2004).

Andrews, Jim. 2003. "Arteroids, Poetry, and the Flaw." *poemsthatgo,* no. 14 (Fall). http://www.poemsthatgo.com/gallery/fall2003/arteroids/article.htm (accessed October 24, 2004).

Andrews, Jim. 2004. "Avant Auteur: An Interview with Jim Andrews." *Avant Gaming.* http://www.avantgaming.com/andrews.html (accessed February 4, 2005).

Andrews, Jim, and Peter Howard. 2002. "Continuing Conversation on Flash." http://www.webartery.com/ (accessed October 1, 2002).

Artaud, Antonin. 1958. *The Theater and Its Double.* Trans. Mary Caroline Richards. New York: Grove Press.

Attali, Jacques. 1985. *Noise: The Political Economy of Music.* Trans. Brian Massumi. Minneapolis: University of Minnesota Press.

Bakhtin, Mikhail. 1984. *Rabelais and His World.* Bloomington: Indiana University Press.

Baldwin, Sandy. 2003. "Process Window: Code Work, Code Aesthetics, Code Poetics." In *Cybertext Yearbook 2002–2003,* ed. Markku Eskelinen and Raine Koskimaa, with a special section on ergodic poetry edited by John Cayley and Loss Pequeño Glazier, 107–119. Publications of the Research Centre for Contemporary Culture. Jyväskylä: University of Jyväskylä.

Baraka, Amiri [LeRoi Jones]. 1973. "Hunting Is Not Those Heads on the Wall." In *Poetics of the New American Poetry,* ed. Donald Allen and Warren Tallman, 378–382. New York: Grove Press.

Baraka, Amiri [LeRoi Jones]. 1973. "State/Meant." In *Poetics of the New American Poetry,* ed. Donald Allen and Warren Tallman, 382–383. New York: Grove Press.

Barthes, Roland. [1973] 1990. *S/Z.* Trans. Richard Miller. Oxford, UK: Blackwell.

Barthes, Roland. 1979. *Cy Twombly: Catalogue raisonné des oeuvres sur papier de Cy Twombly*. Milan: Multhipla Editions.

Basinski, Michael. 1999. "Robert Grenier's Opems." *Witz* 7, no. 1: 32–34.

Basinski, Michael. 2003. "Program 9." *Radio Radio*. http://www.ubu.com/sound/radio_radio/index.html (accessed September 22, 2005).

Bateson, Gregory. 1979. *Mind and Nature: A Necessary Unity*. New York: Dutton.

BeeHive. http://beehive.temporalimage.com/archive/index.html.

Beiguelman, Giselle. 2001. *Wop Art*. http://www.desvirtual.com/wopart/index.htm (accessed December 5, 2004).

Beiguelman, Giselle. 2002. *egoscope*. http://www.desvirtual.com/egoscopio/english/about_more.htm (accessed February 11, 2005).

Beiguelman, Giselle. 2002. *egóscopio* (*egoscope*). http://www.desvirtual.com/egoscopio/index.htm (accessed December 5, 2004).

Beiguelman, Giselle. 2002c. *Leste O Leste?* (*Did You Read the East?*). http://www.pucsp.br/artecidade/novo/giselle/index.htm (accessed December 5, 2004).

Beiguelman, Giselle. 2003. *Poétrica*. http://www.poetrica.net/ (accessed December 5, 2004).

Belgum, Erik. 1998. *Raymond Federman's Take It or Leave It*. Smart Noise. CO173.

Belgum, Erik. 1999. *Blodder*. Innova Recordings. CD 26708 65272.

Benjamin, Walter. 1969. "The Work of Art in the Age of Mechanical Reproduction." Trans. Harry Zohn. In *Illuminations*, ed. Hannah Arendt, 217–251. New York: Schocken Books.

Berger, Maurice. 1989. *Labyrinths: Robert Morris, Minimalism, and the 1960s*. New York: Harper and Row.

Bergvall, Caroline. 1999. *ambient fish*. http://epc.buffalo.edu/authors/bergvall/amfish/amfish.html (accessed June 29, 2004).

Bergvall, Caroline. 2001. "Flèsh." *How2* 1, no. 5 (March 2001). http://www.scc .rutgers.edu/however/v1_5_2001/current/new-writing/bergvall/index.html (accessed June 29, 2004).

Bergvall, Caroline. 2001. "Flèsh" [print form]. In *Foil: Defining Poetry 1985–2000*, ed. Nicholas Johnson, 84–91. London: Etruscan.

Bergvall, Caroline. 2001. *Goan Atom*. San Francisco: Krupskaya.

Bergvall, Caroline. 2001. "Notes to Flèsh." *How2* 1, no. 5. http://www.scc.rutgers .edu/however/v1_5_2001/current/new-writing/bergvall/index.html (accessed June 29, 2004).

Bergvall, Caroline. 2002. Email to Marjorie Perloff. September 9, 2002.

Bergvall, Caroline. 2003. Email to Marjorie Perloff. January 13, 2003.

Bernstein, Charles. [1976] 1987. *Veil*. Madison, WI: Xeroxial Editions.

Bernstein, Charles. 1986. *Content's Dream: Essays, 1975–1984*. Los Angeles: Sun & Moon.

Bernstein, Charles. 1992. *A Poetics*. Cambridge, MA: Harvard University Press.

Bernstein, Charles. 1996. "Littoral." http://epc.buffalo.edu/authors/bernstein/visual/ littoralht.html (accessed July 26, 2004).

Bernstein, Charles. 1997. "Alphabeta." UbuWeb. http://www.ubu.com/contemp/ bernstein/alphabeta.html (accessed June 26, 2004).

Bernstein, Charles. 1997. "An Mosaic for Convergence." *electronic book review* 6 (Winter). http://www.altx.com/ebr/ebr6/ebr6.htm (accessed July 20, 2004).

Bernstein, Charles. 1997. "Politics." UbuWeb. http://www.ubu.com/contemp/ bernstein/politics2.html (accessed July 26, 2004).

Bernstein, Charles. 1997–1998. "Access." *electronic book review* 6. http://www.altx .com/ebr/ebr6/6bernstein/access.htm (accessed July 26, 2004).

Bernstein, Charles. 1997–1998. "Avant." *electronic book review* 6. http://www.altx .com/ebr/ebr6/6bernstein/avant.htm (accessed July 26, 2004).

Bernstein, Charles. 1997–1998. "Defaults." *electronic book review* 6. http://www .altx.com/ebr/ebr6/6bernstein/defaults.htm (accessed July 26, 2004).

Bernstein, Charles. 1997–1998. "On_Veil." *electronic book review* 6. http://www .altx.com/ebr/ebr6/6bernstein/On_Veil.htm (accessed July 20, 2004).

Bernstein, Charles. 1997–1998. "Punic." *electronic book review* 6. http://www.altx.com/ ebr/ebr6/6bernstein/punic.htm (accessed July 26, 2004).

Bernstein, Charles. 1997–1998. "Realpolitick." *electronic book review* 6. http://www .altx.com/ebr/ebr6/6bernstein/realpolitick.htm (accessed July 26, 2004).

Bernstein, Charles. 1997–1998. "Textuaì." *electronic book review* 6. http://www.altx .com/ebr/ebr6/6bernstein/Textuai.htm (accessed July 26, 2004).

Bernstein, Charles. 1998. "Introduction." In *Close Listening: Poetry and the Performed Word*, ed. Charles Bernstein, 3–26. New York: Oxford University Press.

Bernstein, Charles. [1994] 1999. "I Don't Take Voice Mail: The Object of Art in the Age of Electronic Textuality." In *My Way: Speeches and Poems*, 73–80. Chicago: University of Chicago Press.

Bernstein, Charles. 1999. "An Interview with Manuel Brito." In *My Way: Speeches and Poems*, 25–32. Chicago: University of Chicago Press.

Bernstein, Charles. 1999. *My Way: Speeches and Poems*. Chicago: University of Chicago Press.

Bernstein, Charles. 1999. "Riding's Reason." In *My Way: Speeches and Poems*, 255–267. Chicago: University of Chicago Press.

Bernstein, Charles. 2001. "Electronic Pies in the Poetry Skies." *electronic book review* 3. http://www.electronicbookreview.com/v3/servlet/ebr?command=view_essay&essay_id =bernsteinaltx (accessed June 14, 2004).

Bernstein, Charles. 2001. *With Strings*. Chicago: University of Chicago Press.

Bernstein, Charles. 2002. "Electronic Pies in the Poetry Skies." Design by damian lopes. http://www.chbooks.com/online/electronic_pies/index.html (accessed June 14, 2004).

Bernstein, Charles. 2002. "Every Which Way But Loose." In *Reimagining Textuality: Textual Studies in the Late Age of Print*, ed. Elizabeth Bergmann Loiseaux and Neil Fraistat, 178–185. Madison: University of Wisconsin Press.

Bernstein, Charles. N.d. *Veil* [electronic version]. http://www.ubu.com/contemp/ bernstein/bernstein.html (accessed June 14, 2004).

Bohn, Willard. 1996. "From Hieroglyphics to Hypergraphics." In *Experimental–Visual–Concrete: Avant-Garde Poetry Since the 1960s*, ed. K. David Jackson, Eric Vos, and Johanna Drucker, 173–186. Amsterdam and Atlanta, GA: Rodopi.

Bolter, J. David. 1991. *Writing Space: The Computer, Hypertext, and the History of Writing*. Hillsdale, NJ: Lawrence Erlbaum.

Bolter, J. David. [1991] 2003. "Seeing and Writing." In *The New Media Reader*, ed. Noah Wardrip-Fruin and Nick Montfort, 680–690. Cambridge, MA: MIT Press.

Bolter, J. David. 2001. *Writing Space: Computers, Hypertext, and the Remediation of Print*. Mahwah, NJ: Lawrence Erlbaum.

Bolter, Jay David, and Richard Grusin. 1999. *Remediation: Understanding New Media*. Cambridge, MA: MIT Press.

"Bootleg Remixes: Music's Latest Craze." 2002. MTV Asia News. http://www. mtvasia.com/News/200208/02001383.html (accessed August 2, 2002).

Bootz, Phillipe. 2003. "Hypertext: Solution/Dissolution." Trans. John Cayley. In *Cybertext Yearbook 2002–2003*, ed. Markku Eskelinen and Raine Koskimaa, with a special section on ergodic poetry edited by John Cayley and Loss Pequeño Glazier, 56–82. Publications of the Research Centre for Contemporary Culture. Jyväskylä: University of Jyväskylä.

Bory, Jean François. 1968. "The worldWord is. . . ." In *Once Again*, ed. Jean François Bory, 86–95. New York: New Directions.

Brogan, T. V. F., ed. 1994. *The New Princeton Handbook of Poetic Terms*. Princeton, NJ: Princeton University Press.

Bronzell, Sean, and Ann Suchomski. 1986. "Interview with John Cage." In *The Guests Go in to Supper*, ed. Melody Sumner, Kathleen Burch, and Michael Sumner, 20–27. Oakland, CA: Burning Books.

Bürger, Peter. 1984. *Theory of the Avant-Garde*. Trans. Michael Shaw. Minneapolis: University of Minnesota.

Burroughs, William S. 1987. *The Ticket That Exploded*. London: Paladin Books.

Bush, Vannevar. [1945] 2003. "As We May Think." In *The New Media Reader*, ed. Noah Wardrip-Fruin and Nick Montfort, 37–47. Cambridge, MA: MIT Press.

Cage, John. [1958] 1961. "History of Experimental Music in the United States." In *Silence: Lectures and Writings*, 67–75. Middletown, CT: Wesleyan University Press.

Cage, John. 1961. *Silence: Lectures and Writings*. Middletown, CT: Wesleyan University Press.

Castellin, Philippe. 1998. "Le Poème est la somme." http://www.sitec.fr/users/akenatondocks/DOCKS-datas_f/collect_f/auteurs_/f/C_f/CASTELLIN_f/anim_f/lasomme_F/poeme.html (accessed November 10, 2003).

Castells, Manuel. 2000. *The Rise of the Network Society*, 3 vols. Oxford, UK: Blackwell.

Castro, E. M. de Melo e. 1996. "Videopoetry." *Visible Language* 30, no. 2: 138–149.

Caws, Mary Ann, ed. 2001. *Manifesto: A Century of Isms*. Lincoln: University of Nebraska Press.

Cayley, John. 1998. "Of Programmatology." *Mute* (Fall): 72–75.

Cayley, John. 1998. "Performances of Writing in the Age of Digital Transliteration." Paper presented at the Digital Arts Conference, University of Bergen, Norway, November.

Cayley, John. 1999. *noth'rs*. http://www.shadoof.net/in?nothrs.html (accessed June 15, 2004).

Cayley, John. 2002a. *riverIsland*. http://www.shadoof.net/in?riverisland.html (accessed August 20, 2003).

Cayley, John. 2002. "The Code Is Not the Text (Unless It Is the Text)." *electronic book review* 3. http://www.electronicbookreview.com/v3/servlet/ebr?command=view_essay&essay_id=Cayleyele (accessed December 1, 2003).

Cayley, John. 2002. *What We Will*. http://www.z360.com/what/ (accessed June 28, 2004).

Cayley, John. 2002. "What Is Transliteral Morphing?" Text file accompanying *riverIsland*. http://shadoof.net/in?transliteral.html (accessed August 20, 2003).

Cayley, John. 2003. "Digital Wen: On the Digitization of Letter- and Character-Based Systems of Inscription." In *Reading East Asian Writing: The Limits of Literary Theory*, ed. Michel Hockz and Ivo Smits, 277–294. London: RoutledgeCurzon.

Cayley, John. 2003. "Inner Workings: Code and Representations of Interiority in New Media Poetics." *Dictung-digital* 29, ed. Loss Pequeño Glazier. http://www.dichtung-digital.de/2003/issue/3/Cayley.htm (accessed June 20, 2004).

Cayley, John. 2004. "Literal Art: Neither Lines nor Pixels but Letters." In *First Person: New Media as Story, Performance, and Game*, ed. Noah Wardrip-Fruin and Pat Harrigan, 208–217. Cambridge, MA: MIT Press.

Cayley, John. 2004. "Overboard: An Example of Ambient Time-Based Poetics in Digital Art." http://www.dichtung-digital.org/2004/2-Cayley.htm (accessed February 9, 2005).

Cha, Theresa Hak Kyung. 1995. *Dictee*. Berkeley, CA: Third Woman Press.

cheek, cris. 1999. "how can this hum be human." *Riding the Meridian*. http://www.heelstone.com/meridian/cheek.html (accessed June 29, 2004).

cheek, cris. 2003. "Program 4." *Radio Radio*. UbuWeb. http://www.ubu.com/sound/radio_radio/cheek.html (accessed June 29, 2004).

Chevrel, Seb, and Gabe Kean. 2002. *You and We. Born Magazine*. http://www.bornmagazine.org/youandwe/ (accessed June 28, 2004).

Chomsky, Noam. 2002. *Cartesian Linguistics: A Chapter in the History of Rationalist Thought*. Christchurch, NZ: Cybereditions.

Chopin, Henri. 1983–1989. *Le Corpsbis*. Audio recording. http://www.ubu.com/sound/chopin.html (accessed June 29, 2004).

Chopin, Henry. 1956. "Rouge." *UbuWeb Sound Poetry*. http://www.ubu.com/sound/chopin.html (accessed March 21, 2004).

Clover, Joshua. 2003. "American Ink." *Village Voice* (February): 19–23.

Coleridge, Samuel Taylor. [1817] 1983. *Biographia Literaria; or, Biographical Sketches of My Literary Life and Opinions*. Ed. James Engell and W. Jackson Bate. Princeton, NJ: Princeton University Press.

Conte, Joseph M. 1991. *Unending Design: The Forms of Postmodern Poetry*. Ithaca, NY: Cornell University Press.

Coolidge, Clark. 1974. *The Maintains*. San Francisco: This Press.

Coolidge, Clark. 1980. *Smithsonian Depositions and Subject to a Film*. New York: Vehicle Press.

Coover, Robert. 1992. "The End of Books." *New York Times Book Review*, June 21.

Coover, Robert. [1999] 2000. "Literary Hypertext: The Passing of the Golden Age." *Feed*. http://www.feedmag.com/documents/cb2911ofi.html (no longer available).

Coverley, M. D. 2003. Email to N. Katherine Hayles, November 20.

Cramer, Florian. 2001. "Digital Code and Literary Text." *BeeHive Hypertext/Hypermedia Literary Journal*. http://beehive.temporalimage.com/content_apps43/app_d.html (accessed February 17, 2005).

Creeley, Robert. 1970. *A Quick Graph: Collected Notes and Essays*. Ed. Donald Allen. San Francisco: Four Seasons Foundation.

Creeley, Robert. 1998. *Day Book of a Virtual Poet*. New York: Spuyten Duyvil.

Crisell, Andrew. 1994. *Understanding Radio*. London: Methuen.

Crisell, Andrew. 2000. "Radio Signs." In *Media Studies: A Reader*, ed. Paul Marris and Sue Thornham, 210–219. New York: New York University Press.

Cummings, Allison M., and Rocco Marinaccio. [1996] 2000. "Interview with Charles Bernstein." *Contemporary Literature* 41: 1–21.

Cybergraphia. 2002. Bard College. http://cg.bard.edu (accessed December 15, 2003).

Dalai Lama XIV. 2001. *Dalai Lama in America: Training the Mind.* New York: Simon & Schuster Audio CD.

Damasio, Antonio. 1999. *The Feeling of What Happens: Body and Emotion in the Making of Consciousness.* New York: Harcourt.

Davidson, Dan. 1998. "Bureaucrat, My Love." *Poetics Journal,* issue 10: 74–78.

Davies, Alan. 1987. *Signage.* New York: Roof Books.

de Campos, Augusto, Décio Pignatari, and Haroldo de Campos. 1968. "Pilot Plan for Concrete Poetry." In *Concrete Poetry: A World View*, ed. Mary Ellen Solt, 71–72. Bloomington: Indiana University Press.

de Man, Paul. 1996. "Phenomenality and Materiality in Kant." In *Aesthetic Ideology*, ed. Andrzej Warminski, 70–90. Minneapolis: University of Minnesota Press.

de Vinsauf, Geoffrey. [1210] 1974. "Poetria Nova." Trans. Margaret F. Nims. In *Classical and Medieval Literary Criticism: Translations and Interpretations*, ed. Alex Preminger, O. B. Hardison, Jr., and Kevin Kerrane. New York: Frederick Ungar.

Debord, Guy, and Gil J. Wolman. [1956] 1981. "Methods of Détournement." Trans. Ken Knabb. In *Situationist International Anthology*, ed. Ken Knabb, 8–14. Berkeley, CA: Bureau of Public Secrets.

Deleuze, Gilles, and Félix Guattari. 1983. *A Thousand Plateaus: Capitalism and Schizophrenia.* Trans. Brian Massumi. Minneapolis: University of Minnesota Press.

Derrida, Jacques. 1978. "Freud and the Scene of Writing." In *Writing and Difference*, trans. Alan Bass, 196–231. London: Routledge.

Derrida, Jacques. 1988. "Signature Event Context." In *Limited Inc.*, trans. Samuel Weber, 1–23. Evanston, IL: Northwestern University Press.

DJ Spooky [Paul Miller]. 2003. "Program 12." *Radio Radio*. UbuWeb. http://www. ubu.com/sound/radio_radio/miller.html (accessed June 29, 2004).

DJ Spooky, and Scanner. 2000. *The Quick and the Dead*. Sulfur Records. CD BBSUL 004.

Doll, William E., Jr. 1993. *A Post-Modern Perspective on Curriculum*. New York: The Teachers College Press.

Dragomoshchenko, Arkadii. 1998. "The Eroticism of Forgetting." *Poetics Journal*, issue 10: 79–87.

Drucker, Johanna. 1996. *The Century of Artists' Books*. New York: Granary Books.

Drucker, Johanna. 1998a. *Figuring the Word: Essays on Books, Writing, and Visual Poetics*. New York: Granary Books.

Drucker, Johanna. 1998b. "Language as Information: Intimations of Immateriality." In *Figuring the Word: Essays on Books, Writing, and Visual Poetics*, 213–231. New York: Granary Books.

Drucker, Johanna. 2002. "Intimations of Immateriality: Graphical Form, Textual Sense, and the Electronic Environment." In *Reimagining Textuality: Textual Studies in the Late Age of Print*, ed. Elizabeth Bergmann Loiseaux and Neil Fraistat, 152–177. Madison: University of Wisconsin Press.

Drucker, Johanna. 2002. "Theory as Praxis: The Poetics of Electronic Textuality." *Modernism/Modernity* 9, no. 4: 683–691.

Drucker, Johanna, and Bethany Nowviskie. 2003. "Temporal Modelling." In *ALLC/ACH Conference Abstracts 2003*, ed. Eric Rochester and William A. Kretzschmar, Jr. Handout at ALLC/ACH Joint International Conference, May 29–June 2, The University of Georgia, Athens.

Drucker, Johanna, and Bethany Nowviskie. 2003. "Temporal Modelling Project: Storyboard." http://www.iath.virginia.edu/time/storyboard/orig.html (accessed June 27, 2004).

Drucker, Johanna, and Jerome McGann. 2004. *IVANHOE: Design and Development*. October. http://www.patacriticism.org/ivanhoe/credits.html (accessed February 23, 2005).

Duborgel, Pierre. 1992. *Imaginaire et pédagogie*. Toulouse: Privat.

Duguid, Paul. 1996. "Material Matters: The Past and Futurology of the Book." In *The Future of the Book*, ed. Geoffrey Nunberg, 63–101. Berkeley: University of California Press.

Dworkin, Craig, ed. 2003. *The UbuWeb Anthology of Conceptual Writing*. UbuWeb. http://www.ubu.com/concept (accessed June 29, 2004).

Electronic Poetry Center. SUNY Buffalo. http://wings.buffalo.edu/epc/ (accessed December 13, 2003).

Eskelinen, Markku, and Raine Koskimaa, eds. 2003. *Cybertext Yearbook 2002–2003*, with a special section on ergodic poetry edited by John Cayley and Loss Pequeño Glazier. Publications of the Research Centre for Contemporary Culture. Jyväskylä: University of Jyväskylä.

Feldman, Morton. 1995. "Radio Happenings." In *Exact Change Yearbook*, ed. Peter Gizzi, 254–261. Boston: Exact Change.

Filreis, Alan. 1997. "On Frets about the Death of the Book." March 4. http://www.english.upenn.edu/~afilreis/sanders-etext.html (accessed December 16, 2003).

Foucault, Michel. 1979. *Discipline and Punish: The Birth of the Prison*. Trans. Alan Sheridan. New York: Viking.

Freud, Sigmund. [1915] 1991. "The Unconscious." In *On Metapsychology: The Theory of Psychoanalysis*, ed. Angela Richards, 161–222. Vol. 11, The Penguin Freud Library. Harmondsworth: Penguin Books.

Futurism and Futurists. http://www.futurism.org.uk/ (accessed June 29, 2004).

Genette, Gérard. [1987] 1997. *Paratexts: Thresholds of Interpretation*. Trans. Jane E. Lewin. In *Literature, Culture, Theory* 20, ed. Richard Macksey and Michael Sprinkler. Cambridge, UK: Cambridge University Press.

Georgel, Pierre. 1989. "Portrait de l'artiste en griffonneur." In *Victor Hugo et les images*, ed. Madeleine Blondel and Pierre Georgel, 75–119. Dijon: Aux Amateurs de Livres.

Georgia Tech School of Literature, Communication & Culture. *IDT: Information Design & Technology.* http://www.lcc.gatech.edu/idt/index.html (accessed December 18, 2003).

Gitelman, Lisa. 2002. "'Materality Has Always Been in Play': An Interview with N. Katherine Hayles." *The Iowa Review Web.* http://www.uiowa.edu/~iareview/tirweb/feature/hayles/interview.htm (accessed June 14, 2004).

Glazier, Loss Pequeño. 2002. *Digital Poetics: The Making of E-Poetries.* Tuscaloosa: University of Alabama Press.

Glazier, Loss Pequeño. 2002. "Io Sono At Swoons." http://epc.buffalo.edu/authors/glazier/java/iowa/iosono.html (accessed June 30, 2004).

Goldsmith, Kenneth. 1999. *Fidget* [electronic version]. http://www.chbooks.com/online/fidget/index.html (accessed June 29, 2004).

Goldsmith, Kenneth. 2000. "UbuWeb Wants to Be Free." http://www.ubu.com/papers/ol/ubu.html (accessed December 13, 2003).

Goldsmith, Kenneth. 2001. *Soliloquy.* New York: Granary Books.

Goldsmith, Kenneth. 2001. *Soliloquy* [electronic version]. http://www.epc.buffalo.edu/authors/goldsmith/soliloquy/index.html (accessed June 29, 2003).

Goldsmith, Kenneth. 2002–2003. "Uncreativity as a Creative Practice." *Drunken Boat* 5 (Winter). http://drunkenboat.com/db5/goldsmith/uncreativity.html (accessed February 20, 2005).

Goody, Jack. 1987. *The Interface between the Written and the Oral.* New York: Cambridge University Press.

Gould, Glenn. 1967. *The Idea of North.* Audio recording. http://www.gould.nlc-bnc.ca/ineye/eeye2.htm (accessed May 27, 2002).

Gourmont, Remy de. 1966. "The Dissociation of Ideas." In *Selected Writings,* 11–29. Ann Arbor: University of Michigan Press.

Greenberg, Clement. [1940] 1992. "Towards a Newer Laocoon." In *Art in Theory, 1900–1990: An Anthology of Changing Ideas*, ed. Charles Harrison and Paul Wood, 558. Oxford: Blackwell Publishers.

Greimas, Algirdas Julien. 1987. *On Meaning: Selected Writings in Semiotic Theory*. Trans. Frank Collins. Minneapolis: University of Minnesota Press.

Grenier, Robert. 1978. *Sentences*. http://www.whalecloth.org/grenier/sentences.htm (accessed April 10, 2004).

Grenier, Robert. [1982] 1985. "Language/Site/World." In *Writing/Talks*, ed. Bob Perelman, 230–245. Carbondale: Southern Illinois University Press.

Grenier, Robert. 1986. "May Dawn Horizon Many Graces Pollen." In *Phantom Anthems*. Oakland, CA: O Books.

Grenier, Robert. 1986. "On Speech." In *In the American Tree*, ed. Ron Silliman, 496–497. Orono, ME: National Poetry Foundation.

Grenier, Robert. 1996. "10 Pages from RHYMMS." http://www.thing.net/~grist/l&d/grenier/lgrena00.htm (accessed June 14, 2004).

Grenier, Robert. 1997. "For Larry Eigner." http://www.thing.net/~grist/l&d/grenier/lgl00.htm (accessed June 14, 2004).

Grenier, Robert. 1998. "Realizing Things." Unpublished talk, State University of New York, Buffalo, October 28. http://epc.buffalo.edu/authors/grenier/rthings.html (accessed April 10, 2004).

Grenier, Robert. 2001. [Untitled essay.] In *Poetry Plastique*, ed. Jay Sanders and Charles Bernstein, 71–73. New York: Marianne Boesky Gallery and Granary Books.

Grenier, Robert. n.d. "Greeting." http://www.thing.net/~grist/l&d/grenier/rggrt01.htm (accessed April 8, 2004).

Grenier, Robert. n.d. "Pond I." http://www.thing.net/~grist/l&d/grenier/rgpnd01.htm (accessed June 14, 2004).

Grenier, Robert. n.d. "[saplling]." http://www.thing.net/~grist/l&d/grenier/rgpnd28.htm (accessed July 27, 2004).

Hansen, Mark B. N. 2000. *Embodying* Technesis: *Technology Beyond Writing*. Ann Arbor: University of Michigan Press.

Hansen, Mark B. N. 2004. *New Philosophy for New Media*. Cambridge, MA: MIT Press.

Haraway, Donna. 1991. "A Cyborg Manifesto: Science, Technology, and Socialist-Feminism in the Late Twentieth Century." In *Simians, Cyborgs, and Women: The Reinvention of Nature*, 149–181. New York: Routledge. Also in *Socialist Review* 80 (1985): 68–108.

Harrison, Gilbert A. 1974. "Introduction." In *Gertrude Stein's America*, ed. Gilbert A. Harrison, 9–17. New York: Liveright.

Havelock, Eric A. 1986. *The Muse Learns to Write: Reflections on Orality and Literacy from Antiquity to the Present*. New Haven, CT: Yale University Press.

Hayles, N. Katherine. 1992. "The Materiality of Informatics." *Configurations* 1.1: 147–170.

Hayles, N. Katherine. 1996. "Virtual Bodies and Flickering Signifiers." In *Electronic Culture: Technology and Visual Representation*, ed. Timothy Druckery, 259–277. New York: Aperture.

Hayles, N. Katherine. 1997. "Voices Out of Bodies, Bodies Out of Voices: Audiotape and the Production of Subjectivity." In *Sound States: Innovative Poetics and Acoustical Technology*, ed. Adalaide Morris, 74–96. Chapel Hill: North Carolina University Press.

Hayles, N. Katherine. 1999. *How We Became Posthuman: Virtual Bodies in Cybernetics, Literature, and Informatics*. Chicago: University of Chicago Press.

Hayles, N. Katherine. 2000. "Open-work: Dining at the Interstices." Commentary on "The Dinner Party." *Riding the Meridian* 2, no. 2. http://califia.hispeed.com/RM/haylesfr.htm (accessed June 10, 2004).

Hayles, N. Katherine. 2002. *Writing Machines*. Cambridge, MA: MIT Press.

Hayles, N. Katherine. 2003. "Translating Media: Why We Should Rethink Textuality." *The Yale Journal of Criticism* 16, no. 2: 263–290.

Hayles, N. Katherine. 2005. *My Mother Was a Computer: Digital Subjects and Literary Texts.* Chicago: University of Chicago Press.

Heizer, Michael. 1991. *Double Negative.* New York: Rizzoli.

Hejinian, Lyn. 2000. *The Language of Inquiry.* Berkeley: University of California Press.

Hejinian, Lyn. 2001. *A Border Comedy.* New York: Granary Books.

Hennessey, Neil. 2004. "Jabber: The Jabberwoky Engine." *poemsthatgo* 15 (Winter). http://www.poemsthatgo.com/gallery/winter2004/jabber/index.htm (accessed February 4, 2005).

Hitchens, Christopher. 2001. *Letters to a Young Contrarian.* New York: Basic Books.

Holman, Bob, and Paul Skiff. 2000. *Nuyorican Poets Symphony.* Knitting Factory. Audio CD 138.

Holtzman, Steven. 1997. *Digital Mosaics: The Aesthetics of Cyberspace.* New York: Simon & Schuster.

Howard, Peter. 2001. *Ugly. BeeHive Hypertext/Hypermedia Literary Journal.* http://beehive.temporalimage.com/archive/51arc.html (accessed June 28, 2004).

Howard, Peter. 2001. *Xylo.* Wordcircuits. http://www.wordcircuits.com/gallery/xylo/ (accessed June 28, 2004).

Howe, Susan. 1985. *My Emily Dickinson.* Berkeley, CA: North Atlantic Books.

Jackson, Laura (Riding). 1928. *Anarchism Is Not Enough.* London: Jonathan Cape.

Jackson, Laura (Riding). 1980. *The Poems of Laura Riding: A New Edition of the 1938 Collection.* New York: Persea Books.

Jackson, Laura (Riding). 1992. *First Awakenings: The Early Poems of Laura Riding*, ed. Elizabeth Friedmann, Alan J. Clark, and Robert Nye. New York: Persea Press.

Jackson, Laura (Riding). 1992. "A Prophecy or a Plea [1925]." In *First Awakenings: The Early Poems of Laura Riding*, ed. Elizabeth Friedmann, Alan J. Clark, and Robert Nye, 275–280. New York: Persea Press.

Jaeger, Peter. n.d. "Steve McCaffery's Visual Errata." UbuWeb. http://www.ubu.com/papers/jaeger.html (accessed April 10, 2004).

Jameson, Fredric. 1981. *The Political Unconscious: Narrative as a Socially Symbolic Act.* Ithaca, NY: Cornell University Press.

Joyce, James. [1922] 1993. *Ulysses.* New York: Oxford University Press.

Joyce, Michael. 1990. *afternoon* [electronic resource]. Watertown, MA: Eastgate Systems.

Joyce, Michael. 1995. *Of Two Minds: Hypertext Pedagogy and Poetics.* Ann Arbor: University of Michigan Press.

Kac, Eduardo. 1996. "Holopoetry." *Visible Language* 30, no. 2: 184–213.

Kahn, Douglas. 1999. *Noise, Water, Meat: A History of Sound in the Arts.* Cambridge, MA: MIT Press.

Kahn, Douglas, and Gregory Whitehead, eds. 1992. *Wireless Imagination: Sound, Radio and the Avant-Garde.* Cambridge, MA: MIT Press.

Keep, Christopher J. 1999. "The Disturbing Liveliness of Machines: Rethinking the Body in Hypertext Theory and Fiction." In *Cyberspace Textuality: Computer Technology and Literary Theory*, ed. Marie-Laure Ryan, 164–181. Bloomington, IN: Indiana University Press.

Kelly Writers House. 2003. http://www.writing.upenn.edu/wh/ (accessed December 13, 2003).

Kendall, Robert. 2002. "Faith." http://wordcircuits.com/faith (accessed November 1, 2002).

Kirschenbaum, Matthew. [2001] 2003. "Materiality and Matter and Stuff: What Electronic Texts Are Made Of." *electronic book review* 12. http://www.altx.com/ebr/riposte/rip12kir.htm (accessed April 10, 2004).

Kittler, Friedrich A. 1990. *Discourse Networks 1800/1900.* Trans. Michael Metteer, with Chris Cullens. Stanford, CA: Stanford University Press.

Klein, Melanie. [1923] 1967. "Le Rôle de l'école dans le développement libidinal de l'enfant." In *Essais de psychanalyse*, 90–109. Paris: Payot.

Knabb, Ken, ed. 1981. *Situationist International Anthology.* Trans. Ken Knabb. Berkeley, CA: Bureau of Public Secrets.

Kosuth, Joseph. 1991. *Art After Philosophy and After: Collected Writing, 1996–1990*, ed. Gabriele Guercio. Cambridge, MA: MIT Press.

Krauss, Rosalind E. [1979] 1998. "Sculpture in the Expanded Field." In *The Anti-Aesthetic: Essays on Postmodern Culture*, 2nd ed., ed. Hal Foster, 31–42. New York: The New Press.

Lamarque, Jean-Luc. 1996. "pianographique." http://pianographique.com/datas/inter_fr.php (accessed May 4, 2003).

Landow, George P. 1992. *Hypertext: The Convergence of Contemporary Critical Theory and Technology.* Baltimore, MD: Johns Hopkins University Press.

Landow, George P. 1996. "Twenty Minutes into the Future, or How Are We Moving Beyond the Book?" In *The Future of the Book*, ed. Geoffrey Nunberg, 209–237. Berkeley: University of California Press.

Lanham, Richard. 1993. *The Electronic Word: Democracy, Technology, and the Arts.* Chicago: University of Chicago Press.

Laurillard, Diana. 1993. *Rethinking University Teaching: A Framework for the Effective Use of Educational Technology.* London: Routledge.

Leroi-Gourhan, André. 1993. *Gesture and Speech.* Trans. Anna Bostock Berger. Cambridge, MA: MIT Press.

Lieberman, Jethro. 1970. *The Tyranny of the Experts: How Professionals Are Closing the Open Society.* New York: Walker.

Lippard, Lucy, ed. 1997. *Six Years: The Dematerialization of the Art Object from 1966 to 1972.* Berkeley: University of California Press.

Lockard, John. 1997. "Progressive Politics, Electronic Individualism and the Myth of Virtual Community." In *Internet Culture*, ed. David Porter, 219–232. New York: Routledge.

Logan, Robert K. 1986. *The Alphabet Effect.* New York: William Morrow.

Logan, Robert K. 1995. *The Sixth Language: Learning a Living in the Computer Age.* Toronto: Stoddart.

Loseby, Jessica. 2001. "code scares me." http://www.rssgallery.com/code.htm (accessed February 17, 2005).

Loseby, Jessica. 2001. "Code Scares Me [Commentary]." *New Media Line.* http://www.kanonmedia.com/news/nml/code.htm (accessed February 17, 2005).

Lukka, Tuomas. 2001. "GZigZag: A Platform for Cybertext Experiments." In *Cybertext Yearbook 2000*, vol. 68, ed. Markku Eskelinen and Raine Koskimaa, 141–151. Publications of the Research Centre for Contemporary Culture. Jyväskylä: University of Jyväskylä.

Lukka, Tuomas. 2002. *GZigZag Glossary.* http://gzigzag.sourceforge.net/gl/gl.html (accessed December 19, 2002).

Lyon, Janet. 1999. *Manifestoes: Provocations of the Modern.* Ithaca, NY: Cornell University Press.

Mac Low, Jackson. 1971. *Stanzas for Iris Lezak.* Barton, NY: Something Else Press.

Manovich, Lev. 2001. *The Language of New Media.* Cambridge, MA: MIT Press.

Manovich, Lev. 2001. "Post-Media Aesthetics." http://www.manovich.net/ (accessed June 29, 2004).

Manovich, Lev. 2003. "New Media from Borges to HTML." In *The New Media Reader*, ed. Noah Wardrip-Fruin and Nick Montfort, 13–25. Cambridge, MA: MIT Press.

Marghen, Alga. 2002. *Revue Ou: Sound Poetry, The Anthology.* 4 CD boxset. ALGA045.

Marinetti, F. T., and Pino Masnata. [1993] 1992. "La Radia." Trans. Stephen Sartarelli. In *Wireless Imagination: Sound, Radio, and the Avant-Garde*, ed. Douglas Kahn and Gregory Whitehead, 265–268. Cambridge, MA: MIT Press.

Marsh, William. 1999. "Six String Aria." http://www.factoryschool.org/btheater/works/6strA/aria.html (accessed November 18, 2003).

Mauss, Marcel. 1973. "Les Techniques du corps." In *Sociologie et anthropologie*. Paris: PUF. Originally published in *Journal de Psychologie* 32 (1935): 3–4.

McCaffery, Steve. 1973. *Carnival: The First Panel, 1967–1970*. Toronto: Coach House Books.

McCaffery, Steve. 1977. *Carnival: The Second Panel, 1970–1975*. Toronto: Coach House Books.

McCaffery, Steve. 1986. *North of Intention: Critical Writings, 1973–1986*. New York: Roof Books.

McCaffery, Steve. 1997. "From Phonic to Sonic: The Emergence of the Audio Poem." In *Sound States: Innovative Poetics and Acoustical Technologies*, ed. Adalaide Morris, 149–168. Chapel Hill: University of North Carolina Press.

McCaffery, Steve. 1998–2001. *Carnival* [electronic version]. Coach House Books. http://www.chbooks.com/online/carncvil/index.html (accessed April 10, 2004).

McCaffery, Steve. 2000. *Seven Pages Missing*. Volume One: Selected Texts 1969–1999. Toronto: Coach House Books.

McCaffery, Steve. 2001. *"Carnival* Panel 2 (1970–1975)." In *Poetry Plastique*, ed. Jay Sanders and Charles Bernstein, 69–70. New York: Marianne Boesky Gallery and Granary Books.

McCaffery, Steve, and bpNichol. 1992. *Rational Geomancy. The Kids of the Book-Machine. (The Collected Research Reports of the Toronto Research Group 1973–1982.)* Vancouver: Talonbooks.

McGann, Jerome. 1993. *Black Riders: The Visible Language of Modernism*. Princeton, NJ: Princeton University Press.

McGann, Jerome. 2001. *Radiant Textuality: Literature after the World Wide Web*. London: Palgrave Macmillan.

McLuhan, Marshall. 1962. *The Gutenberg Galaxy: The Making of Typographical Man*. Toronto: University of Toronto Press.

McLuhan, Marshall. 1964. *Understanding Media: The Extensions of Man*. New York: McGraw-Hill.

Meltzer, Eve. 2003. "How to Keep Mark Making Alive." Unpublished doctoral diss., University of California, Berkeley.

Memmott, Talan. 2000. *Lexia to Perplexia. The Iowa Review Web*. http://www.uiowa.edu/~iareview/tirweb/hypermedia/talan_memmott/index.html (accessed June 28, 2004).

Memmott, Talan. 2000. "Toward Electracy: A Conversation with Gregory Ulmer." *BeeHive* 3, no. 4. http://beehive.temporalimage.com/archive/34arc.html (accessed October 7, 2004).

Memmott, Talan. 2001. "Narcisystems" (from "Delimited Meshings: A White Paper"). *Cauldron & Net* 3 (Spring). http://www.studiocleo.com/cauldron/volume3/confluence/talan_memmott/delimited_meshings/meshings/narcisys.html (accessed January 28, 2005).

Menacker, Peter. 2004. "The Futurist Uterus = F. T. Marinetti + Digital Poetics." Unpublished paper.

Mencia, Mária. 2002. *Another Kind of Language*. http://www.m.mencia.freeuk.com/ (accessed June 28, 2004).

Messerli, Douglas, ed. 1987. *"Language" Poetries*. New York: New Directions.

Meyer, Ursula, ed. 1972. *Conceptual Art*. New York: E. P. Dutton.

Mez [Mary Anne Breeze]. [Homepage.] http://www.hotkey.net.au/~netwurker (accessed June 27, 2004).

Mez [Mary Anne Breeze]. 1998. "Fleshistics." *Internal damage report vers 1.1.* http://ctheory.concordia.ca/multimedia/dirt/fleshistics/page_1.html (accessed November 18, 2003).

Mez [Mary Anne Breeze]. 2000. "The Art of M[ez]ang.elle.ing: Constructing Polysemic & Neology Fic/Factions Online." *BeeHive Hypertext/Hypermedia Literary Journal.* http://beehive.temporalimage.com/archive/34arc.html (accessed June 27, 2004).

Migone, Christof. 2001. "Head Hole: Malfunctions and Dysfunctions of an FM Exciter." In *Experimental Sound and Radio*, ed. Allen S. Weiss, 42–52. Cambridge, MA: MIT Press.

Migone, Christof. 1996. *Hole in the Head.* OHM/AVATAR AB-AVTR005-CD.

Miller, Laura. 1998. "www.claptrap.com." *New York Times Book Review*, March 15, Bookend. http://www.nytimes.com/books/98/03/15/bookend.html (accessed December 2, 2004).

Mitchell, William J. 2003. *Me++: The Cyborg Self and the Networked City.* Cambridge, MA: MIT.

Moirenc, Élodie. 1998. "Akenaton." http://www.sitec.fr/users/akenatondocks/AKENATON_f/TEXTES_f/Moirenc_f/moirenc.html (accessed February 1, 2003).

Montfort, Nick. 2003. "Introduction to 'As We May Think.'" *The New Media Reader*, ed. Noah Wardrip-Fruin and Nick Montfort, 35–36. Cambridge, MA: MIT Press.

Montfort, Nick. 2003. *Twisty Little Passages: An Approach to Interactive Fiction.* Cambridge, MA: MIT Press.

Morris, Adalaide. 1997. "Introduction." In *Sound States: Innovative Poetics and Acoustical Technologies*, ed. Adalaide Morris, 1–14. Chapel Hill: University of North Carolina Press.

Morris, Adalaide. 1997. "Sound Technologies and the Modernist Epic: H.D. on the Air." In *Sound States: Innovative Poetics and Acoustical Technologies*, ed. Adalaide Morris, 32–55. Chapel Hill: University of North Carolina Press.

Morris, Adalaide, ed. 1997. *Sound States: Innovative Poetics and Acoustical Technologies.* Chapel Hill: University of North Carolina Press.

Morris, Robert. 1993. *Continuous Project Altered Daily.* Cambridge, MA: MIT Press.

Murray, Janet H. 1997. "The Pedagogy of Cyberfiction: Teaching a Course on Reading and Writing Interactive Narrative." In *Contextual Media*, ed. Edward Barrett and Marie Redmond, 129–162. Cambridge, MA: MIT Press.

Nelson, Theodor Holm. [1974] 2003. "Computer Lib/Dream Machines." In *The New Media Reader*, ed. Noah Wardrip-Fruin and Nick Montfort, 303–338. Cambridge, MA: MIT Press.

Nelson, Theodor Holm. [1981] 1993. *Literary Machines 93.1.* Sausalito, CA: Mindful Press.

Nelson, Theodor Holm. 2001. *Zigzag.* http://xanadu/zigzag (accessed May 12, 2003).

Ness, Sally Ann. 1992. *Body, Movement, and Culture: Kinesthetic and Visual Symbolism in a Philippine Community.* Philadelphia: University of Pennsylvania Press.

Nichol, bp. 1967. "eyes." In *An Anthology of Concrete Poetry*, ed. Emmett Williams, n.p. New York: Something Else Press.

Nunberg, Geoffrey, ed. 1996. *The Future of the Book.* Berkeley: University of California Press.

Odin, Jaishree K. 2002. "Into the Space of Previously Undrawable Diagrams: An Interview with Stephanie Strickland." *The Iowa Review Web.* http://www.uiowa.edu/~iareview/tirweb/feature/strickland/interview.html (accessed August 20, 2003).

Olson, Charles. 1966. "Projective Verse." In *Selected Writings of Charles Olson*, ed. Robert Creeley, 15–26. New York: New Directions.

Olson, Charles. 1966. "The Resistance." In *Selected Writings of Charles Olson*, ed. Robert Creeley, 13–14. New York: New Directions.

Olson, Charles. 1966. *Selected Writings of Charles Olson.* New York: New Directions.

Ong, Walter J. 1982. *Orality and Literacy: The Technologizing of the Word.* New York: Methuen.

Papert, Seymour. [1980] 2003. "Excerpt from *Mindstorms: Children, Computers, and Powerful Ideas*." In *The New Media Reader*, ed. Noah Wardrip-Fruin and Nick Montfort, 414–431. Cambridge, MA: MIT Press.

Parrish, Katherine. 2002. "Teaching in the Splice: MOO Pedagogy and Poetics." http://www.meadow4.com/mooped/mpfrmset.html (accessed December 17, 2003).

Perelman, Bob. 1996. *The Marginalization of Poetry: Language Writing and Literary History.* Princeton, NJ: Princeton University Press.

Perloff, Marjorie. 1991. *Radical Artifice: Writing Poetry in the Age of Media.* Chicago: University of Chicago Press.

Perloff, Marjorie. 2002. "'ex/Crème/ental/eaT/ing': An Interview with Caroline Bergvall." *Sources: Revue d'études Anglophones* 12 (Spring): 123–135.

Perloff, Marjorie. 2002. "The Poetics of Click and Drag: Problems and Possibilities of Digital Technology." Paper delivered at New Media Poetry: Aesthetics, Institutions, Audiences conference, University of Iowa, Iowa City, October 11–12.

Perloff, Marjorie. 2002. "'Vocable Scriptsigns': Differential Poetics in Kenneth Goldsmith's *Fidget* and John Kinsella's *Kangaroo Virus*." In *Poetry and Contemporary Culture: The Question of Value*, ed. Andrew Roberts and John Allison, 21–43. Edinburgh, Scotland: Edinburgh University Press.

Perloff, Marjorie. 2003. "A Conversation with Kenneth Goldsmith." *Jacket*, issue 21 (February). http://jacketmagazine.com/21/perl-gold-iv.html (accessed June 29, 2004).

Pignatari, Décio. 1968. "beba coca cola." In *Concrete Poetry: A World View*, ed. Mary Ellen Solt, 108. Bloomington: Indiana University Press.

Poets Against the War. http://www.poetsagainstthewar.com. Redirected to Living Poets Society webpage (accessed June 28, 2004).

Pornolizer. http://www.pornolize.com (accessed March 20, 2004).

Poster, Mark. 1990. "Derrida and Electronic Writing: The Subject of the Computer." In *The Mode of Information: Poststructuralism and Social Context*, 99–128. Chicago: University of Chicago Press.

Poster, Mark. 1990. *The Mode of Information: Poststructuralism and Social Context.* Chicago: University of Chicago Press.

Pound, Ezra. 1960. *ABC of Reading.* New York: New Directions.

Poundstone, William. 2002. "3 Proposals for Bottle Imps." http://www.william-poundstone.net/Bottle.html (accessed June 27, 2004).

Project Achieve: A Collaborative Learning Environment. 2002. http://projectachieve.net (accessed January 4, 2004).

Queneau, Raymond. 1982. *Cent mille milliards de poèmes.* Paris: Gallimard/NRF.

Raley, Rita. 2002. "Interferences: [Net.Writing] and the Practice of Codework." *electronic book review* 3. http://www.electronicbookreview.com/v3/servlet/ebr?command=view_essay & essay_id=raleyele/ (accessed August 20, 2003).

Rasula, Jed. 1996. *The American Poetry Wax Museum: Reality Effects, 1940–1990.* Urbana, IL: National Council of Teachers of English.

Rasula, Jed, and Steve McCaffery, eds. 1998. *Imagining Language: An Anthology.* Cambridge, MA: MIT Press.

Ratcliffe, Stephen. 2000. *Listening to Reading.* Albany: State University of New York Press.

Rosenberg, Jim. 1993. *Intergrams.* Watertown, MA: Eastgate Systems.

Rosenberg, Jim. 1996. *The Barrier Frames: Finality Crystal Shunt Curl Chant Quickening Giveaway Stare.* Watertown, MA: Eastgate Systems.

Rosenberg, Jim. 1996. *Diffractions Through: Thirst Weep Ransack (Frailty) Veer Tide Elegy.* Watertown, MA: Eastgate Systems.

Rosenberg, Jim. 2003. "Questions about the Second Move." In *Cybertext Yearbook 2002–2003,* ed. Markku Eskelinen and Raine Koskimaa, with a special section on ergodic poetry edited by John Cayley and Loss Pequeño Glazier, 83–87. Publications of the Research Centre for Contemporary Culture. Jyväskylä: University of Jyväskylä.

Roussel, Raymond. [1914] 1965. *Locus Solus.* Paris: Pauvert.

Ryan, Marie-Laure. 1999. "Cyberspace, Virtuality, and the Text." In *Cyberspace Textuality: Computer Technology and Literary Theory,* ed. Marie-Laure Ryan, 78–107. Bloomington: Indiana University Press.

Sanders, Barry. 1994. *A Is for Ox: Violence, Electronic Media, and the Silencing of the Written Word.* New York: Pantheon Books.

Sapner, Megan. 2002. "'The Letters Themselves': An Interview with Ana Maria Uribe." *The Iowa Review Web.* http://www.uiowa.edu/~iareview/tirweb/feature/uribe/uribe.html (accessed February 4, 2005).

Scalapino, Leslie. 1990. *How Phenomena Appear to Unfold.* Elmwood, CT: Potes and Poets Press.

Scalapino, Leslie. 1998. "War/Poverty/Writing." *Poetics Journal*, issue 10: 62–70.

Schama, Simon. 1989. *Citizens: A Chronicle of the French Revolution.* New York: Knopf.

Scharf, Michael. 2003. "Nations of the Mind: Poetry, Publishing and Public Debate." *Publisher's Weekly*, March 31, 29–32.

Sebald, W. G. 1998. *The Rings of Saturn.* Trans. Michael Hulse. New York: New Directions.

Seltzer, Mark. 1992. *Bodies and Machines.* New York: Routledge.

Shaner, Tim, and Michael Rozendal. 2000. "Introduction: 'the new is the old made known.'" *Verdure* 3–4 (September): 47–48.

Silliman, Ron. 1978. *Ketjak.* San Francisco: This Press.

Silliman, Ron. 1987. *The New Sentence.* New York: Roof Books.

Silliman, Ron, ed. 1985. *In the American Tree*, 1st ed. Orono, ME: National Poetry Foundation.

Slattery, Diana. 2000. Glide. http://www.academy.rpi.edu/glide/apps/collabyrinth.html (accessed October 1, 2002).

Smithson, Robert. 1979. "Smithson's Non-Site Sights: Interview with Anthony Robbin." In *The Writings of Robert Smithson*, ed. Nancy Holt, 157–159. New York: New York University Press.

Smithson, Robert. 1996. *The Collected Writings*. Ed. Jack Flam. Berkeley: University of California Press.

Solt, Mary Ellen. 1968. "Introduction." In *Concrete Poetry: A World View*, ed. Mary Ellen Solt, 7–66. Bloomington: Indiana University Press.

Sonic Youth. 1999. *Goodbye 20th Century*. Sonic Youth Recordings. SYR 4.

Spinelli, Martin. 2003. *Radio Radio*. http://www.ubu.com/sound/radio_radio/ (accessed January 4, 2004).

Stefans, Brian Kim. 1992. "Rational Geomancy: Ten Fables of the Reconstruction." http://www.arras.net/RNG/director/geomancy/geomancy_index.html (accessed April 10, 2004).

Stefans, Brian Kim. 1999. *the dreamlife of letters*. UbuWeb. http://www.ubu.com/contemp/stefans/dream (accessed October 3, 2002).

Stefans, Brian Kim. 2002. [Index to *New York Times* Vaneigem détournements.] http://www.arras.net/vaniegem (accessed June 26, 2004).

Stefans, Brian Kim. 2003. Circulars. http://www.arras.net/circulars (accessed June 29, 2004).

Stefans, Brian Kim. 2003. *Fashionable Noise: On Digital Poetics*. Berkeley, CA: Atelos.

Stefans, Brian Kim. 2003. "Stops and Rebels or, The Battle of *Brunaburh*." In *Fashionable Noise: On Digital Poetics*, 63–169. Berkeley, CA: Atelos.

Stein, Gertrude. 1998. "Composition as Explanation." In *Gertrude Stein: Writings 1903–1932*, ed. Catherine R. Stimpson and Harriet Chessman, 520–529. New York: Library of America.

Stein, Gertrude. 1998. "Portraits and Repetition." *Gertrude Stein: Writings 1932–1946*, ed. Catherine R. Stimpson and Harriet Chessman, 287–312. New York: Library of America.

Sterne, Jonathan. 2003. *The Audible Past*. Durham, NC: Duke University Press.

Stock, Hausen & Walkman. 1999. "Flogging." *Ventilating Deer.* LP. Hot Air QRMVDLPOO1.

Strickland, Stephanie. 1997. "Poetry in the Electronic Environment." *electronic book review* 5. http://altx.com/ebr/ebr5/strick.htm (accessed February 1, 2005).

Strickland, Stephanie. 1997. *True North.* Notre Dame, IN: University of Notre Dame Press.

Strickland, Stephanie. 1998. *True North* [hypertext version]. Watertown, MA: Eastgate Systems.

Strickland, Stephanie. 2001. "Moving Through Me As I Move: A Paradigm for Interaction." http://califia.hispeed.com/Strickland/ (accessed February 14, 2003).

Strickland, Stephanie. 2002. V: Vniverse. http://www.vniverse.com (accessed August 20, 2003).

Strickland, Stephanie. 2002. *V: WaveSon.nets/Losing L'una.* New York: Penguin.

Strickland, Stephanie. 2003. Email to N. Katherine Hayles, August 23.

Strickland, Stephanie. 2006. "Quantum Poetics: Six Thoughts." In *Media Poetry: Poetic Innovation and New Technologies*, ed. Eduardo Kac. Bristol, UK: Intellect Press.

Strickland, Stephanie, and Cynthia Lawson. 2002. "Making the Vniverse." http://vniverse.com/essay (accessed June 27, 2004).

Surman, Mark, and Darren Wershler-Henry. 2001. *Commonspace: Beyond Virtual Community.* Toronto: FT Prentice-Hall.

Swiss, Thomas, ed. 2002. "New Media Literature: A Roundtable Discussion on Aesthetics, Audiences, and Histories." *NC1* (Spring/Summer): 84–110.

Tisseron, Serge. 1994. "All Writing Is Drawing: The Spatial Development of the Manuscript." *Yale French Studies* 84: 29–42. Special issue on Drawing and Writing.

Turing, Alan. 1950. "Computing Machinery and Intelligence." *Mind* 59: 433–460.

Tynjanov, Jurij. 1978. "On Literary Evolution." In *Readings in Russian Poetics: Formalist and Structuralist Views*, ed. Ladislav Matejka and Krystyna Pomorska, 66–78. Ann Arbor: Michigan Slavic Publications.

Tzara, Tristan. 1981. "Note on Poetry." In *Seven Dada Manifestos and Lampisteries*, 75–78. New York: Riverrun Press.

UbuWeb. http://www.ubu.com/ (accessed March 20, 2004).

Ulmer, Gregory. 1994. *Heuretics: The Logic of Invention*. Baltimore, MD: Johns Hopkins University Press.

Uribe, Ana Maria. 2003. *Anipoems*. http://amuribe.tripod.com/anipoems.html (accessed February 4, 2005).

Utterback, Camille. 1999. "Text Rain." http://www.camilleutterback.com/textrain.html (accessed February 28, 2003).

Varela, Francisco J., Evan Thompson, and Eleanor Rosch. 1991. *The Embodied Mind: Cognitive Science and Human Experience*. Cambridge, MA: MIT Press.

Varnedoe, Kirk. 1994. *Cy Twombly: A Retrospective*. New York: MOMA.

Viola, Bill. 1995. "The Porcupine and the Car." In *Reasons for Knocking at an Empty House: Writings 1973–1984*, ed. Robert Violette, 59–72. Cambridge, MA: MIT Press.

Viola, Bill. 1995. "Statements 1985." In *Reasons for Knocking at an Empty House: Writings 1973–1984*, ed. Robert Violette, 149–152. Cambridge, MA: MIT Press.

Voices in the Wilderness. http://www.vitw.org/. June 21, 2004.

Vos, Eric. 1996. "New Media Poetry." *Visible Language* 30.2: 214–233.

Waltuch, Michael. 2003. "Letter to Jessica Lowenthal." http://ronsilliman.blogspot.com/2003_03_01_ronsilliman_archive.html (accessed July 22, 2004).

Warburton, Dan. 1999. "Erik Belgum: Interview with Dan Warburton, September 1999." *Paris Transatlantic Magazine*. http://www.paristransatlantic.com/magazine/interviews/belgum.html (accessed June 6, 2003).

Wardrip-Fruin, Noah. 2004. "Screen." *The Iowa Review Web.* http://www.uiowa.edu/~iareview/tirweb/feature/cave/index.html (accessed June 27, 2004).

Wardrip-Fruin, Noah, ac chapman, Brion Moss, and Duane Whitehurst. 1999. *The Impermanence Agent.* http://www.impermanenceagent.com/agent (accessed June 28, 2004).

Wardrip-Fruin, Noah, and Nick Montfort, eds. 2003. *The New Media Reader.* Cambridge, MA: MIT Press.

Wardrip-Fruin, Noah, and Pat Harrigan, eds. 2004. *First Person: New Media as Story, Performance, and Game.* Cambridge, MA: MIT Press.

Warhol, Andy. 1968. *A: A Novel.* New York: Grove Press.

Watten, Barrett. 1984. *Total Syntax.* Carbondale: Southern Illinois University Press.

Watten, Barrett. 1985. *Progress.* New York: Roof Books.

Watten, Barrett. 2002. "Breaking Codes, Constructing Paradox: Beyond the Demon of Analogy." Unpublished talk, Cyberculture Working Group, University of Maryland, April.

Watten, Barrett. 2003. *The Constructivist Moment: From Material Text to Cultural Poetics.* Middletown, CT: Wesleyan University Press.

Watten, Barrett. 2003. "Zone: The Poetics of Space in Post-Urban Detroit." In *The Constructivist Moment: From Material Text to Cultural Poetics*, 321–348. Middletown, CT: Wesleyan University Press.

Watten, Barrett. 2006. "Modernist Posthistoire: Laura Riding as Finality." Forthcoming in *Horizon Shift: Progress and Negativity in American Modernism.*

Weiss, Allen S. 1995. *Phantasmic Radio.* Durham, NC: Duke University Press.

Weiss, Allen S. 2002. *Breathless: Sound Recording, Disembodiment, and the Transformation of Lyrical Nostalgia.* Middletown, CT: Wesleyan University Press.

Wershler-Henry, Darren. 2002. *Free as in Speech and Beer: Open Source, Peer-to-Peer, and the Economics of the Online Revolution.* Toronto: Financial Times.

What Is Cybergraphia? 2000. Bard College. http://cg.bard.edu/whatis.html (accessed January 4, 2004).

Whitehead, Gregory. 1991. "Degenerates in Dreamland." http://www.somewhere.org/NAR/work_excerpts/whitehead/main.htm (accessed June 28, 2004).

Whitehead, Gregory. 2001. "Radio Play Is No Place." In *Experimental Sound and Radio*, ed. Allen S. Weiss, 89–94. Cambridge, MA: MIT Press.

Whitehead, Gregory. 2003. "Program 1." http://www.ubu.com/radio/whitehead.html (accessed June 30, 2004).

Wiener, Norbert. 1948. *Cybernetics; or, Control and Communication in the Animal and the Machine.* New York: Technology Press.

Williams, Emmett, ed. 1967. *An Anthology of Concrete Poetry.* New York: Something Else Press.

Williams, William Carlos. 1963. *Paterson.* New York: New Directions.

Williams, William Carlos. 1970. *Imaginations.* Ed. Webster Schott. New York: New Directions.

Williams, William Carlos. 1986. "The Pure Products of America Go Crazy [To Elsie]." In *The Collected Poems of William Carlos Williams*, vol. 1, ed. A. Walton Litz and Christopher McGowan, 217–221. New York: New Directions.

Wittgenstein, Ludwig. 1953. *Philosophical Investigations.* Trans. G. E. M. Anscombe, and R. Rhees. Oxford, UK: Blackwell Publishers.

Wordsworth, William, and Samuel Taylor Coleridge. [1798] 1975. *Lyrical Ballads*, 2nd ed. Ed. Derek Roper. Plymouth, UK: MacDonald and Evans.

xStream. http://xstream.xpressed.org (accessed March 20, 2004).

Young, Karl. n.d. "10 pages from RHYMMS by Robert Grenier: Introductory Note." http://www.thing.net/~grist/l&d/grenier/lgrena00.htm (accessed April 10, 2004).

Zervos, Komninos. 2004. "Beer." http://www.gu.edu.au/ppages/k_zervos/beer.html (accessed February 28, 2004).

Žižek, Slavoj. 1997. "Cyberspace, or, The Unbearable Closure of Being." In *The Plague of Fantasies*, 127–167. New York: Verso.

Zuern, John. 2003. "Matter of Time: Toward a Materialist Semiotics of Web Animation." *dichtung-digital-journal für digitale ästhetik* 1. http://www.dichtung-digital.org/2003/1-zuern.htm (accessed June 1, 2004).

Contributors

Giselle Beiguelman   is a multimedia essayist and Web artist living in São Paulo, Brazil, where she was born. She is Professor of Digital Culture at Pontifical University Catholic of São Paulo and a former fellow of the VITAE Foundation. Her Web works are exhibited at festivals and scientific events devoted to new media art. Since 1998, she has run desvirtual at http://www.desvirtual.com.

John Cayley   is a London-based poet, translator, publisher, and book dealer. Links to his writing on networked and programmable media are available at http://www.shadoof .net/in. Cayley is an Honorary Research Associate in the Department of English, Royal Holloway College, University of London. His most recent work explores ambient poetics in programmable media.

Loss Pequeño Glazier   is a poet, Professor of Media Study at SUNY Buffalo, and Director of the Electronic Poetry Center (http://epc.buffalo.edu), an extensive Web-based digital poetry resource. He is the author of the digitally informed *Anatman, Pumpkin Seed, Algorithm* (Salt Publishing, 2003) and *Digital Poetics: The Making of E-Poetries*. His work has been shown at various museums and galleries, including the Kulturforum, Berlin; the Royal Festival Hall, London; and the Guggenheim Museum, New York.

Alan Filreis   is Kelly Professor of English, founder and Faculty Director of the Kelly Writers House, and Director of the Center for Programs in Contemporary Writing at the University of Pennsylvania. He is the author of *Wallace Stevens and the Actual World* (1991), *Modernism from Left to Right* (1994), and *The Fifties' Thirties: The Conservative Attack on Modern Poetry, 1945–1960* (forthcoming), and editor of Ira Wolfert's *Tucker's People* and *Secretaries of the Moon: The Letters of Wallace Stevens and José Rodríguez Feo*. His innovative teaching has won him numerous awards, including the Ira Abrams Award. In 1999–2000 he was named Pennsylvania Professor of the Year by the Carnegie Foundation. He maintains one of the oldest and most often visited Web sites in the literary academy. With Charles Bernstein, he is Codirector of PennSound (http://www.writing.upenn.edu/pennsound).

Alan Golding is Professor of English at the University of Louisville, where he teaches American literature and twentieth-century poetry and poetics. He is the author of *From Outlaw to Classic: Canons in American Poetry*, a CHOICE Best Academic Book Award winner. Works in progress include *Writing the New Into History*, which combines essays on the history and reception of avant-garde poetics with readings of individual writers, and a book on the relationship between experimental poetics and pedagogy. With Adalaide Morris and Lynn Keller, he coedits the Contemporary North American Poetry Series at the University of Iowa Press.

Kenneth Goldsmith is the author of seven books, including *I'll Be Your Mirror: The Selected Andy Warhol Interviews*. He is the founding director of the online resource *UbuWeb* (http://www.ubu.com) and the host of a weekly radio show on New York City–based WFMU. He lives in New York City with his wife, the artist Cheryl Donegan, and their son, Finnegan.

N. Katherine Hayles, Hillis Professor of Literature at the University of California, Los Angeles, teaches and writes on the relation of literature, science, and technology in the twentieth and twenty-first centuries. Her book *How We Became Posthuman: Virtual Bodies in Cybernetics, Literature, and Informatics* won the René Wellek Prize for the Best Book in Literary Theory for 1998–1999. Her next book, *Writing Machines*, won the Susanna Langer Award for Outstanding Scholarship. Her new book, *My Mother Was a Computer: Digital Subjects and Literary Texts*, was published by the University of Chicago Press in 2005.

Cynthia Lawson is a new media artist, technologist, and educator. Her work has been seen at the Modern Museum of Art (Bogota), the UCLA Hammer Museum, Macy Gallery, NY Arts Space, CalArts, Rhode Island School of Design, and in online journals and publications. She has taught courses in interactive technologies and the arts at New York University and elsewhere. She lives in New York City and is Associate Director and a member of the faculty of the Integrated Design Curriculum at Parsons School of Design. Her Web site is at http://www.cynthialawson.com.

Jennifer Ley created her first hypermedia poem in the mid-1980s using an Amiga computer so primitive it lacked a hard drive. A member of the online literary community since 1996, she founded a number of Web-based literary arts magazines, among them the new media journal *Riding the Meridian* (http://www.heelstone.com/meridian). Her own new media work has been published, performed, and exhibited internationally.

Talan Memmott is a hypermedia artist and writer originally from San Francisco, California. His work has appeared widely on the Internet. He is the editor of the online literary hypermedia journal *BeeHive*. Memmott holds an MFA in Literary Arts from Brown University and has taught at Rhode Island School of Design, Georgia Institute of Technology, and the University of Colorado, Boulder.

Adalaide Morris, John C. Gerber Professor of English at the University of Iowa, teaches and writes on modern and contemporary poetry and poetics. Her books include *Wallace Stevens: Imagination and Faith, How to Live/What to Do: H.D.'s Cultural Poetics,* and the edited collection *Sound States: Innovative Poetics and Acoustical Technologies.* With Alan Golding and Lynn Keller, she edits the Contemporary North American Poetry Series at the University of Iowa Press.

Carrie Noland teaches avant-garde literature and critical theory in the Department of French and Italian at the University of California, Irvine. She is also the Director of an interdisciplinary major, Arts-Humanities, that encourages theorists to become practicing artists and artists to engage in the practice of theory. Her most recent publications include the book *Poetry at Stake: Lyric Aesthetics and the Challenge of Technology.*

Marjorie Perloff has written numerous books on modern and contemporary poetry and poetics. Her most recent publications include *21st-Century Modernism: The "New" Poetics* (2002), *The Vienna Paradox* (2004), and *Differentials: Poetry, Poetics, Pedagogy* (2004). She is Sadie D. Patek Professor Emerita of Humanities at Stanford University and is currently scholar-in-residence at the University of Southern California.

William Poundstone is an author, critic, and Web poet living in Los Angeles. As an MIT physics student, he was exposed to Claude Shannon's experiments in computer-generated texts and to Noam Chomsky's game of devising grammatically correct statements that say nothing. Poundstone's Web projects have been featured in *BeeHive, The Iowa Review Web*, and UbuWeb.

Martin Spinelli is Senior Lecturer in Media and Film at the University of Sussex. His radio work has been heard on public, commercial, and alternative radio throughout North America, Europe, and Australia, and is included in the permanent collections of the Museum of Television and Radio (New York) and the National Sound Archive (London). His essays on media history, politics, art, and semantics have been published in *Postmodern Culture, The International Journal of Cultural Studies, Social Policy, Object*, and elsewhere.

Brian Kim Stefans has published several books and chapbooks of poetry, most recently *Jai-lai for Autocrats, Poem Formerly Known as "Terrorism" and other poems*, and *Fashionable Noise: On Digital Poetics*, a collection of dialogues, poems, and poetics. His new media poetry and poetics Web site arras.net has been active for over five years as a show-case for electronic publications such as the journal *Arras*. He is currently working on an MFA in electronic writing at Brown University.

Stephanie Strickland is a print and new media poet. Her poem *V: WaveSon.nets/ Losing L'una* has a Web component (http://vniverse.com) created with Cynthia Lawson. *V* was awarded the Di Castagnola Prize. Her poem *True North* was chosen by Barbara Guest for the Di Castagnola Prize and is also a prizewinning hypertext. *The Ballad of Sand and Harry Soot* garnered simultaneous awards in both print and digital forms. Strickland is the author of the poetry volumes *The Red Virgin: A Poem of Simone Weil* and *Give the Body Back*. A director of the Electronic Literature Organization, she produced TechnoPoetry Festival 2002 at the Georgia Institute of Technology and has taught hypermedia literature as part of experimental poetry at Brown University, Hollins University, University of Montana-Missoula, Boise State University, Sarah Lawrence College, Georgia Institute of Technology, Columbia College Chicago, and Parsons School of Design.

Thomas Swiss, Professor of English and Rhetoric of Inquiry at the University of Iowa, is the editor of *The Iowa Review Web*, a journal of new media writing and art. His collaborative poems appear online as well as in museum exhibits and art shows. Author of two collections of poems, his most recent book is *Unspun*, an edited anthology on key concepts for understanding the World Wide Web.

Barrett Watten is Professor of English at Wayne State University, where he teaches modernist studies and poetics. He is the author of *The Constructivist Moment: From Material Text to Cultural Poetics* (Wesleyan University Press, 2003), awarded the René Wellek Prize in 2004. His essays have appeared in *Critical Inquiry*, *Genre*, *Poetics Today*, *Modernism/Modernity*, *Qui Parle*, *The Impercipient Lecture Series*, *Postmodern Culture*, *Textual Practice*, and *Cultural Studies*. *Total Syntax*, essays on modern and contemporary poetics, appeared in 1984. Other books include *Frame: 1971–1990* (Sun & Moon, 1997). As editor, he brought out two journals of poetry and poetics, *This* (1971–1982) and *Poetics Journal* (1982–1998).

Darren Wershler-Henry is a writer, critic, and author of two books of poetry, *NICHOLODEON: A Book of Lowerglyphs* and *The Tapeworm Foundry*. He is also the author or coauthor of five books about technology and culture, including *Commonspace: Beyond Virtual Community* (with Mark Surman) and *FREE as in Speech and Beer: Open Source, Peer-to-Peer, and the Economics of the Online Revolution*. He currently teaches in the Communications Studies program at York University.

Index

Electrostasis, 256

Embedded journalism, 77

Embodying Technesis: *Technology Beyond Writing* (Hansen), 12

Engelbart, Douglas, 10

Epic theater, 76

Ergodic literature, 16

Establishment culture, 145

Ethnopoetics, 144

"Every Which Way But Loose" (Bernstein), 274

Evoba (McCaffery), 252

Exaggeration, 115

Expanded fields
  context and, 342–343
  diacritical process and, 343
  diminished use and, 336
  genre structure and, 340–366
  interanimation and, 338
  Krauss and, 335, 343, 345, 348–349, 351, 365–366
  Language school and, 335–337, 341–343
  Memmott and, 351–366
  postmodern negativity and, 339–348
  radical poetry and, 338–340
  self-reflexive mode and, 335
  shock of impact and, 340

Explorer, 8, 272

"Faith" (Kendall), 218

Farrell, Joe, 126

Fashionable Noise: On Digital Poetics (Stefans), 159–160

Federman, Ray, 112

Fibonacci sequence, 24

Fidget (Goldsmith), 146–147

Figueroa, Jose, 110

Figuring the Word (Drucker), 134

File sharing
  disinformation and, 55–58
  MP3 format and, 51–52, 58
  peer-to-peer, 59–60
  recontextualization and, 57–62
  sampling and, 58–62

Filreis, Alan, 269, 403
  kinetics and, 123–140
  poetics theory and, 5–6, 15, 32

Finlay, Ian Hamilton, 145, 184

Finnegans Wake (Joyce), 14

Firefox, 8

Fisk, Robert, 77

Flaubert, Gustave, 83

Flèsh (Bergvall), 153–155

Fluxus, 24, 144, 146

Fonts, 52–57, 269, 288–289

Ford, Ford Madox, 83

"Forensics" (Stein), 2

"For Larry Eigner" (Grenier), 261

Foucault, Michel, 222–223

Fountain pens, 274

Frauenfelder, Mark, 78

Free as in Speech and Beer (Wershler-Henry), 68

Freud, Sigmund, 28

Futurism and Futurists, 146

Galaher, Eliza, 110

Gameboys, 6

Geisler, Kirsten, 12

Gesamtkunstwerk, 246

Gilbert, Alan, 68

Gillespie, William, 116

Gins, Madeline, 256

Glazier, Loss Pequeño, 403
  digital writing and, 251
  e-poetry and, 266
  "Io Sono At Swoons" and, 210–216
  kinetics and, 128, 131–132, 135, 137